KINSHIP
AND THE
SOCIAL ORDER

THE LEWIS HENRY MORGAN LECTURES/1963
presented at
The University of Rochester
Rochester, New York

KINSHIP
AND THE
SOCIAL ORDER

The Legacy of Lewis Henry Morgan

MEYER FORTES

ALDINE PUBLISHING COMPANY
Chicago

First published 1969 by Aldine Publishing Company
529 South Wabash, Chicago, Illinois 60605

Library of Congress Catalog Card Number 68-8147
SBN 202-01022

Designed by Chestnut House
Printed in the United States of America

Foreword

<small>Lewis Henry Morgan was associated with the University of Rochester</small> from its founding. At his death he left it his manuscripts and library, and money to establish a women's college. Save for a wing of the present Women's Residence Halls that is named for him, he remained without a memorial at the University until the Lewis Henry Morgan Lectures were begun.

These Lectures owe their existence to a happy combination of circumstances. In 1961 the Joseph R. and Joseph C. Wilson families made a gift to the University, to be used in part for the Social Sciences. Professor Bernard S. Cohn, at that time Chairman of the Department of Anthropology and Sociology, suggested that establishing the Lectures would constitute a fitting memorial to a great anthropologist and would be an appropriate use for part of this gift. He was supported and assisted by Dean (later Provost) McCrea Hazlett, Dean Arnold Ravin, and Associate Dean R. J. Kaufmann. The details of the Lectures were worked out by Professor Cohn and the members of his Department.

The Morgan Lectures were planned initially as three annual series, for 1963, 1964, and 1965, to be continued if circumstances permitted. It was thought fitting at the outset to have each series focused on a particularly significant aspect of Morgan's work. Accordingly, Professor Meyer Fortes' 1963 Lectures were on kinship, Professor Fred Eggan devoted his attention to the American Indian, and Professor Robert M. Adams considered a particular facet of the development of civilization, concentrating on urban society. Professor Eggan's Lectures and those of Professor Adams were published in 1966. The present volume completes the foundation of the Lewis Henry Morgan Lectures, for although the series have been continued annually and are to be published, the first three years' Lectures have a special unity and importance as a whole, particularly in relation to Morgan's work.

The visit of Professor Fortes and his wife, Mrs. Doris Fortes, came when the Department at Rochester was just beginning its expansion. The informality favored by these circumstances enabled the Department's faculty to reap the maximum in pleasure and benefits from many unhurried conversations, seminars and evening gatherings, in which all were able to take part at one time or another.

In this greatly expanded version of his original Lectures, Professor Fortes has made it possible for readers who did not hear them or the discussions that went on daily to appreciate more fully (if still imperfectly) his impact on those who did. The Lectures, on which this book is based, were delivered at the University of Rochester on April 2 through April 18, 1963.

ALFRED HARRIS
Department of Anthropology
The University of Rochester

Preface

THIS BOOK IS AN EXPANSION OF THE LEWIS HENRY MORGAN LECTURES I WAS privileged to deliver at the University of Rochester in the spring of 1963. In thus enlarging what was originally a short course of lectures, I have had a special aim in view. It seems to me that the controversies among anthropologists of the past two or three generations relating to the subjects I deal with in this book have turned more often on misunderstandings, or even frank disregard, of the relevant source data than on conceptual inadequacies. The picture that has become traditional of Lewis Henry Morgan's contributions to our studies is a case in point. My thesis is that the structuralist theory and method of analysis in the study of kinship and social organization developed in modern British and American social anthropology stems directly from Morgan's work. This is not a novel point of view, but it has been smothered by the biased interpretations of Morgan's ideas and discoveries that have long prevailed. In order, therefore, to establish my thesis, I felt it to be essential to exhibit the evidence in full.

Here lies a difficulty. We do not, in social anthropology, have the notations and techniques to sum up complex researches and theories in compact formulas. Despite the valiant typological and statistical efforts of G. P. Murdock and others, we still have to go back to the monographic sources to test the value of a generalization or the validity of an argument. In a short course of lectures one may be allowed the liberty of making the categorical pronouncements that flow so easily from the pens of most of us. When it comes to the permanent record, one has a choice. One can stay brief and leave it to the reader to search out for himself the evidence by which to check the argument, or, one can copy Morgan and, instead of a clutter of bare bibliographical references, lay out for the reader the data on which the analysis is based.

Rightly or wrongly, I have chosen the second road, setting out in detail the steps in my argument, and citing at appropriate length the evidence to which I could at best only allude in the lectures. My biggest dilemma has been how to take into account the many publications bearing on my subject matter that have appeared in the past five years. In the event, I have not hesitated to draw on such recent work where it has seemed particularly apposite and have reluctantly put it aside where it would make no difference to an already rounded-off argument.

The idea of tracing out systematically the connections between modern structural theory in the study of kinship and social organization and Morgan's investigations has long been in my mind. But I doubt if I should ever have ventured upon this daunting task if it had not been for the invitation to give the Morgan Lectures at Rochester. Bernard S. Cohn, at that time Chairman of the Department of Anthropology at Rochester, initiated it. I am deeply grateful for this. I am equally indebted to Alfred Harris, the present Chairman of the Department, for the considerate and patient friendship with which he has kept an eye on the progress of this work. The warmth and cordiality with which President Allen Wallis received and introduced me to the academic community at Rochester made the occasion truly memorable. I wish to thank him and his colleagues, in particular Provost McCrea Hazlett and Dean Arnold Ravin for honoring me with the invitation to give the first series of Morgan Lectures. Rella Cohn, Grace Harris, and many others gave generously of their time and hospitality to make my wife and me feel at home in Rochester.

This book is a tribute to Lewis Henry Morgan's abiding influence. If this were not so, I should have dedicated it to the great American foundations for the advancement of learning and human welfare. Tributes to the part they have played in sustaining the studies and researches of anthropologists have become a matter of routine. But it is not often realized how much their generous and disinterested support contributed to the survival and growth of British social anthropology in the critical years before the last war.

More particularly, I have a special debt to an institution that eloquently typifies this tradition of disinterested support for learning. The final revision of this book has been accomplished during my tenure of a Fellowship at the Center for Advanced Study in the Behavioral Sciences at Stanford, California. It must suffice to say that if it had not been for the freedom to concentrate on this book and the facilities to process it provided for me at the Center, its completion would have been yet further delayed. But the Center has played a bigger part than this, for it was during my earlier Fellowship at the Center, in 1959, that the principal ideas explored in this book began to take the shape they now have. My debt to the seminars and discussions I shared with G. P. Murdock, Fred Eggan, Raymond Firth and the other anthropologists and sociologists who were in residence there at the time can only be acknowledged, not specified.

Nor can I state in detail what I owe to my colleagues in the Department of Archaeology and Anthropology at Cambridge, and to the postgraduate students who have, over the years, taken part with us in our research seminar. There is hardly a topic dealt with in this book that has not been debated and clarified for me in our seminar. I have drawn heavily on the publications of its members. Among others who have helped to clarify for me problems dealt with in this book, I must make special mention of Max Gluckman and Isaac Schapera. Discussion with them has helped me over some difficult hurdles in the development of the analysis, especially where it touches on the field of political and legal anthropology.

I am grateful to Ailsa Allan, Mrs. M. E. Molyneux, and, in particular, Mrs. Agnes Page for their patient and efficient secretarial services in preparing the type-script for publication, and to Mrs. Gail Petersen for bibliographical assistance. And I am under a very special obligation to Priscilla Jones for the vigilance with which she has scrutinized the text and checked the bibliographical references, to the reader's great advantage.

Finally, I wish to thank my wife Doris Y. Fortes for bearing with me at discouraging moments and for assistance in the task of revision.

MEYER FORTES

Contents

The Opposition between the two viewpoints, the synchronic and the diachronic, is absolute and allows of no compromise.

—Ferdinand de Saussure: *Course in General Linguistics*

Reality is the embodiment of structure;
Structures are the embodiment of properties;
Properties are the embodiment of harmony;
Harmony is the embodiment of congruity.

—Kuan Tsi, Chapter 55, Section ix (Fourth Century B.C.)
Written by Ts'ao T'ien-ch'in, translated by Gustav Haloun (1951)

PART I

RETROSPECT

CHAPTER I

Morgan: The Founding Father

I

LEWIS HENRY MORGAN'S SCHOLARLY INTERESTS, LIKE HIS PARTICIPATION IN PUBLIC affairs, had a wide range, but in this book I confine myself to his achievements as an ethnologist and his enduring intellectual legacy to us, his posterity in the discipline he helped to found.

History, we are often warned, is a fickle jade. Morgan was by all accounts as robust and uncompromising an American of his day as could have been found anywhere in the United States. Yet his ideas and discoveries, revolutionary as they were for the science of man, suffered eclipse in his own country at a critical time. Like the proverbial prophet, his following was greater outside than within his native land at that time. Nevertheless, you might well ask what special claims a British anthropologist could have to merit the honor of giving the first of these lecture courses dedicated to his memory.

It is due, I am sure, to a turn curious in the history of our discipline. It was a British anthropologist, W. H. R. Rivers, as all students of the subject know, whose rediscovery of Morgan restored him to his rightful place in the main stream of anthropological scholarship—and this was the beginning of a method and theory of research which took deep root in British anthropology. Our science is by its very nature incapable of existing as an insular study. Morgan's observations and theories excited worldwide ethnological interest in his own lifetime, but leading authorities in the United States soon turned away from him, perhaps not without justification. For what chiefly attracted attention about his work was what we now know to be its ephemeral facade. His fundamental discoveries were either ignored or misunderstood. Then came their vindication by Rivers, and the discipline thus founded now stands at the center of anthropological science.

I am going to argue that the primary source of what is nowadays called structural theory in the study of kinship and social organization is to be found in Morgan's work, and this not only in the purely historical sense but also, and more significantly, in the conceptual sense. This is true almost in spite of Morgan himself. For one of the curious and instructive features of this story is that he himself overemphasized what eventually proved to be of merely incidental importance in his work, thus failing to make the most of what eventually proved to be his discoveries of lasting value.

I am concerned then with the emergence and growth of a discipline in the science of anthropology. "An academic discipline," says Robert Redfield, in one of those dazzling papers in which he blazed many a trail, "an academic discipline is at once a group of men in persisting social relations and a method of investigation" (1953: 728). Spelled out, his dictum applies to any autonomous branch of art or science or scholarship. It is marked, firstly, by the craft or skill or body of knowledge that is distinctive of it. But if it is a living activity, it can be equally well identified by the manner in which its practitioners are set apart from the laity, by which I mean all the rest of the world as far as the practitioners are concerned. They will have an organization that is exclusive, institutions that are peculiar to their community as a profession, distinctive customs and norms. In short a specific culture. This is how they appear to the outsider. He knows that they are different because he is unable to comprehend the idiosyncrasies of their activity even if he can to some extent appreciate the products of their labors.

But how do the insiders, the practitioners, represent the autonomy of their craft and their calling to themselves? How do they perceive their collective identity, as opposed to the uninitiated laity? As anthropologists, we know where to look for the answer. We may expect to find it crystallized in myth and pedigree and accounted for by tradition—that is the process of handing on from generation to generation. And we shall not be surprised to find this sense of in-group identity symbolized in figures of ancestors and heroes and their opponents, the false prophets and factionmongers.

II

I first heard of Lewis H. Morgan as one of these false prophets. It was in Malinowski's seminars in 1931. Morgan was presented to us as a regrettable example of deluded genius, personifying the Reign of Error in anthropology which functionalism had come to overthrow. He stood for many of the things that were anathema to Malinowski's view of human social life—the discredited and repugnant hypothesis of primitive promiscuity and group marriage, the preposterous scheme of stages of social evolution, the dreary addiction to kinship terminologies as an end in itself.

Rivers was Malinowski's *bête noire* and Morgan loomed behind him as the misguided inventor of primitive communism in women and in property and as the inspiration of his misleading emphasis on forms of marriage as the main causal factors in kinship institutions. Morgan's canonization, as Lowie has called it, by Marx and Engels, and the blind adherence of Marxists ever since to his theories was a further black mark. If it was not his fault, it was added evidence of the wrongheadedness and sterility of his ideas. The touchstone was elementary: Morgan's theories were all wild conjecture. They collapsed in the face of the ethnographic facts and of functionalist criticism. Lowie, who was more respected than admired by Malinowski, received praise for refuting Morgan's reconstruction of the origin of the clan, while Westermarck, hero of Malinowski's apprentice days, was held up for special honor because he had so early demolished the dogma of group marriage.[1]

At that point, then, Lewis H. Morgan was to me, and I suspect to all of Malinowski's pupils, one of the leading anti-heroes of our discipline. His theories, his methods, his whole approach, represented in starkest shape tendencies to which the new movement in social anthropology was most antipathetic.

III

I confess with shame that it was not till nearly a decade later that I first read Morgan's works with an open mind. My own field experience, illuminated by Evans-Pritchard's studies of Nuer lineage organization, had forced me to come to grips with kinship and descent theory. Happily for me, Radcliffe-Brown was there to show the way. He was critical of Morgan, indeed more so than Malinowski or most of Morgan's other critics, for the simple reason that he understood what Morgan was trying to do. He made a present to me, when he was disposing of his library, of the copy of *Ancient Society* (1877) which he had acquired as a student at Cambridge University in 1906. And one need only turn the pages and note the passages he marked to realize how closely he had read it and how he had penetrated to what was fundamental in Morgan's work.[2]

Coming to Morgan then, and reading him side by side with the works of his

1. I have discussed Malinowski's stand in kinship studies elsewhere (Fortes, 1957: 157–88). His antipathy to the approach which Rivers derived from Morgan, was noted in the position he arrived at in his first theoretical work, *The Family Among the Australian Aborigines* (1913). It remained fixed throughout his life. His main objection to Morgan was the current one based on Westermarck's criticism of Morgan's distorted theories of the nature of parenthood and marriage, and his alleged assumption that all kinship institutions expressed "ideas of community of blood through procreation" (*ibid.*: 168–69). What Malinowski specifically scorned was Morgan's purported disregard of the parental family as the source of all kinship ties and as the basis of social organization. (*Sex and Repression*, 1927: 223).

2. It is well to remember that Radcliffe-Brown was Rivers's student at Cambridge at the very time (1901–06) that Rivers was launching out on his study of kinship and social organization with Morgan's works to guide him. This was the beginning of Radcliffe-Brown's lifelong interest in kinship and allied aspects of social life. Professor Eggan tells me that Radcliffe-Brown had an exhaustive knowledge of *Systems of Consanguinity and Affinity of the Human Family* (hereafter referred to as *Systems* or as *Systems of Consanguinity and Affinity*) and used it as the basis of the researches on American Indian social organization which he and his students at Chicago initiated (see references in chap. IV below).

contemporaries and successors, put his contributions to the development of anthropology in a new light for me. I was reminded of this recently when reading an essay by Kroeber. In this paper Kroeber looks back from 1950, over the half-century since the official establishment of anthropology at the University of California. He divides the history of our subject into two major periods. He calls the first period "unorganized" and measures it from Herodotus, our quasi-mythological founding ancestor. This period ends, he says, with the revolutionary decade of the 1860's. Then began what he calls the "organized" portion of our history. It was, as he observes, the phenomenal decade which started with Maine's *Ancient Law* (1861) and Bachofen's *Das Mutterrecht* (1861) and ended with Morgan's *Systems* (1870) and Tylor's *Primitive Culture* (1871). Not only that, for Darwin's *Origin of Species* (1859) and *Descent of Man* (1871) appeared at the beginning and the end respectively of this intellectual explosion. It did not matter, Kroeber comments with characteristic wisdom, if the views held were right or wrong. "What did matter," he concludes, "was that there was a direction, an attitude, a notion of method, above all a set of problems" (1952: 144–45).

In retrospect, then, if we follow Kroeber (and other authorities support him) we see Morgan not as a false prophet but as one of the inspired band of mid-nineteenth-century pioneers who brought order and method into the studies that are now distinctive of our calling, where previously random speculation and casual curiosity had been the rule.

How does Morgan appear today in this light? To judge of this we must note, first of all, the controversies that blazed up at once around and among these innovators. Morgan in particular drew plenty of fire. In fact, he became one of the central figures in a debate that went on for half a century. But I must not linger over details of this, pregnant though it was for the future of our science. Morgan's contributions to this great movement of thought have been amply described in biographical and historical studies of his life and work, notably through the devoted scholarship of Leslie White. What we must remember is that the issues were not just academic in nature. The very foundations of the nineteenth-century conception of humanity were at stake. No wonder that passions flew high and that the most eminent scholars and scientists were engaged.

What chiefly aroused Morgan's contemporaries was his radical and grandiose vision of the origins and development of mankind's basic social institutions. I call it a vision rather than a theory for one cannot read his works, even from the sober perspective of modern anthropology and archeology, without being swept along by the ardor and enthusiasm that suffused them. Here is learning enough but it is not the dry erudition and the studied aloofness of Tylor. Nor is it the persuasive accumulation of detail that we find at the other extreme in Darwin. Nor is Morgan even in his most rhetorical and involved arguments carried away by the poetical licence of which Starcke (1889: chap. VII) accused Bachofen. Morgan often refers to his hypotheses as "conjectures." But when he presents them he does so in the spirit of a man who has made—to quote a favorite word of his—"stupendous" discoveries:

> . . . like some watcher of the skies
> When a new planet swims into his ken.

So he had, as was in due course recognized.

But what loomed foremost for him, and for his contemporaries, was not these discoveries, but as I have said, the extravagant vision of the development of human society which he derived from them. Historians of our science have shown how this came about. The zeitgeist demanded it. Darwin wrote *The Descent of Man* to demonstrate that man "like every other species is descended from pre-existing forms" and in order to refute those by whom "it had often and confidently been asserted that man's origins can never be known." Morgan's theme was as urgent for him, and as momentous, in his estimation, for the work of fashioning the new conception of mankind that was to replace "The theory of human degradation to explain the existence of savages and barbarians," which came in "as a corollary from the Mosaic cosmogony" (1877; 1878 ed.: 4–5). He set out, we remember, to show that "the history of the human race is one in source, one in experience and one in progress" (*ibid.*: vi), that it was created by a "common principle of intelligence" (*ibid.*: 533) and culminated in Civilization with all its promise for ages to come. He spoke for his time—and a De Tocqueville of the period would, no doubt, have added tartly, for his country's social philosophy too. And that was why it was his large generalizations, rather than the empirical and scholarly investigations with which he believed he was merely underpinning them, that caught most attention.

We must bear in mind, as his biographers have emphasized (Stern, 1931), that the hypothesis which he took over and built upon in elaborating what to us is his preposterous scheme of social stages, was widely current at the time.[3] Eminent scholars in Europe and America, as well as men of affairs, took for granted the notion of development by stages in the growth of society. Many, moreover, accepted in some shape or another, the assumption of a primordial stage of marital communalism coupled with matriarchy as the *terminus a quo* of the history of the human family.

In relation to this frame of thought, and more particularly to the nature and paucity of the observational data that could be drawn upon, Morgan's contribution was sensational. The criticism that broke loose, even from some who were broadly in agreement with his ideas testified to this. The story has been well told by others,[4] but what I wish to underline is that the focus of attention was then, and so remained for fifty years, Morgan's speculative hypotheses. The glaring fallacies in his reasoning and the shaky foundations of his conjectures were easily exposed. Darwin, arguing from the analogy of sexual selection and mating habits among the lower primates, was one of the first to express reservations amounting to a rejection of the

3. And, like his basic orientation and his method of "conjectural history," had a respectable scholarly pedigree going back to the social philosophers and historians of the previous century. As is well known, the method of "conjectural history" was first proposed by the eighteenth-century Scottish social philosopher, Dugald Stewart. Manifestly fallacious as it appears to us now in the light of modern knowledge, its historical importance should not be overlooked. As Teggart has shown, it was a "most serious effort to lay the foundations for a strictly scientific approach to the study of man" (Teggart, *Theory of History*, 1925: 87, quoted in Bryson, p. 112).

4. By Stern, 1931, and, among others, by Lowie, 1936; Tax, 1937; White, 1948. A recent biographical study by Carl Resek, *Lewis Henry Morgan: American Scholar*, 1960, also touches on the topic.

promiscuity and group marriage hypothesis (1871: vol. II, 358–63). But even he couched his objections in terms of deference to the prevailing ethnological opinion of his day. When in 1891 Westermarck stepped into the arena with his *History of Human Marriage*, it was with the primary, if not sole purpose of disproving the doctrine of original group marriage and its implications.

On the other hand, as others have recorded (Stern, 1931; Lowie, 1936; Tax, 1937; White, 1948), Morgan's speculative theories had partisans too. I am thinking not only of their adoption by Marx and Engels as the gospel source for their theory of the origin of the family and the state, nor of the cordiality of Maine or the enthusiasm of Bachofen (cf. Stern, 1931: 145 ff.). I have in mind rather such (from our point of view) more respectable and influential support as these views received from people like Lord Avebury (1870) and from Sir James Frazer even as late as 1910.

IV

To realize what this means in relation to our own times, let us remember that it was in the early 1900s that Malinowski fell under the spell of *The Golden Bough* (1890–1915) and that Radcliffe-Brown wrote the first draft of *The Andaman Islanders* (published 1922). By this time Boas was the unquestioned leader of American anthropology, Kroeber was already vigorously pursuing research, and Lowie was serving his apprenticeship with Wissler (cf. Lowie, 1959: chap. 2). We are by this date on the threshold of today, linked to Morgan by a brief intellectual pedigree, and by a tradition which is as green as that which binds us to our own parents and grandparents. Since then, the theory of primitive promiscuity and group marriage—outside the U.S.S.R. and apart from such Marxist scholars as Professor George Thomson (1949)—has been liquidated, helped by a strong push from Malinowksi with his study of the Australian family (1913). More significantly, the seemingly endless matriarchy controversy has been pulled down from the realm of inspired guesswork to the solid earth of ethnographical field research.[5]

It is this, particularly, that marks the big change since Morgan's lifetime in the direction and organization of anthropological research to which Kroeber referred. True, the main currents of ethnographical research in the first decade of this century, especially in the United States under Boas's influence (cf. White, 1948), moved strongly away from the beacon set up by Morgan; but his presence never ceased to be felt and soon it was authoritatively recognized. *The League of the Iroquois* (1851)[6] influenced ethnographic field research in America before Morgan became internationally known.

But what was more to the point was the recognition of Morgan as a discoverer, one not unworthy to be ranked with a discoverer of a new planet. And it is this that marked the real break between the period of anthropological history inaugurated by

5. Cf. the admirable evaluation of how the issue appears today by David F. Aberle, "Matrilineal Descent in Cross-cultural Perspective" in Schneider, and Gough (ed.), 1961: 655–727.

6. Full title, *League of the Ho-dê-no-sau-nee or Iroquois*; hereafter referred to as *The League* or as *The League of the Iroquois*.

Morgan and its earlier, amorphous anticipations; from this stemmed the shift in method and direction to which Kroeber drew attention.

By *discovery* I mean bringing to light previously uncomprehended or totally unknown facts and principles—in this context, facts and principles relating to human social life. What was significant for Morgan and critical for the subsequent development of anthropology was that his discoveries were made by direct observation in the field. Nor did he stop there. He added the necessary complement of theoretical interpretations which could be verified or falsified by recourse to further direct observation. This is something quite different from the reliance on speculation and conjecture which had prevailed before and which still held sway among the leading ethnologists of the day.

V

Morgan's greatest discovery, as every anthropologist knows, and as has often been stressed, was, in Leslie White's words, "the fact that customs of designating relatives have scientific significance." (1957: 257). Stated so modestly, its momentous importance would not be apparent to the layman. To us as anthropologists whose work it is to seek knowledge of the springs of man's social life, it has a clarion ring, for we know that it was from this discovery that some of the most far-reaching explorations of our subject matter first took their impetus. With all due respect to the memory of Malinowski, honor must be given in particular, as I have already suggested, to W. H. R. Rivers. He was, as Sol Tax reminded Radcliffe-Brown's followers "the founder of the modern study of social organization" (1955: 471). It is surely relevant that Rivers came to this study, as Morgan did, through direct observation in the field. In this lay the stimulus which led him to acclaim, to his everlasting credit, "the great theoretical importance" of what he described as Morgan's "new discovery" (1914a: 5).

We should remember that Morgan's analysis of classificatory kinship systems had been ignored for thirty years as the result mainly of McLennan's criticism. This explains why Rivers thought it necessary to refute McLennan's contention (1876; 1886 ed. p. 273) that classificatory systems (in Rivers's words) "formed merely a code of courtesies and ceremonial addresses" (1914a: 6). He rejected with equal firmness Kroeber's early (and subsequently discarded) thesis that they were "determined primarily by language" and "reflect psychology, not sociology" (1909: 84).

What Rivers did was to go back to Morgan. He commented astutely that the controversy about primitive promiscuity and group marriage had obscured the true import of Morgan's great discovery. Appealing to his own field observations, he emphatically confirmed Morgan's analysis of kinship and concluded that this—not his speculative theories—was Morgan's important and fundamental contribution.

If I might digress for a moment, the history of science offers many instances of revolutionary discoveries being temporarily smothered by the clamor of orthodoxy, or at best escaping recognition because the state of knowledge is not yet ripe for them. Mendel affords a classic example. Morgan's partial eclipse in the last quarter of the nineteenth century was doubtless due in part to the rarity, at that time, of ethnologists with first-hand field experience. There are grounds for such a conclusion if we bear in mind how Rivers was led by his field experience to return to Morgan. For this empirical starting point, as I shall repeatedly argue, is crucial. Lowie, who surely deserves to rank beside Rivers as an architect of modern kinship studies, was also influenced in that direction by field research. It was his field work among the Crow Indians that opened his eyes to Morgan's prowess as an ethnographer.

Should we then conclude that Morgan's novel discoveries failed to take root in the ethnology of his time because the ground was barren through lack of the fertilizing waters of ethnographical field research? Here, I think, some caution is necessary. We need only recall Boas and Malinowski to see that empirical research, even when it is pursued with complete integrity, has provided material for the rejection, or, at best, the misinterpretation rather than the confirmation of the analysis of social organization put forward by Morgan. It depends, really, on the frame of mind, or rather the apparatus of theory and method with which the field work is conducted and interpreted. And here lies the crucial issue for a just assessment of Morgan's legacy to us.

Rivers's explanation, incidentally, is worth bearing in mind because I think it has a lesson for us. As I have already indicated, Morgan himself never doubted that what deserved pride of place in his investigations, what was, from his point of view, most conclusive, was what I have called his visionary conception of mankind's social progress. Yet this is the part which is now generally dismissed as nothing more than a fallacious excrescence on the discoveries of substance embedded in his two great treatises. This applies also to the more restricted pseudo-historical conjectures to which he yoked the enquiries recorded in *Systems of Consanguinity and Affinity*. What has remained of permanent value, both as a testimony to his genius and as a springboard for advances in knowledge, is the body of data and the ancillary interpretations which he thought of primarily as the raw material for his speculations.

Morgan is not unique in this respect. Other great men have fallen for phantom aims, only to reach spurious conclusions on the basis of major discoveries which they failed to assess rightly. Our branch of science, I fear, is peculiarly prone to attracting this type of intellect. Perhaps indeed there is no anthropologist, nor ever has been one, who is really free from this propensity. Perhaps this is because we are particularly vulnerable to the political, moral, and spiritual climate of our time and culture, and therefore succumb easily to illusory ideals about our work; or maybe at bottom it is simply the price we pay for our scientific underdevelopment—that is, for the insufficiency of our apparatus of theory and method—for the tasks of rigorous and disciplined research.

VI

Be this as it may, as regards Morgan, one consequence of the exaggerated importance he himself and his contempories—as well as many of his successors—gave to his speculations is that, ever since, too much attention has been directed to them. Again, I am not here thinking of Engels and the other Marxist admirers and followers he has had. As I have mentioned, Malinowski exploited these extravagant hypotheses (and not without reason or precedent) to make a straw image of Morgan as a foil to functionalist theories. Even those who, like Rivers, Lowie, Radcliffe-Brown and, in our own generation, Leslie White and G. P. Murdock, have had the perspicacity to seize on the fundamental discoveries he made, have been hampered by this tradition. We see this in the paper I have previously cited which was contributed by Lowie to the Kroeber *Festschrift* in 1936, where he makes an assessment in retrospect of Morgan's total contributions to anthropology. Before paying his tribute to what he calls the "positive side" of Morgan's contribution, he finds it necessary to refute at length Morgan's evolutionist scheme and the deductions tacked on to it. Then only can he discuss what he elsewhere (1937; 1960, p. 62) describes as "Morgan's unique distinction . . . in literally creating the study of kinship systems as a branch of comparative sociology".

Morgan's field observations have been regularly taken into account for their ethnographical and historical bearing on later findings, as by Swanton, Lowie, and many others since. The revelation by Rivers of what was truly original and fundamental in Morgan's work on kinship and social organization has stimulated frequent reappraisal of his concepts and interpretations by later theoretical criteria. Yet the formative influence of his methods and ideas throughout the whole later development of the anthropological study of kinship and social organization has, to my mind, never been properly evaluated. Inquiry has been too much side-tracked by his evolutionist aberrations.

This formative influence was effective by degrees, making itself felt almost more by contagion than by willing acceptance. To appreciate it one has to go back to the sources. One has to immerse oneself particularly in the two great treatises, *Systems of Consanguinity and Affinity* and *Ancient Society*, without prejudice and, I should add, without impatience with their pedantic and repetitious form.

However, different ways of approaching the work of our predecessors are open to us. If we examine them in an historical spirit, we try to assess them in relation to the times in which they lived. In Morgan's case, biographers, critics and commentators, some of them already referred to, provide plenty of guidance and material. The revolutionary decade, the sixties of last century, singled out by Kroeber, is tremendously interesting to us today because of the parallels and contrasts in method, theory, and aims discoverable among the founders of our science in that period. Take for instance Sir Henry Maine and compare him with Morgan. In retrospect we can see that they exercised convergent influences on the birth of modern social anthropology. Jurist and ethnologist respectively, they started, as Stern notes, from almost opposite kinds of data and premises (1931: 88). They disagreed on what to them seemed to be basic conclusions, principally over the hypothetical issue of which came first, patriarchy or matriarchy. Now suppose we ignore this, realizing that it was the accidental result of Maine's absorption in the history of Roman and Hindu family law and of Morgan's Iroquois predilections. We cannot then fail to be impressed by the compatibility of their points of view and their theories, and we can see why it is that modern structuralist anthropology has derived much of its inspiration from them. Whether or not, for example, Morgan borrowed the division he made between *societas* or gentile society, and *civitas* or political society, from Maine's celebrated contrast between status and contract, is immaterial. The fact is that he found it apposite to his thought and improved on it theoretically by lifting it from its narrow legal associations to the sociologically more significant political plane. Yet matchless scholar though he was, Maine's ethnological naïveté was exposed when he commented as follows on Morgan's analysis of classificatory kinship systems: "May I suggest," he wrote, "that it is at least worthy of consideration whether all or part of the explanation may not lie in an imperfection of mental grasp on the part of savages? . . . the comprehension of a large body of complex relationships demands a prodigious mental effort, even now requiring for its success the aid of a special notation." Perhaps, he added, classificatory kinship represents "a rude and incomplete attempt at the mental contemplation of a tolerably numerous tribal body" (1883: 289–90). Today we would not take this kind of explanation seriously.

On the other side, there was Morgan blinded, as Lowie pointed out in 1936, by his Iroquois experiences and his preconceived hypotheses to such an extent that he failed to grasp the relevance of Maine's analysis of the concept of the corporation to his own theory of the gens and its passage into political society. Today of course we can see that they were complementary to each other. Patriarchy versus matriarchy, *patria-potestas* versus the democracy which Morgan tended to overrate in the matrilineal gens, the principle of the corporation as a legal entity by contrast with the structure of the corporate gens as a political unit based on kinship—in all these respects their researches complemented each other.

Now compare Tylor, the true founding ancestor of what has come to be called cultural anthropology. Like Morgan and Maine, he was a social evolutionist. He believed in progress and his scientific aim was the recovery of the origins of social institutions. But his idea of the subject matter of anthropology, that is to say, of the stuff of human social evolution, was poles apart from Maine's and Morgan's. His disciple and biographer R. R. Marett (1936) testifies to Tylor's lack of interest in "sociological matters," in other words, in social organization and related institutions, until nearly the end of his career. Dominated by his image of the "complex whole," as he called it, to which he gave the name of Culture, and committed as he was to a psychological mode of explanation (derived straight from the eighteenth-century Scottish social and moral philosophers), he simply did not know what to make of the bones and sinews of social organization that support and direct the manifestations of Custom. In his first major work, which appeared in the middle of the formative decade of the sixties, he alludes to the little that was then known about rules prohibiting marriage between kin and comments on affinal avoidances. But he throws them into a grab-all chapter labeled "Some Remarkable Customs" and dismisses them with the reflection that they belong "properly to that interesting, but difficult and almost unworked subject, the Comparative Jurisprudence of the lower races"— in fact, to Maine's and Morgan's field (1865; 1878 ed.: 279).

This judgment, incidentally, shows that Tylor was well aware of the difference between his interests and proclivities and those that were reflected in contemporary researches on kinship and marriage. His image of primitive culture as a jumble of variegated customs unified primarily by the superstitious beliefs generated by the all-prevailing principle of animism had no place for kinship and social organization. These topics are not even mentioned in his massive and famous book *Primitive Culture* (1871), whereas Morgan, in his work, reverses the emphasis and treats religious beliefs and ideas as secondary attributes of gentile and political structure.

We can see now that what Tylor lacked was the idea of a social system, of a society as a system of interconnected institutions that regulate social relations and embody norms of right and duty. I hope I will not be accused of invidious imputations if I add that this deficiency, transmitted through Frazer, Haddon, Boas, Kroeber, and others, has continued to characterize much of what goes by the name of cultural anthropology. Maine had the idea of a social system by way of the logical and analytical apparatus of Roman jurisprudence, though he too dressed up his findings in the positivist and evolutionist idiom of his time. Morgan came to it via the paradigm of formal regularity he discerned in kinship terminologies—influenced too, no doubt, by his thorough study of Roman civil law. Tylor, on the other hand, had only his evolutionist orientation and his comparative procedure to bring order into the atomistic assemblages of custom which he brought together. When, eventually, he came out with his famous paper on marriage and descent (1889), he still adhered to his method of dismembering institutional complexes and correlating (albeit now numerically) the traits he separated out. But the idea of a system, which Morgan and Maine had, is the key to the subsequent development, through Radcliffe-Brown and his successors, of our current structural theories.

These comparisons could profitably be extended but there is no need for this.[7] I have paused to consider them because I wanted to illustrate what I mean by examining our predecessors' work in an historical spirit. When we do so, we do not of course divest ourselves of all that we have learned since their day. It would be false, and indeed silly, to think that we can effectively put ourselves back in their place and time. We can only evaluate them fruitfully for our own instruction if we judge them frankly by our own standards of theory and practice.

This holds even more strongly if we approach their work in what I should like to call a genealogical spirit. I mean by this the frame of mind of someone who traces back his ancestry to see what he has got from it. As we all know, Radcliffe-Brown and Lowie, the two outstanding authorities in the generation just antecedent to ours on the subject which Morgan opened up for science, were inspired to study kinship and social organization by Rivers, who was thus passing on the insight he had derived from Morgan's original researches. If this is not tantamount to transmission "through the blood" (if I might be allowed to parody one of Morgan's more fanciful notions), it is, without disrespect, almost an apostolic succession.

To read Morgan in this spirit, but without renouncing our own criteria of theory

7. For example, by including Herbert Spencer, McLennan, and other nineteenth-century protagonists in the controversies concerning social evolution. For a concise assessment of their significance today see Evans-Pritchard's *Social Anthropology*. The intellectual climate in which their theories developed and the specific contributions of Maine, Spencer and Tylor, to evolutionist ideology are authoritatively analysed in J. W. Burrow's recent (1966) book.

and fact is no mere gesture of piety. For me it was a revelation. It made me realize that two distinct lines of descent are represented in the intellectual heritage of modern social anthropology.[8] I see one as going back through Radcliffe-Brown, Lowie, and Rivers, to Morgan and Maine in particular, and the other as going back through Kroeber, Malinowski, and Frazer, to Tylor and to some extent Boas. I see the first line as the source of our structural concepts and theories, the second as the source of our speciality in the study of the facts of custom, or culture. Naturally, I am oversimplifying, leaving out many names on the family tree that are no less distinguished and influential than those I have cited, not to speak of the collateral connections to Durkheim, Weber, and Freud. I do this to pin down my argument. But do let us remember that a double descent system specifies a person's place and capacity in society along both coordinates simultaneously. Even if a position has no value on one axis, it still signifies a stance in relation to what that axis stands for. We must never forget that "structure" and "culture" stand for indissociably conjoined frames of analysis in our studies. What matters is how they are mutually balanced in any particular kind of inquiry.

VII

In short, if we want properly to understand in what ways Morgan's work remains significant for us, we must look behind the intellectual conventions and the dominant forms of thought of his time, those in which he dressed up his observations and ideas, and we must try to see what he was really getting at. We must, as it were, read between the lines of his writings. For one thing, just as there was in the 1930's, and still is in some quarters, an anti-hero prejudice against Morgan, so there also was (and is) a hero-worshipping reverence for him in other quarters;[9] and both attitudes distort our judgment. For another, the historicist position[10] (better still, illusion, as Radcliffe-Brown used to say) has a mysterious fascination. When we try to understand human behavior in any of its manifestations, we are apt spontaneously to slip into looking for explanations of what is before our eyes—in the "here and now" of custom and behavior—in terms of sequences of antecedent actions and circumstances. I imagine that it is a tendency which is a projection outwards of the individual's experience of growth and change within the continuity of his personal identity. Professional historians have a good excuse for following this pattern, though among them too there are now many dissidents who have aligned themselves to all intents with functionalist and structuralist methodology (cf. Carr, 1961). At the other end of the continuum of human existence, in dealing with the phenomena of personality and individuality, psychoanalysis and genetic psychology have

8. As I pointed out in my Inaugural Lecture, *Social Anthropology at Cambridge since 1900* (1953a).

9. Again, I am not referring to his Marxist admirers but cf., e.g., Roland B. Dixon's "Some Aspects of the Scientific Work of Lewis Henry Morgan" (1919).

10. I use this term in the sense given to it by Professor K. R. Popper in his well-known work, *The Open Society and Its Enemies* (1945).

invested historically oriented theory with exceptional prestige.[11] In anthropology, however, it has been a perennial source of confusion, not only with regard to aims and methods but also with detriment to the tasks of empirical research. How it has also held back the advance of theory has been demonstrated in the generation-long debate begun with the joint assault by Malinowski and Radcliffe-Brown, fighting under the banner of functionalism, on the ultra-diffusionists, on the one hand, and on the Boasian empiricists, on the other.

If we now apply functional and structural criteria of analysis, we can see where the confusion resides and how Morgan himself was affected by it. It comes from failure to discriminate between synchronic and diachronic systems and relations. As a result, the things which are analytically discontinuous, but not dissociated within the synchronic frame of observation are interpreted as if they were dia-chronically related, therefore discontinuous in time, and therefore sequential. Maine had an inkling of this when he suggested, in criticism of Morgan, that it was not necessary to postulate that descent in the gens changed from the female line to the male line. "One of these two groups" he wrote "did not really succeed the other, but the two co-existed from all time, and were always distinct from one another. We must be careful, in theorizing on these subjects, not to confound mental operations with substantive realities" (1883; 1886 ed.: 287). A more familiar illustration of this point is Lowie's demonstration (1920) that territory and kinship are not successive but coexistent principles of political organization in simple societies. Morgan's supreme vice of method was to leap indiscriminately from what was effectively synchronic observation to pseudo-historical deduction. But his scrupulous regard for the facts as observed, coupled with his logical naïveté, make it quite easy to separate the one from the other.

This is the frame of analysis I shall apply in order to disentangle from his work and thought the ideas and conceptions which helped to shape our modern theories and methods. I shall examine *Systems of Consanguinity and Affinity* and *Ancient Society* by this procedure,[12] and I hope to show that, surprising as it may sound, if these works of Morgan are examined in a genealogical spirit and in the light of subsequent developments, they can be seen to constitute the basic charter of modern structural theory in social anthropology. My interest does not lie in the fact that

11. The conceptual and methodological parallels between historical and psychogenetic forms of explanation are classically exhibited in such works as Freud's *Totem and Taboo* (1913) as well as in Tylor's and Frazer's writings. It is interesting to find that Rivers was aware of this and even went so far as to argue that they are complementary. In *The History of Melanesian Society* (1914b: vol. II, pp. 6–7.) he declared that the "historical study of human culture" should go on "side by side" with its psychological study as each casts light on the other.

12. What I am here stating is a point of view often expressed by Radcliffe-Brown and expounded with his usual lucidity in a lecture on "The Development of Social Anthropology" which he gave at Chicago in December, 1936, and which was not, to the best of my knowledge, ever published. In the mimeographed record kindly made available to me by Professor Fred Eggan, Radcliffe-Brown explains how "pseudo-historical" theories are intelligible from a logical and scientific standpoint if they are thought of as "logical fictions" cast in a form that fitted in with the philosophical notions and intellectual conventions of the time. Eighteenth-century social philosophers, such as Hume and Dugald Stewart himself, were, he adds, quite aware of this. The confusion between suppositious history and true history seems to have developed in the nineteenth century, no doubt as a result of the coincident emergence of evolutionary biology and historical scholarship.

Morgan broke new ground ethnographically in the study of kinship and social organization, though I agree with those who consider *Systems* to be an imposing compendium of empirical field data judged by any standards. What I specifically wish to examine is an aspect of its construction that has hitherto been almost entirely ignored. To my mind this book (and *Ancient Society*, too) is remarkable for the intuitive analytical methods developed in it. It is a method which I claim to be thoroughly congenial to our current theoretical approaches and which indeed foreshadows them. It reflects a procedure and a theory which, in my view, are recognizably structural in our accepted sense today, if only embryonically so. Of course, there is all that bizarre nonsense about "streams of the blood" and all that fancy guesswork about the historical origins of the American Indian peoples. There is also the master hypothesis derided by Lowie, and curtly dismissed by Radcliffe-Brown as "one of the most fantastic in a subject that is full of fantastic hypotheses" (1941: 59), that is to say, the assumption that classificatory kinship terminologies are the precipitates of extinct forms of marriage and family institutions. It is salutary to remember, however, that this hypothesis was accepted by a number of highly qualified ethnologists, including no less a person than Rivers himself. It survives in Soviet ethnology as a fixed premise of kinship theory; and it is perhaps no exaggeration to see a trace of it in the priority given to the relations of marriage over those of descent in the theories of Lévi-Strauss and his followers today (Lévi-Strauss, 1949; cf. also Dumont, 1957). I mention this because we know well enough now that kinship terminologies do, in certain respects, reflect marriage rules and practices, though not in the way that Morgan asserted, and that the elucidation of these conceptions was in no small measure due to confronting his erroneous views with the facts of field research. This is a warning against the doctrinaire rejection of what are thought to be false theories which Malinowski, for example, was guilty of in respect to Morgan. Properly reinterpreted, they may stimulate valid discovery. It is my aim to demonstrate that Morgan requires and repays reinterpretation in the light of hindsight conferred by the later developments in anthropological theory and research. More precisely, what I propose to show is that the development in the study of kinship and social organization which culminated in what we today describe as structural theory has its roots and precedents in Morgan's work.

VIII

There are signs that we are coming to the end of this phase. New prospects are opening. Yet the continuity is, to my mind, unmistakable. I can easily imagine some future Kroeber—looking back fifty years hence on the first century of scientific anthropological research and theory in the field of kinship and social organization— seeing it as all of one piece. I can imagine him describing it as the Morganian classical period and setting its termination in our present decade. He will no doubt see it as subdivided by a succession of critical events. The first will be Rivers' reinstatement of Morgan as the discoverer of the key significance of kinship systems in human social organization. He will single out Rivers' insistence on Morgan's principle that kinship terminologies and customs depend on social causes, have social functions, reflect socially ordained rights and duties, as against Alfred Kroeber's earlier view that their connotation is purely psychological and linguistic. This latter-day Kroeber would, I believe, next select Lowie's early work *Primitive Society* (1920) and show how its general theme and the particular topics he dealt with derive straight from Morgan. He will not fail to perceive that Lowie's great service to our science was to map out the subject matter that falls within the ambit of the anthropological study of kinship and social organization, delineate its constituent parts, and set out the problems to be investigated in this field. After Lowie he will surely regard as the next landmark Radcliffe-Brown's *Social Organization of Australian Tribes* (1930–31). He will be struck by the close parallels between Radcliffe-Brown's and Morgan's frames of analysis, noting in particular the crucial importance both attach to the concept of system in the study of kinship. I imagine him going on to the next landmark, which in my view, is the Chicago volume on *Social Anthropology of North American Tribes* (Eggan, 1937a), in which Radcliffe-Brown's conceptual framework and analytical methods are tested out in an ethnographic area that was peculiarly Morgan's. And here he will note how the separation of the synchronic dimension of social structure from the diachronic dimension, which—as I hope to show—was intuitively grasped by Morgan but smothered in his presentation, is made a basic rule of procedure. He could hardly avoid contrasting this line of development with what might seem on the surface to be the very different one best epitomized in Malinowski's slight but arresting study of the psychological and cultural dynamics of the matrilineal family in *The Father in Primitive Psychology* (1927b). But coming next to our own times he will find in Lévi-Strauss's ambitious work, *Les Structures Elémentaires de la Parenté* (1949), these two tendencies reconciled in a new leap forward and he will note the dedication to Lewis H. Morgan as testimony of the author's recognition of his scientific ancestry. From the point of view of such an historian, I think the conclusion will be inevitable that structural social anthropology has its roots and its origins, conceptually no less than historically, in Morgan's work.

I began with a reminiscence of how Lewis Henry Morgan was first presented to me and to many of my contemporaries as the arch-enemy of all we stood for, worthy only of ridicule and contempt for his preposterous theories. To counter blinkered prejudice with blind hero worship is absurd and I have no intention of playing this game. My position is, quite simply, that, far from being an anachronistic hindrance to the development of modern theory in social anthropology, Morgan's discoveries and procedures of analysis in fact foreshadowed it and set the course for it in important and fundamental respects. "As the births of living creatures at first are ill-shaped," Sir Francis Bacon wisely warns us (*Essays*, 24), "so are all innovations which are the births of time." We must not be deceived by the unprepossessing shape Morgan adopted for presenting his discoveries, and so fail to grasp their true significance.

CHAPTER II

The Line of Succession:
From Morgan to Radcliffe-Brown

I

MORGAN HAS BEEN A CONTROVERSIAL FIGURE IN ANTHROPOLOGY, IN SOCIAL philosophy, and in political theory for nearly a century. A large and varied literature has accumulated concerning him and his theories. I have suggested that it would be profitable to take a fresh and unprejudiced look at his major treatises, ignoring his speculative hypotheses and making allowance for the backward state of ethnographical field research in his day. To do this it is necessary to put aside the critical, exegetical, and expository literature to which I have previously referred, and begin from the beginning. I say this in no spirit of disparagement of the many eminent scholars who have contributed to this literature, for, as stands to reason, some of my conclusions have been anticipated by them. My main thesis, however, has, I believe, hitherto escaped adequate recognition. I claim that Morgan's substantive discoveries and intuitively elaborated methods of analysis constituted the foundations of what we now call structural theory in social anthropology. I maintain that the analytical procedure implicit in his work foreshadowed and stimulated, in a striking manner, the development of theory which we owe above all to the lead given by Radcliffe-Brown. The proof, as I hope to show, lies in the Morganian sources.

It is essential to return to the sources because Morgan has been consistently

THE LINE OF SUCCESSION

misunderstood, or rather misread, by generation after generation of scholars. I am not thinking here of the hypnotic attraction his conjectural stages and fanciful evolutionist ideas had—and still have—for many doughty and learned investigators. For this has been largely a matter of preconceived doctrine and ideology. (A good example is V. Gordon Childe's attempts to adapt and preserve Morgan's pseudo-historical framework.[1])

I am thinking rather of how Morgan's concepts and hypotheses in relation to kinship and social organization have been misconstrued by anthropologist after anthropologist in the past sixty years, not excluding Rivers himself. We owe a piquant example of this to Leslie White (1958). The distinction Morgan drew in exact and rigorous terms between classificatory and descriptive systems of terminology was and remains the linchpin of his and of subsequent kinship theory. Yet anthropologists of the highest repute and competence have, as White reveals, persistently misinterpreted it. His list—enlivened with telling verbatim quotations—of those who have made this mistake includes Kroeber, Lowie, Goldenweiser, and other leading anthropologists of their generation, and convicts even such contemporary authorities as Hoebel and Murdock of muddling the conceptual distinction. A common objection to it is that descriptive systems have classificatory elements; but, as White remarks, Morgan himself drew attention to this and explained it convincingly. It is not without significance for my theme that White specifically exonerates Radcliffe-Brown and his followers—among whom I am gratified to find myself named—from this error. He adds that, useful as some of the refinements of terminology proposed in recent studies may be, they do not cover or invalidate the distinction Morgan made, and I fully agree with him. In view of this widespread carelessness in the understanding of Morgan's basic concept, it is not surprising that the deeper theoretical implications of his work have escaped recognition.

II

Let us turn, then, to the first of Morgan's theoretical treatises, *Systems of Consanguinity and Affinity*. If I describe it as the basic charter of what subsequently became structural theory and method, this is not because it broke open for the first time in the history of the human sciences the golden vein of kinship and social organization for scientific mining. It is because of the procedure of exposition and method of analysis followed in the development of the argument. Crucial to the whole, and fundamental for later development, is the empirical basis of field observations, whether Morgan's own or those of his correspondents.[2] We must not lose sight of

1. Cf., e.g., Childe's *Social Evolution* (1951). I cite him because he was an erudite and balanced scholar distinguished among the archeologists of his time for his understanding of modern anthropological ideas.

2. Morgan's own description of how he first came upon the fact of classificatory kinship terminology and established that it was not a unique and peculiar Iroquois custom but probably general among American Indians, has often enough been referred to in anthropological literature to need no attention here. This applies also to his account of how he

this, nor of the fact I have previously emphasized, to wit, that Morgan worked with systems of relationships, not with traits of custom. He dealt with taxonomically distinguished units of human social organization, that is, societies, not with isolated properties or characters of man's behavior. But his investigations proceeded at two levels. At one, he was concerned with the internal constitution of systems and families of systems of relationships; at the other, he sought for the congruences and connections between systems and families of systems. But like Darwin and the evolutionary biologists before the advent of modern genetics, he failed to see that these correspond to both logically and analytically discrete dimensions of social organization. The result was the confusion of aims symptomatized in his pursuit of the chimera of pseudo-history.

Morgan introduces the concept of the *classificatory system* right at the beginning of the treatise (p. vi). Characteristically and significantly, it is presented in juxtaposition to the complementary concept of the *descriptive system*, which is defined as the "reverse" of it in "fundamental conceptions"; and each is said to contain "a plan, for the description and classification of kindred." After this, the master hypothesis of primitive promiscuity and group marriage is introduced; but it is tacked on, avowedly as a conjectural inference.

Morgan was a punctilious, even pedantic writer, as the much corrected and rewritten manuscripts of *Ancient Society* in the library of the University of Rochester testify. Now there is one thing about pedants which one must not overlook. They weigh their words carefully. Thus when Morgan writes of a "plan," there is a point to it which no other words would convey. This is evident from the way in which the statement I have quoted is repeated over and over again, like a formula, sometimes superfluously, frequently with the inconsequential corollary that "the important question . . . [is] how far these forms become changed with the progressive changes of society" (p. 13).

Let us consider a typical passage from the treatise in which he expounds the meanings he attaches to his key concepts. I quote the explanation which introduces the discussion of the "Ganowanian" system, but similar pieces abound *passim*:

In contradistinction from *descriptive* the term *classificatory* will be employed to characterize the system of consanguinity and affinity of the Ganowanian, Turanian, and Malayan families, which is founded upon conceptions fundamentally different. Among the latter families consanguinei are never described by a combination of the primary terms; but on the contrary they are arranged into greater classes or categories upon principles of discrimination peculiar to these families. All the individuals of the same class are admitted into one and the same relationship, and the same special term is applied indiscriminately to each and all of them. For example, my father's brother's son is my *brother* under the system about to be considered; and I apply to him the same term which I use to designate an own brother: the son of this collateral brother and son of my own brother are both my *sons*. And I apply

obtained his world wide sample of kinship terminologies (*Systems*, pp. 4–6). How he came to write the book is related Leslie White (1957). Who can fail to admire the rigor and caution with which Morgan checked his inferences and set up the comparative survey by which to test and validate his hypotheses ?

to them the same term I would use to designate my own son. In other words, the person first named is admitted into the same relationship as my own brothers, and these last named as my own sons. The principle of classification is carried to every person in the several collateral lines, near and remote, in such a manner as to include them all in the several great classes. Although apparently arbitrary and artificial, the results produced by the classification are coherent and systematic. In determining the class to which each person belongs, the degrees, numerically, from *Ego* to the common ancestor, and from the latter to each kinsman, are strictly regarded. This knowledge of the lines of parentage is necessary to determine the classification. As now used and interpreted, with marriage between single pairs actually existing, it is an arbitrary and artificial system, because it is contrary to the nature of descents, confounding relationships which are distinct, separating those which are similar, and diverting the streams of the blood from the collateral channels into the lineal. Consequently, it is the reverse of the descriptive system. It is wholly impossible to explain its origin on the assumption of the existence of the family founded upon marriage between single pairs; but it may be explained with some degree of probability on the assumption of the antecedent existence of a series of customs and institutions, one reformatory of the other, commencing with promiscuous intercourse and ending with the establishment of the family, as now constituted, resting upon marriage between single pairs.

From the complicated structure of the system it is extremely difficult to separate, by analysis, its constituent parts and present them in such a manner as to render them familiar and intelligible without close application. There are, however, several fundamental conceptions embodied in the system, a knowledge of which will contribute to its simplification. The most of them are in the nature of indicative characteristics of the system, and may be stated as follows: First, all of the descendants of an original pair are not only, theoretically, consanguinei, but all of them fall within the recognized relationships. Secondly, relations by blood or marriage are never described by a combination of the primary terms, but a single special term is applied to each of them... (pp. 143–44).

What I wish to draw attention to is the plan of the argument. If we brush aside the pseudo-historical and pseudo-biological interpretations of the data and examine the analytical side of the argument, we cannot but be struck by the way it is presented. It is done in terms of a dichotomous opposition quite on the lines of the most up-to-date precepts of methodology in linguistics and the social sciences. We might almost say that "descriptive" and "classificatory" are presented as the two terms of a binary opposition. Moreover, this opposition is consistently followed through. "Primary terms" are counterposed to "categories," and "lineal" to "collateral" relationships; and what is most important, the coherent and systematic nature of the data comprised within the conceptual scheme is particularly emphasized.

Thus what we have here, so far, is the identification of a couple of paradigms which are claimed, on the basis of the empirical evidence, exhaustively to delineate the universe and to specify within it the distribution of all known forms of "systems of consanguinity and affinity." The parallel with classical biological taxonomy is obvious, though it goes no farther than a rudimentary distinction such as that of metazoa and protozoa.

III

So much for the form of the argument. But if we look at the substance, we can see that the data adduced and the distinction Morgan draws between the two kinds of system pertain wholly and strictly to their synchronic constitution. The "plans" he elicits are synchronic in their reference; and it is my contention that Morgan intuitively understood quite clearly what this implies.

The procedure he follows in order to reach the general propositions he aims at witnesses to this. The essential step is embodied in the concept of system, as I have already suggested. It is no empty word for Morgan. His introductory remarks (pt. I, chap. II) show him grappling with the problem of justifying its use. The critical observation is the one which established the standard form of presenting a kinship terminology with Ego at the center. The way Morgan put it (quotations in this and the following paragraph are from Pt. I, chap. II–III) was that every person can be thought of as "the central point, or *Ego*, from whom outward is reckoned the degree of relationship of each kinsman, and to whom the relationship returns" in other words, as standing at the center of a "circle or group of kindred." It is thus a self-balancing and, *eo ipso*, systematic arrangement. Morgan repeatedly insists that this is a "formal arrangement" not *ad hoc* usage, that it is a formal and systematic method for distributing kindred in accordance with "lines of descent" and for "distinguish[ing] one relative from another." Moreover, he regards these systems as so fundamental for human social life that he believes them to have been "one of the earliest acts of human intelligence." Put in more modern terms, we might say that he considers kinship systems to be so intrinsic to social organization that they must be accepted as irreducible components of it.

Now one of Morgan's preconceived notions reflecting the values of his own time and culture, was that the "marriage of single pairs," as he called it, was the most natural as well as the most refined and advanced form of human mating. Single-pair marriage, he contends, gives rise to "definite . . . lines of parentage" and so to a "natural system" of degrees of proximity among the descendants of one pair which can be numerically computed. He recurs to this theme repeatedly, though its true import is often obscured behind the fustian phraseology in which it is clothed. The point is that descriptive terminologies reflect one kind of "definite ideas," those enshrined in the "natural system" ensuing from single-pair marriage. Classificatory systems reflect another set of definite ideas. It is these which make them into systems and, what is more, make them all systems of that one type. Translating again, what the argument asserts is that the essence of the dichotomous opposition lies in the definite ideas.

One instance of this line of thought must suffice. It is reiterated with Morgan's customary prolixity. Summing up his gratification at finding complete coincidence between the Seneca-Iroquois system and that of the "Dakota nations" he writes:

It thus appears that every indicative feature of the Seneca system is not only present in that of the Dakota nations; but that they are coincident throughout. The diagrams used to illustrate the Seneca-Iroquois form will answer for either of the Dakota nations as well. Every relationship I believe, without exception, would be the same in the six diagrams. This identity of systems is certainly an extraordinary fact when its elaborate and complicated structure is considered. The significance of this identity is much increased by the further fact that it has remained to the present time, after a separation of the Iroquois from the Dakota nations, or from some common parent nation, for a period of time which must be measured by the centuries required to change the vocables of their respective stock languages beyond recognition. The maintenance of a system which creates such diversities in the domestic relationships, and which is founded upon such peculiar discriminations, is the highest evidence of its enduring nature as a system. Ideas never change. The language in which they are clothed is mutable, and may become wholly transformed; but the conceptions which it embodies, and the ideas which it holds in its grasp, are alone exempt from mutability. When these ideas or conceptions are associated together in such fixed relations as to create a system of consanguinity, resting upon unchangeable necessities, the latter is perpetuated by their vital force, or the system, in virtue of its organic structure, holds these ideas in a living form. We shall be led step by step to the final inference that this system of relationship originated in the primitive ages of mankind, and that it has been propagated like language with the streams of the blood (p. 176).

The emphasis, we note, is on the identity of the underlying ideas behind the variability of the language in which they are clothed; and it is the association together of the ideas which creates the system of consanguinity. Even the fanciful nonsense about the streams of blood is meaningful as a pointer to the question raised by Morgan elsewhere as to how these systems are maintained generation after generation. His solution, that they are maintained by constant use and are transmitted by virtue of the fact that they form part of what he calls the domestic organization, is surely the obvious and indisputable one. It is the observation of an ethnographer intuitively alert to function and structure.

IV

It would be tedious to go over all the statements made by Morgan on the meaning he gives to his notion of system, for they are repetitious to a point of surfeit. But the concept is so important in his frame of analysis that it is worth tarrying over one more illustration. In presenting the Tamil system, his meticulous procedure reveals the terminology for the children of cross cousins which, he declares to be "the only particular wherein it differs materially from the Seneca-Iroquois form" (p. 391). He adds that "the Seneca is more in logical accordance with the principles of the system than the Tamilian." This divergence, he frankly admits, baffles him. But he insists that, in spite of its seeming complexity and arbitrariness, it is a system "coherent, self-sustaining, and harmonious throughout" embodying, though not apparently based upon, the same fundamental conceptions as the ideal, generalized Ganowanian system (p. 394).

System, to Morgan, means therefore a self-balancing, internally coherent, and harmonious arrangement of recognized relationships centered on Ego and based upon fundamental conceptions common to all humanity. It is essentially a synchronic system with which he is concerned. This is evident in his emphasis on the utility and necessity of kinship systems in daily life, particularly in the domestic organization, and in the explanation he gives of their internal coherence. In all systems it depends upon the strict application of the "principle of correlative relationship" by which reciprocally related kin use reciprocal terms. In classificatory systems it is assured also by the strict and logical application of the principle of classification (*passim*, e.g., p. 390).

Let me turn back now to the procedure Morgan devised for establishing what these "fundamental conceptions" are. He is fumbling and prolix in elaborating it, but the principle is clear, and it is the principle which has guided fruitful search for generalizations in social anthropology ever since. What he does is to set up a prototypical model or paradigmatic case for each class of systems and he then allocates each specimen to its proper class by comparing it with the paradigm. Our own system is his norm for the descriptive category, but he prefers the Roman system as the paradigmatic case. Its "characteristic features," as Morgan (curiously anticipating the "distinctive features" of modern phonemics) appositely terms what have been more vapidly designated as *traits* by later ethnologists, are formally specified. Then the other specimens of the descriptive system are taken in turn and juxtaposed with the model to show up correspondences and deviations. They are not, I must repeat, compared trait by trait. Finally, a generalized paradigm is established which subsumes a family of models each member of which constitutes a distinctive variant of the common structure. Thus we get the Semitic, the Aryan and the Uralian submodels of the common descriptive system.

The same principle is followed, only more discursively owing to the nature of the data, in the case of the classificatory systems. For each ethnic cluster or, as he calls it, family, he begins by setting up a paradigm for which all the "indicative features" as he now calls them are specified in full. Then follows the procedure of comparison as before. And, incidentally, one cannot withhold admiration for the rigorous and scholarly examination by which the eligibility of each tribal system for inclusion in the family, and its position in the cluster as a whole, is established by linguistic, geographical, historical and ethnological criteria. How trivial by contrast is the Tylorian comparative method—which even Lowie, otherwise so critical of slipshod thinking, approved of and in part followed.

It would take too long and serve no purpose to review the 26 Indicative Features presented for the Ganowanian generalized model, or the 23 that are listed for the Turanian system (interestingly enough, in a footnote, and stated explicitly to be for checking against the Ganowanian model which it is claimed to reproduce), or the Hawaiian features. What it amounts to is an enumeration and analysis of each of the categories of relationship that is isolated. The six diagnostically most sensitive features, those in which "deviations from uniformity" as Morgan calls it (p. 148), are found in some tribes are, however, worth noting. Those specially emphasized are the relationships of uncle and nephew or niece, that is, cross-sibling's children, which is said to be one of the most striking indicative features of the system, and the relationships of cross-cousins.

It is in respect of this relationship, so perennially prominent in controversies on the subject of kinship and social organization to our own day, that, as Morgan observes, the principal deviations from uniformity occur. The complications of cousin terminologies were a puzzle and a trial to Morgan. He tells how he first discovered from an informant the apparently anomalous Omaha usage by which mother's brother's son is mother's brother to Ego, with the result, as he puts it that "A mother's brother and his lineal male descendants are thus placed in a superior relationship over her children with the authority the avunculine relationship implies in Indian society" (p. 179). Then he records an actual observation of the kind frequently reported by later ethnographers. He describes how an informant pointed to a small boy and designated him as his "uncle" because he was the son of the speaker's mother's brother who was also "uncle" to him. This is typical of Morgan's shrewd and scrupulous field work. At all events, the cross-cousin puzzle, the analytical recognition of which came to mean so much for later theoretical developments, merely plunges Morgan into silly pseudo-historical conjectures. He believes that the relationship of cousins was developed by the more advanced nations "to remove a blemish" and to "improve [the] symmetry" of the classificatory system (p. 179).

V

So far, we must conclude, Morgan remains, methodologically, wholly within the framework of synchronic analysis. Furthermore, he presses this analysis forward in logically consistent directions, as when he takes pains repeatedly to insist that the systems of nomenclature described are actually used in social life and are not merely linguistic curiosities or expressions of courtesy. American Indians, he points out, never address each other by name. Instead they employ kinship terms, both in address and for reference. Everybody, even young children, must therefore have an exact knowledge of their genealogical relationships. Far from being an idle exercise,[3] a kinship terminology represents a body of specialized knowledge which is indispensable for the individual in regulating and organizing his social relations. Morgan carefully checks on this correlation and expresses great satisfaction when it is reported for the Tamils. (I may add that a definitive investigation of the relationship between naming customs and kinship institutions and terminology has yet to be made.) Morgan's implicit hypothesis that kinship terminologies and names may be mutually exclusive functional equivalents has only recently begun to receive the attention it merits.[4] Likewise, in commenting on the terminological specification of the mother's brother in the Iroquois system, he relates this to the mother's brother's authority as the real head of his sister's family, gives some ethnographic illustrations, and concludes that it is rooted "in the tribal organization . . . which limits descent to the female line" so that "the children of a man's sister are of the same

3. It will be remembered that McLennan asserted classificatory kinship to be "a system of mutual salutations merely" (1876; 1886 ed.: 273).
4. The possibilities are illustrated in Thomson (1946) and Needham (1954).

tribe with himself" (p. 158); that is, what we should today call a clan or a lineage.

One item of incidental evidence deserves to be recorded. Introducing the discussion of the descriptive system, Morgan delivers himself of a remarkable warning: "It is impossible," he says, "to recover the system of consanguinity and affinity of any people, in its details, from the lexicon, or even from the literature of their language, if it has ceased to be a living form" (p. 17). If it has not been codified, as a law of the state, as was done by the Romans, it can only be obtained in detail "by a direct resort to the people"—in other words, by field research in living communities, a desideratum which Malinowski would certainly have applauded. The Roman system stirred him almost to rapture by its "beauty" and "perfection" and its comprehensive and precise discrimination of lines and degrees of consanguinity and affinity. But he particularly insisted that it was not merely a means of describing relationships. It had "the more important object of making definite the channel, as well as the order of succession to estates" (p. 27).

In all these examples, and they could be added to, Morgan is concerned to bring out the interconnections between kinship nomenclatures and other institutions and arrangements in what might be called a protofunctional and protostructural sense. It is the contemporaneous interdependence of the indicative features of the model, their connection with descent grouping, family authority, inheritance and succession, and behavior patterns, which he labors. This is what Rivers found in Morgan's work and summed up as the discovery of "the close connection between the terminology of the classificatory system of relationship and forms of social organisation" (1914a: 5).

Without laboring the point further, we can see that it was this analytical substratum, as I regard it, of Morgan's investigations and hypotheses synchronically oriented and empirically validated, which was the spur to the ethnographical and theoretical study of kinship and social organization initiated by Rivers. This applies not only to the general pattern and objective of research but also to particular nodal problems and issues which have engaged attention ever since. I have already mentioned cross-cousin terminologies and their significance. The so-called avunculate is another case in point; and, indeed, the root problem of how classificatory terminologies are generated and what they serve and stand for still remains open. Radcliffe-Brown's theory, summed up in his two principles of the unity of the lineage and the unity of sibling group, convincing as it is, is only part of the solution.

I return to this later. Here let me note again that the momentum set going by Rivers' rediscovery of Morgan was reflected in the contents and interests of Lowie's first major work, *Primitive Society* (1920), which I have suggested might without derogation be described as a revision and expansion of Morgan's ideas and subject matter. Kroeber's periodical sorties into the field of kinship and social organization readily fit into the scheme of Morgan's investigations and are, indeed, little more than extended reappraisals of constructions put on his data by Morgan. Coming to our own day, one cannot read Murdock's influential book on *Social Structure* (1949) without being reminded of *Systems of Consanguinity and Affinity*. More particularly, chapter 7 of Murdock's book immediately brings to mind Morgan's "Indicative Features." But there is a crucial divergence between them. It is illustrated by an instance which I take almost at random. Murdock attributes "the classification of two or more relatives under a single term" to the psychological process of " 'stimulus generalization' " occurring, he says, "only on the basis of regular and perceptible similarities" (1949: 132). I am not sure that I understand what Dr. Murdock means by this hypothesis—whether, for instance, he locates the process in the realm of each individual's experience as he grows up, much as Malinowski did with his theory of the extension of kinship attitudes and terminologies at successive stages of the life cycle (for further discussion, see chap. IV), or whether he thinks of it as having happened once for all in a people's history and having then been perpetuated by custom. In any event, I am confident that Morgan would have firmly rejected Murdock's explanation. By what "perceptible similarities" he might have asked could one arrive at a term which classified together a mother's brother of my parents' generation by birth and age with a relative of my grandchild's generation by birth and age as the Omaha do? For Morgan, the crucial principle was that relatives are classified together in accordance with relationships which are "arbitrarily" and "artificially" defined and recognized by reference to the "lines of parentage" laid down in each system. Not psychological mechanisms but institutional arrangements and structural criteria are the decisive factors. Fifty years later this became the central pillar of Radcliffe-Brown's approach.

VI

There is, as I have claimed, a direct conceptual as well as historical line of descent between Radcliffe-Brown's frame of thought and Morgan's. It may be said that this is equally true of others who were stimulated by Rivers, or even directly by the controversies among Morgan and his contemporaries, to take up the study of kinship and social organization. But there is a striking difference between what Radcliffe-Brown took or perhaps simply absorbed from Morgan and what others found in him. We need look no further than Rivers himself to see the contrast. For what *he* took from Morgan was the conviction that kinship nomenclatures and institutions derive, in the last resort, from, or are determined by, historically antecedent marriage forms, a supposition which eventually led to the preposterous theories typified by his hypothesis of Melanesian gerontocracy.[5] What Radcliffe-Brown, on the other hand, seized upon was the idea of the synchronic system of kinship relations, focused on

---

5. For the benefit of the record, I will give just one short quotation to illustrate Rivers's confusion. It is taken from *The History of Melanesian Society* (1914b, vol. II, p. 48.): "Henceforward I propose to regard it as established that the anomalous features of the Pentecost system, whereby members of alternate generations are classed together, are connected with an ancient social condition in which it was the normal occurrence for a man to marry the granddaughter of his brother, using the term brother either in the English or the classificatory sense." There is more to the same effect in this extraordinary chapter in which speculations about dual organization, gerontocracy, and systems of marriage are sweepingly mixed together. I should add the reminder that Rivers here represents an approach to kinship and marriage which was widely current in the half century after the publication of Morgan's *Systems*. To give but one example, he was anticipated in his general line of thought by the distinguished German ethno-jurist, R. Kohler in his essay "Zur Urgeschichte der Ehe" (1897) and other publications in which he followed Morgan. Gifford was another whose views were not far apart from those of Rivers.

Ego, as the center of an arrangement of kindred, grouped lineally and collaterally by recognized categories of relationship expressed in the terminology. It is a frame of analysis that would commend itself immediately to an ethnographer alert to the actualities of social relations in the field. Why, therefore, so practiced and (for his time) perceptive an ethnographer as Rivers, was tempted to search for chimerical marriage regulations to explain classificatory kinship remains a puzzle. Perhaps it is enough to say that he too was caught up in the methodological confusions of evolutionist and, what was later even worse, diffusionist theory, and therefore simply took over the explanatory formula which was most conspicuous in Morgan's theory.[6] But he also investigated and described forms of marriage empirically. In this he went farther than Morgan, for one of the curious deficiencies in Morgan's major treatises is the paucity of observational data on marriage; and this is perhaps understandable in view of the use to which he put his imaginary constructs of primitive promiscuity and group marriage. He acknowledged only one true, "natural" form of marriage and that was "the marriage of single pairs." To other forms of marriage practice he was, if not blind, at any rate insensitive and averse. Hence the caricatures he made of them—and their relegation to the mythological past he conjured up.

The contrast enhances the significance of the synchronic paradigm he intuitively built into his analysis of kinship systems. And my thesis is that it was an obvious and quite straightforward step to move from Morgan's paradigm of a system of consanguinity and affinity to Radcliffe-Brown's concept of a system of kinship and marriage relationships, as utilized, for instance, in his first (1913) publication on Australian social organization. (I discuss this more fully in chap. IV.)

The next step was to generalize the concept of a kinship system to subsume what was later distinguished as "the sum total of the social relations of the individuals making up the social group" (Eggan, 1937; 1955 ed.: 39) and to equate this with the social structure. I am here quoting Eggan's formulation, and it confirms the association I am suggesting between Morgan's and Radcliffe-Brown's concepts to find Eggan going on to define social relations—quite along Morganian lines—as "composed largely of social usages—customary ways of behaving. . . ." The advance on Morgan, at this stage, was that kinship terminologies are here explicitly correlated with other customary ways of behaving, not examined in isolation. Morgan's "principle of correlative relationship" is also incorporated in a more specific form in the method of identifying customary usages by their functions and emergence in dyadic social relations as it is employed by all the contributors to the book I am citing. This is the method that is turned to such brilliant analytical advantage in Lloyd Warner's *A Black Civilization* (1937), which must, I think, be regarded as the most sophisticated and fruitful ethnographical application of Radcliffe-Brown's earlier (1930–31) theoretical scheme.

To point the moral from another angle, let me revert for a moment to Lowie. I doubt if he ever completely sorted out the distinction between synchronic and diachronic, or rather, genuinely historical modes of investigation and reasoning in ethnology. In confusing them he fell into the same trap as Rivers and Morgan did

6. Cf., for instance, his posthumously published lectures (1924).

and the marks of this are patent in *Primitive Society*. There he still maintains that cross-cousin marriage, the levirate and the sororate, "tend to produce a definite terminology of kinship" (p. 34), though it is unclear whether he means this in an historical sense or in the sense of concomitant variation. More revealing is his handling of the "avunculate." It clearly had him foxed. The best he could do was to suggest that where it was found among a patrilineal people it could be due either to borrowing from matrilineal neighbors or was connected with cross-cousin marriage (pp. 171–72).

Compare this approach with Radcliffe-Brown's of the same date and the gap is striking. The test is found in Radcliffe-Brown's almost contemporary study of the same institution based in part on the same ethnographic sources and published only three years later. I refer, of course, to the famous paper on the mother's brother in South Africa (1924). Here strict synchronic analysis showed the patrilineal avunculate to fit consistently into a segmentary patrilineal lineage organization. It made sense of the ethnographic facts in a way that such pseudo-historical explanations as Lowie's (and Rivers's before him) failed to do. Lowie himself conceded this by implication when in 1948, with characteristic integrity, he recorded his agreement with Radcliffe-Brown's theory. (I deal with this in chap. IV.)

It is the more curious still to meet with throw-backs to an even more primitive form of conjectural history, outside of Eastern Europe, such as Dr. Murdock's (1959) revival of the hypothesis which explains the avunculate as a relic of an earlier and submerged stage of matriliny.

Where the parallel between Radcliffe-Brown's conception of a system of social relations and Morgan's notion of a system comes out most explicitly, however, is in *The Social Organization of Australian Tribes* (1930–31). In this fundamental inquiry Radcliffe-Brown follows Morgan—and not, for example, his own mentor Rivers—in taking as his units for comparison total systems of kinship and social structure and grouping them by types which represent local variants of a generalized model. What he is interested in is how best to delineate his generic model and to relate the members of the family of models it subsumes to one another and to the inclusive paradigm. They are investigated strictly as synchronic systems, with the avowed aim of eliciting the laws or principles of social structure by which the models are generated. Thus he arrives at "the one essential principle of what are known as 'classificatory systems of terminology,'" that is to say the famous principle of the equivalence of siblings. This step, to be sure, took the study of kinship to a level not reached by Morgan or by any previous investigator. But this is not the point of immediate concern to me—I shall return to it presently. I want only to demonstrate the connection between Radcliffe-Brown's method and Morgan's, though it may well have commended itself to Radcliffe-Brown also because it fitted in with the conception of social morphology which he shared with the school of Durkheim, and thus lent itself to "functionalist" treatment.[7]

7. It is to be understood that I am focusing attention on Radcliffe-Brown's work in the field of kinship and social organization. How he came to the general theoretical position projected in his concepts of function and structure is not the question here. Nor do I mean to imply that his debt to Morgan has hitherto been ignored. Tax (1955), for one, has made it clear enough.

The pattern of inquiry transmitted from Morgan and improved and refined by Radcliffe-Brown has been followed and elaborated by later investigators working in this tradition of what we now appropriately call structural analysis. Representative works are *Social Anthropology of North American Tribes* (Eggan, 1937a), Fortes and Evans-Pritchard's *African Political Systems* (1940) and Eggan's *Social Organization of the Western Pueblos* (1950), in all of which the paradigmatic method is used in much the same way as by Radcliffe-Brown. But this is not the only contribution to the theoretical study of kinship and social organization which we owe to Radcliffe-Brown. That I will return to presently.

CHAPTER III

Morgan and the Analytical Approach

I

WE HAVE NOT YET FINISHED WITH MORGAN AND I CRAVE THE READER'S INDULGENCE for going back on my tracks.

I have, I hope, successfully shown that at the level of synchronic observation and analysis intuitively followed by him, Morgan's insight and discoveries were pregnant with the constructive possibilities that were later realized. Where he went wrong, and grotesquely so, was at another level. It was when he made the leap from observation to explanation. It would be unrewarding to resuscitate this issue if it were not for the incorrigible persistence of Morgan's error. His point of departure was a legitimate question that arose from his analysis of the synchronic data. His question was: Why are there two and only two grand paradigms of kinship system? His answer was to fall back on the prevailing idiom of thought and definition of aims and think up a pseudo-historical explanation. To do this he had to misread the distinctions he perceived analytically as having chronological or rather sequential significance. The complementary dichotomy of descriptive and classificatory systems was turned into major stages of "progressive" development. This entailed supplementary hypotheses to explain how the observed facts came to be what they were. Here he was misled partly by mistakes of analysis due to the limited nature of the ethnographical data at his disposal, but mainly by the blindly accepted aim of demonstrating the unity of origin and therefore of mentality of the different branches of mankind.

We can see now that he was misled by his *a priori* judgment. He thought that the descriptive system not only corresponds to an advanced stage of social development but is also the "natural" one, since it follows the "nature of descents." He connected this system rightly with the marriage of single pairs. Hence came the inference that marriage was the key to the understanding of the classificatory system too. And given the dominance of the historicist mode of thought, the rest followed by a leap of deduction fully representative of the tradition of scholarship in which he was bogged down.

To give him his due, though, we must not forget that Morgan went to great pains to consider alternative explanations. In the final chapter of *Systems* he discusses such alternatives as the possibility that classificatory systems were spontaneously invented to meet special conditions of social life. The argument is so involved that it is not worth while trying to dissect it. He sensed a connection with another of his analytical dichotomies which he twisted to fit his pseudo-historical bias. (This is a version of the hypothesis he later developed in *Ancient Society*.) He argued that a wide recognition of kindred, especially of collateral kin, was necessary as a bond of mutual protection in the conditions of primitive social life, since the state and the law which are the sources of protection in civilized society were lacking (*passim* and p. 474 ff.). He also sensed a relationship between classificatory systems and what he calls tribal organization, that is, descent group structure. But, he sensibly concludes, it is impossible to see how these "external causes" could give rise to the particular "plan of consanguinity" exhibited in classificatory systems. Therefore they must be regarded as results rather than causes of the system.

Again, Morgan perceived that it is not enough to postulate causes that are no longer operative. Some explanation must be found for the persistence of their effects or else they would have vanished too. Hence the hypothesis—also concordant with the idiom of thought of his time—that the effects are preserved in language.

Finally, and with the same combination of insight and confusion, he realized that some explanation was necessary of the process of change from one stage of marriage and consanguinity to the next; and here he produced his trump card, the "rights of property and the succession to estates" (p. 493). This he declared (anticipating *Ancient Society*) "is the only conceivable agency sufficiently potent to accomplish so great a work as the overthrow of the classificatory, and the substitution of the descriptive system." But singularly little justification is here offered for this bold claim. It is pure guesswork—a projection of his private values as an American of his day in a society undergoing rapid economic expansion.

To us it is plain that these diverse explanatory hypotheses simply do not knit together and I will not waste space in further discussion of them. Let me just round off the tale.

II

A survey of the lines that have been followed in the study of kinship and social organization during the past half century or so shows up a number of different tendencies. Leaving aside those which put primary emphasis on motivational factors and general psychological dispositions, or on the learning aspect, and therefore look to psychology and psychoanalysis for their guiding concepts, we can range the majority of recent and current approaches broadly under two rubrics. On the one hand are the scholars who believe in historical methods and historical or quasi-historical explanations; on the other are those whose interest lies in the search for functional and structural generalizations. Both forms of inquiry have been widely pursued in the study of kinship and social organization since Morgan's day. Both are found in Morgan's works, as I have tried to make clear, but so entangled with one another and distorted by preconceived ideas as to leave nothing but a trail of confusion. We realize better today than Morgan did that they are calculated to pose and find answers to quite different kinds of questions. They are, as Eggan puts it, "different procedures giving different results, but aiding and abetting each other when properly utilized" (1950: 9); and his book is a masterly demonstration of how historical and analytical methods should be used to complement one other.

The questions of aims and methods here at issue have, indeed, been exhaustively ventilated during the past generation of anthropological controversy.[1] Yet confusion still reigns. The documented and dated records of the past used by Eggan and Schapera to give a perspective of a determinable run of generations to their descriptions of Pueblo and Tswana social and political organization represent a totally different kind of history from the speculative constructions we meet with in Morgan's works. Furthermore, these are both different from the consideration of the time factor in social relations and social structure to which I drew attention in a paper published some years ago (1949a). There is a time factor in the cycle of development through which the domestic group passes in every society (cf. Goody, 1958), but this is not history in any precise sense. It is not a-synchronic, no more than the lapse of time between the beginning and the end of a spoken sentence is.

This lack of clarity in regard to the nature and place of historical explanation in the study of kinship and social organization shows itself in the persistence of some of Morgan's wrong theories and faults of reasoning in the most unexpected quarters. I have already instanced Dr. Murdock's recent reversion to the hypothesis of a prior stage of matriliny to account for the mother's brother's status in patrilineal African kinship systems.[2] However, this well-worn item of pseudo-historical currency is not solely of Morgan's coinage.

But a much more obvious symptom of the historicist urge is the recurrent pursuit of a single all-embracing causal factor in order to account—historically—for

1. For the most recent and, to my mind, most balanced appreciation of these issues, cf. Schapera (1962).
2. It is staggering to find so sophisticated a "structuralist" as Dr. Rodney Needham to all intents (though apologetically) coming into line with Murdock on this issue (1962: 36) solely out of zeal to confute Radcliffe-Brown.

general features of social organization, as Morgan did with property. Tylor, in his much quoted paper on marriage and descent (1889) concluded that the rule of post-marital residence was the critical, if not the only important factor that determined the reckoning of descent. Lowie more prudently plumped for a combination of "the transmission of property rights and the mode of residence after marriage" (1920: 157–62). Kroeber, nearly twenty years later, argued with characteristically tantalizing ambiguity that "place of residence" was one of the "underlying phenomena" in relation to which "Traits having to do with . . . formal social organization—clan, moiety [etc.]" were "secondary or superstructural" (1938: 307). The theme runs through much current research,[3] but the selection of residence rules as the prime mover in social organization has, perhaps, nowhere been so firmly advocated as by Murdock. This is how he sums up his conclusion: "It is in respect to residence that changes in economy, technology, property, government, or religion first alter the structural relationships of related individuals to one another, giving an impetus to subsequent modifications in forms of the family, in consanguineal and compromise kin groups, and in kinship terminology" (1949: 202).

Substitute "property" for "residence" here and the proposition becomes authentic Morgan.

The alternative method is implied in Morgan's own realization of the fallacy of looking for "external" or extrinsic causes to explain social organization. Appeals to history come dangerously close to this mistake, and Morgan himself succumbed to it. Yet, as I have shown, the alternative procedure of structural and functional analysis was implicit in his concept of system, in his discrimination of the Indicative Features of kinship systems, and in his paradigmatic analysis of their internal order and common characteristics. This is what Radcliffe-Brown built on.

An analogy to Radcliffe-Brown's analytical method suggests itself to me. It is the method of Mendelian genetics,[4] by contrast with that of the Darwinian theory of heredity, notably as it was espoused by Karl Pearson and the biometrical school in the early years of the present century. This is a highly technical subject and I make no pretence of expounding it adequately. As is now commonly accepted,[5] there is a radical distinction between the Darwinian theory of "blending inheritance" and the Mendelian theory of particulate inheritance. The unity and discreteness of the genes, their segregation and recombination in mating, their autonomous transmission relatively to their somatic environment and their variant phenotypical manifestations, which are ruled but not immutably fixed by the genetic material—all this represents a contrast to the biometric view of quantitatively varying characteristics arising from the blending of parental contributions to inheritance.

I have no means of knowing whether or not Radcliffe-Brown was consciously influenced by the Mendelian revolution. It is difficult to believe that he was unaware of its significance, seeing that Cambridge in the first few years of this century, when

3. Cf., for instance, Goodenough's (1956) penetrating observations on this subject.
4. Lévi-Strauss, with characteristic flair for such parallels, has previously drawn attention to this resemblance between genetic analysis and the structural analysis of kinship and descent. He rightly puts modern linguistic methods alongside (1949: 139).
5. See the authoritative review of the whole subject by Julian Huxley (1942), and the more recent reassessment of Darwin's theories in Barnett (1958).

he was studying anthropology with Haddon and Rivers, was the base from which William Bateson campaigned for the new teaching.[6] In any case, what I am concerned to point out is not a direct connection but a conceptual and methodological parallel. This is the more suggestive since one of the merits of the Mendelian theory is that it provides a model for a generalizing theory. "There is," says Huxley, "an astonishing similarity in the genetic systems of the great majority of organisms" (1942: 131). The similarity lies in the way their "hereditary machinery" is organized and in the processes by which genes are segregated and recombined. The mechanism of heredity is the same for all higher plants and animals.

To follow up the analogy, what I want to draw attention to is this. Having established his generic model of the Australian kinship system, what Radcliffe-Brown went on to do was to isolate a limited number of strictly intrinsic factors as the constitutive principles of the system. Subsequently these were generalized to account for the features common to the internal structure of all kinship systems, in a way reminiscent of the generalizations of geneticists about the uniformities in genetic systems. Like Mendelian genes, these factors are shown to be segregated in their operation but to combine in different ways in specific kinship systems. Phenotypically, kinship systems are generated which are suited to maintain the social organization required by particular communities, in particular natural environments, and with particular traditions of life, at a given time in their history. Genotypically, a strictly limited number of general principles rooted in the universal facts of parentage underlies all kinship systems. Significantly, the two basic principles enunciated by Radcliffe-Brown, the principle of the unity of the lineage and that of the unity of the sibling group are correlated to distinct, in certain respects opposed though universal, dimensions of the kinship system. (I describe the development of Radcliffe-Brown's theories in detail in chap. IV.)

Let me make quite clear what I am inviting attention to. I am not here claiming finality or even validity for these general factors. It is the method of analysis and the kind of theory attained that I am concerned with. Nor do I wish to suggest that Radcliffe-Brown had a monopoly in the application of an analytical procedure in the study of kinship and social organization. In a way, Rivers was getting at the same kind of thing when he postulated—albeit somewhat rashly—the virtual universality of the dual organization in Melanesia (1914b: vol. II, passim). Again, Malinowski's concept of reciprocity (cf. Fortes, 1957), and Mauss's theory of the gift (1925), especially as elaborated by Lévi-Strauss into the theory of exchange, are also analytical, at least in form. But these are not structural principles on the same footing as Radcliffe-Brown's. They are not meant to account for the internal constitution of social relations, but purport to state universally regulative processes of social

6. This is pure guesswork on my part, for in drawing parallels between his ideas about method and theory in a "natural science" of "comparative sociology" and the principles followed in the established natural sciences, Radcliffe-Brown resorted to classical physics and mechanics as often as to biology. There can be little doubt that he was influenced by the developments in mathematical philosophy due to Russell and Whitehead, as can be seen from his remarks on ."relational analysis" in his posthumously published lectures (1957: 69 ff.). It should be remembered that this movement had its focus at Trinity College, Cambridge, where Radcliffe-Brown was a scholar from 1901 to 1906. (Cf. Fortes, 1949b: v–xiv.)

organization. Reverting to my starting point, it can be seen that Radcliffe-Brown's structural principles belong to the same class of theoretical constructs as Morgan's distinction between primary terms and classificatory terms, and between the principles underlying descriptive systems and classificatory systems, respectively. In both cases, the concept of a kinship system is prerequisite. By contrast Murdock's "Determinants of Kinship Terminology" (1949: chap. 7) are, as I have previously noted, reminiscent of Morgan's Indicative Features. These, as Morgan realized, are in the nature of diagnostic signs, not of constitutive principles, and therefore easily lead on to trait counting, as in Murdock's treatment. To all these questions I will presently return.

III

The later development of Morgan's thought, which culminated in *Ancient Society*, leads on even more directly to modern theory. In *The League of the Iroquois*, Morgan declared his purpose to be the analysis of their "civil and domestic institutions." He proposed, he said, not "to narrate their political events; but to inquire into the structure and spirit of the government, and the nature of the institutions, under and through which these historical results were produced" (1851; 1904 ed.: 53). It was thus that he discovered what he called the "tribe" or as we should now say, the matrilineal clan. But unlike some later students of social organization, he perceived that, though it was based on the selective recognition of kinship relations, it was a civil, that is a political, rather than a domestic unit. This insight lies at the heart of *Ancient Society*. Whereas in *Systems* his main focus of interest is the domain of domestic, i.e., familial, relations, in this book it is the complementary domain of political organization.

The pivot of the argument is the analysis of the gens.[7] As in *Systems*, he sets up a paradigmatic model—in his idiom, the gens "in its archaic form" (p. 65)—and then proceeds to compare a worldwide sample of organizations of the same kind taken one at a time, as total systems, not trait by trait, and over a large stretch of recorded history. The model he delineates, for all the elements of bias imparted to it by the matrilineal Iroquois form with which he started, has only been rivalled in the ethnography of the past 25 years. What it chiefly lacks, by modern standards, is the dynamic dimension reckoned with in our attention to such processes as fission and fusion, segmentation and accretion. And yet the presentation Morgan attempts is truly diachronic, i.e. developmental, rather than pseudo-historical. He tries to depict his specimen systems as extended in time and in process of growth. In this undertaking he is, indeed, remarkably successful, considering his dependence on the secondary authorities of his time for his data on classical antiquity, and having regard to the state of ethnographical research. And we can see why this is so. It is

7. Strictly speaking, according to the Roman usage the term "gens" should be reserved for patrilineal descent groups (e.g., Lowie, 1920. Chap. VI) and Morgan's usage is a solecism. But this is after all a minor point of terminology.

because he confines his inquiry, by and large, to the structural aspects of political organization.

If we ignore the framework of pseudo-historical reconstruction and evolutionary stages, we are left with the fundamental observations and hypotheses which lead straight on to modern research. For what Morgan in effect does is to explore the interconnections and operations over a stretch of time of the basic principles of political organization posited in his paradigmatic model. He states his findings in terms of his scheme of the progressive development of forms of government from the gentile stage, through democratic tribal confederations, to constitutions based on the idea of property and culminating in what he calls "political society" in which the state founded upon territory and law supervenes. But let us transpose his stages into a comparative order, and think of them as representative types of political systems diversified according to the combinations of the basic principles of descent, territory, law, etc., which they display. Then we cannot fail to be impressed by his remarkable sociological insight.

I say this advisedly because one of the intriguing features of *Ancient Society* is the evidence it affords of how Morgan himself visualized his task and objectives. To put it in the language of today, the facts of custom, or culture, were of subsidiary interest to him. He cites them only for their structural relevance. Thus when he describes Iroquois gentile organization he refers to the ceremonies and ritual associated with it—but only in brief footnotes. He is his own best witness. This is how he defines his notion of the kind of study he is engaged upon:

In Indian Ethnography the subjects of primary importance are the gens, phratry, tribe and confederacy. They exhibit the organization of society. Next to these are the tenure and functions of the office of sachem and chief, the functions of the council of chiefs, and the tenure and functions of the office of principal war-chief. When these are ascertained, the structure and principles of their governmental system will be known. A knowledge of their usages and customs, of their arts and inventions, and of their plan of life will then fill out the picture. In the work of American investigators too little attention has been given to the former (p. 148).

The distinction Morgan draws between "the structure and principles of the governmental system" and the "usages and customs" which are put in the second place sums up his general standpoint. It anticipates almost exactly Radcliffe-Brown's habitual juxtaposition of the system of social relations, on the one hand, and the customs and usages in which they are expressed, on the other, and it is pretty well taken for granted by most of us today. Yet we must not forget that the utility, let alone the validity, of a distinction along these lines was in the thirties—and indeed still is—contested by leading exponents of the Tylorian tradition. In 1950 we find Kroeber (1950/51; 1952: 152–66), at that date surely the veritable Solon of American anthropology, reluctantly conceding the distinguishability of a "societal segment" from the "cultural segments" of human social life—but allocating its study to sociology, as opposed to anthropology. Significantly, the reproach to American ethnographers with which my quotation from Morgan ends is now no longer justified.

Judged from today's standpoint, what is most notable about *Ancient Society* is

Morgan's demonstration already alluded to, that "gentile" organization, in his terminology (lineage organization as we now prefer to term it), belongs to the realm of government and therefore of political institutions, and not—or, to be more accurate, as well as—to the domestic sphere. He perceived and emphasized the critical significance of unilineal descent as the distinctive feature. Lowie (1920) harps critically on Morgan's mistaken interpretations, yet tacitly follows him in recognizing and emphasizing the distinction between kinship and descent or, as Morgan stated it, kindred and gens. Morgan repeatedly reminds us that kindred is always bilaterally reckoned through both parents, whereas the gens is always unilaterally exclusive. In his description of Greek and Roman political development, we find him inveighing against those scholars who (like their counterparts to this day) dogmatically declared "the family" to be "the basis of the social system." The gens, he protests, and not the family, is the basic unit of political organization. It could not be the family because the family could not be a constituent of the gens since husband and wife must, by definition, belong to different gentes. Elaborating the argument by citing laws and customs which differentiate spouses by gens, he concludes by observing that the modern European and American family is likewise not the elementary unit of political society. Townships, counties and states—corresponding, respectively, to the gens and to phratries and confederacies in primitive society —are, he shrewdly comments, our elementary political units.

IV

These distinctions laid down by Morgan, so critical for both the empirical and the theoretical study of kinship and social organization, are now familiar, largely as a result of the ethnographic researches of the past 25 years on tribal political structure and on the part played therein by unilineal descent groups. But in 1940, when Evans-Pritchard and I brought out *African Political Systems*, it was still necessary to labor the point (1940: 6–7). At that date the theory that descent concepts are one-sided extensions of domestic kinship relations originating in the nuclear family had wide support, chiefly through Malinowski's advocacy. Indeed, it continues to crop up even today. Rivers and Radcliffe-Brown did appreciate the distinction Morgan made, and they incorporated it in their theoretical work. But even they did not fully take Morgan's point. They perceived the juridical properties and functions of the descent principle but overlooked its political functions.[8] Lowie (1920: chap. XIII) paid handsome tribute to Morgan, rightly coupling him with Maine in the penetrating discussion of primitive government which is, to my mind, the most impressive and original part of his analysis of kinship and social organization. But he fell into the trap of the historicist controversy and set out to prove that democracy was not, as Morgan claimed, universal in primitive society. We must remember, however, that this led him to the findings, previously noted

8. In this connection following Starcke (1889) as Radcliffe-Brown acknowledges (1941: 5; 1952: 59). I am speaking here of Radcliffe-Brown's earlier work. In his later writings, after 1940, as I shall explain in the next chapter, he took cognizance of the political, as well as the jural aspects of descent group structure.

and often confirmed by later research, that kinship and territory are jointly effective in the political organization of all societies, even those without overt governmental institutions.

To finish the catalog, Malinowski, by contrast with those I have mentioned, failed to understand the jural and political aspects of unilineal descent (cf. Fortes, 1957). He was too engrossed in the intrafamilial constitution and dynamics of kinship. Nowadays we interlink the two sides in ethnographic research, thus, in a sense, coming back full circle to Morgan's main scheme.

We see how the two frames intersect when we consider the internal structure of the unilineal descent groups (cf. Fortes, 1953b). And when we turn to Morgan's discussion of this aspect of the gens we must admit that it brilliantly anticipates modern accounts. At the outset, when he is deriving his paradigm from the Iroquois gens he states (*Ancient Society*, p. 71):

The gens is individualized by the following rights, privileges, and obligations conferred and imposed upon its members, and which made up the *jus gentilicium*.

Then follows a list of what we should now describe as the distinctive politico-jural features of the gens, as follows:

I   The right of electing its sachem and chiefs.
II   The right of deposing its sachem and chiefs.
III   The obligation not to marry in the gens.
IV   Mutual rights of inheritance of the property of deceased members.
V   Reciprocal obligations of help, defence, and redress of injuries.
VI   The right of bestowing names upon its members.
VII   The right of adopting strangers into the gens.
VIII   Common religious rites, query.
IX   A common burial place.
X   A council of the gens.

The descriptive elaboration of each item—setting aside some wild inferences and pseudo-historical distortions—covers every significant matter. There is one striking deficiency, though. He does not specifically discuss marriage, though he makes a special point of one of his favorite observations, that is to say, the necessary separation by descent of husband and wife, even to the extent of their receiving separate burial in their respective gentile cemeteries. He appreciates but does not explicitly mark the corporate nature of the gens when he comments on the effect of mutual rights of inheritance in strengthening the autonomy of the descent group and on the importance of personal names as gentile property conferring gentile rights. Here, perhaps, is the germ of Lowie's later generalizations about incorporeal property (1920: 235–43). Another anticipation of later ideas is his inclusion of the rule of exogamy among the juridical attributes of the gens. Finally, we cannot but admire the sure grasp of the political system indicated in his panegyric on the council.

Judged by subsequent research, we can see that the generalized description he developed and applied comparatively is by no means out of date. And we can also see where the crux of his theory lies. It is the question of what determines citizenship—"*societas*" or "*civitas*"—as he himself puts it; and it is with respect to this question that he and Maine overlap, as I pointed out earlier. The issue is fundamental for the theory of unilineal descent structure in its political aspects. Whether we think typologically or genetically, there is a critical dividing line between social systems in which citizenship, or, to put it more formally, status in the politico-jural domain, is conferred by membership in a corporate descent group or by some other genealogically determined title, and those in which it is otherwise mediated, e.g., by residence, or else accrues to a person in his own right, by virtue of autonomous status in, or unmediated relationships to the politico-jural system. Restating it thus in a more modern terminology brings us to the essence of Morgan's theory. Its general validity cannot be disputed.

V

It would be an unforgivable omission to end without some reference to the subject of property, which figures so largely in *Ancient Society*. Morgan did not, of course, discover for himself that there is a connection between property relations and social organization. The eighteenth-century legal and social philosophers debated the subject voluminously. What was new in Morgan's use of the idea of property was the ethnological content he gave to it and the almost mystical force he attributed to it. In *Ancient Society* he takes up again and elaborates his earlier thesis that property was the revolutionary mechanism which finally created the Aryan system of consanguinity, the monogamian family, and the civilized state. It is, in my judgment, the weakest link in the tortuous chain of conjectural history he constructed, and that is partly because it is the least supported by empirical evidence. But the prominence he gave to the formative influence on kinship institutions which he attributed to property had important results. Again, it is not the polemical use made of these notions by Marx and Engels and their followers that I am referring to, but the impetus it gave to the anthropological study of the institution of property itself—this "ubiquitous human institution," as Hallowell calls it (1943: 134). The vast literature that has grown up around this subject is fortunately not relevant to my theme, so I need say no more about it here; there will be occasion to refer to particular aspects of it later. Just for the record, however, let me briefly note some of the significant developments in the anthropological study of property stimulated primarily by Morgan's ideas. Rivers comes to mind first. His quixotic adoption of the theory of primitive communism (1924: chap. VI) helped to set Malinowski off in the opposite direction in defense of the universality of individual property rights (1926) and this in turn provided one of the main themes in such classical functionalist reappraisals of primitive economic organization as Firth's study of Maori economics (1929). However, the chief credit for placing Morgan's ideas on property in the sober perspective of later field research must go to Lowie. His closely reasoned discussion of the subject (1920: chap. IX) anticipated Malinowski's conclusions and, as I have already mentioned, he went further than Morgan in the association he postulated between property, post-marital residence patterns, and "unilateral" descent; and the issues he thus raised still remain open.

VI

I have confined myself to Lewis Henry Morgan's legacy to modern social anthropology and more particularly to the genetic connection, as I see it, of his discoveries and methods with those of one special branch of contemporary anthropological scholarship. I have done so in part because I can make no pretensions to a knowledge of his influence on anthropological science in all its worldwide ramifications. Mainly, however, it is because my concern in this book is with the tradition and practice in social anthropology to which I myself belong. What I have done, in effect, has been to give an account of a personal pilgrimage to the sources of this tradition, and so to justify the division I made in my Inaugural Lecture at Cambridge (1953a) between Tylor's heirs and Morgan's heirs and my claim by implication to be counted among the latter.

I must guard against one possible misunderstanding. I am not asserting that everything in modern kinship theory and in recent research on social organization comes from Morgan. I have just pointed out his relative neglect of the subject of marriage, for instance, which today looms conspicuously and controversially in kinship theory. Eggan points out (1955: 530) that he was apparently unaware of the custom of cross-cousin marriage and failed to observe that it was reflected in the Plains Cree kinship terminology which he recorded. Some might argue, also, that the highly sophisticated application of linguistic theory in the analysis of kinship terminologies is nowhere foreshadowed in Morgan, though it would surely be agreed that a necessary preliminary was the concept of a system of kinship relations primarily exhibited in the terminology, and serving to replace prohibited names. Farthest, perhaps, from the general orientation traceable to Morgan is the study of kinship from the angle of psychology and psychoanalysis, due, preeminently, to the inspiration of Freud. But the richest contribution of all to the branch of anthropological science founded by Morgan has come from the field researches of the past fifty years, in particular those that were inspired by the functionalist revolution led by Radcliffe-Brown and Malinowski. Some consideration of the theoretical basis of these developments is therefore appropriate; and this to my mind, means mainly Radcliffe-Brown.

CHAPTER IV

Radcliffe-Brown
and the Development of
Structural Analysis

I

I HAVE MADE IT PLAIN THAT IN MY PERSONAL PERSPECTIVE OF THEORY AND METHOD THE modern era in the study of kinship and social organization is first firmly established with the publication of Radcliffe-Brown's 1931 monograph on the social organization of Australian tribes.

As I have already noted, his affinity with Morgan (as opposed to the then prevailing bias in American ethnology) stands out in this inquiry, though he makes a special point of criticizing Morgan for having "obscured the fact . . . that the whole [Australian] kinship system is based on the family (1930–31: 436). But much more significant is the break both with Morgan's pseudo-historical frame of interpreta- and with such alternatives as Kroeber's pseudo-psychological ideas. The critical innovations are the shift to a rigorous synchronic methodology and the "functionalist" thesis that kinship systems are intelligible only in relation to the total social organization which they subserve.

The revolutionary effect of this innovation is most directly confirmed in the famous Chicago symposium on North American Tribes to which I have already referred. And since then so much has been written by way of criticism, appreciation, and elaboration of Radcliffe-Brown's thesis and methods that further discussion of them might seem superfluous.

Nevertheless, the specific question to which I want to address myself still needs attention. It is the question of Radcliffe-Brown's part in the development of modern structural theory. The ground is ably cleared in Tax's introduction (1937) to the Chicago symposium, but it is to later developments, or at least changes in emphasis, in Radcliffe-Brown's theoretical position (as Eggan has shown, 1955) that modern structural theory owes most (cf. Fortes, 1955).

To keep the record straight, let me begin with the reminder of how much Radcliffe-Brown owed to W. H. R. Rivers. He disagreed radically with Rivers's general theoretical position, but he built directly on concepts and methods developed by Rivers. His concept of social structure, his notion of the relationship between genealogical connexion and kinship system, his approach to the analysis of descent groups, all benefited from Rivers's lead. Indeed, it is fair to say that all that is of permanent value for kinship theory in Rivers's researches is embodied in Radcliffe-Brown's.

Radcliffe-Brown's basic theoretical position was already foreshadowed in 1913. It is not, however, fully worked out until the 1931 monograph. I have stressed that its starting point was his concept of the social system. This is a structural and functional concept—morphological and physiological, to use the terms which Radcliffe-Brown took over from Durkheim and Spencer. It is not a blanket concept; it implies the possibility of analytically discriminating the processes, mechanisms, and principles which work together to maintain the total system. The first question that arises is purely descriptive: how to present and organize the empirical data of field observation in their synchronic association. Here the notion of social structure becomes relevant. This is how Radcliffe-Brown first defines it:

In the strict and narrow sense of the term the "social structure" of a people consists of the system of formal grouping by which the social relations of individuals to one another are determined, *i.e.*, it is a grouping of human beings in relation to one another. But there is also a larger structure in which the society and external nature are brought together and a system of organized relations established, in myth and ritual, between human beings and natural species or phenomena (1930–31: 60).

Thus social structure, at this point, means the system of formal grouping as seen from the outside; and its basis is the kinship system. But there follows an analytical distinction of key importance. This is the distinction between the "system of genealogical relationships" traceable to common parentage, on the one hand, and the "kinship system" built upon it, on the other (1930–31: 43).[1] The latter is the product of society, depending on the kind of "recognition" given to the natural genealogical connections in the rules by which kin are classified and grouped in the social

1. Cf. Morgan's reiterated emphasis on the "arbitrary" and "artificial" character of classificatory systems. Rivers, of course, had worked with this distinction before, in the Toda monograph (1906). This thesis is reiterated in one form or another in Radcliffe-Brown's later publications, e.g., in his last theoretical statement (1950): "There is the purely physical relation between a child and a woman who gives birth to it or the man who begets it. The same relation exists between a colt and its dam and sire. But the colt does not have a father or a mother. For there is the social (and legal) relation between parents and children which is something other than the physical relation" (1950: 25).

structure, and, more visibly, in the usages and customs by which the behavior of relatives so recognized and classified, is ordered and regulated. From this point of view, the terminology of kinship and affinity is regarded as primarily meaningful as a component part (albeit the most important part) of the body of rules and usages in which the kinship system is brought into action. Rules, customary behavior (which includes linguistic usages) and forms of grouping people—these are the empirical data of kinship and social organization. Thus regarded, kinship systems are seen to have a "job of work" to do in and for society, as Eggan later put it, a "function" in the plain, instrumental sense of playing a determinate part in maintaining the structure as a whole.[2]

At the theoretical level, however, we are concerned with explanation. Given that social organization rests upon what Radcliffe-Brown elsewhere described as the "relations of actual interconnectedness",[3] e.g., by kinship, that subsist between persons, and are mediated through their customary behavior, how do they add up to the unity and persistence of social structure, as a totality? The answer, in "morpho-logical" terms, is found in the concept of range, exhibited, in the Australian case, in the all-inclusive range of the kinship system. The structure persists because all its elements and parts are bound together within the all-embracing framework of kinship forms. In "physiological" terms, it is found in the postulate that the usages, rules, and forms of grouping have functional value and work together consistently to maintain the social system. Thus patrilineal descent, in Australia, is said to have a "real advantage" in adaptation to a difficult environment (Radcliffe-Brown, 1930–31: 439),[4] and division into moieties is said to systematize and stabilize a kinship structure which would be unstable if there were no segmentary organization for grouping individuals into permanent and recognizable divisions embracing the whole society (pp. 440–43).

But there is a further problem of explanation. It concerns the *mechanisms* of social organization on which I remarked in the last chapter. To restate it in Radcliffe-Brown's own words, the problem is to seek out the "active principles, which not merely help to produce the institutions at their origin but serve to maintain them in existence. . ." (1930–31: 441). "The task of the sociologist" he proceeds, "is to isolate these active principles by a process of analysis, formulate them as precisely as possible, and endeavour to reduce them to terms of universal sociological law" (p. 441). He gives point to his thesis by contrasting his plan with the pseudo-historical approach. An example is Rivers's conjectural theory of the origin of the classificatory kinship system "in a social structure founded on the exogamous social

2. Rather than branch out into a discussion of the status of the concept of function in kinship studies—which would lead me from my main theme—I refer the reader to the excellent review of its place in social science in Dorothy Emmet's *Function, Purpose and Power* (1958: chaps. IV, V) and to the analysis of its methodological utility in Robert Brown's *Explanation in Social Science* (1963: chap. IX).

3. In the lectures of this period posthumously published under the title of *A Natural Science of Society* (1957). Note the implication, to which I allude later, that these relations are autonomously given.

4. The advantage of patrilineal descent comes from the fact that a "detailed knowledge of the animals and plants . . ." is necessary for adaptation to the environment, and this knowledge is transmitted in the localized horde.

group" (1914a: 71–72). By contrast, Radcliffe-Brown derives classificatory kinship from the "principle" of the equivalence of brothers with its underpinning in their solidarity. This principle, he asserts, can be seen at work in the family and the clan. It is therefore empirically substantiated. But on the theoretical plane it accounts for the most characteristic feature of classificatory systems by invoking a continuously operative, universal, and verifiable mechanism of social organization, not suppositious antecedent factors.

I have already indicated that (like Eggan) I regard the formulation of this principle and its correlate, the principle of the unity of the lineage, as it came to be designated, as marking a major breakthrough in kinship theory. Now in 1931 Radcliffe-Brown still tried to combine a Durkheimian "functionalist" interpretation of Australian social organization with a more explicitly structural interpretation drawn out of his own ethnographic experience. Hence he veered between an *external* view of how institutions function in a social system adapted to a particular environment, and an *internal* analysis which sought to understand them genotypically, that is, in terms of particular factors inherent in the system. The outcome is an unresolved inconsistency in his conceptual scheme. Thus when he ascribes adaptive value to horde patriliny, he is judging by the *externally* discernible relationships of a society with its natural environment. Extraneous utilities such as the advantage of a knowledge of terrain are adduced. But the "active principles" are inferred from observations of the *internal* structural arrangements, the norms of usage regulating the relationships and evinced in the behavior of persons within the encompassing social organization taken in its own right.[5] There is here a methodological ambiguity that confuses the study of kinship and social organization to this day, I mean the failure to discriminate between "external" and "internal" fields of structure.[6] I shall try to make this clearer in the next chapter.[7]

Without stating it in so many words, Radcliffe-Brown came nearer to recognizing the problem than any other student of social organization in the thirties and forties. It comes out in the paradigm of the kinship system which he formulated in 1941, though this is a revision of his earlier model, not a completely new construction. For its focus is on the internal constitution of kinship systems and the genotypical principles, or factors, operating within them. Their external functions and relationships are to all intents disregarded.

II

We have seen that the generic paradigm of Australian social systems put forward by Radcliffe-Brown in 1930–31 visualizes a totality made up of component systems

5. They are at this stage, as he remarked at a later date, the results of "an immediate abstraction from observed facts" (1941: p. 12).

6. The confusion is patent in all reductionist theories, for example those that purport to reduce kinship relations and institutions to technological, economic, biological, or even residential factors. I shall consider some of these later.

7. A valiant but unsuccessful attempt to resolve this dilemma is made by Kathleen Gough in her theoretical contribution to the volume on matrilineal kinship (Schneider and Gough, ed. 1961).

held together and working together in functional interdependence. It follows that any of the component systems can be analytically isolated and examined as a relatively self-contained, internally comprehensible structure. And this, in effect, is what Radcliffe-Brown does with the kinship system. It is true that he makes specific mention of the totemic and mythological components of what he calls the "larger structure" in which man and nature are united and emphasizes their connection with the kinship system through the local organization (1930–31: 60–61). But he sets them on one side and concentrates on the kinship system. His task was probably made easier just because, in the Australian case, the kinship system is coextensive with the total social organization of a tribe, and thus ultimately regulates all economic, jural, and ritual relations. Tacitly, I think, this picture remained his prototype through all his later work, and he never overcame a tendency to regard social structure primarily from the point of view of kinship. In this paradigm, the elementary situation of kinship is the dyadic relationship of one person with another, as this is laid down by membership within the parental family or is derived therefrom through the operation of the basic structural principles, and as it is expressed in customary usages, in "patterns of behaviour." The formula applies to groups as well as to individuals. Hence the common usage, by which all the members of a given parent's recognized descent group are identified with that parent both in terminology and in conduct, is reduced to a dyadic formula.

This procedure was taken over by Radcliffe-Brown's immediate followers, and as I have previously noted, used to great advantage, for example, by Lloyd Warner (1937), Eggan and the other members of the Chicago group (1937a), and it has been widely followed in kinship study ever since (Evans-Pritchard, 1951b; Firth, 1936; Fortes, 1949c).

Now Rivers and Morgan also referred kinship terminologies and institutions to dyadic relations and reciprocities of conduct. But Radcliffe-Brown went a step further in his differential analysis of the norms and usages distinctive of the elementary relations of kinship, formulated in the well known tetrad of respect and joking, avoidance and familiarity. The significant step was establishing how each is coupled with a discrete category of consanguineal or affinal relations defined by opposition to other categories of elementary relations. The tetrad proved to be a searching diagnostic scheme, as in the clarification of American Indian social organization by the Chicago group and Murngin kinship by Warner. It remains a standard analytical tool in kinship studies. For it was not for Radcliffe-Brown merely a set of descriptive labels for empirical facts, as is evident from such studies as his papers on joking relationships (1940a, 1949) and in the application of the scheme by the Chicago group and by Warner.

The tetrad is an analytical classification. Behind it lies the constellation of dyadic relations deemed by Radcliffe-Brown to be generated in the elementary situations of parenthood, siblingship, and marriage. He sees them as falling into mutually exclusive categories. But he sees them also as forming a system because these elementary relations are bound together by a second order of social relations, namely, relations of opposition between successive generations, of solidarity within a generation derived from the sibling bond, of reciprocity and complementarity, as between cross-kin and affines, and of coalescence, as between alternate generations. Thus respect and familiarity, joking and avoidance are significant, both in the normative sense and discriminatively, not only because they are discrete "patterns of behaviour," but also because they are coordinate with this constellation, and are, consequently, counterpoised to one another within a unitary system or set (cf. Eggan, 1937b: 76). Given that they serve critically to differentiate, they also and *a fortiori* interconnect, in balanced opposition, the basic categories of kinship relations. Diagnostically used, therefore, the tetrad serves as a set of generic norms by reference to which culturally specific expression, in custom and behavior, of the underlying principles of social structure can be located and identified. True, it has limitations, as I will presently argue; but the germ of the notion of structural opposition later developed by Evans-Pritchard lies in it.

This method of looking at social structure through the prism of the customary usages in which its elements are diffracted, so to speak, dates back to *The Andaman Islanders* (1922). It is further developed in the famous (1924) paper on the mother's brother to which I have already made a passing reference, though it is not methodically applied until 1930. The point of that paper, let us remind ourselves, is to show how the "avunculate," meaninglessly historicized by the majority of contemporary ethnologists, proves to be "functionally" intelligible. Synchronically analysed, it reflects the distribution of attitudes and sentiments amongst familial kin which corresponds to the arrangement of the structurally differentiated and complementary relations of ego with the authority-vested (and therefore respected) father and his kin on the one side and the indulgent (and therefore familiar) mother and her kin on the other in a segmentary, patrilineal descent system.

The seminal influence of this paper on the development of kinship theory over the past forty years has been without parallel, as even its severest critics testify (Goody, 1959; Lévi-Strauss, 1958a). Seldom a year passes without a re-examination of Radcliffe-Brown's hypothesis in relation to new ethnographic data. What is this due to? Partly, no doubt, to the diagnostic importance of the "avunculate" in the classification of kinship systems, but primarily on account of the method of analysis demonstrated in Radcliffe-Brown's paper and the hypothesis advanced in it. In the first place, it shows how structural and functional analysis makes sense of custom and social relationship at what might be called the histological level of social morphology no less than at the level of the total system. Secondly, it demonstrates that the customary attitudes and alignments exhibited in a component part—albeit a crucial part—of the total social structure are determined by principles operative throughout the whole structure.

As to the interpretation offered by Radcliffe-Brown, he himself later admitted that it needed to be expanded and modified (1952: 1–14; cf. also the shift of view implied in his 1940 paper on joking relationships). Its main weakness (apart from the inadequacy of the ethnographic data available at the time) as we now see it, springs from the residue of traditional ethnology tempered with Durkheim in Radcliffe-Brown's theoretical approach at that date. The "behaviour patterns" in the dyadic situation were still, for him, the data of primary functional significance. The structural determinants were adumbrated rather than put clearly in the foreground. What more recent structural analysis has elicited is that the critical factor in the "avunculate" is the jural status of the parties in relation to one another, not the sentiments and attitudes in which it is expressed. I drew attention to this in my study of Tallensi kinship (1949c: 299 ff., 313 ff.). This conclusion provides the essential modification made by Homans and Schneider (1955) in their application of Radcliffe-Brown's hypothesis to the problem of cross-cousin marriage. It has been elaborated and verified by Goody, who shows just how the constellation of "behaviour patterns" characteristic of the "avunculate" reflects the jural relations of the parties based on their differential alignments by descent, siblingship, and complementary filiation (1959). This sets out a framework for a more general theoretical analysis than Radcliffe-Brown's, one which can accommodate all the varieties of the "avunculate"—patrilineal, matrilineal and cognatic.

Of other attempts to supersede Radcliffe-Brown's interpretation, the most challenging has been that of Lévi-Strauss (1958). Insofar as it is more than a reformulation of Radcliffe-Brown's analysis, it adds nothing of explanatory value. It takes cognizance only of the same descriptive facts of attitude and sentiment, and throws no light on the structural mechanisms responsible for the differential assignment of authority and indulgence by status in the constellation. This however is the real problem at issue, as Goody has made clear. Lévi-Strauss does not appreciate this because there is no place in his theoretical scheme for the analytical distinction between (phenotypical) affective behavior and (genotypical) jural roles which is the key to the problem of mechanism and process.[8]

To return to Radcliffe-Brown's theoretical scheme of this period when it was adopted in the thirties by many functionally orientated ethnographers, its only effective rival was Malinowski's biographical scheme, and this rested on parallel functional premises. Handled complementarily, the two approaches could be, up to a point, reconciled for descriptive purposes, as Firth showed (1936).[9] In both, the actual relations of persons in the parental family was the starting point; and for

8. This point is worth laboring, even at the risk of some repetition. The "plus" and "minus" ties so neatly balanced in Lévi-Strauss's notation represent the same kind of customary attitudes and sentiments in the context of dyadic relations as those that are adduced in Radcliffe-Brown's scheme. The notation is reminiscent of Lloyd Warner's in his description of the relations between successive generations of mother's brother and sister's son among the Murngin (1937) and is just as misleading. The contrast drawn by Lévi-Strauss between "free and familiar" relations on the one hand and relations of "hostility, antagonism or reserve" on the other (1958: 55), comes straight from Radcliffe-Brown's tetrad. Granted that these customary "behaviour patterns" constitute a "language" (the signs and symbols) in which the complementary kinship relations that make up the configuration are acknowledged and signified, they explain nothing. What is ignored is that the "minus" stands for a very positive relationship of jural authority on one side and right on the other in both the Tongan and the Trobriand situation and the "plus" for its complementary absence. This is the basic structural factor not the purely phenotypical "system of four parties," which is, in fact, not even correct as the parties are interrelated not as individuals in the family structure but as right- and duty-bearing members of descent groups, siblings, spouses, and filial dependents. It is only by considering the problem in terms of the locus of jural authority that the structural principles underlying all forms of the so-called avunculate can be elicited.

9. By contrast, for instance, with the more strictly Radcliffe-Brownian method followed by Lloyd Warner (1937). Firth's eclectic functionalist approach has been followed by other British ethnographers writing on the familial and kinship institutions of particular peoples—for example, Fortes (1949c), Evans-Pritchard (1951b).

both the central task was to establish the rationale of customary kinship behavior, more particularly in regard to obligatory attitudes and sentiments in the dyadic situation.

In this phase of functionalist theory, then, the kinship system is envisaged as a bilateral network of recognized dyadic relations radiating outwards from the elementary family. These are thought of as embodied in the behavior patterns and customary usages, notably the terminologies, which differentiate precisely among, and interlink them, in a system of reciprocals making a balanced, overall arrangement. It is interesting to observe how strong a hold this dyadic paradigm had, not only in kinship studies but in functionalist studies of other aspects of social life. In 1939 Radcliffe-Brown himself resorted to it in his analysis of taboo, and in 1940 he generalized it to cover all categories of social relations.[10] Mauss, for example, assumed it in his theory of the gift (1925), and Malinowski in his theory of primitive law (1926). Its appeal was and remains obvious,[11] for it enables us to regard custom and institutional forms as behavior, as action. It implies reciprocity and thus fits the symmetrical configuration of a system of kinship relations. In particular, it justifies treating kinship terminology as a mode of "behavior" and therefore as simply the "linguistic mechanism of the kinship system" (Firth, 1936: chap. VII). Pushed to the extreme, this notion seriously misled Malinowski and caused difficulties for Radcliffe-Brown, too.

Dyadic analysis accords well with a genealogical interpretation of kinship relations, since the dyads can be genealogically specified. It is not surprising, in view of his biographical scheme and his extension theory of classificatory kinship, that Malinowski should be attracted to a genealogical reduction of kinship relations. It is odder that Radcliffe-Brown should have yielded to the same bias. For the dyadic paradigm inhibited him from following out to its logical conclusion the distinction he had himself laid down between genealogical connection and kinship relation. Committed like Malinowski to the familial origin of Australian kinship systems, he referred them back always to "real genealogical relations of parent and child or sibling and sibling" (1930–31: 436) which he claimed was the way the natives themselves dealt with them. This lay behind his treatment of the regulation of marriage in Australian societies, right down to his last major contribution to the subject in 1951. The differences of degree in the recognition of kinship relations to which he attached so much importance were interpreted in genealogical not jural terms. Yet the data he himself examined showed what later research has repeatedly demonstrated: that knowledge of actual genealogical connections among Australian aborigines is too

10. Compare, for example, the following statements: (a) "It is perhaps necessary for the avoidance of misunderstanding to add that a social system also requires that persons should be objects of interest to other persons. In relations of friendship or love each of two persons has a value for the other. In certain kinds of groups each member is an object of interest for all the others, and each member therefore has a social value for the group as a whole. Further, since there are negative values as well as positive, persons may be united or associated by their antagonism to other persons. For the members of an anti-Comintern pact the Comintern has a specific social value" (1939: 22–23). (b) "Social relations are only observed, and can only be described, by reference to the reciprocal behaviour of the persons related" (1940b: 8).

11. It is the basis of Lévi-Strauss's method of analysis, e.g., in his previously cited paper on the avunculate as well as in his *Structures Élémentaires de la Parenté*.

limited for the exact specification of classificatory kinship relations except among the closest kin. It is clear that over a large part, if not the largest part, of an actor's field of kinship, the calculus of relations is operated by recourse to terminological and institutional equations and contrapositions, not by genealogical reckoning.[12] Persons are located in status positions relatively to other status positions by the system of terminology and custom, not in specifiable genealogical positions. It is a common experience to find the same status position—designated by the same kinship term—assigned to persons who, by a genealogical mode of reckoning, are connected with ego by mutually exclusive routes[13] and, vice versa, one person being assigned to different kinship statuses in different contexts. How this works is common knowledge. The genealogical phrasing tells us what the shape or the form and the minimally distinctive content of a kinship relation is by matching it implicitly with its elementary prototype. It tells us that if, by the calculus of relations, I place X in the category of mother's mother's brother and X places Y in the category of daughter, then I am entitled, in certain circumstances, to place Y in the category of mother's mother's brother's daughter and, *ergo*, potential mother-in-law, in accordance with the genealogical prototype of this relationship. But no genealogical reckoning is necessarily entailed. This is the essential point of what the earlier writers quoted by Radcliffe-Brown (and, as it happens, Warner, too, after him) referred to as "tribal" relationships in contradistinction to "blood" or "consanguine" relationships. The genealogical fallacy has been the cause of much confusion in the study of kinship systems and marriage institutions. It underlies the confusion which has led some theorists to assert that the mother's brother in, for instance, South Indian patrilineal systems, is primarily an affine not a consanguineal kinsman to ego, whereas in truth he has both statuses.

III

Concern with kinship custom and behavior in the dyadic situation did not, however, blind Radcliffe-Brown or Malinowski to other dimensions of relevance in kinship institutions. Neither of them, for example, disregarded the specifically linguistic connotations of kinship terminologies. I shall come back to this presently, but here let me first note the step which took Radcliffe-Brown to a different level of structural analysis. This came when he tackled the problem of unilineal succession in his famous paper of 1935. Here he confronted what he later described as the jural aspect of kinship relations. The analysis of matrilineal and patrilineal succession as alternative modes of perpetual corporate succession serving to establish unequivocally where rights *in personam* reside and thus stabilizing their transmission, breaks away from the dyadic formula. It presents kinship institutions not as customary

12. Or as Rivers put it (1941b: I, 8–9), by "relationships rather than relatives." I shall come back to this point later.

13. This has general applicability in classificatory kinship systems, as Firth demonstrated for Tikopia, in a classical study of this problem (1930). Firth's conclusions have been confirmed in numerous anthropological studies. The Tikopia pattern described by him is common among the Tallensi, for example (cf. Fortes, 1949c).

patterns of interaction between persons but as the vehicles of interests and requirements that flow from the overall constitution of society. There are obvious links
between this line of thought and both Morgan's theory of the gens and Maine's
analysis of corporate succession. But it goes further, firstly in the generality of the
hypothesis advanced, and, secondly, in relating it directly to necessary conditions
of existence of the total social structure. Furthermore, it emerges in juxtaposition
to, rather than in the framework of, the bilateral network paradigm, thus implicitly
echoing the distinction between "kindred" and "gens" established by Morgan.
Here lies one reason why the hypothesis of this paper opened the way for the
analysis of unilineal descent groups which led on to the next major advance in
kinship theory (cf. Fortes, 1953b).

IV

But I am anticipating. I want to go back again briefly to Radcliffe-Brown's treatment
of kinship terminologies. It is true that Radcliffe-Brown opposed Kroeber's extreme
position; but he did not put kinship terminology exactly on a par with other kinship
custom. He recognized that a kinship terminology has diverse aspects. Designating
the social relations expressed in such behavioral customs as joking and avoidance is
but one of them. Viewed from the outside, it also serves to classify and systematize
the total range of kinship relations recognized in a given society; and considered
from within, it is the instrument by means of which the individual's field of kinship
is ordered and registered for him. Thus, "the nomenclature of kinship," he stated,
is commonly used as a means of establishing and recognizing the "*categories* [italics
added] . . . into which the various relatives of a single person can be grouped"
(1941: 6). This is reminiscent of Morgan and Rivers. In fact, Radcliffe-Brown's
search for underlying principles was first evoked by Morgan's problem of finding
an explanation for the classificatory form of kinship terminology, assuming that
actual degrees of "consanguinity" are always recognized, as in the distinction
between close and distant kin. The "principles" enabled inferences to be made
from terminologies about the categorization and grouping of kinsfolk and suggested
predictions of the institutional forms these might take. This was tantamount to
accepting the specificity of kinship terminologies as "lexical sets" (if I may borrow
Lounsbury's term [1956]), ordered to an empirically as well as analytically distinguishable domain of social life—the "universe of kinship" as Goodenough (1956)
aptly calls it.[14] Certainly, Radcliffe-Brown was not alone in this interest. The
literature of the period is choked with disquisitions on kinship terminologies lifted
from their observable social and cultural contexts and referred to suppositious
origins. Hypotheses about their origins and causes proliferated, a favorite one being

14. It is important to realize that Radcliffe-Brown's point of view did not imply lifting
kinship terminologies from their social and cultural environment, though he did not go so far
as to assert with Rivers that they were rigorously determined by social conditions. Radcliffe-
Brown was strongly opposed to treating them as self-contained logical constructions, intelligible without reference to their specific cultural and social content. This is the point of his
objections to Dumont's presentation of Dravidian kinship terminology "as an expression of
marriage" (Radcliffe-Brown, 1953).

some variation on that hardy survivor from Morgan's period—and one of Radcliffe-Brown's pet aversions—the rules of marriage past or present.[15]

The difference lay in the sterility of these theories, in contrast to Radcliffe-Brown's. Their common fault was the perennial one of transposing synchronic terminological connections to a diachronic—or rather pseudo-historical—frame of reference and so falling into the error of attributing causal efficacy to institutions like the levirate or the sororate, or preferential marriage, which are often correlative with, but in no sense antecedent to, classificatory kinship terminologies. The climax of this tendency is surely Dr. Murdock's attempt at an eclectic theory to compass all possibilities (1949: chap. 7). He needs no less than thirteen assumptions for it and extracts no less than thirty so-called theorems from his calculations. How elegant, by contrast, is the parsimony and generality of Radcliffe-Brown's theory.[16]

However, the supreme merit of Radcliffe-Brown's set of "principles" by contrast with its competitors, lay and lies in its applicability to the observed facts. It provides a key, which no other theory can match, to the basic rules followed in the construction of classificatory terminologies. Applied to a particular system, the "principles" give us the elementary features on which its structural logic is built up. They also demonstrate a form of genotypical analysis that can be extended to disclose variations of and additions to the original "principles."[17]

V

Having said this (and other tributes to the utility of the "principles" will be referred to later) I must concede that they raise difficulties by reason of their very generality. Are they to be regarded primarily as identifying the irreducible genealogical connections, the given relations of actual connectedness, which are universally utilized in building up kinship relations and categories?[18] Or are they rather to be thought of as the mechanisms by which genealogical connections are transposed into kinship relations, the bridge, as it were, between the two levels? Or are they—despite Radcliffe-Brown's claims to the contrary—valid only for the interpretation of kinship terminologies? We are brought back thus to the central question: what

15. Murdock's survey covers most of them (1949: chap. 7).

16. "Thus a single method of interpretation is applied throughout, and this gives a simplification or economy of theory" (Radcliffe-Brown, 1950: 34). Cf. also the general argument and examples of the 1941 paper. The "single method," we should recollect, was applied to account for a variety of descriptively distinct kinship institutions: the levirate, the sororate, the patrilineal avunculate, the opposition of successive and the merging of alternate generations, and the corresponding avoidance, joking, respect and familiarity customs.

17. For example, stretched farther, the unity of the sibling group becomes the unity of the generation group which may of course, by functional criteria, be extended to a group of, e.g., age-mates or village-mates who will thus be terminologically equated by ego. Similarly, reduced to its nucleus, the unity of the lineage becomes the unity of a person and his filial successor (e.g., father and son, mother's brother and sister's son) in relation to a third party.

18. Cf., e.g., the following characteristic remark: "What I am trying to show you is that the classificatory terminology is a method of providing a wide-range kinship organization, by making use of the unity of the sibling group in order to establish a few categories of relationship under which a very large number of near and distant relatives can be included" (1941: 8). The "category" is taken to include both near and distant relatives.

is the function of kinship terminologies in the creation of kinship systems out of genealogical connections—in the "recognition" of these connections? It is a question engulfed in such an ocean of scholarship and controversy that I shrink from embarking on a discussion of it. I should like, however, to digress and present a point of view which seems to me to follow from Radcliffe-Brown's theory and to illustrate better than abstract discussion both its empirical utility and its limitations.

How, if we follow Radcliffe-Brown, should we define the relationship between genealogical connections and kinship terminologies? Let us start from the idea of a "kinship universe." A kinship terminology (including affinal and derived terms) is a special vocabulary-complex. The native speaker of a language can at once recognize a word as belonging to this vocabulary-complex, or not. There is frequently a concept for kinship in the most inclusive sense embracing all "lines" and "categories."[19] Even when they are used in the most attenuated metaphorical or figurative sense, kinship words never lose their genealogical resonance.[20] But to think of a kinship terminology as no more than a collection of specialized words is to miss the point. It is not comparable to a technical vocabulary, for example, that of an engineer or a physiologist. Kinship terms are more directly comparable with such verbal elements as personal names—for which, as Morgan taught us, they are sometimes obligatory substitutes—or titles, which sometimes replace them. What is important to emphasize is that kinship terms designate not individuals but status relations between persons.[21] Their distinctive character arises from the generally recognized fact that the relations they designate have their origin in a distinct sphere of social life, the sphere which, for both observers and actors, is demarcated by reference to the base line of genealogical connection. Tautologous as it may sound, the fact to be reckoned with is that a kinship word in any language is not identifiable as such if it cannot ultimately be referred to a "genealogical" datum, that is to say, either a connection between persons generated or deemed to be generated by their own or others' parentage—begetting and bearing—immediate or at a remove, or by marriage.[22]

19. As in Tallensi, *dogham* and Nuer, *mar*, which might well be translated by Morgan's term—consanguinity. I cite other examples in chap. XII.

20. Our own language is full of such usages; cf. mother-ship, mother-country, father-land, sister-college, and so on. The use of terms like "father" and "mother" to designate Roman Catholic clergy is still less remote from its familial source. Even when they are applied in such unexpected quarters as atomic physics, kinship words retain and are indeed chosen for this resonance. The fissionable material in a chain reactor is said to undergo 'fissions per generation"; and compare such a remark as: "Even the primary fission neutrons have a good chance of producing daughters for the chain." (I quote from the article by Philip Morrison, "The Physics of the Bomb", 1950. The diagrams of "divergent" and "balanced" chain reaction in Sir John Cockcroft's essay on "Nuclear Reactors", 1950, look exactly like the charts of segmentary lineage systems customary in anthropological studies.)

21. As Morgan intuitively appreciated, Rivers stressed, and later authorities like Lowie implicitly accepted (Cf. the suggestive discussion of this important point by Service, 1960). I referred to this earlier. And here I must add that his ambiguous handling of the genealogical fallacy did not prevent Radcliffe-Brown from recognizing this point. His use of the concept of the "person" (1950) and, to go back farther, his 1935 paper on succession are proof enough.

22. I am talking about kinship words not kinship relations. But cf. Radcliffe-Brown's dictum (1950: 13): "Two persons who are kin are related in one or other of two ways: either one is descended from the other or they are both descended from a common ancestor."

These are anthropological commonplaces. But here Radcliffe-Brown's thesis that genealogical facts become kinship data when they are "recognized" by discriminative rules, actions and, most conspicuously, words, becomes relevant. Stated differently, genealogical connections though indispensable are latent by nature and only become structurally manifest in the kinship relations imputed to them. This does not mean that either element is prior genetically or in efficacy to the other. Genealogical connections are *innucleated*, if I might coin a word for Radcliffe-Brown's axiom, in kinship relations, but are nevertheless precisely distinguishable from them. This holds both for the actors and for the observer. The variations among different "types" of kinship systems all referable to the same irreducible genealogical nuclei, illustrate this. And terminologies are the medium through which this distinction is bridged. (Cf. Murdock, 1949, Ch. 6.)

Discovering kinship shows this at work. Among the Tallensi I often witnessed a situation that every anthropological field worker comes across. Two men, A and B, from widely separated clan settlements, meet for the first time at a ritual celebration held in the homestead of X, who is related to both by kinship or marriage. Presently A and B, assisted by others, begin to "trace out parentage," or, more literally, "bearing and begetting" (cf. Fortes, 1949c: 16). It turns out, shall we say, that A's mother's mother and B's mother's mother's mother were the daughters of one mother. At once they know they are *soog* to each other (Fortes, 1949c: 30 ff.) and clasp hands with joy. Where before they regarded and treated each other with the ordinary courtesy due from one guest to another at the house of a common kinsman, they now act as if they were the closest of siblings. Established genealogical connection is converted into a kinship relation. Such encounters are common in all societies.[23] With us the revelation of previously unknown kinship has been the theme of myth, fiction, and drama from *Oedipus Tyrannus* to *Great Expectations*—not to speak of the biblical story of Joseph and his brethren.

The separability of genealogical connection and kinship relation is the foundation of Rivers's classical "genealogical" method in kinship research. It is a mode of inquiry that is possible only because informants make and use the distinction in their own lives. But from the observer's point of view it contains the germ of contradictions. This is what underlies the problem summed up in Morgan's insistence on the "artificiality"—that is, the cultural or institutional derivation—of classificatory kinship, or as Radcliffe-Brown put it, its customary recognition.

VI

The example from the Tallensi shows us a kinship word used initially to place a person in a recognized category of relationship to another person. This is not the same thing as classification. The category word assigns status. It is, so to speak, a package of definitions, rules and directions for conduct. It is a store of information but also a tool of action. All adult Tallensi can explain what the concept of *soog*

23. And as we know well from the reiterated textbook example of the Australian aborigines, there are many societies in which social relations cannot be entered into between persons who are unable to discover or invent kinship relations. I discuss the significance of this in chap. VII.

means: that witchcraft "follows" *soog*, so that if a person is a witch or is clairvoyant, his *soog* kin, known or unknown, will be potential witches and clairvoyants, too; that *soog* posits intimacy and trust like that of matri-siblings, so that if you want to say of another person, related or not, that he is as close to you as your own brother, you say he is a kind of *soog* to you; that *soog* must help and support one another without question; and that *soog* may not marry or have sexual relations. It is as I have suggested a word loaded with the moral imperatives distinctive of the status it assigns as well as connoting a particular kinship relationship.

But if we want to know how persons come to be *soog* to one another, we must find out how the term serves in classification. Tallensi say that people are classified together as *soog* relatives if they have "single mother-birth", however remote. This is a genealogical criterion. Tallensi give it a special kinship meaning, some peoples do not. Their kinship system selects uterine linkage for recognition as a criterion of classifying persons for certain social purposes, and it does this by explicit contraposition with agnatic descent, which is selected for the classificatory grouping of persons for other social purposes.

The distinction between the category aspect and the classifying aspect of a kinship concept like *soog* is empirically demonstrable. It is shown by the fact that a person cannot be classified among—that is, have membership within—a group of *soog* kin if he is not genealogically of common uterine origin with them, whereas he can, as I have noted, be brought into the category of *soog* for a particular person whose feelings for, and relationship with, him partake of what we might call *soog*-ship. Classification is determinate, categorization not necessarily so, in the universe of kinship. According to the criterion adopted, a person is either in or out of a classificatory group or division, and such a group would not be distinguishable if everybody in the whole society were in a single such group.

We can put this somewhat differently and say that the kinship categories utilized in a particular society form a distinctive set of customary axioms embodied in their language. They embody the rules in accordance with which genealogical connections are sorted into kinship kinds and arrangements. They also embody and signify defining properties, directions for behavior, and santioned norms of right and duty. The Tallensi category of *soog* predicates a rule of classification, to wit, that persons of common uterine descent—of "single mother-birth"—belong together in what is ideally a strictly determinable aggregate. This implies that a person cannot be *soog* to two or more persons who are not also *soog* to one another. As a category word, *soog* imposes bonds and commands subject to norms such as the incest law. It also imputes congenital identity of certain potentialities of personality. As a classifier, it is discriminative because the Tallensi are also grouped and segmented by other structural criteria—by patrilineal descent, by residence, by ritual allegiance, and so forth—and individuals thus associated may be distributed among mutually exclusive *soog* sets. Kinship categories are used to define kinship classes or to classify persons together only if the kinship universe comprises more than one kind of class and if membership in different divisions of a class and in different classes can be exclusive for a given purpose.

We must not forget, of course, that we are speaking all the time of the way the kinship universe is constituted for those who are inside the system. The anonymous Ego of our kinship charts symbolizes this. An outsider has no means of knowing *a priori* what the categories and classifications accepted in a particular society are.

VII

This brings up what might be called the registering function of kinship terminology, that is, its use "as a means of ordering relationships for social purposes" (Radcliffe-Brown, 1950: 34). For Ego, the categories provided for him by his kinship system serve not only to direct his conduct and specify his rights and duties in the normative sense, but also to establish a particular arrangement of persons in his field of kinship in which these are actualized.[24] They serve him as a scheme built up by social learning from childhood, as Malinowski insisted, by which to sort out and organize the relationships that constitute his personal "kinship universe."[25] Among the Tallensi, for a man in the middle years of life, his kinship field will commonly include, for example, "fathers", "aunts" (lit. "female fathers") "mothers" and "uncles", "siblings", "children", and if we extend it to affines, parents-in-law and siblings-in-law. These categories comprise known and named persons, for the most part, who fall into discrete, structurally interlinked classes. In practice, any of these classes will have members not known to him at any given moment but knowable in the appropriate circumstances. A man does not necessarily know all the male members of his mother's patrilineage but all are potentially relevant for him in respect, for instance, to certain ritual obligations and are therefore knowable by him. Departed ancestors have places in his kinship register and are reckoned with in his kinship-regulated activities.

Kinship terms and categories are thus deployed in all domains of Tale social structure. Directly or indirectly, kinship status has either operative or potential relevance for the actor in all domains, and this is true for most tribal societies. It is a determinant of rights, duties, and capacities and a directive of customary conduct in all domains. This deserves reiteration, for the omni-functional valency of kinship relations has been misinterpreted. It has given rise to the illusion that kinship concepts and institutions are no more than an "idiom" for "expressing" what are alleged to be more fundamental social realities. The underlying reality, it

24. It is convenient to speak of Ego as an individual, but it should be remembered that full siblings have the same field of kinship, barring their conjugal and affinal relations.

25. My argument is cogently anticipated in the following observation by Evans-Pritchard: "Kinship categories are limited in number and they have a definite arrangement to any person. It is not merely that the anthropologist perceives that they have a pattern. The Nuer himself perceives it and can describe it without reference to any particular person, or as an abstract system. Also, when the pattern is enunciated in behaviour and there is no one to fill one of the roles, it is recognized that the actual configuration does not correspond to the ideal configuration, and that it should be made to conform to it by substitution, if this is possible." (Evans-Pritchard. 1951b: 152). Cf. my remark about the Tallensi lineage paradigm (1945: 30). The thesis so well formulated here by Evans-Pritchard was previously expounded at length by Firth (1936, chap. VII).

is argued, consists of economic, political and jural relations and interests and it is these that are given expression in the "idiom" of kinship. Misinterpreting the point of view that goes back to Radcliffe-Brown and Rivers, supporters of this thesis argue that the concepts and categories and social relations commonly given the label of kinship, are "socially" and "culturally" not "biologically" defined. They conclude, therefore, that the "biological" element presupposed in the genealogical formulations of kinship relations and institutions is of accidental, or at best contingent significance. (Cf. Beattie 1964, for a review of the debate.)

I will return to the question later and consider where the fallacies lie in this view. They have been trenchantly exposed by Gellner (1960), who, in effect, reaffirms the more usual anthropological view, which assumes recognition of parentage as a fact of nature to be a necessary factor in the construction of kinship systems.

To return to kinship terms and categories, by their means a person appropriates statuses to himself in relation to specified other persons, assigns statuses to them, and regulates his conduct accordingly. Naturally, the schedule of categories and scheme of classification a person draws upon to register the makeup of his personal field of kinship must be the same for all members of his society (allowing for sex, age, and generation), or consistent and coordinated social action would be impossible. However, the fact, for example, that everybody has a father, and uses the same kinship terminology as I do to identify the relationship, does not obliterate the significance of the term "father" as an index of a relationship with features that are unique for myself and one other person (or class of persons) in my kinship field. Conversely, whether or not there is in my field of kinship, at a given time, a person to whom I can as of right apply the term "father" (or whose relationship to me can be specified by this term) does not alter the fact that the category of relationship designated by it is terminologically identified and is recognized in customary usages and norms in all spheres of social life. A person may be fatherless through being orphaned, and this may influence his status and well being. Among the Tallensi, it is when a man no longer "has a father alive" that he attains complete jural and ritual autonomy (cf. Fortes, 1949c: 147 ff.). Likewise, illegitimacy by birth in tribal societies with patrilineal descent systems, and equally, of course, in most European and American societies, means having no legally identified father. The extensive provisions that exist in modern legal systems to mitigate the social and juridical disabilities of illegitimacy assume this.[26] Most striking is the observation that inspired Malinowski's "Principle of Legitimacy."[27] It is a fact, as he maintained, that legitimacy by birth, in matrilineal systems, generally depends on

26. The subject is well covered in the *Encyclopedia of Social Science* (1937 ed.), *s.v.* "Illegitimacy," though the article is in some factual respects out of date.

27. Repeatedly enunciated by Malinowski, it is summed up thus in his challenging article on "Kinship" (1930): The Principle of Legitimacy, he says, "declares that, in all human societies, a father is regarded by law, custom and morals as an indispensable element of the procreative group. The woman has to be married before she is allowed legitimately to conceive, or else a subsequent marriage or an act of adoption gives the child full tribal or civil status. Otherwise the child of the unmarried mother is definitely stigmatized by an inferior and anomalous position in society." He cites the polyandrous Todas and the matrilineal peoples of Melanesia as well as the monogamous Christians of Europe as all equally proof of his contention.

the recognition of jural paternity. In Ashanti, for instance, a bastard is a person whose legal paternity is unknown or unacknowledged (as I shall explain in a later chapter).[28] Thus a particular individual may be fatherless, but the category of fatherhood is given and is available in the kinship system and the social structure, and this is true for all familial status categories recognized in a particular kinship system.

To take another example, among the Tallensi, as in many other tribal societies, it is uncommon for a man to live long enough to have personal contact with ("to reach," as they say) a great-grandchild. But the category exists in the kinship terminology, and the status is recognized and occasionally seen in action,[29] and customary definitions and norms distinctive of the relationship are known to all adults and older children—though there are kinship systems which do not recognize this category of relationship, for example, Australian systems.

The point is elementary, yet it is still too often overlooked. We all agree that a kinship terminology is a customary apparatus for the management of certain kinds of social relations, but it is a special kind of apparatus, nowadays often described as a lexicon, a term which very well underlines its linguistic identity. Thus regarded, it can be treated as if it were self-contained, as the componential analysts and other kinship-linguists have so ingeniously demonstrated,[30] and as has indeed been commonly accepted since Kroeber asserted it in 1909. But if, as is now commonly agreed, it is stultifying to treat the lexicon purely as a linguistic system suspended in a social and cultural void, it is also a distortion to treat it as an apparatus that is intelligible solely in its instrumental use in the dyadic, genealogically described situation.[31] Its character as an inventory and classification of a distinct domain of social relations (and the elements of which they are composed) "recognized," either in one particular society or in a class of societies (at the limit all societies), is thus lost sight of.

To repeat, the function of a kinship terminology as an inventory by means of which a person maps out and manages the total constellation of kinship relations within which he must conduct himself as a bearer of kinship statuses, presumes the application of rules of arranging, grouping and classifying persons by criteria of status in society at large. This is not the same thing as the use of kinship terms as counters in dyadic intercourse, where it is justifiable to regard them as most like other kinds of kinship custom.

The Trobriand kinship system has become a classical example of the mistakes

28. The rule holds for all matrilineal peoples known to me, even the Nayar, among whom the penalty falling on a woman for whose child no *sambandham* lover would accept paternity was expulsion from the caste; cf. Gough, 1959. It is common with African matriliny; cf. Richards, 1950, and for a particularly interesting example where a man's civic status depends on being able ritually to demonstrate legitimate patrifiliation, cf. Colson, 1955.

29. I have known some half dozen great-grandparents among the Tallensi.

30. I refrain from further discussion of this movement as it is not germane to my argument, and content myself with mentioning again the elegant examples afforded in the papers by Lounsbury (1956) and Goodenough (1951). But I must emphasize the "as if" in my remark. One of the weaknesses of componential analysis in the study of kinship systems, it seems to me, is that in fact it cannot avoid smuggling into the analysis the minimal ethnographic content without which the linguistic manipulations make no sense.

31. This being at the opposite extreme to disregarding the cultural and social setting which gives it particular meaning.

that can arise from neglecting this distinction. Malinowski attributed only pragmatic, that is instrumental, validity to Trobriand kinship terminology[32] and thus landed himself in an impasse. Confronted with what are quite obvious Crow-type terminological usages, he was forced by his theory to regard them as anomalous (1929a: 447; and see below, p. 68), and adduced the hypothesis of chance homonymy to account for them (cf. Fortes, 1953b). How this blinded him is ingeniously suggested in Leach's 1958 reanalysis of Trobriand clan and kinship categories. I do not find Leach's analysis wholly convincing; but it does draw attention to the significance of the extra-familial—that is, primarily the politico-jural—dimension of kinship categories and concepts. It does bring out the significance of kinship terms in defining status relations at key points in the life cycle, as opposed to their instrumental use in dyadic intercourse. This puts the instrumental function of the kinship terminology emphasized by Malinowski in a context of social structure he failed to appreciate.[33]

Malinowski's error was one that Radcliffe-Brown never fell into, for Radcliffe-Brown understood that the linguistic, the normative, the "behavioral," and the structural components of kinship institutions, consistent though they must be, are not therefore coterminous. For Malinowski, language, kinship, law, morals, religion, etc. were just different "aspects" of culture conceived as a global entity harnessed to the task of ensuring social survival.[34] For Radcliffe-Brown, these "aspects" were partially autonomous departments or subsystems of an all-inclusive social system. As a part of a language, a kinship terminology is subject to rules and principles that are peculiar to language. Analogously, other forms of kinship custom and behavior fall into the partially autonomous subsystems of law, morals, and ritual. Not fusion but interdependence characterizes the relations between the component subsystems of a total social system. They can even be compared among themselves to seek out common underlying principles of organization. Thus in 1941 he drew a parallel between his comparative approach to the question of "how workable kinship systems have been created by utilising certain structural principles and certain mechanisms" and the "morphological comparison of languages" (1941: 6) aimed at discovering how such principles as, for instance, inflection, agglutination, and word order have been used in building languages.[35]

32. The "ill-omened kinship nomenclatures", as he contemptuously dubbed them (1929a: xx). He went even farther when he declared with characteristic rhetorical hyperbole: "Any problem starting from the classificatory nature of kinship terminologies, must be spurious, because the plain fact is that classificatory terminologies do not exist and never could have existed" (1930: 22).

33. Leach's argument is open to the objection that he has simply turned Malinowksi's theory of the extension of kinship terms and categories inside out. Instead of the family, Leach postulates external factors such as locality, age and jural status as the determinants of kinship categories and relationships. Where he errs is in denying independent validity to the genealogical reference of kinship terms and concepts. How for example, could a Trobriander arrive at the notion of *tama* as "domiciled male of my father's sub-clan hamlet" (Leach, 1958, p. 132) if he has no concept of father as opposed to male non-father, and no referent for this concept that is independent of the local, hamlet association? There is no escaping the genealogical reference of kinship terms and their ultimate source in the familial domain.

34. Cf. the summary of his ideas in his posthumous book, 1944.

35. It should be borne in mind that Radcliffe-Brown was well acquainted with the linguistic scholarship of his time. As is well known, he took the concepts of "synchrony" and "diachrony" from de Saussure.

CHAPTER V

Toward the Jural Dimension

I

THE PROBLEMS I HAVE BEEN CONSIDERING IN THE PRECEDING CHAPTER LIE AT THE heart of kinship studies. They arise from the very nature of social relations. Textbooks always remind us that social relations are abstractions, since they are not directly visible and tangible, as individuals and activities are, but have to be established by inference. This does not mean that social relations are not real. It is only that they are implicit and general, wrapped up, as it were, in the particular occasions in which they emerge. From the observer's point of view, these occasions are disparate and discontinuous; most social relations, by reason of their generality, emerge in action in many phenotypically distinct situations and contexts of social life. "Siblingship" is manifested in kinship words, in eating customs, in incest taboos, in jural rights and duties, in ritual activities, etc. But let us turn the matter inside out. We can then say that in order to be at the disposal of those who engage in them, social relations must become discernible, objectified. They must be bodied forth in material objects and places, in words, acts, ideas, attitudes, rules and sanctions; in short, in all the features of public meaning that custom provides. Ego knows that he is B's sibling and acts accordingly because custom, through rules of genealogical collocation and norms of status and of value codified *inter alia* in a kinship terminology, provides for this category of relationship. He signifies his engagement in the relationship by the nomenclature he uses towards and about B, by his attitudes, claims, and conduct in situations where it is significant. It is distinctive custom that makes a social relation signifiable by those who participate in it and cognizable by those who are external to it. This is what "recognition" of genealogical connection implies. This is what emerges, in Radcliffe-Brown's tetrad.

There is ground enough here for divergence of interpretation. We can, with Radcliffe-Brown, fix our attention primarily on the social relations projected in custom, or we can follow Malinowski and give precedence to the personal and collective ends subserved by social relations and custom, or we can deny any analytical distinctions between custom and social relations and regard everything as "culture" in the manner of Tylor, Frazer, Boas, Kroeber, et al. The data of kinship, as I said before, lend themselves to different frames of interpretation, and it leads to confusion if we do not keep them apart. It is only by keeping them conceptually apart that we can fit together findings made from different analytical positions.

II

Some tricky issues arise here. To recur to one touched on before, what is the logical or empirical justification for making general statements about social, and, more immediately, kinship relations, as if they existed in their own right, seeing that we have cognizance of them only in the particular occasions of social action in which they emerge? Is the truth of the matter—to put it in extreme terms—that there are no such phenomena as kinship relations but only kinship words and behavior, rules and customs, sentiment and belief mobilized in residential or economic or other tangible forms in the service of economic or jural or ritual interests? The classificatory principle accentuates the dilemma. It is brought out sharply in a recent theoretical discussion by Raymond Firth (1954 and 1955). His argument ranges too widely to follow all the way. I confine myself to one or two of the issues germane to my present theme.

Let us consider the connection between what Firth calls "type relations"—for example, a generic (classificatory) kinship relationship such as that of "mother's brother" and "sister's son"—and the diversity of actual situations and personal circumstances in which they appear. What he means by "type relations" is indicated in the following quotation:

In the authoritative essay of Radcliffe-Brown (1924) . . . the [Firth's italics] mother's brother holds the field. But this is reasonable, since he was concerned with establishing the type relationship. Only in a footnote is it implied that if the mother's brother is dead his sons fill the same role (1954: 13).

Later (p. 14) Firth divides the "obligations and ties" of such relationships into three classes. First, are those of "generic implication . . . use of the kin term; freedoms and restraints in behaviour; advice in time of trouble. . . . Here is no need for individual differentiation. All mother's brothers—or sister's sons—can behave alike. . . ." Second, are specific conditions such as the inheritance of personal names or of a widow which only apply to a particular individual at a time. And thirdly come "intermediate or optional" features as in the case of "inheritance of land rights," where giving to one person may represent favoritism or reflect tensions.

Ethnographical objections to this classification can easily be raised, but let us accept it for argument's sake. Then it must surely be agreed that the one element that is constant and critical through all these vicissitudes of generic, specific, and optional activities is the relationship as such. It is always precisely definable and identifiable by terminology and by norms, rules and customs that mark it.[1]

More concretely, when a classificatory kinsman of the right category assumes the status of Mother's Brother in relation to Ego, he does so in conformity with definite rules, for example the rule of lineage unity, or patrilineal succession, not arbitrarily. He assumes consequential rights and obligations and accommodates his actions to sentiments and values that are distinctive of the status of Mother's Brother in the most general sense, in contrast to other statuses of the same kinship order. Surely this is one of the main functions of a classificatory terminology—to designate such status constancies in a social structure. Differences of magnitude or degree alone do not invalidate this proposition, as seems to be implied by Firth in the second of the two papers cited.[2] The threadbare old joke about the wayward daughter who returns home with an illegitimate baby and protests, when she is disowned by her angry father, "but it is only a very tiny baby," points this moral. And it is palpably brought home to us by the contraposition of different categories of kinship relations with one another and of kinship with other categories of social relations in everyday activities and encounters.

No matter how close or how distant the genealogical connections may be, if Ego recognizes Alter A as an actual or classificatory son, and Alter B as an actual or classificatory sister's son in a patrilineal African system, he will differentiate precisely between these two relationships by the contrasting forms of customary behavior, "ties and obligations," which he displays and expects in each, as well as by the terms he uses. There is a core of prescribed conduct and of normative rules that is distinctive of each relationship and is fixed regardless of "genealogical distance." There are significant differences of substance as well as of degree in the relations of a Tallensi father with his begotten son, as opposed to a classificatory son. But every male he designates by the term for "son" is deemed, by definition, to belong to the generation of his begotten son, and has attributed to him, in particular

1. That is why, among other things, kinship relations, like all social relations, can be referred to and discussed in abstraction from any actual situations in which they emerge. Ethnographical literature abounds in texts obtained from non-literate informants which explain the meaning of kinship terms and the nature of kinship relations in the abstract. This is analogous to looking up the meaning of words like "father" and "mother" in a dictionary.

2. Firth writes (1955: 16): "Terminologically persons are called siblings . . . But in the more concrete aspects of rights and duties to kin—observance of taboos, performance of economical obligations, etc.—there is a sharply decreasing magnitude." This is the problem that has troubled every student of classificatory kinship systems since Morgan. But Firth's contention seems to be that these quantitative variations reduce the "type" relationships to the level of fictions devoid of content. Anyone who has worked with classificatory kinship relations knows that this is not correct.

situations, something of that status. This means (to apply Radcliffe-Brown's tetrad) that the person so designated must not act towards him with the kind of familiarity that is appropriate between equals. And if the son is a classificatory son by the rules of lineage unity and generational sequence, he would not be permitted to marry any woman who could be designated as the same man's daughter. The example I have previously given of the *soog* relationship is apt here too.

Such distinctions also pertain to other social relations. For instance, Tallensi, like other African peoples, draw a sharp contrast between the involuntary, inescapable, immutable bonds of kinship, *however distant*, for which they have a particular concept (*dogham*), and the voluntary, optional, and flexible relationship of friendship, for which they also have a special term (*zoot*).[3]

I agree with Firth that magnitude, in the form of frequency of incidence, or duration, or intensity or range is a critical coefficient of social relations. I myself put forward this contention some years ago (1949a), supporting it with an analysis of Ashanti domestic organization.[4] But the variables that exhibit magnitude must be independently isolated and conceptualized to be susceptible of measurement or counting (cf. Fortes, 1953c), and, what is most important, they must be conceptualized in relation to one another, as a system—operationally speaking, as a matrix—for the recognition of variability to be meaningful at all. This is what Radcliffe-Brown's "principles" and "type relations" are better designed to deal with than analogous isolates of other kinship theories. In short, far from being placed in doubt by such qualifications as Firth makes, they prove to be methodologically indispensable for establishing the conceptual basis for dealing with the very problems of magnitude and situational variability he emphasizes. The pitfall to be wary of is the genealogical fallacy, and this I believe is at the bottom of Firth's objections.

III

Nevertheless, I do not deny that there are ambiguities and gaps in the particular hypotheses of Radcliffe-Brown to which Firth raises objections. The reason, I believe, is that Radcliffe-Brown failed to connect his "principles" precisely with the analytical distinctions adumbrated in his (1935) theory of descent and succession. He failed, therefore, to develop his insight that kinship relations are multidimensional in the dyadic situation no less than in group structure. The relations of husband and wife, parent and child, sibling and sibling belong not only to the familial domain but also, and at the same time, to the politico-jural domain, the economic domain, and the religious domain. What we represent, from Ego's point of view, as only variations in the range and incidence of his kinship relations are, in their total structural setting, correlated with distinctions between the domains

3. Cf. Goody's observations (1962) on this contrast. Incidentally, the point did not escape Malinowski's ethnographic eye. He notes that Trobrianders distinguish between a kinsman and a friend, who must not be either a kinsman or a member of the same clan (1929a: 422).

4. One could not attempt to assess the effect of the conjugal bond in post-marital residence without first isolating it and without balancing it against the contrary pull of matrifilial and sibling relations.

in which they are implicated. A mother's brother is not indispensable for a Tallensi's economic activities and relations; but in the religious domain the correlative statuses of mother's brother and sister's son are, in certain circumstances, indispensable and must be produced *ad hoc* if necessary. It is here that the classificatory principle comes into its own, serving as a bridge between the different domains in which Ego's field of kinship lies.

The language of kinship is a guide to these dimensional factors.[5] For the structural differentiae which I am discussing are, as one might expect, partly embedded in the nomenclatures of kinship and social status, both as incorporated in the lexicon and as used in social action. Grown-ups in our society often address and even refer to their parents as "daddy" and "mummy" in the intimate setting of the family. They would not use these terms in a court of law. Similarly, Tallensi use the same kinship words—*ba*, father, *ma*, mother, and so forth, with or without qualifying suffixes to show that they are being used in a classificatory sense—in all situations where the relationship in question is effective. But in some situations it is the familial component of meaning that is uppermost, indicating, for instance, the affection and trust parents and children have for one another in the routine of daily life, whereas in others it is the politico-jural component, stressing the authority of the parents and the subordination of the children in relation to the wider social structure, or their ritual statuses in the ancestor cult.[6] And there are special expressions that mark these differences of signification. When a man's status in his lineage is defined in terms of his father being alive or not he may declare "*mba be*" my father is alive or "*mba ka*" my father is dead. Everybody knows that he is referring to his "father" in the jural connotation the term has in the lineage context, not in its intimate familial sense. This is typical of the way kinship and other status words are used. It shows that classificatory distance, so-called, is not merely a matter of quantitative variation along a uniform line of extension, but is an index of structural location.

IV

The difficult question, which I brought up earlier, however, still remains open. Is it possible to account for the institutional forms through which the "principles" come into operation? What kind of forces or factors or conditions do we have to look for in order to account for the ways in which genealogical connections, on one side, and the "principles," on the other, are "recognized" in social organization? It could plausibly be argued that how custom "recognizes" genealogical connection

5. Examples abound, for instance in such treatises as *African Systems of Kinship and Marriage* (Radcliffe-Brown & Forde, 1950) and *Matrilineal Kinship* (Schneider & Gough, 1961), and curiously enough, nowhere is this so well documented as in chap. VII of Firth's *We, the Tikopia* (1936).

6. Cf. Fortes. 1949c: 204–5: "The Tallensi regard the economic relations, the jural relations, and the moral and ritual relations of father and son as different aspects of the same thing. . . . [Its] elements . . . stand out more clearly when the consolidating effect of the emotional ties between own parent and own child is absent."

can only be established for each particular social system in its own right. As an internally coherent system it might be assumed to invest genealogical material with kinship meaning in ways that are unique to itself. But then the widespread pheno-typical uniformities, such as appear in the patrilineal mother's brother-sister's son relationship and a host of other kinship relations, as well as the diversities, such as those listed in Firth's remarks (1955: 4) on the sibling relationship,[7] must be reckoned with. The same kinship customs are found in a great variety of social systems, as Morgan discovered and as scholars from Rivers to Murdock have sought to explain.

There is another aspect, too, to this problem. As I have previously pointed out, kinship customs conform to definite rules which qualified informants can formulate. That they are sometimes flouted does not destroy their force and validity—no more than the occurrence of crime or blasphemy destroys (though it may lead to changes in) laws and morals. If this were not so, a kinship system would become chaotic.[8] The mechanisms of "recognition" must include the sanctions that enforce kinship custom—the constraints behind avoidance, respect, and familiarity, behind the rules of marriage, inheritance, property rights, and legal responsibility—for that matter, behind the terminology itself. How did Radcliffe-Brown deal with these questions? At one stage (1941, for instance) the onus seems to be thrown somewhat non-committally on history. A people's social system is the product of their particular history and this can, for the most part, not be known for non-literate peoples. Therefore, all we can do is to accept it as it is.

But in the 1950 "Introduction," structural analysis is turned on to this problem. Reverting to the postulate that the elementary and irreducible genealogical connec-tions utilized in the construction of kinship categories are generated in the parental family, Radcliffe-Brown now concentrates on the internal structure of kinship systems. He reformulates a number of earlier generalizations,[9] of which the most important concerns the relations of proximate generations. He claims that it is an intrinsic feature of this relationship for parents to exercise authority, control, and protective care, and for children to respond with respect and dependence. These relations are counterpoised by the friendly familiarity of members of a single generation through the extension of sibling solidarity, and of alternative generations by the merging rule. All this follows inherently from the requirement that traditional culture must be passed on to each generation by its immediate predecessors for an orderly social life to be sustained.[10] We conclude that not only are the basic genealogical categories utilized in kinship systems derived from the natural structure

7. It is enough to remind ourselves of the differences between the kinship relations of patrilineal father and child and those of matrilineal father and child to see the point of this.

8. It will be remembered that Malinowski made an allegedly inevitable divergence between formulated rules and their observance in practice a central plank in his theory of primitive law. More realistically, Lévi-Strauss recognizes the normative force of rules and takes this as the starting point for his analysis of cross-cousin marriage (1949). His theory of structural models (1953) also presupposes this. Indeed, most writers on kinship and social organization accept this position.

9. Set out, e.g., in the 1930–31 monograph, Part III.

10. Cf. Radcliffe-Brown, 1950: 27 ff. The argument links up directly with the correlation of kinship and affinal relations with the tetrad customs.

of family relations (1950: 31), but that the norms of behavior distinctive of these categories are also naturally generated within the family.

I have paraphrased and sharpened the thesis maintained in this statement, but the essential point is not in doubt. He still considers the basic categories of kinship, like the elementary genealogical relations innucleated in them, to be given, or at least potential in the structure of the parental family. A kinship system, then, is particular insofar as it represents special modes of selection, elaboration, and combination of universally given social relations and categories to form an internally consistent arrangement integrated into the total social structure. The "principles" stand for factors present in all kinship systems and expressed in generic norms. Only the customary forms of expression (which are presumably artifacts of history) differ from society to society. It is essentially the same theory as before—and, incidentally, it involves psychological assumptions, though Radcliffe-Brown always professed to eschew psychology.

In postulating the elementary family as the source of the genealogical substratum of all kinship relations and categories, Radcliffe-Brown was following common opinion in post-Morgan anthropology. Lowie and Malinowski, though they differed in their ideas of what kinship contributes to social organization, were unanimous and in accord with Radcliffe-Brown in allotting pride of place to the family as the matrix of kinship institutions.[11] They were, indeed, particularly insistent on this assumption, partly in reaction against evolutionist ideas derived from Morgan and his followers. And they were echoed by leading authorities, not only in anthropology but in such related disciplines as psychology and sociology too.[12]

It is an assumption that continues to hold the field, such classical exceptions as the Nayar being quoted more to prove than to refute it, as by Radcliffe-Brown himself (1950: 72). Nor is this the only correspondence between Radcliffe-Brown's standpoint and those of other anthropologists contemporary with him. The same climate of thought affected all of them. Thus, to take an extreme example, he always

11. Lowie, 1920: 63 ff.; Malinowski, 1929b, and generally in his writings. It should be borne in mind, as I mentioned before, that some of Morgan's ideas, e.g., about earlier forms of marriage and primitive matriarchy, were still influential at this time. For example, Rivers in the 1920's (cf. 1924: v and 78) still supported the hypothesis of group marriage, and, as I noted earlier, believed classificatory kinship to be "founded on the clan" or other exogamous groups (1914b: vol. I, p. 7). It should be realized, too, that evolutionist theories of marriage, sexual behavior, and the family had a considerable vogue at that time (and still have, cf. Fortes. 1957) in "progressive" intellectual and political circles. Freud, newly discovered, and the Marxist version of Morgan's theories via Engels were the main influences. One representative popularizer of this trend was Robert Briffault. He espoused the cause of matriarchy in a large, diffuse and uncritical treatise called *The Mothers* (1927) in which he drew on current theories of sexual behavior as well as on evolutionist hypotheses concerning the connection between property, marriage, parenthood, and family systems. Though not taken seriously by professional scholars, his popularity was such as to sting Malinowski into refuting him.

12. But I must emphasize again that in addition to postulating primitive promiscuity and the intermarriage of brothers and sisters to account for the beginnings of classificatory kinship, Morgan also made some prescient observations, such as the following from *Systems*: "Some method of distinguishing the different degrees of consanguinity is an absolute necessity for the daily purposes of life. The invention of terms to express the primary relationships, namely, those for father and mother, brother and sister, son and daughter, and husband and wife, would probably be one of the earliest acts of human speech" (1870. *op. cit.*, p. 470).

professed to be vehemently opposed to Freudian theory,[13] but I do not believe that he was uninfluenced by it. Indeed it is my guess that the importance of the sibling group might have been suggested to him through reading *Totem and Taboo* (just as his theory of joking relationships undoubtedly owes much to Freud's theory of jokes and the unconscious). So also the function he attributes to parental authority in the relations of proximate generations is not incompatible with the psychoanalytically tinted hypotheses Malinowski put forward, for instance, in his theory of incest.[14]

V

Granted Radcliffe-Brown's adherence to the prevailing theory of the priority of the family in kinship structure, what then was peculiar to his views? The answer is clear if we compare them, for example, with Malinowski's. For Malinowski the family was, first and foremost, the workshop of child-rearing. Founded on the instinctive desire for parenthood, it is the place where the primary ties of kinship, symbolized in the primary meanings of kinship words, are forged (Malinowski, 1929b; see also Fortes, 1957). Culture builds on these biological imperatives and turns the family into the arena of a drama in which the culturally defined and channeled emotional and social interactions of the individual members are played out. At the heart of the drama lies the conflict (intrinsically an emotional, not a social one) between the "principle of discipline, authority, and executive power" (typified for him by the Trobriand mother's brother), on the one hand, and the "loving care and tender companionship" or just friendly concern (typified by the Trobriand father) on the other (1927a: 10–11). And this conflict, let me emphasize, is traced to the composition of the family and specifically Trobriand cultural values.

That there is an ultimate biological basis for parenthood and therefore for all genealogical connections is undeniable and was taken for granted by Radcliffe-Brown. It is not in this direction that the essential divergence between him and Malinowski lies. Where it lies is best illustrated by Malinowski's theory of substitute parenthood as the source of the "extensions" that underlie classificatory kinship custom and terminology. The standard example is the extension of the term for "mother" and its concomitant sentiments and attitudes to the mother's sister. The picture is well known. Through frequent contact during childhood, when the mother's sister acts for the mother and lavishes affection on the child, but above all because she is the "natural substitute" for the mother in case of illness, death, and other crises, the mother's sister comes to be regarded as a secondary mother and is treated and addressed as one. Other "extensions" of primary kinship, that is of intrafamilial patterns, follow the same course. The incest taboo, for example, eliminates sex from the parental and sibling relationships and is extended to establish a division between "natural associates" who are assimilated to the family, and the others who are friendly rivals and marriageable.

13. In discussion and when the subject came up in his lectures. I know of no published statement of his views on Freud.
14. As expounded in *Sex and Repression in Savage Society* (1927a), for instance.

I do not mean to denigrate Malinowski when I suggest that this is a dubious theory (cf. Fortes, 1957). Let us grant that it fits, near enough, the way in which a kinship terminology and its concomitant body of norms and usages is acquired by the individual—even so, it still depends on circular reasoning. It not only falls into the genealogical fallacy, but it also assumes the prior availability of the classificatory concept and the paradigm of extension in the corpus of a people's language and custom.[15] Our children do not learn to call an "aunt" by the term for "mother" even if she is frequently in their home. Where then does the essential contrast between Malinowski's and Radcliffe-Brown's conception of the family matrix lie? It is not easy to pinpoint, since there is so much overlap between them. Broadly stated it comes to something like this: For Malinowski, the familial relationships of husband and wife, parent and child, sibling and sibling, etc., are required by each generation of the individuals who enter into them for the legitimate fulfillment of biological and cultural "needs." The kinship relations are means, not ends in themselves. Parental authority is necessary in order to transmit culture; incest is prohibited in order that sexual passion should not confuse the emotional and educational relationships of successive generations.

For Radcliffe-Brown, by contrast, the starting point is the relations as such. They are intrinsically given from the outset. The elementary familial relations are not the by-products of the regulation of sexual needs or of the need for parental authority and affection to ensure the upbringing and cultural formation of the next generation. These relations are irreducibly and universally constitutive of familial structure. They form the *terminus a quo*, the inherent framework upon which the emotional relationships, the sentiments and activities, the cooperation of siblings, and the incest barrier between parent and child, must everywhere be built.

And it is because they are precisely identifiable, distinctive and intrinsic to family structure, that the elementary genealogical connections and the correlative kinship relations serve as the building blocks of kinship systems and social organization in all societies. Customary "recognition" refers to the mode of sanctioned deployment of these elementary relations that is adopted in a particular society. If a mother's sister is classified with the mother, this is not because of the adventitious conditioning experience of being partly brought up by her. Nor has it anything to do with the ultimate ends of cultural transmission. It follows from the kind of recognition

15. Malinowski's article in the *Encyclopaedia Britannica* (1929b) sums up these well known hypotheses which are further elaborated in the Trobriand monographs, e.g., *Sexual Life of Savages* (1929a: 442–44). Having asserted that "the mixing up of the individual and the 'classificatory' relation, kept apart by the natives in law, custom, and idea, has been a most misleading and dangerous cause of error in anthropology. . . .," he goes on to the argument about the extension of the term for "mother" to the mother's sister. The "new use of the word," he contends, "remains always what it is, an extension and a metaphor" taught to the child. Then follows the provocative statement on the extension of the term for 'sister' to the extremity of the clan "sister" "with whom sex intercourse is legally forbidden, but . . . may be indulged." It is interesting to see that here as in many other places in this and in his other monographs, Malinowski was on the brink of perceiving that the critical feature of classificatory kinship is its "legal," or as Radcliffe-Brown later said, its "jural" meaning. However, his theoretical bias diverted him from following up this idea. Is there an echo of Malinowski's bias in Firth's previously cited critique of Radcliffe-Brown?

accorded in the social structure at large to the equivalence that is an inherent property of the sibling relationship.

We could, I suppose, describe this point of view as narrowly synchronic and sociological in contrast to Malinowski's eclectic and dynamic approach. Its main merit is that it fixes attention on the strictly structural components of kinship systems, seen from within. Analytically extraneous factors are set aside. This includes not only the biological parameters and psychological variables given precedence by Malinowski but also such factors as the spatial contexts of residence and locality, the economic context of modes of livelihood or forms of property, and such hypothetical, final determinants as generalized reciprocity or exchange. There are no determinants, let alone prime movers, of kinship institutions extraneous to the central core of genealogical connection.

I am, perhaps, exaggerating, for Radcliffe-Brown's conceptual scheme is by no means so clear-cut. But this draws better attention to the main gap in his kinship theory. The famous "principles" identify the genotypical parameters in kinship relations that are the basis of the recognition given to them in particular systems. They do not account for the specific modes of their recognition. For this, it is necessary to consider the connections between kinship relations in the familial matrix and the extra-familial politico-jural order. It is true that Radcliffe-Brown was early aware of this. It is evident, for example, in his suggestions in 1931 and earlier that the wide range of Australian kinship systems is conditioned by their lack of chiefship and other governmental institutions. Later on, responding to new ethnographic material, he paid increasing attention to the jural and political dimension of kinship institutions, but he stopped short of seeing their full implications for the problem of the social recognition of kinship. It is arguable that his synchronic rigor, in this regard, led him to too narrow a view of kinship structure.

I shall return to this presently. Meanwhile I shall make the claim that, granted these reservations, Radcliffe-Brown's "principles" and, in particular, the frame of analysis from which they stem, are the foundation of modern structural theory and method in the study of kinship and social organization. Lowie, as I have previously recorded, virtually acknowledged this in the authoritative recognition he gave to the principle of the unity of the sibling group and the principle of the unity of the lineage in his last work on kinship and social organization (1948). But let me add a more recent and in some ways more telling tribute. It comes from Floyd Lounsbury's previously cited paper on Pawnee kinship terminology. One of the conundrums raised by the defective information in his main source, Morgan's *Systems*, concerns the terminological merging of father's father's father and father's father's father's brother "types" with mother's brother's "types" of "uncle." He derives this hypothetically from a "three-generation cycling of the agnatic line among the uterine lines" and suggests that "a pattern of preferential mating of a man with his female patrilateral second cross cousin must have been responsible for the cycling . . ." (1956: 182–83). The merits of this hypothesis need not concern us. I refer to it because it represents the very approach which Radcliffe-Brown regarded as diametrically opposed to his own. It is all the more striking, then, to find that examination of Pawnee kinship custom from the side of "sociology"—in effect, the descriptive ethnography of the social organization—brings Lounsbury to the following conclusion: "The social equivalence and substitutability of brothers which is found in the social structure is fully reflected in the structure of the terminological paradigm" (1956: 188).

VI

In what ways, then, do Radcliffe-Brown's "principles" fall short in explanatory value? One fallacy critics have committed is to take them in isolation. Taken by itself alone, the principle of the unity of the sibling group, and its corollary, the rule of the equivalence of siblings, cannot account for both the matrilineal Trobriand customs of strict avoidance between adult brother and sister and the matrilineal Ashanti customs of their lifelong intimacy and frequent co-residence. But comparison in this form would be totally at variance with the method of structural analysis initiated by Radcliffe-Brown. It is the first rule of this method (as has been emphasized by others than Radcliffe-Brown's immediate followers[16]) that the systematic character of social organization be kept in the forefront of every analysis. The "principles" cannot be understood in isolation from one another or from the constellation as a whole; they must be seen in relation to one another in a given social system. To interpret the differences between Trobriand and Ashanti sibling-ship, we must consider its connection, in each society, with the structure of descent groups and the rules of filiation and succession. We must take into account how conjugal rights and genetrical obligations are reconciled with the distribution of jural authority and economic control in lineage and clan. We must consider the ritual and metaphysical, as well as the material indices of the unity of the lineage (Fortes, 1959a; Robinson, 1962).

All the same, the critics have a case of sorts, for the procedure I have described is largely implicit, not fully developed in Radcliffe-Brown's own investigations. This was due, I think, to his failure, until 1950, to fuse the line of thought followed in his analysis of succession and descent with his method of dealing with the bilateral network of familial kinship. With his essentially morphological concept of social structure, he never gave up thinking in terms of customary patterns of behavior correlated to the actual connections—prototypically in the dyadic situation—between persons and within groups.[17] He spoke of customs and institutions "maintaining" the social system as a whole and of "integration" as the end aimed at. But he did not, at first, adequately consider the nature of the overall framework within which the component systems of this whole are held together, and what constraints, or what components of social relations, emanate from it. Presumably, with his Australian paradigm always in the background of his thought, he found it difficult to bring into a unified conceptual scheme both the politico-jural frame-

16. Thus Spoehr, reviewing the state of kinship studies in 1950, selects this feature of Radcliffe-Brown's theory for particular commendation (Spoehr, 1950).

17. This, as I understand it, is the main point of Lévi-Strauss's criticism of Radcliffe-Brown's concept of social structure (1953).

work of social structure assumed, for example, in his analysis of descent, and the kinship system of his paradigm. Most of the functionalist kinship studies of the thirties, whether influenced by him or by Malinowski, have the same shortcoming. This was no doubt due as much to the small scale of the societies which provided the models as to the theoretical convictions of the investigators. Thus it is only now, as a result of the researches carried out by Powell (1960) under the stimulus of post-war political anthropology, that we have a reasonable picture of Trobriand politico-jural organization and can see how the familial vicissitudes made so much of by Malinowski reflect orderly politico-jural norms and constraints.[18]

What I am reverting to is the rules and sanctions that lie behind kinship relations and institutions everywhere; and I am arguing that these cannot be understood without regard to the political and jural constraints that are generated in the extra-familial domain of social structure.[19] It hardly needs saying that neither Malinowski nor Radcliffe-Brown—nor, of course, any of their early followers—was oblivious of this consideration. Hogbin's pioneering study, *Law and Order in Polynesia* (1934), coming as it did on the heels of *Crime and Custom*, testifies to this. But it was not until the final statement of his kinship theory in 1950 that Radcliffe-Brown formally distinguished the jural dimension of kinship and descent institutions. Relating what he held to be the distinctive features of "mother right" and "father right," he now ascribes them to the "corporate" character of unilineal descent groups. To elucidate this he distinguishes between "jural relations, which are confined within the lineage, and the personal relations of affection, esteem, and attachment" (1950: 78). Hence he now defines the contrast between matrilineal systems (in which possessory rights over children are vested in the united sibling group of brothers and sisters) and patrilineal systems (in which such rights are vested in the father, and cross-sex siblings are dissociated) as a jural opposition. The test is that jural severance does not obliterate the affective attachment of patrilineal cross-siblings.

This analytical dichotomy joining together into one scheme descent status and familial kinship is new, and it hinges, clearly, on his conception of the nature of jural relations.

Here let me interpolate that, to the best of my knowledge, Radcliffe-Brown first used this concept, and that rather tentatively, in his 1940 paper on joking relationships (pp. 206–07). I have a particular interest in this as I had, at that date, the advantage of discussing with him the concepts and the method I proposed to use in describing the lineage and kinship structure of the Tallensi. And it was then that the concept of jural relations, or rather, of the jural dimension, or factor, of kinship and descent structure, became crystallized for me, and, I think, commended itself to Radcliffe-Brown as a logical categorization of the determinants of sanctioned right and duty that enter into kinship and descent relations.[20] His use of it in the analysis

18. The subject is dealt with at length in Powell's unpublished Ph.D. thesis submitted to the University of London. I am indebted to Dr. Powell for permission to refer to it.

19. The following is one of several observations made by Powell which exemplify my point: "Malinowski stressed the dyadic aspect of marriage relationships generally and of the *urigubu* presentations. . . . In fact the *urigubu* responsibilities of a sub-clan are in principle as well as in practice corporate, as are its rights in land, magic, etc. . . ." (1960: 127; cf. also Fortes, 1957).

20. I leave the development of this point for the next chapter.

of joking relations is a cautious recognition that jural elements are critically associated with dyadic kinship relations, not just contingent to them.

This shift of emphasis was, it is true, consistent with the whole trend of his thought and work (cf. Fortes, 1955). Even at this stage, however, he did not follow up all its implications. As far as he went, though, it is my belief that it was brought to a head through the influence of the ethnographic studies of the previous decade, due chiefly to what has sometimes been described as the "British" school of structural anthropology. These dealt with societies of much larger scale than those of Australia, North America, and New Guinea, and this required consideration of an overall framework of social structure which was palpably political and juridical in character. Evans-Pritchard's first analysis of the Nuer lineage system (1940) and *African Political Systems* (1940) set the course. A dimension of kinship structure not so systematically investigated since Morgan and Maine thus came under renewed[21] theoretical scrutiny. The theoretical importance of this development lay, as I have pointed out elsewhere (1953b), not only in the impetus it gave to political anthropology, but even more in the analysis it offered of kinship groups and institutions from the angle of their connection with the political organization.

Though the 1950 synopsis appears in the context of African systems of kinship and marriage, it is patently intended to have general applicability. Had he considered the matter, Radcliffe-Brown would have recognized that the jural and the affective dimensions of kinship institutions are distinguished even in the Australian systems. This much is implied in his observation, repeated in the "Preface" to *African Political Systems* (1940), that kinship institutions have political functions in Australian society.

VII

It is my contention that the major advance in kinship theory since Radcliffe-Brown, but growing directly out of his work, has been the analytical separation of the politico-jural domain from the familial, or domestic domain within the total social universe of what have been clumsily called kinship-based social systems. It is true that constitutive principles and determinants of social organization perceived as operative in the narrower field of kinship, descent, and marriage relations, but deemed to be of extra- or supra-familial origin, have repeatedly been postulated since Morgan made property his prime mover. The principle of reciprocity, which I mentioned earlier, came near to serving the same universally explanatory purpose for Malinowski; and its sophisticated elaboration in Lévi-Strauss's theory of matrimonial exchange has been both applauded and criticised for the universal

21. I say "renewed" because, among others, Rivers gave some attention to it (cf. 1924. chap. IX) and in particular Lowie, as I have mentioned before, paid close regard to political and juridical institutions. Radcliffe-Brown himself (1941: 5) quoted with approval Starcke's (1889) view of kinship nomenclature as "the faithful reflection of the juridical relations which arise between the nearest kinsfolk in each tribe," but he did not explicitly connect this with political organization.

validity claimed for it.[22] But, as I said before, hypotheses of this level of generality are of a different order altogether from the kind of generalization contained in Radcliffe-Brown's statement. They purport to isolate universal mechanisms of the kind that I am calling prime movers which are supposed to operate over the whole sweep of social life, analogously, one imagines, to the way in which gravity works in the physical universe. The more modest objective I am discussing is to seek out directly observable mechanisms that play a formative part in social structure. The principle of reciprocity, for example, does not help us to understand or explain the structural differences between a social system that makes use of unilineal descent groups and one that rests upon cognatic kindreds. Yet it is exactly such problems of structural variation that lie at the heart of kinship theory, and "final cause" theories throw no light on such problems (as Homans and Schneider argue). By contrast, it is in the clarification of just such problems that the analytical discrimination of the politico-jural dimension of kinship systems has proved most significant.

I must repeat what I said in a different context in an earlier chapter. I am not proposing to substitute for Radcliffe-Brown's "principles" more general principles of a politico-jural order. I regard the politico-jural aspect as complementary to the familial aspect of kinship relations to which Radcliffe-Brown's "principles" are primarily applicable. This is relevant to all fields of social structure, in dyadic no less than in polyadic and collective situations, in what are traditionally regarded as purely kinship relations, no less than in the sphere of what are conventionally accepted as legal and political relations. Further discussion of this topic must wait, but I cannot refrain from calling on the support, once again, of a scholar whose authority no one will question—Floyd Lounsbury. His review (1962) of Rodney Needham's *Structure and Sentiment: A Test Case in Social Anthropology* bears directly on my argument. Discussing the antithesis between "prescriptive" and "non-prescriptive" rules of marriage, he comments:

It is not the incidence of marriages according to a given rule that is decisive, but the *consequences* of such marriage. We would think that the distinction should rest rather on an aspect of the *legal structure* of a society. . . (p. 1308).

Continuing, he says of kinship terminologies:

for kinship terminologies, when completely analyzed and reduced to the rules that generate the totality of terminological assignments, can be shown, we think, to be diagnostic of certain aspects of the *legal structures* of societies—especially of those two aspects that concern succession and inherited affinity (p. 1309).

I cannot assert that Lounsbury's notion of "legal structure" corresponds exactly

22. In his masterly critique of Lévi-Strauss's theory, Professor J. P. B. de Josselin de Jong credits Lévi-Strauss with having "convincingly" demonstrated "the significance of the principle of reciprocity as a panchronic and universal dynamic factor in social life . . ." (1952). But as Lévi-Strauss himself explains, the idea has a longer history, going back to Mauss, Malinowski and others. The reservations I am stating, it is almost superfluous to add, are mild compared to some of the criticism Lévi-Strauss's method and theory have incurred. I here follow Homans and Schneider (1955), who have previously raised similar reservations more forcefully and cogently. The controversy between them and Needham is referred to later (cf. f.n. 35 below).

to what I mean by the politico-jural order; but he is unquestionably describing an important and characteristic part of it, and he connects it precisely with the kinship system. What is more, this is his chief ground for rejecting the central premise of Needham's reasoning. The essential point is the following: Orthodox functionalist theory taking dyadic genealogical relations as the fixed base, emphasizes the step by step attenuation for Ego, with increasing "genealogical" distance, of the relationships signified in a classificatory kinship terminology. But this applies only to the affective and interpersonal components of kinship relations. The invariant core of every kinship relation specified in a classificatory terminology, to which I drew attention when I considered Firth's objections to Radcliffe-Brown's principles, remains unaccounted for. What makes it invariant? In my view, and, as I read him, in Lounsbury's too, the answer lies in the politico-jural domain; and supposing we grant that every kinship relation is built up on an elementary genealogical connection, by extension or generalization or some other such process, its invariant component derives from its jural status. The leviratic, sororatic, cross-cousin, inheritance, and such like rights, claims and duties, as well as the conventional patterns of behavior and sentiment, are not extinguished by mere genealogical distance. They can be asserted, in appropriate circumstances, irrespective of personal and affective attitudes and bonds and this is enforceable, in the last resort, by sanctions that emanate from the politico-jural domain.

To avoid misunderstanding let me add a gloss. Surely, it might be objected, what is characteristic of such kinship institutions as the patrilineal avunculate and matrilineal paternity is the absence of jural sanctions in the relationship. My answer, to revert to an earlier argument in this discussion, is that, nevertheless, kinship relations of this type cannot be understood without taking into account the jural constraints in the kinship systems of which they form an integral part. For as I indicated in reconsidering Radcliffe-Brown's theory of the patrilineal avunculate, its form and content directly reflect the complementary moral role it serves in contraposition to the jurally defined and sanctioned relationship of father and son, within the total system of kinship and politico-jural relations. We shall see that the principle here implied is well illustrated and clearly understood by the Lozi and the Ashanti. In their legal systems, formally non-jural claims and privileges, of the kind exemplified by those that arise between matrilineal father and son, are dealt with in the courts by recourse to the concepts of equity and justice; whereas those that arise in the structurally complementary and formally jural relationships, such as those of matrilineal mother's brother and sister's son, are deemed to fall under strict rules of legality.

I have suggested that, even when he thus took explicit cognizance of the jural dimension of kinship structure, Radcliffe-Brown yet fell short of filling the gap in his theoretical system. His last discussion of unilineal descent and corporate group structure reveals this (1950: 39–43). He still takes the essential characteristics of corporate descent groups to lie in their collective solidarity. The criteria he emphasizes are collective action in ritual, representative leadership as by a chief or a council, and collective control of property. There is no real advance here on the 1935 paper. Corporate descent groups are seen as arrangements of persons in fixed social segments. He makes no attempt to investigate what is critical for corporate group organization, that is, the external status of such groups within the overall politico-jural structure.

VIII

We see this better if we compare Evans-Pritchard's analysis (1940) of the Nuer lineage system. The corporateness of the descent group is here presented as a function of its external relations with like units in a lineage system that constitutes the overall political armature of Nuer society. Moreover, lineage structure is shown to emerge characteristically in such jural and political norms and procedures as prescribed exogamy, the settling of homicide disputes by negotiation or feud, the regulation of territorial association, and the range of what Evans-Pritchard designates as Nuer Law.[23] In particular, he brings out the cardinal significance of continuity in time for descent group structure. He takes the morphological concept of segmentary organization from Durkheim and Radcliffe-Brown, but shows that it subsumes the structurally counterposed processes of "fission and fusion." He shows that these are continually operative at all levels of lineage and clan structure in strict alignment with the morphological pattern laid down by the rules of descent and the distribution of political solidarity.[24] Thus a general process of differentiation and integration is demonstrated to underlie corporate group organization, and it pertains to the system as a whole and is governed by political and jural norms and principles. It is these that mobilize the factors of lineage unity, sibling equivalence, and generation division to maintain the system, as Radcliffe-Brown would have put it. Morphology is exhibited as present in process, and process is shown to shape morphology. If the analogy I earlier suggested between Radcliffe-Brown's "principles" and the particulate units of Mendelian genetics is not too far-fetched, then we might compare Evans-Pritchard's contribution to the discovery of the reproductive mechanisms, such as mitosis and meiosis, which bring about the segregation and combination of genes and link them to the constitution of the organism as a whole.

The analysis of corporate descent group structure first developed by Evans-Pritchard (and further elaborated in my study of Tallensi social structure) enables us to see very clearly how the familial order and the politico-jural order are inter-meshed. Though jurally validated, and politically implemented, descent group structure is rooted in kinship relations generated within the familial system and constituted in accordance with Radcliffe-Brown's "principles."

23. *Op. cit.* pp. 168–69: "We speak of 'law' here in the sense which seems most appropriate when writing of the Nuer, a moral obligation to settle disputes by conventional methods, and not in the sense of legal procedures or of legal institutions. . . . The first point to note about Nuer Law is that it has not everywhere the same force within a tribe, but is relative to the position of persons in social structure. . . ." This definition would not be inconsistent with my notion of the jural (see next chapter). Incidentally, Evans-Pritchard also emphasized the importance of distinctive ritual observances as indices of lineage identity (1940: 211). In *Nuer Religion* (1956), this theme is developed at length.

24. Cf. Fortes. 1953b. Gluckman offers an interesting commentary on the emergence of this analytical scheme in *Order and Rebellion in Tribal Africa* (1963: 50 ff.).

A corollary must be added. One result of recognizing the jural coefficient in kinship relations is to draw attention to the element of constraint in them. But when we examine this closely we see that kinship relations, or rather the basic kinship norms, are commonly deemed to be binding *ab initio*, in their own right. Constraint is felt to be inherent in the elementary relations themselves. But we must not forget the limiting factor of jural legitimization for marriage and for parental control and responsibility within the familial organization. In the experience of the actor, the elementary relations of kinship thus emerge as irreducible moral relations (Fortes, 1949c: chap. XII), in the sense that they are felt to be axiomatically binding and to stipulate the rule of amity as the basis of kinship behavior. Thus they are maintained through the force of conscience as well as in compliance with the jural code. This comes out in what Radcliffe-Brown defined (1953) as the "affective" components of kinship relations and is frequently expressed in mystical notions and sanctions.

Malinowski perceived but was unable to deal analytically with this aspect of kinship; Radcliffe-Brown mostly took it for granted.[25] We need, however, to keep it openly in sight. For it is the normative counterpart of the fact that in the social structure as a whole the familial domain and the politico-jural domain are interdigitated in a reciprocal and complementary relationship.

IX

I should like to round off this discussion with an ethnographic example. I want to consider briefly some aspects of the sibling relationship, with reference, particularly, to the Tallensi.[26] I thus take up a topic that has come up several times in the course of my argument. But I turn to it again more directly in tribute to the pregnant remark with which Radcliffe-Brown introduces the concluding paragraphs of his 1950 synopsis. Restating the "principle" of the unity of the sibling group in structural terms, he writes: "The unit of structure everywhere seems to be the group of full siblings—brothers and sisters" (1950). It is one of the few generalizations in kinship theory that, in my opinion, enshrines a discovery worthy to be placed side by side with Morgan's discovery of classificatory kinship; and, like Morgan's, it has been repeatedly validated and has opened up lines of inquiry not previously foreseen.

The Tallensi have a word for the patri-sibling relationship as such (*sunzot*) which is as abstract as our own and is employed at all levels of social structure—in the context of the domestic family, the corporate lineage, the clan, and the ritual congregation (cf. Fortes, 1949c: chap. X). It has the institutional correlates we would predict from Radcliffe-Brown's paradigm of a segmentary patrilineal descent group

25. One of Radcliffe-Brown's favorite theses was that there is a "principle of justice" or of "just retribution" at work in all social systems. He described it as "an abstract structural principle" (1957: 131–32) and derived from it the secondary "principle of equivalent returns" with its corollary, the notion of expiation (p. 133 ff.). But he did not make use of this hypothesis in a systematic way. If I understand him correctly, the point I am making is implied in Lévi-Strauss's notion of "*le fait de la règle*" (1949, p. 39).

26. Relevant details are given *passim* in Fortes, 1945 and 1949c.

system, for example, the levirate, the "male mother" avunculate, and the "female father" amitate. In addition to these expressions of the equivalence of siblings, Tallensi cite one feature above all: Siblingship implies equality of status among like-sex siblings in contraposition to the inequality of status that characterizes other relations of kinship, descent, and affinity; they are "in parage",[27] and an index of this is the mutual substitutability of like-sex siblings in jural and ceremonial relations. This follows from their identification in the structure of the lineage. In this context they appear as a nuclear corporate unit. They are defined as equals for the assignment of such jural rights as those of inheritance and succession by the rules of patrilineal descent. But they are equals also at another level, that is, vis à vis one another within the sibling group. In this context, they are morally equal by filiative status, and this is reflected at the level of lineage structure in the segmentary organization of the lineage.

Siblingship, then, is both a familial status and a lineage status; and a distinctive feature of the relationship is the right of equal sharing, differences of birth order and sex being allowed for. In fact, wherever there is sharing on equal terms, there siblingship can be inferred to be the normative criterion, even if the participants are not genealogically siblings either of the same parentage or by lineage reckoning. It is from this feature of siblingship that the rights, duties, sentiments, and values exhibited in such institutions as the levirate and in such processes as lineage segmentation are thought ultimately to flow. To emphasize it, Tallensi quote maxims which contrast siblingship with social relations that rule out sharing. Parents and children, for instance, do not share; they are not mutually substitutable in the internal[28] arrangements of the family; thus parents give or apportion, children receive and make returns. Friends give and reciprocate freely in ways that look like sharing but are in fact not the same thing, since there is no element of right in it.

It is evident that siblingship cannot be defined simply in genealogical terms or as a kinship category or by the rule of patrilineal descent. Descriptively it can be thought of as a configuration of relationship that comes under all these rubrics, but how it works, among the Tallensi, can be seen only by considering the moral and jural norms which govern its different manifestations.

This is not to say that genealogy, terminology, kinship category, and descent are merely contingent. Far from it. They constitute the calculus for determining siblingship. An interesting reflection of this occurs with configurations of social

27. I lift this medieval juristic term, which sums up the principle of sibling equivalence and equality so beautifully, from Pollock and Maitland (1895). In English constitutional law of the eleventh and twelfth centuries, they state (bk. II, chap. VI, no. 2, p. 263), brothers were equal—"they are in parage; one of them cannot be called upon to do homage to his peer." In a footnote they record that "Richard Coeur de Lion refused to do homage to his brother Henry, 'the young king,' saying, 'It is not meet that the son of the same father and the same mother should admit that he is in any way subject to his elder brother.' " This is a good illustration, by the way, of the manner in which social relations constituted primarily in the familial domain pertain, equally, to the politico-jural domain, and thus mark, as it were, the overlap of these two domains. (*Parage*, is defined in the Shorter Oxford Dictionary as an obsolete word which meant (1) lineage or descent, or (2) equality of birth or station, as in the equality of duty or service among brothers and sisters in feudal tenure.)

28. N.B., as opposed to the external relations of a domestic group or its lineage core, when representative status may be assigned to any member regardless of generation.

relations that do not belong to the domain of kinship and descent but in which moral and jural norms characteristic of siblingship are effective. These emerge in connection with the ancestral and Earth cults, for example, where the mode of distributing the duties and apportioning the sacrificial animals corresponds to the sharing patterns among siblings. In these cases, presumptive genealogical, terminological, and categorical bonds are invoked to assimilate the configuration to the appropriate structural model of siblingship.

To conclude, there are two dimensions to Tallensi siblingship. By filiation, Tallensi siblings perceive themselves as equals, bound and entitled by moral and affective norms to share on equal terms. By descent, they see themselves as a unit in contraposition to other like sibling groups in the lineage, and think of their right to share as jural equality of participation in the corporate unity of the group.

We can see that if sharing by equal division is a jurally enforceable rule, then fission, partition of patrimonial property, and, in the extreme case, dissension and dispersion might well be the paradoxical climax in the assertion of jural equivalence among siblings. Among the Bedouin of Cyrenaica, Peters informs us (1960), intralineage fission is precipitated by the competitive claims made by half-brothers in assertion of their agnatic equality in such matters as inheritance. But lineage unity remains unimpaired in the organization of the vengeance groups which are the politico-jural units in external relations for exacting and paying blood money. The Arab saying "to hate like a brother" is apt here. But even better instances are found, as we might expect, in systems that lack corporate descent groups designed to contain the sibling group as a unitary element of its internal structure. The sibling relationship among the Iban (Freeman, 1958) and in the Sinhalese community of Pul Eliya described by Leach (1961a) are of this type. But it is nevertheless true to say—of these societies as of many that are economically or politically simpler— that "The sibling group is the fundamental structural unit," at any rate within the familial domain.[29] It is evident, in short, that the rule of equal sharing among siblings (for accuracy, we should add "of like sex") which is *prima facie* a norm of the internal structure of the sibling group, is implemented in diverse ways, depending upon the extra-familial social structure in which the sibling group is contained. Sibling relations are laid down in the familial setting by genealogical reckoning and defined by kinship criteria, but they are manifested in accordance with jural norms pertaining to property, status, marriage, etc., that stem from the overall structure of society as implemented in politico-jural institutions. Indeed the qualifications to take account of sex and age factors are not only morally and affectively given in the familial setting, they are also a jural requirement.[30]

29. I am quoting from the short but incisive (1954) analysis of Lapp social organization by Pehrson, later expanded in his monograph of 1957. A parallel example in which the analysis is supported by an unusual wealth of descriptive and demographic data is Dunning's study of the Northern Ojibwa (1959).

30. This is patent in the contrast between the "patrilineal" and the "matrilineal" avunculate. I have, of course, only touched on the fringes of a subject about which a treatise could be written. One need only think of such institutions as the cattle-linked cross-siblingship of the Lovedu and other Southern Bantu peoples, or at the other end of the spectrum, the mythological elaboration of the sibling concept among peoples as widely separated in space and culture as the Murngin and the Dogon to see the possibilities.

It may seem that I have overemphasized the importance of the jural dimension in the rule of the unity of the sibling group and the equivalence of its members. That this is not so can be seen from the often-discussed and superficially anomalous treatment of fratricide in many societies where extra-familial killing either provokes vengeance or requires the payment of blood-compensation or even, in some instances, incurs penalties imposed by political authorities. The "sin of Cain," as Schapera explains (1955) is apt to be left either to the arbitrament of supernatural agencies, or to be dealt with by the family or clan itself, sometimes even when cognizance is taken of the occurrence by the political authorities, as among the Tswana. To be sure, this is connected with the fact that citizenship, in these societies, is mediated through membership in the lineage, clan, or family, with the corollary that dissension among kinsfolk, provided it does not infringe on the rights of outsiders, is left to be settled among themselves. But the notion that brothers are equivalent and form a unit in relation to society at large is implicated. The definition of fratricide as sin and sacrilege, not as crime or tort, reflects the assumption that it is a kind of self-inflicted injury for which the perpetrator is not accountable to society at large, as he would be if the victim were, in jural terms, another person.

The treatment of twins and other plural births—where, as has often been pointed out, the acme of sibling equivalence is encountered—exemplifies the same situation particularly clearly. It is enough to note that plural births are rarely accepted with indifference by society at large. Public, extra-familial recognition, whether by approbation and reward, or by condemnation and punishment as sinful or criminal, is common.

This granted, it is all the more important not to lose sight of the fact that sibling-ship is a relationship and a status in the familial domain as well as in the politico-jural domain. We must not lose sight of the affective and moral underpinning of the total configuration. Affective solidarity and jural discrimination are both involved in the cross-sibling linkage that underlies the patrilineal avunculate. Testimony to the efficacy of the affective and moral bonds rooted in the filial experience of siblings is familiar to us from ethnographic studies in tribal and other non-Western societies. It is worth noting, though, that there is ample evidence of their efficacy also in Euro-American societies. In the present context, it is not only such features as the advanced technology, the complex economic organization, and the universal literacy of these societies that are significant but much more the elaborate differentiation of the politico-jural domain in contraposition to the familial domain. In modern American and European countries, citizenship accrues to each individual regardless of his familial status. Family and kinship relations have little or no politico-jural validity in the extra-familial social structure. Marriage, occupational mobility and other circumstances of normal social life continually disperse family members. Sibling solidarity would seem, in these conditions, to have little chance of outlasting early childhood. Yet the evidence shows that it remains a dominant affective and moral force for most ordinary people throughout life.[31] Thus, sibling solidarity remains a prized familial value in our society, too, as most of us know

31. As is excellently demonstrated in the study by Cumming and Schneider (1961).

from our own life experience, though sibling equivalence (medieval "parage") in the jural sense, is no longer recognized in our legal systems.

I have discussed siblingship as if it occurs only in the form of the relationship between brothers and sisters by the same parent or parents. We should remember, however, that it is a category of wider connotation especially where classificatory kinship concepts and institutions are operative. It may be extended to embrace an age-grade, or age-set, as, for example, among the Nilo-Hamitic peoples of East Africa (cf. Peristiany, 1939: 29–45), and, at the limit, a whole generation, as in classical Hawaiian systems. The significant point is that wherever siblingship is imputed, there some features of the equality and equivalence that are distinctive of this relationship will be assumed or imputed. It may be so whittled down as to have no jural force or to receive no recognition outside the family circle; but if it is recognized at all there will be associated patterns of conduct to mark it, perhaps only on the affective level of sibling solidarity, as a relationship of peculiar mutuality and equality and moral binding-force between the parties to it, and as one of equivalence in relation to the external social order. Where the nomenclature of familial relationships is customary in designation and address in non-familial contexts such as, for example, Roman Catholic monastic institutions and Masonic lodges, this may seem to have only figurative implications. But it is common knowledge that brotherhood in these and similar organizations implies patterns of value and of conduct that are distinctly fraternal in ways corresponding to the analysis I have here given.

X

These examples must suffice, for the time being, to illustrate how consideration of the politico-jural factors brings to light the mechanisms and processes through which the elementary principles of kinship structure identified by Radcliffe-Brown are put to work—and thus "recognized"—in a society. They illustrate, also, a procedure of analysis which, to my mind, stems directly from Radcliffe-Brown's method, though it was not clearly envisaged by him. The essential step is to discriminate the internal constitution from the external context of a social group or relationship or institution. Judged by this procedure (which I elaborate in the next chapter), Radcliffe-Brown's principal concern was with the familial, or domestic domain of social relations, customs, and institutions, viewed from within, as an internal system. Aware though he was of them, he made no systematic analysis of the constraints from the complementary politico-jural domain that help to shape familial organization in every society.

In the matter of anthropological method, Radcliffe-Brown's outstanding contribution lay in his consistent adherence to the synchronic frame of analysis. Guided by this, he was able to propose hypotheses which could be tested by criteria of synchronic consistency and interdependence among the rules, principles, and structural arrangements he formulated. This gave his method a degree of sociological rigor not attained by other anthropologists of his generation (cf. Fortes, 1953b,

1955). It provided the measure of theoretical parsimony which saved him from the pitfalls of historicism that entrapped so many of his contemporaries. But his self-imposed limits of method, combined with the kind of ethnographic material at his disposal until his last years, held him back in one important respect: Except for general statements, he had no place in his system for the part played by the factor of time in social structure (Fortes, 1949a). He ignored the fact that the synchronic structure of a social system contains within itself a temporal extension which is neither historical nor diachronical in the narrow sense of successive concatenation.[32] Leaving this aside, it is to Radcliffe-Brown's theoretical system that modern structural anthropology, British-style, owes its main frame of analysis. It is not invidious to compare Kroeber, whose insatiable catholicity of interests led him to try many lines of investigation and to experiment with a diversity of frames of reference. He bequeathed stimulating, and even inspiring, ideas and vistas to us but not a disciplined methodology or a systematic conceptual apparatus for any one branch of our subject. Malinowski, too, master that he was of empirical field technique, bequeathed brilliant and original theoretical ideas to us, but not a productive methodology of analysis.

I speak here of the British style of structural anthropology in deference to certain other theoretical trends in the study of kinship and social organization which operate with a structural frame of discourse but are firmly distinguished from, and even opposed to it by their exponents. I have in mind, especially, the work of G. P. Murdock and his colleagues, and the school of thought, for such it is, created by Lévi-Strauss and his followers. Murdock's chief interest has been in the classification and typological ordering of kinship and affinal systems and institutions.[33] I have commented in passing on some of his generalizations. Though his cross-cultural statistical methods serve his taxonomic aims well, like öKbben (1952) and some other critics, I do not find them relevant to my inquiry.

Lévi-Strauss and his followers, on the other hand, deal in more radical ways with some of the problems and data that occupied Radcliffe-Brown's attention and remain central to the work of his successors. But such is the divergence between their theories and those derived from Radcliffe-Brown, that anyone working within the latter tradition must find it difficult to assimilate the former. Formally, as Schneider points out (1965),[34] it lies in an alleged antithesis between a theory which regards kinship and descent as the critical determinants of any system of kinship and affinity, and one which puts marriage, or more generally alliance, in this place. The former is ascribed to the Radcliffe-Brown group, the latter is claimed by the Lévi-Strauss group (cf. Dumont, 1965; Needham, 1962). This, to my mind, is pure casuistry. I share my colleague Jack Goody's judgment on this issue (with which Schneider obviously concurs) when he rejects the exclusiveness this implies for one

32. And, *inter alia*, therefore took no cognizance of the actual processes of inter-generational transmission—the so-called socialization processes—which figured so largely in Malinowski's scheme.

33. As is amply documented in his major work, 1949. Cf. also his introduction to *Social Structure in Southeast Asia* (1960).

34. Unfortunately, Dr. Schneider himself confuses some of the fundamental issues, (cf. n. 11, p 287) but they are exhaustively stated.

axis of relationship as against the other. This is not merely a question of definitions. The arguments of the "alliance" theorists are often based on presentations of the ethnographic data that can at best be described as unwarrantedly one-sided. As Needham admits (echoing Leach, 1951) the "great book" with which Lévi-Strauss launched the movement "suffers from serious lacks as regards sources, and it contains a number of ethnographic errors and misinterpretations of the facts" (1962: 3).

But supposing we overlook this fault, since no ethnography is free of imperfections. What then of the theoretical concepts and method of analysis characteristic of "alliance" theory? A serious difficulty arises here. The analytical procedures of its proponents turn on their special concept of the "model." The "model" has a structure, that is, its elements—kinship terms, descent rules, marriage regulations, discriminative customs, and so forth—have an ordered arrangement and are mutually consistent. It is expressly the observer's construct—as of course any conceptual label for observed data is; only here comes the rub: the "models" put forward by alliance theorists are apt to be so formal and abstract that it is frequently impossible to connect them unequivocally with the data they purport to represent.

Thus Needham (1962: 81) says of his model of Purum "alliance cycles": "In the model this is a single cycle . . . but, as we should expect, the factual situation which this so simply represents is very much more complex."[35] Subsidiary qualifications therefore become necessary to enable us to read back from the model to the reality.[36] Dumont, again having set up his "model," is able to declare that "If we say [presumably on the basis of what informants tell us] that 'one marries one's cross-cousin,' we merely state a condition to be observed in order to maintain a certain pattern of intermarriage"; and he adds, "the regulation causes marriage to be transmitted much as membership in the descent group is transmitted" (1967: 4)—a state of

35. The Purum case and Needham's "model" have been subject to a great deal of controversy. Since the above was written, the debate has waxed furiously. Charles Ackerman claims to have shown that Needham's "model" is irreconcilably at variance with the actualities of Purum marriage (1964). The same numerical data are claimed by others, using different statistical methods, to support Needham's thesis (cf. the discussion of Ackerman's article). Needham's own defense of his position in this discussion points the moral. It is that ethnographic and numerical data as defective as those on which his Purum "model" is based can be manipulated to satisfy quite contradictory "models" of the formal and hypothetical type that is the stock-in-trade of "alliance" theorists.

36. In *The Dynamics of Clanship among the Tallensi* (1945) I introduced the analysis with an account of what I called the "Paradigm of the Lineage System" (chap. III). I presented it as, firstly, an observer's "paradigm by which to orient our analysis"; but I added, secondly, that "Something of this sort, though less systematic and abstract, is in the mind's-eye of every well-informed native when he discusses the structure of his society or takes his part in public affairs" (p. 30). The point of principle here implied is, I believe, of general validity. The theoretical paradigm (sc. model) set up by the observer, and the pragmatic paradigm used by the actors in a social system are not antinomic as Lévi-Strauss and others seem to maintain. (Cf. Lévi-Strauss. 1953; Leach, 1954; Needham, 1962.) There is a distinction, of course, if only because the observer constructs his model from the outside, the actor from within. But a good theoretical model—that is, one which tells us (in Leach's words, 1954: 8) "how the social system works"—must correspond to the pragmatic model. One need only recollect the controversy over the Murngin kinship system (cf. Leach, 1951; Radcliffe-Brown, 1951) to see how wide of the mark a theoretical model divorced from its pragmatic counterpart can be.

affairs I find difficult to visualize. The claim seems to be that the "model" tells us what really matters, what is the true meaning of the custom. The notions held by the actors of the rules and the kinship relations that regulate their marriages (what Lévi-Strauss called their "home-made model") are, by this argument, one might almost think, illusory.

I find this mode of reasoning confusing and unilluminating. Alliance theory does not, for me, shed light on the problem which I consider to be fundamental. It does not concern itself with the mechanisms and processes of social structure or reckon with the politico-jural determinants of kinship, descent, and marriage relations. This surely is the gravamen of the criticism made by Homans and Schneider of Lévi-Strauss's theory of cross-cousin marriage. Whatever objections may be raised against their theory, it follows in the tradition of Radcliffe-Brown's structuralism in seeking for the mechanism and process behind the customary usage. Heuristic, interpretative, and explanatory schemes, whether we call them models, theories, or what you will, are indispensable to our study. But caution is needed. "The price of the employment of models", Braithwaite warns, "is eternal vigilance" (1953: 93). For if our models drift too far away from the empirical facts, we run the risk of relapsing into the habits of mind that almost ruined ethnological research and scholarship in Morgan's day.

Happily, Dr. Needham himself provides me with a fitting conclusion to this digression. His book is a furious attack on Homans and Schneider for their temerity in disputing Lévi-Strauss's theory of cross-cousin marriage. Since the principal source of the hypothesis they advance, in lieu of Lévi-Strauss's, is Radcliffe-Brown's 1924 theory of the patrilineal avunculate, Needham has to discredit this theory in mounting his onslaught. I do not want to discuss Needham's strictures on the arguments of Homans and Schneider, justified though I think some are, nor his objections to Radcliffe-Brown's theory, which are not particularly original. What is of interest to me is that even so uncompromising a critic cannot dispense with the conceptual tools forged in the Radcliffe-Brown workshop. So we find him contrasting "jural" and "sentimental" features of social relations, applying the concept of "jural authority" to castigate Radcliffe-Brown and, *ipso facto*, Homans and Schneider, and discoursing on "attitudes associated conventionally with jural persons." Yet he never mentions the fact that Radcliffe-Brown himself gave authoritative recognition to these concepts and distinctions; nor is there any allusion to the ethnographic studies which commended them to Radcliffe-Brown in the first instance.

To forestall critics, let me, finally, insist again that I am very well aware of aspects and dimensions of kinship and social organization that cannot be compressed within the bounds of structural analysis. Not for nothing did I receive lessons in this branch of our studies from Malinowski, Evans-Pritchard, and Firth. I know that family and kinship relations are the nursery of fundamental emotional dispositions and personality patterns, as well as being the media of jural and moral and, of course, economic and ritual institutions. I even readily grant that history must be consulted where necessary. Ashanti nowadays often use *maami* and *papa* instead of the Ashanti terms for "mother" and "father". This terminology is used by both old and young people, non-literates as well as literates, in a classificatory as well as a primary sense, mainly in non-ceremonial situations. It would surely be fatuous to ignore the derivation of these usages from European missionary and school teaching especially with regard to Christian marriage and parenthood. Again, as several investigators have shown, there is a demographical side to kinship and social organization and I have myself paid some attention to it (1954). And I wholly agree that no study of a family and kinship system can be complete if it ignores the emotional currents that run through it. The Trobriand sibling relationship is not exhaustively accounted for without considering the emotional undercurrents in the incest taboo and the cleavages symbolized in cross-sibling avoidances. All that I wish to maintain is that there is a distinctive range of problems presented by the facts of kinship and social organization which can be better isolated, probed, and made sense of within the framework of structural analysis, as we have developed it in succession to Radcliffe-Brown, than by any other discipline yet available in social anthropology. This is what I shall try to demonstrate.

PART TWO

PARADIGMATIC ETHNOGRAPHICAL SPECIMENS

CHAPTER VI

A Methodological Excursus

I

STRUCTURAL THEORY MARKS OUT A BROAD BUT DEFINABLE FIELD OF INQUIRY IN THE
manifold universe of kinship facts. The length and breadth of it can hardly be better
plotted than in the terms of Morgan's original discoveries. One dimension stands
for the province of familial or, as he put it, domestic kinship connecting person to
person in a scheme of dyadic relations. The other epitomizes the principle implied
in his analysis of the gentile organization and its supposed territorial successor.
What this is concerned with is the part played by kinship rules and concepts in the
allocation of civic status—in other words, the determination of citizenship in the
political community. This, essentially, is the matter at issue in a great deal of current
controversy and research on those aspects of kinship and social organization to which
Radcliffe-Brown devoted his last theoretical statement. For what is "civic status"
or "citizenship" but a comprehensive label for the collection of rights and duties,
privileges and responsibilities presupposed in the notion of jural relations?

Social relations are governed by rules and norms; but not all rules and norms fall
into the category of the jural. What precisely does this notion amount to then? I
have used the concept freely in my account of the main developments in structural
theory. But I have not stopped to define it. I have trusted rather that its import
would show in its usage. I admit that this is not only an expository device; it also

87

reflects a personal bias. I have a prejudice against definitions. For in an empirical subject like ours, they can easily turn into dogmas that blind us to what is in front of our eyes. But some attempt at definition seems necessary at this point, if only because the concept of the jural is now so lavishly used in kinship studies.[1]

I can do no better than to begin with a quotation from my late friend David Tait's posthumous monograph on the Konkomba. He is speaking of the fact that certain standards of conduct are subject to quasi-legal sanctions that do get enforced in this politically acephalous society.

[But] the standards were at no time laid down by a legislature, are not interpreted by a judiciary and are not enforced by an executive. Therefore, if the term 'law' is to be used only in the strict sense of Radcliffe-Brown's definition, some new term should be found to cover the quasi-legal or para-legal methods of peoples like the Konkomba. I will speak of jural activities. This is a term used by Fortes; he says that jural relations involve lineage segments: "What we find . . . is that all jural relations involve a configuration of rights on the one side and a configuration of responsibilities on the other, both corresponding to the range of lineage segments involved. And no jural transaction is complete until the whole configuration of rights, and responsibilities, on both sides, is brought into action" (Fortes, 1945, p. 230).

Tait's own definition then follows.

By the term 'jural' I seek rather the quasi-legal executive activities: those acts of individuals, as in retaliation, or of groups, as in ostracism, which are a reaction on the part of those offended against an offender, acts of retribution which are approved by Konkomba society as a whole. An offender who calls out against him the anger of his society has failed to attain the required standards of behaviour, and in retributive acts or jural acts by individuals or groups against the offender the moral support of the society is always with the offended person. A jural act in this sense is a punitive act which has the moral backing of the society. (1961: 62).

To this Tait adds the rider that his reference to punitive acts must not be taken too literally. When elders exert their authority, which rests on moral or ritual status rather than on powers of direct punishment or retaliation, this also results in measures of jural constraint.

My own notion of the jural fits in with Tait's definition. I make no pretense of using it in a sense that would pass muster in jurisprudence, though (inspired by Radcliffe-Brown's 1935 paper on succession) I borrowed the term from Roman law. It is in line, also, with the authoritative analysis of law in primitive society advanced by Hoebel (1954) and with Gluckman's (1955) interpretation of the Lozi conception of the nature of law in their society.[2] Hoebel, in fact, makes a special point of what

1. Before Radcliffe-Brown adopted it in 1950, the concept "jural" was, to the best of my knowledge, not in the usual vocabulary of British or American ethnography and social anthropology. Having no precedents, I had difficulty in applying it strictly when (after discussion with Radcliffe-Brown, as I have mentioned) I decided to use it in my analysis of Tallensi social structure. This lack of precision was rightly criticized by Firth in his review (1951) of *The Web of Kinship among the Tallensi*. Wider circulation, together with the clarification of our ideas about primitive law by such studies as those of Hoebel and Gluckman (cited below) should help to define it more exactly.

2. Both rest their arguments squarely on modern sociological and jurisprudential theories of law, but it is outside my scope (and indeed my competence) to go into this background.

(following Julius Stone and other jurists), he calls the "jural postulates" which "find expression in the juridical institutions" of a society (1954: 16). I have the impression, however, that he has in mind a more determinate category of normative imperatives than is intended in my usage and Tait's. Nevertheless, it is a difference of degree only. For what Hoebel proves in presenting his type-cases of primitive systems of social control is that quite definite jural norms, sanctions and procedures, as distinct from rules and practices of morality or of religion or of etiquette, regulate the conduct and social relations of people, even in societies ostensibly as anarchical as the Eskimo and the Ifugao.

In Roman law *ius* is contrasted with *lex*, much in the way implied in Tait's observations. The applications of the term *lex* says Buckland (1925) "embody the notion of enactment . . . of declaration." *Ius*, he continues, has "ambiguities which attach to . . . the same notion in other languages (*Recht, Right, Droit, Diritto*)." It may, *inter alia* mean law in the objective sense, or a right in the subjective sense (*ius in rem, ius in personam*) or even the "unwritten part of the law as opposed to *lex, edictum*, etc."

However, in the usage which I propose, the adjectival form, also preferred by Hoebel, is more appropriate than the substantive. I define "jural" as denoting certain aspects or elements of right and duty, privilege and responsibility, laid down in the rules that govern social relations. They enter, I suggest, into all social relations and not only into those that are conventionally described as legal, however wide a meaning may be given to this term. If they are not actually contained in the relationship, they come into it as constraints from the outside, so to speak. It is, furthermore, distinctive of these features of right and duty, privilege and responsibility that, in Tait's words, they have the backing of the whole society. That is to say, they derive their sanction from the political framework of society. They thus have "public" legitimacy in contrast to the "private" legitimacy of rights and capacaties based solely on moral norms or metaphysical beliefs. Jural norms are guaranteed by what some authorities on jurisprudence classify as "external" sanctions, though we should have to include among these such unspecialized sanctions as those mentioned by Tait. Characteristically, then, breach of jural norms disrupts a person's relations with society rather than with individuals only and is, by this token, dereliction of civic obligation. Thus, compliance with jural norms appertains to civic status. It is behavior in conformity with what Gluckman (1955: 201) designates as the "right-and-duty bearing" characters of persons.

My notion of the jural has much in common, it seems to me, with Hoebel's and Gluckman's rather similar ideas of the nature of law in primitive society. Gluckman shows that it is characteristic for this type of law to be thought of by responsible members of the society as being made up of a body of rules, norms, and sanctions which can quite properly be described as a *corpus juris* (1955: 164). Lawful conduct means conformity to this general body of jural custom; particular items of right and duty are meaningful only in the context of this total configuration. This is evident in situations such as those referred to by Tait. What these show, moreover, is that any segment of the total body of jural custom pertains to a distinguishable segment of the total social structure, just as the *corpus juris* as a whole pertains to society in its totality. More exactly, as I said before, it emanates from the political constitution of the society, being in its working regulated by the political organization of society. This is what I mean when I say that the jural components of social relations derive from the politico-jural domain as I shall presently define it. Yet it is important to bear in mind a consideration which Tait adduces and both Hoebel and Gluckman emphasize. The norms and rules of law—of jural custom, as I would like to say adapting Allen's (1958: 143–44) notion of "legal custom"—are not necessarily upheld only by legal institutions such as courts and other formally jucidial methods. There are also what Gluckman calls "alegal" institutions and procedures that embody the jural consensus of a society (1955: 230–31), as Malinowski taught us a generation ago and jurists from Blackstone to Allen have long recognized.

To speak of jural features, elements or aspects of social relations, is tacitly to contrast them with their non-jural counterparts. We are here on the time-hallowed grounds of jurists and political philosophers, from Aristotle onwards, debating how to distinguish between law and custom, law and morality, legal rules and ethical precepts, conduct regulated from without (by "the will of organized society") and behavior controlled by "the dictates of . . . [the individual's] own conscience."[3] Indeed the contrast or, as I would prefer to say, the contraposition of jural and moral frames of conduct in social relations is fundamental for my argument, too. It corresponds to critical divisions in the social structure, as the Lozi recognize and many of the cases recorded by Gluckman vividly illustrate. And the line commonly drawn by such authorities on jurisprudence as Vinogradoff and Allen would be acceptable to African elders and judges, provided that the term "legal" and "law" are understood more in the sense of the Roman notion of *ius* than in that of *lex*. Which reminds us that Roman law clearly recognizes this distinction, contrasting *ius* and *lex*, on the one hand, with *fas* (rules subject to moral and religious sanction), and *mos* (habitual custom), on the other (cf. Buckland, 1925: chap. II).

However, this is looking at the matter from the side of the body of rules and norms recognized in a society. The other side is to be found in the actual conduct of persons and the actual social relations in which they engage. These are rarely elementary by analytical criteria. In the relations of parent and child among the Tallensi, a father has authority over his children. But this, as I implied in the last chapter, is compounded of a number of features. He exercises direct or indirect jural authority in respect of a daughter when she is sought in marriage. He can, for instance, refuse the prestations which are essential to establish the jural validity of the marriage and he will be supported in this by his whole lineage and clan even if he is acting in a way that many would regard as needlessly selfish. He also exercises moral authority over his children, as when he punishes them if they are lazy or ill-mannered, and when he directs their work on the farm or at home.[4] Again, he has

---

3. I am quoting from Sir Paul Vinogradoff's *Common Sense in Law* (1914; 1959 ed.: 43); but see also the exhaustive discussion of these matters by C. K. Allen (1958: 126–47 and 389–94). He concludes that "Legal custom is distinct from other social customs in that its obligatory sanction is complete and uniform" (p. 143).

4. The repressed conflict between paternal authority and filial aspiration given symbolic outlet by means of the concept of personal Destiny (*Yin*—cf. Fortes, 1959b) is graphically illustrated in the following case, which I quote here, however, to show how moral authority,

religious authority over them since he alone is entitled to offer sacrifices to the ancestors on their behalf, and is responsible to the ancestors for them. Lastly, he has the affective authority which superior knowledge and power give to parents in the process of upbringing.

An example from the filial side makes the distinction even clearer. When O. died his oldest son was working in Southern Ghana. Messages were sent urging him to return at once since, as he well knew, the funeral ceremony could not be performed without his presence. He pleaded inability to leave his work just then and promised to return as soon as possible. After two years he had still not come back, though he continued to send messages promising that he would soon do so. However, he sent his senior wife and her children back to his father's house, as was his right. Some difficulties over bride price had arisen with his in-laws and the responsibility for dealing with this jural issue which would have fallen on his father now devolved on his father's brother and the head of their lineage segment. Indignant though these men and his own brothers were with him, they were obliged to deal with the matter and did so. In former days, disputes over bride-price payments could culminate in a fight between the lineages, this being the ultimate jural sanction. At the same time, they were powerless to compel him to honor his moral and religious obligation to return and perform his father's funeral ceremonies. Another year passed without avail. And then one of his children got ill and died. Divination revealed that this was a punishment inflicted on him by the ancestors for neglecting his filial duty to his father. But he still procrastinated; then another child got ill. This time he submitted and returned to perform the funeral.

The distinctions I am considering are not novel. When Aristotle concludes, in book III, chap. iv of the *Politics* that "a man who is an excellent citizen may not possess that virtue which constitutes a good man," he is separating jural status from moral caliber, and later political and legal philosophers have followed him in this. As anthropologists, however, what we seek particularly to understand is the connection between these variables of status and of norms of conduct, and the social structure. This is where Radcliffe-Brown's statement (1950) linking jural norms particularly with unilineal descent—Morgan's gens—is pertinent. Moral and affective norms, *per contra*, have their roots in the familial organization. And what

---

as distinct from jural authority, prevails in the relationship of father and son. T. aged around 60, is a highly respected citizen of Tongo, a noted diviner, a confidant of the chief, in fact a leading member of the community. However, his father, well over 80 now, is still vigorous for his age, and in full possession of his faculties, except that he is blind. T. was commanded by his divining ancestors and Destiny to give up farming else sickness and other misfortunes would afflict him and his wife and children. Being not yet *sui iuris*, he was still farming for his father, as well as on a smaller scale for himself. He was therefore obliged to inform his father of the prohibition his divining ancestors and Destiny had placed on him. Not unexpectedly (as T. admitted) the old man raised strong objections. If T. stopped farming for the common food supply, he said, the younger sons would also soon seek pretexts to evade this duty. T could pay a fine of a sheep or a goat to the ancestors and beg their leave to continue farming for the present. T. explained that he could not have been forced to comply with his father's demand. But it would be an insult amounting almost to sacrilege for a man to reject such a claim from his father. By contrast, he was under no obligation to reveal to his father or share with him his private earnings as a diviner and as a craftsman.

is specially pertinent for us is that these distinctions are signified in the terminologies of kinship and in the customary usages (respect, avoidance, etc.) correlated to them.

II

This brings up another item of analytical theory and method that needs further elucidation. In reviewing the development of Radcliffe-Brown's thought, I remarked on the confusion that may be caused by failure to discriminate between the internal structure of any social formation or institutional arrangement we are investigating, and its external relations. We are faced with the difficulty, here, that it is impossible to stipulate criteria, either qualitative or quantitative, by the application of which boundaries between the internal and the external constitution of a selected configuration of custom, behavior, or social relations can be unequivocally established. The structural antipodes are self-evident: the individual, or, in the terminology of Parsons and Shils (1951: chap. I, esp. pp. 18–19), the "personality system" at the one extreme, the total society at the other. But social structure also operates in the area of social existence that stretches between these extremes; and this is where the difficulty lies. As in biology, we find that what we discriminate as a discrete state of affairs relative to its external environment by one set of criteria, dissolves into constituent parts if we follow a different procedure or ask different questions; or again, from another angle, merges with its environment.

However, the predicament disappears if we realize that we are concerned with a rule of procedure and a policy in the use of our conceptual tools, not with a set of mechanically applicable tests. It is a procedural postulate that everything we seek to analyze in social anthropology can be seen as made up of an internal structure relatively to an external structure and that the two are in a relationship of contraposition.

The study of residence patterns provides a straightforward example of what I mean. There is a well-known paper of Ward Goodenough's (1956) which puts it in a nutshell. It seeks to elucidate why he and Fischer come to opposite conclusions about the incidence of "types" of post-marital residence in one small community in Truk, though they both rely on the same census methods. (See also the admirable discussion of the whole problem of classifying forms of residence by Barnes, 1960.) The divergence arises from a difference of approach. Fischer's primary isolate is the residence of a married couple at a given time in relation to the parents of either spouse. Some can be described as living "patrilocally," others "matrilocally," and some "neolocally," and there is no common pattern or rule. In effect, he isolates the residential practices of married couples as if they are internally coherent arrangements not influenced by external factors other than the link with parents. Goodenough, while adhering to this terminology of classification sees the situation differently. He does not regard the residence of married couples, or indeed of single persons, as independent variables indicative of supposedly autonomous choice. His primary isolate is the residential arrangement of the extended family and the descent group. Seen in this context, the different patterns of residence apparently adopted by married couples prove to be variants of a common mode of residing with an extended family associated with one or other of the four matrilineages (wife's, husband's, wife's father's, husband's father's) in which the spouses have rights and claims. Thus regarded, the mode of residence adopted by a couple is intelligible only if it is perceived as an element in the structure of an extended family and lineage. The significant unit of internal structure is the matrilineal extended family, not the married couple. As Goodenough rightly remarks, we explain "what we observe and what our informants tell us" (1956: 36) in the light of our theories, and the difference between him and Fischer finally comes down to this. It springs from different views held by them of what is the significant socio-spatial unit of domestic grouping viewed as an internal structure. But, as I showed in my analysis of Ashanti residence patterns (1949c), there are also socio-temporal variables that have to be be taken into consideration. Phenotypically diverse residence patterns in the same community fall into place in a unitary scheme when it is understood that they are indicative of different standard phases in the developmental cycle of the domestic group (Fortes, 1958). Thus in determining the boundary of what to demarcate as an internal field of social structure for this inquiry, I decided that it was essential to take the time factor into consideration as well as the alignments and collocations of persons, and the interconnections between institutions, at a fixed time.

In short, according to our analytical problem, we have in one case to isolate a determinable socio-spatial region, in another, a process through a stretch of time, in a third an institutional complex, or a configuration of custom or an arrangement of social relations, as the internal field of social structure to be set against an external field. There are more complicated problems for which we may have to use more elaborate analytical criteria than those I have listed, or combine several.

Take the subject of Indian caste. For castes to exist, there must be boundaries between caste and caste in a social universe wholly constituted of an assemblage of castes. Whether at the village and district level, to which so much attention has been given by students of this subject (Leach, 1960a, Marriott, 1959), or at the national level (Hutton, 1946), a caste group is only identifiable from the outside by contraposition with other caste groups in the constellation in which it operates. A caste is a relatively discrete section of an Indian village community and a separate entity in the nation in virtue of its external relations and connections with other castes. But it seems that no single category of relations or of mode of association, no single pattern of privileges and responsibilities or of rights and obligations, definitively fixes caste boundaries. For intercaste relations are compounded of ties and cleavages. different forms and degrees of mutual dependence for economic and ritual services being counter-balanced by different forms and degrees of mutual segregation expressed in rules regulating social and physical contacts, and more especially in the kinds and amounts of commensality permitted. The most rigorous segregating institution is of course the rule of caste endogamy.

I enumerate these well-known attributes of the caste system to emphasize their external structural provenance. They derive from the system as a whole. They reflect the common values and beliefs of a religious and metaphysical nature concerning grades of ritual purity deemed to be signified in the prescriptions and avoidances followed in intercaste relations (Stevenson, 1954). But they also represent, and some would contend more fundamentally than in their ritual symbolization, the jural rules governing the distribution of political status, juridical authority, occupational specilization, and ritual capacities—above all, the last two—among the castes in the local community. Obligatory exchange of economic and ritual services among occupationally specialized castes, which are also differentiated and ranked by status that is imputed and justified by religious ideology, summarily delineates the caste system externally regarded. To speak figuratively, castes are separate and interlinked by a kind of connective tissue, rather than by hard teguments.

Trouble begins when we examine the factors that appear to be critical for the internal structure of a caste. Take the cardinal rule of endogamy; as such, it is jurally and ritually regulative, primarily in the external scheme of caste relations. In the internal structure of most caste groups it is more of a limiting rule setting the bounds within which lineage exogamy or cross-cousin marriage must be adhered to. Again, the internal kinship structure of different castes varies across the entire gamut of known kinship systems. Thus, within his caste a person acts as a lineage member or a family member or by whatever kinship role is relevant; in his intercaste relationships he acts in a representative capacity as a caste member.

In the Tanjore village described by Dr. Gough (1960), the Konans are a non-Brahman, meat-eating inferior caste whose members are hereditary serfs of the dominant Brahman lineages. But within their own caste this servile status is for the Konans, a "right of service" inherited patrilineally, an incorporeal possession of value, giving its holders title to "an assurance of livelihood" (p. 23). The hereditary occupations of the Barber and Washermen caste groups are defined as ritually polluting to Brahmans but they are certainly not so thought of among themselves. Their food habits may fill Brahmans with religious horror, but are not scandalous among themselves. In religious matters, the caste groups of a particular community usually have their respective private deities and cults but also obligatorily participate in certain community rituals and cults. And likewise in the sphere of social control— the internal affairs of each caste are administered by its own headman and council but offences against the rules of caste segregation, notably the prohibition of marriage between castes and wrongs against members of other castes, are dealt with (as a rule) by the recognized authorities of the dominant caste.

It is obvious that the customs and institutions characteristic of Indian caste society have two faces. Descriptively unitary, any caste-bound status, skill, observance, or practice we care to choose is analytically divisible into an inward-turned and outward-turned aspect which have different, possibly even opposed, structural meanings and cultural values. Confusing them is one of the main sources of ambiguity in discussions of such issues as the differential ranking of castes in the total system.

III

To round off this methodological excursus, I must give some explanation of the notion of *domain*, as I use it.[5] The concept of structure has a geometrical, or perhaps it would be more correct to say, a topographical resonance. It tacitly implies a socio-spatial frame of arrangement. The distinction I make between "internal" and "external" aspects of structure reflects this. It is conspicuous in most post-functionalist ethnographic studies of kinship and political organization. Evans-Pritchard's *The Nuer*, Firth's *We, the Tikopia*, and my own *Web of Kinship*, to quote only three relatively orthodox examples, all work in this idiom. Description of kinship institutions, for example, is pinned down to observable socio-spatial arrangements "on the ground." Mitchell (1956), R. T. Smith (1956) and Turner (1957) provide recent examples, with the addition that they take the topographical model a stage further by giving quantitative expression to the relations it subsumes. It is implicit in Schapera's (1956) analysis of tribal political organization which he defines as "that aspect of the total organization which is concerned with the establishment and maintenance of *internal* cooperation and *external* independence" [p. 218; my italics].

An alternative to this frame of analysis is the procedure followed in, say, Malinowski's *Argonauts* (1922), and Evans-Pritchard's *Witchcraft among the Azande* (1937), and other celebrated monographs of the same genre. Their object is to unravel the concatenations and interconnections among the institutions, values, and norms comprised within a particular complex of custom, belief and social organization.

Nor are these the only methods that have been followed with advantage in the anthropological study of society and custom within a broadly functionalist or structuralist frame of theory. Redfield's dichotomy of the "moral order" and the "technical order"[6] envisages a very different scheme for the analysis of the seamless fabric of social life in a given community. Though the concept of "domain" as I use it does not belong to this level of generalization, it has, I think, a distant affinity with Redfield's idea.[7]

I begin from two propositions. Firstly, a "person" in the accepted sociological sense, comprises a variety of statuses. In any given situation or social relationship, he deploys one or some of them, while others remain potentially available for conducting himself in other situations. The ensemble of statuses corresponds to what Radcliffe-Brown at one time called the "social personality", a concept Warner

5. Some indications are given in my "Introduction" to Goody (ed.) 1958. The term was suggested to me by Bertrand Russell's *Introduction to Mathematical Philosophy* (1919: 15–16). It is of course also widely used in linguistic studies, e.g., Voegelin and Voegelin (1957), *Hopi Domains*. My use of the term does not conform strictly to either Russell's definitions or the linguists' usage. It is more in line with one of the OED's definitions: "a sphere of thought or action."

6. "Technical order and moral order name two contrasting aspects of all human societies. The phrases stand for two distinguishable ways in which the activities of man are co-ordinated" (1953: 20).

7. I have elsewhere (1962b) paid tribute to the felicity of insight I find in this hypothesis of Redfield's.

ingeniously applied in his study of Murngin kinship. He showed there that each component of a Murngin's "kinship personality" is the product of a distinctive kinship relation to which he is bound and which is specified in terminology and custom. He has an ensemble of statuses because he participates in "multiplex" social relations, as Gluckman puts it (1955: 19). The basic notion of course has long been familiar. It has been elaborated in a variety of contexts by theoretical sociologists from Simmel (1955) to Parsons (Parsons & Shils, 1951: pt. 2). Karl Marx's often quoted dictum that "the human essence is no abstraction inherent in each single individual. In its reality it is the ensemble of the social relations" (1888) pithily sums up the proposition.

Secondly and conversely, every particular occasion of social relationship and activity is a composite formation. It is compounded of persons-in-relationship acting in customary ways, exercising rights or privileges and discharging obligations or responsibilities in conformity with norms and values that allow them to accomplish culturally legitimate aims and ends in the service of their individual needs and propensities. To be sure, the social occasions which concern us as anthropologists— whether it be something as conspicuous and formal as a marriage ceremony or a sacrifice to ancestors, or as mundane as a conversation or a court case, or a joking situation—have their recurrent shape and unity of structure. But the elements of which they are composed are of diverse structural and cultural provenance, appear and reappear in diverse situations.[8] In the context of my economic occupation, my civic status compels me to pay my income tax; in the context of my home life, it obliges me to send my children to school; in the context of public affairs, it affords me the privilege of casting my vote; and in that of my individual existence, it gives me such rights as freedom of conscience and, at another level, free medical care. But in each of these contexts I also deploy other statuses—of parent, of church membership, of taxpayer, and so forth. These posit different norms and modes of behavior from those that are mobilized in my civic capacity.

The example I previously gave of caste is apt here too. High-caste vegetarianism, whether practiced within the confines of the caste or in external relations, is a custom distinctive of the realm of caste, whereas the accumulation of wealth is not. We read of wealthy non-Brahman caste groups maneuvering to improve their caste rank by adopting vegetarianism. They do not also have to give up customs which are neutral in relation to caste. Analogously, aliens in England make themselves eligible for naturalization by showing that they are able and willing to discharge the duties and responsibilities of citizenship. They do not have to change their family life, or their religion, or their food habits to qualify for naturalization.[9]

8. This was Radcliffe-Brown's point of departure in the method he devised for the analysis of ritual custom in *The Andaman Islanders*.

9. There is a delightful animadversion on this theme at the end of F. W. Maitland's *Constitutional History of England* (1913: 501-4) which begins "It may, I think, be instructive in this context to say a few words as to the active duties which our law lays upon the generality of Englishmen. . . ." After enumerating some of them, he continues with those that are "cast by law upon a person irrespective of any contract, of any special relationship, or of any public office." These are rubricated under the heading of "Active Duties of Citizens." They include the payment of taxes and rates and jury service, for those who are qualified. But for everybody it is, among other duties, obligatory for an Englishman to register the birth of a child born to

But let us take another look at an institution such as the payment of income tax. It is, of course, an economic transaction; it is also a legal obligation; and it is, in England, tied up with the payer's domestic circumstances, being scaled in accordance with his marital, parental, and sometimes filial responsibilities. So we can think of income tax paying as a resultant of certain statuses held by the actor (as employee, citizen, family head) congruently deployed; or we can see it more from the outside as reflecting the intersection in his life-space of various bonds of social relationship (in the firm, the state, the home) or we can evaluate it as a routine pattern of behavior testifying to his compliance with a set of norms corresponding to his several statuses and their respective contexts of social relations—norms of financial probity, civic loyalty, domestic responsibility, etc. Nor does this exhaust the analytical possibilities. The faithful-taxpaying syndrome may well serve to express ideals and values and individual personality dispositions. Indian dietary observances can be analytically dissected along similar lines, for they are religious taboos as well as indices and affirmations of caste and status.

The point I now wish to bring out, obvious as it is, is this: A social occasion, event or institution is not a hodgepodge of casually mixed cultural and structural elements; it has form and texture—that is, an internal structure. And this is because each element of status manifested in it carries with it (or we can turn this around and say is the outcome of) a specific context of social relations to which given norms and patterns of customary behavior are attached. And furthermore, each such nexus—as I have already suggested in discussing the concept of the jural—is also linked with a characteristic socio-spatial substratum, workplace, home, village, community at large. What gives the occasion or event or institution its coherence is the fact that it comes about by the interweaving of such nexuses in the conduct of persons in interaction.

If, then, we can discriminate between the economic, the legal, the domestic, the religious, the caste, and so forth, characters of social nexus formations, what is their source? This is where I find the concept of the domain useful, not as a means of explanation but as an aid to systematization. I suggest that the social and cultural elements and processes that make up a given social system fall into determinate sectors of organization. Each such sector—which I call a domain—comprises a range of social relations, customs, norms, statuses, and other analytically discriminable elements linked up in nexuses and unified by the stamp of distinctive functional features that are common to all. It is, to make a crude comparison, as if everything in one domain were blue, in another red, and so on. The domain of the law in our society embraces judges and courts, police, prisons and lawyers, the statute book and case law, marriage lines, death certificates, voting rights, and a hundred and one more offices and practices. Heterogeneous as these items seem to be, they are all intrinsically bound up with one another and have a common, though very abstract, functional significance, centered on the authority of the state. We have no difficulty in distinguishing the domain of the law from that of the family, which is mirrored

---

him, to have him vaccinated, and to ensure that he receives an elementary education, else he will be fined.

in our vocabulary of kinship and marriage. We can see, moreover, that a domain is not merely a classificatory construct. It is a matrix of social organization in the sense that its members derive their specificity from it. Behind the judge on the bench, the demand for a tax payment, the contract of a sale, lies the whole domain of our law in contradistinction to the domain of kinship, as these are constituted in our society.

IV

A comparison here may help to clarify the argument. I use the concept of a field of social relations in some contexts.[10] Let me give an example. An Ashanti father's model *field* of kinship relations has two parts. On the one side is his wife and children, on the other a sister and her children, the two being residentially separated. In relation to his children he conducts himself solely in accordance with norms of the familial domain. These entitle him, for example, to chastise his children if they misbehave. In relation to his sister's children his behavior is ruled more strictly by reference to the politico-jural domain, the source of his lawful rights over and duties towards them. This corresponds to a field of social relations that extends beyond his domestic field—it includes his lineage, the village political authorities, and the chiefdom of which he is a citizen. Thus if we take such a person's total field of kinship relations, we find that its management involves compliance with norms that emanate from two distinct and in some ways opposed domains of social structure. Jural right and familial privilege enter side by side into his domestic and kinship relations. Gluckman's case records, as I have earlier implied, bring the point out very clearly.

As Gluckman demonstrates, circumstances inevitably arise when the corresponding duties and responsibilities pull in opposite directions. I have elsewhere (1963) described some of the means adopted by Ashanti to reconcile these divergent but equally important interests. I compared the Ashanti situation to the antithesis of *ius* and *fas*, linking this with the principle that Ashanti matrilineal relations are governed primarily by legal (in the narrow sense) rules and sanctions, whereas patri-filial relations are subject to considerations of sentiment, morality, and equity. There is a fascinating parallel to this aspect, too, in Roman law. C. K. Allen, discussing the chief equitable principles of Roman law, cites as his first instance their application "In the triumph of the natural idea of blood relationship over the artificial idea of agnation" and comments "when one considers how profoundly patriarchal that society was . . ., the victory of cognation . . . appears as no mean achievement of juridical development " (1958: 377). However, the Ashanti parallel (and analogous compromises in African patrilineal systems) shows that what really underlies such institutional patterns is a basic structural feature of unilineal descent systems. The descent principle is normally, probably invariably, counterbalanced by the principle of complementary filiation.

10. I first applied this concept to the analysis of clanship among the Tallensi (1945) and have already given examples of it in the present enquiry.

My argument can be summed up in one statement: A status can be defined as a position held by a person in a given domain, specified by the social relations distinctive of that domain, and deployed in activities and attitudes conforming to the norms and customs and material apparatus that are distinctive of that domain.

V

It may be said that the concept of the domain, as here used, is either platitudinous (did not Malinowski speak of the legal, economic, religious, etc., aspects of culture?) or else that it is at best a theoretical abstraction that has no counterpart in the realities of social life. I hope the sequel will show that this is not the case. Though its value to me is primarily heuristic, the concept of the domain does, I believe, reflect the experience people have of their social life. This is shown by the fact that domains and distinctions between domains are commonly given social tangibility in the language, behavior patterns and symbolism of social organization. The judge's black cap is an extreme example; vestments and uniforms of office in general serve this purpose. But most familiar to anthropologists (apart from the language and usages of kinship) are the many forms of totemic beliefs and observances, myths, taboos, and apparently arbitrary rules of behavior by which domains are distinguished as the converse of status elements. Caste is an example.

But let me, rather, quote just one field observation to exemplify how sharply the domain provenance of the actor in a particular role in a specific situation is distinguished and signified. Among the Tallensi, when the final funeral ceremony for an elder is "opened," as they say, the first inaugural act is to consult a diviner to find out what preliminary libations and sacrifices the ancestors demand. When Gieng's funeral was opened, the diviner sent for was a member of the deceased's own lineage. His task complete, he rose to go home. At this point one of the younger men present cried out, "Why is he leaving? Isn't he a kinsman like us? He should stay and take his proper part in the rites." "No, no," an elder called out immediately. "He is not here as a kinsman. He came as a diviner and you know that it is a taboo for the diviner to stay and take part in the ritual that follows the divination. He must go home first and then he can come back as a kinsman and take part in the ritual."

I have no doubt that an inventory could be made of the domains of social structure that are common to human society in general or to any selected sample of societies. It is a plausible hypothesis, moreover, that types of society differ in the number and character of the domains incorporated in their social structure. Simple, or primitive societies are often said to be distinguished from complex societies by the fact that kinship, political, economic, religious, etc., relationships and spheres of activities are not differentiated from one another in the former as they are in the latter. Put in another way, it is said that there is little or no specialization of roles in simple societies in contrast to complex societies. In my formulation, structural domains, even when they are recognizably distinct by the criteria of norms and customs, tend to be fused together in simple societies, whereas in complex societies they tend to be numerous and structurally differentiated.

I make no attempt to pursue these questions any further, for they lie outside of my present objective. However, two domains are of such importance for the study of kinship and social organization that they must be mentioned again, even if it seems needlessly repetitious. From whichever angle we approach the study of kinship, we are always confronted with the implications of Morgan's basic dichotomy between the sphere of consanguinity and the gens (*"societas"*), on the one side, and of civic society (*"civitas"*) on the other. However, it is relevant to observe that Morgan's gens—that is, the unilineal descent group—is, in societies which have it. the nodal institution of what I have called the politico-jural domain; whereas the institutions of Morgan's consanguine kinship belong to the complementary domestic or, more appropriately, familial[11] domain. This links up with the considerations I brought forward in discussing the nature of the jural and the utility of discriminating between internal and external fields of structure. From the point of view of a person acting in accordance with the rules and norms of his familial domain, the politico-jural domain is the locus of external relations and constraints for him. But there are circumstances in which he acts in terms of a status derived from the politico-jural domain; in this case his familial relations may be marked off as the external ones. This happens in forms of initiation ceremonies which segregate the novices from their natal families until they have been incorporated in the appropriate cadre of citizenship.

I have now, I hope, sufficiently explained the basic conceptual distinctions relating to the procedures I shall make use of in the next part of this work. They concern the way in which, in my view, kinship and social organization should be looked at for analytical purposes; they do not refer to the descriptive data as such.

---

11. I am following Southall in the use of this term, but applying it in a somewhat more restricted sense than he does. The distinction I am making between the politico-jural domain and the familial domain closely parallels the distinction he establishes between the "political authority system" and the "familial authority system" (Southall, 1956: 69–75). The theoretical significance of this distinction is admirably substantiated in Southall's study. Indeed the distinction has roots reaching far back in the history of political theory. It is implicit in BK. I of Aristotle's *Politics*. Is not his distinction between the *oikos*, that is, the family in its domestic setting, and the *polis*, that is, civil society, the realm of law and justice, on a footing with the above analysis and with Morgan's contrast between *societas* and *civitas*?

CHAPTER VII

The Kinship Polity

I

LET US NOW LEAVE HISTORY ASIDE AND TURN TO SOME MORE RECENT DEVELOPMENTS in the study of the problems of kinship and social organization first opened up by Morgan. Research and scholarship, both ethnographical and theoretical, grow and ramify so vastly and swiftly in this field that no one can now hope to compass all of it with equal facility. I do not aspire to do so. My concern is not with large generalizations but with a limited number of structural parameters. It is certain mechanisms and processes of social organization and the principles that underlie them that I am interested in elucidating.

In particular, I want to focus attention on the connection between kinship and familial institutions and relationships, on the one hand, and the politico-jural domain, on the other. For this purpose it is more rewarding to examine a few paradigmatic specimens in some depth, much as Morgan did in *Ancient Society* (and others have done since), than to survey the whole gamut of human societies. It is not even necessary, in my opinion, that these specimens should be representative, in a statistical or taxonomic sense, of the total universe of social systems of which we have knowledge, or that they should be related by regional propinquity or cultural affinities. What is required is that they should exhibit clearly the mechanisms and processes I seek to describe, and bring out unequivocally the principles we are trying to understand. If anyone doubts the validity of this procedure, let him remember that Mendel's revolutionary discoveries were made not by regarding a multitude of natural species but by rigorous analysis of experiments with garden peas only. But we do not need to look to the as yet unattainable heights of the natural sciences for precedents. We can cite many examples of crucial discoveries that have been made by intensive research in one or two societes, even before Malinowski.

The ancillary evidence from a wider range of societies which I shall quote will be mainly to confirm and amplify, rather than to establish an argument.

There is one problem of exposition that I must mention. It concerns the conceptual terminology that cannot be avoided. Rather than risk loading the analysis with definitions set down in advance, I shall follow current usage and let modifications that might seem useful emerge as I proceed.

I start with the social systems of the Australian aborigines. They have, of course, an illustrious place in the history of modern kinship theory through their formative influence on Radcliffe-Brown's thought. But for my immediate purpose, their relevance is that they provide a model of a thoroughgoing kinship polity.[1]

We can take it as established that the ideology of kinship pervades, regulates and orders every domain of Australian aboriginal social life. Even the partly esoteric domain of totemic belief, cult, and mythology is tied to the framework of kinship. To examine such systems from the point of view of the politico-jural order might therefore seem to be irrelevant. And indeed, until quite recently students of Australian social organization paid only casual attention to this aspect.

II

Half a century of field research and theoretical discussion, since Radcliffe-Brown first sketched it, has confirmed the uniformity of the ground plan which underlies the diversity of regional and tribal variations and elaborations among Australian social systems. Yet it is only in the past decade or so—and partly under the stimulus of developments in African ethnography—that many of the topics relevant to my theme have been investigated and I shall therefore base my discussion chiefly on these researches.[2]

1. Cf. Fortes and Evans-Pritchard, 1940, "Introduction", sec. V, pp. 6–7. I am very conscious of my temerity in undertaking this analysis. Australian social organization has been and remains a complicated and highly controversial subject, full of obscurities, to the non-adept. I shall not be surprised if I am told that I am wide of the mark in many of the interpretations I venture upon here. In particular, my discussion is open to criticism on the grounds of disregarding the tribal and regional variations. But to an Africanist the broad, common patterns in Australian social organization are conspicuous by contrast with those he is most familiar with; and an Australian paradigm fits my purpose better than any other of the same modality known to me.

2. I draw, in particular (next to Radcliffe-Brown), on the works of Elkin, Lloyd Warner, Meggitt, Berndt, and Hiatt in the following discussion. Strictly speaking, therefore, I am concerned with a limited area of Australia, primarily Arnhem Land. Among theoretical discussions of Australian social organization by armchair scholars, the most illuminating to me has been Lévi-Strauss's analysis of the Murngin system (1949: chap. VII), despite the criticism which it has drawn.

To an Africanist accustomed to sedentary cultivators living in large and stable communities under chiefs or headmen with well-defined politico-jural authority, and subject to recognized laws of property and of persons in their access to and use of their natural and cultural resources, an Australian society presents a paradox. It seems singularly amorphous and yet at the same time internally regimented. The units of collective life variously described as hordes, clans, communities, and language groups, irrespective of their particular composition, hold territorial stretches in some sort of common possession. But it is really only in respect to the totem centers, and other sacred places associated with them, that such a unit has some form of exclusive possession of, or as Meggitt puts it, anchorage in its territory.[3] Its owners, if such they can be called, do not monopolize its economic exploitation or refuse access to other groups. Thus, territorial authority, in either the economic sense or the politico-jural sense, is unknown. As Morgan might have put it, "a *political organization*, founded upon territory" (1877; 1878 ed.: 62) is nonexistent in Australian society. A group's "country" has no fixed geographical boundaries, and indeed even the totemic sites seem to lack boundaries. Moreover the hordes, or clans, or communities, that exploit its surface, are also not fixed in composition, varying especially with the seasons and with ceremonial occasions. As Hiatt has convincingly shown (1965), at some times of the year they melt into one another, at other times disperse into small family groups. People belonging to the same totemic cult group, and therefore having an hereditary attachment to particular totemic sites laid down by its mythological ancestors in a given locality, are often widely dispersed. To be sure, this is connected with their rudimentary productive technology, and their nomadic way of life in ecological conditions which, in extreme circumstances, formerly restricted population to a very low density.[4] But if these external factors undoubtedly help to shape territorial relations, the internal factors of social organization are the most important.

These are all comprised within the classificatory kinship structure. As Radcliffe-Brown emphasized long ago, a person cannot belong to any collectivity, be it a locally anchored group, or a dispersed division of a tribe such as a moiety, or a language community or a ceremonial gathering, if he does not have a kinship status in it. A stranger is an alien unless and until he can demonstrate or have ascribed to him a kinship relation with at least one person in the collectivity. This is what leads Romney and Epling, in their penetrating reanalysis of the Kariera kinship system, to assert that it is a "closed system." In their phrase, "Within Kariera society there are no nonrelatives" (1958: 68). Considered from within the society, every person is related to every other person by bonds of kinship, and all social relations are relations of kinship. All roles are allocated and all activities regulated by kinship status.[5]

3. Cf. especially Meggitt, 1962. But it is of interest to recollect that Radcliffe-Brown maintained that the Kariera "patrilineal" horde was a perpetual corporation possessed of an estate in the form of the locality it was bound to and over which it had rights *in rem*. (1935). This view would seem to be untenable in the light of recent research (cf. Hiatt, 1962).

4. For example, one person to 35 square miles among the Walbiri, a relatively extreme case—cf., e.g. the Murngin, with one person to 8 square miles (Warner, 1937: 16).

5. Cf. Radcliffe-Brown's statement that "it is impossible for an Australian native to have

However, the fact remains that outsiders can be incorporated into a society or a community, or more generally, brought into the ambit of sanctioned social relations, by having kinship status ascribed to them. Different communities, even those of different tribal or linguistic provenance, can exchange personnel by marriage, and can fuse for particular ceremonial occasions by, so to speak, intermeshing their kinship fields. It seems, therefore, that the view that an Australian *community* or *society* is a closed system is in part illusory. It is the kinship calculus that is closed— by its very nature, one might argue—not any community, as such. It is the kinship calculus which, by reason of its exact limitation of range, serves as the basic bound- ary-setting mechanism for the field of social relations that is at one and the same time the maximum kinship field and the maximum politico-jural field for a specified group. Herein lies the essence of the kinship polity and the central theme of the present chapter.

And yet—and here lies the paradox—Australian ethnography, at least from the time of Spencer and Gillen until today, overwhelmingly conveys an impression of relative stability, cohesion, order, and regularity in the patterns of social life. This comes out even in the case records of modern observers (for example, Meggitt and Hiatt), which leave the impression of discord and dissension ever simmering beneath the surface of social life and bursting violently into the open from time to time. Yet this undercurrent of turbulence seems never to have destroyed the general condition of balance and conformity to rules in Australian social systems. The celebrated and crucial rule of mother-in-law avoidance so often stressed by Rad- cliffe-Brown is repeatedly asserted to be meticulously observed (cf. Meggitt, 1962: 153; Warner, 1937: 101–102). More striking is the testimony of Meggitt (1962: 86) and Hiatt (1965: 78–79) to the efficiency and consistency with which the critical norms of marriage are upheld.[6] Again, ethnographic descriptions abound with evidence of the stringency with which esoteric ritual is guarded, and of the efficacy of the rules of hospitality and of obligatory gift giving. All sources confirm the conclusion that mechanisms exist which work very efficiently to ensure the mainten- ance of order and cohesion in an Australian social system.

These mechanisms are inherent in the ideology and the institutions of kinship— above all the classificatory principle, on the one hand, and the totemic system, on the other. We can see what lies behind this if we consider why and how the regulation of social relations devolves finally on the kinship system.

6. Ninety-two per cent of the Walbiri marriages recorded by Meggitt are in the jurally correct, preferred kinship categories. A further 4 per cent are permitted alternative unions and only 4 per cent fall within technically prohibited degrees, but then the spouses are in every case classificatory not close kin. Hiatt shows that of the 35 marriages recorded by him although in only 6 cases (of 33 in which the relationship of the spouses was known) did the husband have a rightful claim on the wife, 25 of the remaining cases were "proper," that is, presumably not in breach of the limiting prohibitions of the incest rule, cross-generational, or intra-moiety marriage.

---

anything whatever to do with any one who is not his relative, of one kind or another, near or distant" (1930–31: 45). I use "kinship status" to stand for the whole gamut of classificatory assignment mediated by the terminology.

III

We have seen that the collectivities bound to tracts of territory chiefly by their totemic allegiances, are not externally bounded and exclusive units. How then are they internally constituted and organized? Meggitt's admirable account of the Walbiri and Hiatt's of the Gidjingali give a clear picture and, *mutatis mutandis*, these conclusions are applicable to the societies described by Warner, Elkin, and others. The Walbiri are divided into four territorially distinct communities numbering from some scores to some hundreds of members each. Social relations and conduct within a community, says Meggitt (1962: 247), are regulated by "the norms of the religious and kinship systems" which "constitute an enduring master-plan." It is a unit of common kinship and common cult. Is it also, looked at thus from within, a political and a jural community?[7]

Introducing his account of the Kariera fifty years ago (1913), Radcliffe-Brown remarked: "There is no tribal chief, nor any form of tribal government"; and, in earlier times, he added, "there was no unity of the tribe in warfare" (pp. 144–45). Warner (1937: chap. 6) presents a similar picture for the Murngin, and Hiatt (1965: 143–47) for the Gidjingali. Murngin wars most commonly occurred between "clans" of the same moiety within a tribe and not between "clans" of opposite moieties or of different tribes.[8] This was due to the fact that the main cause of wars (as of the quarrels in modern conditions) was competition for women. Meggitt carries the analysis further, ably making explicit the structurally significant features. There were formerly and are now no recognized political leaders; there were traditionally no "individuals or groups . . . with permanent and clearly-defined legislative and judicial functions" (1962: 251). "Peoples' behavior in joint activities was initiated and guided largely by their own knowledge and acceptance of established norms" (p. 250). Individuals might act with authority on particular occasions but this depended chiefly on considerations of the kinship status, the "descent lines," and moiety affiliations of the persons actually engaged. And yet, at the same time the Walbiri have a concept of "an established and morally-right order of behaviour", that is, "a body of jural rules and moral evaluations," and adherence to this body of rules is a basic value for the Walbiri (p. 251). It had and has mythological sanction and included man, society, and nature in one system. As to the mechanisms by which the "basic jural norms" were and are maintained, Meggitt reports as follows: "Men argue that, as all intercourse among the people concerns 'relatives', and as everyone has been taught the rules defining the relevant roles, a person cannot plead ignorance of the law in extenuation of misconduct" (p. 255). Social control is very effectively maintained by the due observance of the established and generally accepted norms of kinship and of totemic cult and belief.

As in the secular sphere, so in the conduct of ritual activities there are no regular

7. I borrow this term and its conceptual implications from the "Introduction" by the editors to Middleton and Tait 1958.

8. Warner's "clan" is difficult to interpret. I am taking it here to stand for an (*ad hoc*) aggregate of kinsfolk connected with one another by patrifilial alignment.

offices of authority. Elders who supervise these activities, and who in the case of sacrilege, for instance, have a decisive voice in the punishment of offenders, hold their positions by virtue of their kinship status, their knowledge and experience, and their personal prestige.

One reason why social control can be effective in these societies in the absence of authority-vested agents and offices is no doubt their small numerical and social scale.[9] Their homogeneous social structure also facilitates it. Given their modes of livelihood, their impermanent and limited material culture, and the narrow range of their institutional forms, they are unlikely to be faced with irreconcilable conflicts of interest. Concepts of property, for example, a notorious source of such conflicts in other societies, are stated to be rudimentary (cf. Warner, 1937: 146–47). There is no notion of land ownership by individuals or families. Weapons, implements, decorative and ritual objects, are freely borrowed and exchanged. They are distributed or destroyed on the death of the owner. Such incorporeal possessions as totemic designs, emblems, and songs, together with more lasting articles of ritual use, are not thought of as property, but to quote Warner, "as integral parts of the structure . . . of the cult congregation (1937: 147; cf. also Meggitt, 1962: 120, 139, 209–13). In the same spirit, the objects of prestige value which figure in the remarkable system of gift circulation among the tribes of Arnhem land described by Thomson (1949: chap. 5) are valued not as property but as the material affirmation of the bonds of kinship and alliance which link partners in the exchange cycle. In the absence of any forms of office or of rank, other than the respect conferred by age and generation, the institution of succession is nonexistent. Warner says (1937: 70) that leadership of clan ceremonials is "inherited" by the oldest son or failing him, the deceased's next older brother, but he gives no cases. A province of competitive interests found in most human societies is thus ruled out.

In fact there is only one item of high scarcity value the possession of which is jurally restricted and that is the marital rights over women and the consequential procreative rights over offspring.[10] But even with respect to these there is no strict monopoly of possession. Brothers, conformably with the principle of the equivalence of brothers, habitually exchange wives. The formal exchange of wives for ceremonial copulation between distant classificatory brothers of different tribes during the great totemic ceremonies which figure so vividly in early accounts of so-called sexual license, is a variant of this. It is the more significant, then, that sexual rights over women are the main, perhaps the sole, item for which there is competition and over which conflicts arise. That there are demographic factors in this situation, reflected in the frequent seniority by twenty years and more of husbands over wives, is accepted by all our authorities.[11] But the very fact that

9. Meggitt (1962: 32) estimates the Walbiri to have numbered about 1,000 before the arrival of the Europeans. The Murngin local group numbered 40–50 people occupying 360 square miles of country (Warner, 1937: 16). Most authorities reckon the tribes to have averaged around 500 about the beginning of the nineteenth century.

10. This is, strictly speaking, a misnomer, I believe, but is used here for convenience. Recognized paternal rights would appear to flow from marital rights, not to be of a genitorial nature. The beliefs about "conception" totemism point to this.

11. This is elaborately documented also in the study by Rose, 1960.

licit sexual relations are possible only in marriage and therefore between persons
who are pre-marital kin of specified categories, must give an edge to this competition;
the connivance in adultery, which seems to be common (cf. Meggitt's and Hiatt's
case records) confirms this.

IV

In this system, social relations are regulated by devolving on each person, on the
one hand, the right and privilege of asserting his status-defined interests against
others and, on the other, the duty to comply with the norms of approved conduct in
relation to others.[12]
    This presupposes mutual dependence of person on person in a network of dyadic
reciprocities. It requires also that each person should be in a position to determine
his status unequivocally in relation to any other persons with whom he has dealings
at a given time. Such a "calculus of relations" and of dyadic reciprocities is what the
kinship system provides. First, we must note how Australian kinship systems
emphasize in both terminology and custom, the strictly discrete character of each
status-category recognized. Second, we must note the logic of these systems. They
start from the genealogical foundation given by the fixed incidents of parenthood,
generation, age, and sex, and set up the kinship system by aligning status categories
in accordance with a limited number of elementary rules of structural logic, that
is to say, the well-known rules of sibling equivalence, of the separation of successive
generations, and of reckoning genealogical connection by single degrees. Each
person is thus equipped with a schedule for registering for himself the field of social
relations in which he deploys his repertoire of statuses, asserts his rights, and
responds to claims on him. It is important to bear in mind that this is not the same
thing as a constellation of kinsfolk. The same person may, in different situations,
fall into different kinship categories for ego, and persons connected with ego by
different genealogical or kinship routes fall into the same category. The categorization of rightful spouses in any of the systems here referred to illustrates this. Confusion has been caused by the implicit assumption that a kinship terminology is a
specification of actual kinsfolk.[13]
    As in other kinship systems, only full siblings have identical fields of kinship apart
from their affinal connections, and in Australia even these may coincide in form

---

12. Warner (1937: 105) describes the situation as follows: "Each individual feels it is his
right rather than his duty to keep his part of the system working; hence the proper functioning
of the whole. A proper marriage is preferred because a Murngin man and woman usually
feel that they have a right to each other, since their relationship has destined them to marriage.
This is true of all the behavior of all the personalities in the system." Cf. also Meggitt's
remarks previously quoted, and Hiatt, 1964: chap. 6.

13. Cf. Barnes, "Foreword" to Hiatt, 1965: vii–xi, and such an observation as the following
from Hiatt, 1965: 109: "Some individuals said they were not in favour of adultery with the
wife of a true brother or MMB and addressed such women as 'mother' or 'ZD' to demonstrate an absence of sexual interest." The point is implicit in Warner's notes on the "kinship
personality" and in his reference to the adjustment of kinship terms to fit "wrong" marriages
(1937: 104–105).

owing to the rules of prescribed and preferred marriage. But if they do not coincide, the fields of genealogically connected persons do overlap and this helps to bind them to one another in mutual dependence.

However, an interlocking aggregate of individual fields of kinship does not of itself have contours or boundaries. This is common to all societies in the domain of familial—that is, formally bilateral or cognatic—kinship. Hence the universal "web of kinship" pattern. In the absence of other structural controls, such a web can stretch out indefinitely, and result in a kaleidoscopic fluidity of social relations. This indeed is the impression one gets of the Australian social organization.

In many African social systems this tendency is controlled by the fixed politico-jural framework, be it based on eminent office or on corporate descent groups,[14] and its concomitant ritual, economic, and territorial institutions. Are there corresponding controlling institutions in the Australian kinship policy? With status position maintained by self-assertion and with neither property nor rank nor office to pass on by inheritance and succession and no tribal unity to fight for, what holds successive generations together? What prevents a continual dispersion of individuals when they reach adulthood? This may seem a jejune question; but it helps to bring out a fundamental point. For the answer lies in the irreducible characteristics and values of the kinship structure, on the one hand, and the totemic system, on the other.

Let us look at the religious context first. Descriptively, a person is bound to others—of the same sex as opposed to the other sex, of the same putative ancestry, of the same local allegiance, of the same moral responsibility for a body of sacred knowledge and cult duty, and so forth—by his totemic alignments and attributes. However, these are all in the last resort determined by his parentage. As our authorities constantly remind us, the system of totemic beliefs, mythology, and ritual is inextricably bound up with kinship norms. The well-known institution described as "conception" totemism gives point to this. In this respect and in the localization of totem centers the totemic system provides fixed foci of intergenerational continuity. It also provides a scheme of cross-sexual and intercommunity continuity in the periodical ceremonies and cult activities. Australian social structure can, without undue distortion, be summarily described as an elaborate institutional superstructure on the irreducible datum of parentage. This is the point of the reiterated observation that it is, in Radcliffe-Brown's words, "built up on the family and based on family solidarity" (1930–31: 444).[15] Parentage is, however, the crucial element: it creates the relations between and within generations which form the core of the kinship system. Their focus is the relationship of filiation, which analytically regarded, is the converse of parentage in the overall structure of the relationships of proximate generations.[16] Radcliffe-Brown (1930–31: 442) observed

14. E.g., of the kind typified by Ashanti chiefship and clanship or by the Tallensi maximal lineage.

15. The limitations of this view have been pointed out in chap. v above, but in the present context they are not critical.

16. Cf. Fortes, 1959a: 206. For ease of reference, pending detailed discussion below, chap. XIII, I note that I there define filiation as "the relationship created by the fact of being the legitimate child of one's parents." It subsumes, I add, on the one side, "the bond between

of the section and subsection system that it "generalizes throughout the whole society the parent-child relationship,"[17] but this proposition in fact sums up what is central in the kinship system as a whole.

The recognition of "bilateral" filiation underlies the fundamental and standard division of each person's field of kinship into complementary sides, graphically illustrated in the Kariera opposition of "father people" kin and "other (or matrilateral) people" kin (cf. Radcliffe-Brown, 1913; Romney and Epling, 1958). Murngin kinship structure has a similar form.[18] For the Walbiri, likewise, Meggitt shows how in every significant matter such as a boy's initiation, a girl's marriage, a person's death, patrikin and matrikin are both distinguished and equally involved. The father and possibly the father's father, and the mother's brother and mother's mother's brother are co-responsible and have complementary rights and duties in all jural and ritual issues relating to filial kin. Other authorities offer similar observations. A person's passage through life cannot be managed in customarily proper ways without the collaboration and ministrations of his kinsfolk on both sides, and the classificatory principle ensures that kin of the necessary category are there to be called upon if closer kin are lacking. This in itself is a strong binding force.

How the intergenerational principle of bilateral filiation is elaborated depends upon the kind of differentiation made between brother and sister in the actual, and, by generalization, the classificatory sibling group. The restriction of marriage to persons related by specified kinship is directly associated with this. Warner (1937: 107) maintains that marriage, through "partial destruction of an old family by taking a daughter or sister from it to become a wife and mother of a new family . . ." tends to weaken "lateral" (i.e., intragenerational) as against "perpendicular" (i.e., lineal) relationships.[19] But marriage, as Radcliffe-Brown demonstrated, also pulls together kinsfolk who are disjoined by the divergence of kinship ties deemed to originate in a man and his sister (own or classificatory), respectively, and are also structurally segregated by the locus of the incest barrier. This, surely, is one of the consequences, if perhaps an unintended one, of "sister" and "niece" exchange marriages.[20]

These are mechanisms and institutions that serve to integrate ego's field of kinship "laterally" in Warner's words. The kinship system also includes devices for containing the extension of ego's kinship field over the succession of generations. In

17. This statement must be taken in the classificatory sense, of course.

18. Warner, 1937, e.g., p. 52, where he remarks that a boy's "filial" relationship with his father "places him in his patrilineal clan and moiety and in a marrying relationship with his mother's clan and moiety." Cf. also Meggitt and Hiatt, *passim*.

19. The unfortunate metaphor should not blind us to the important point of principle here implied. The change of status is symptomatic of the structural cleavage between the patrilateral and the matrilateral sides of the kinship field for every ego and of the corresponding opposition between parallel kinship ("siblings") and cross kinship ("cousins") in Australian systems.

20. Cf. Hiatt, 1965: 41, for "niece exchange" marriage.

successive generations" expressed in their identification for inheritance and succession, and, on the other side, the cleavage "symbolized by the incest taboo and in customs of respect and avoidance." Thus, in structural terms, persons are siblings "by virtue of common filiation"—bilaterally for full siblings, patrilaterally or matrilaterally for half-siblings.

such systems as that of the Gidjingali it is easy to see how the merging of alternate generations in terminological reference and customary intercourse compresses all "lineal" relationships into the nuclear categories of filiation and siblingship—that is, the relationship of consecutive generations—and ties in with the rules specifying marriageable kinship categories as well as the section-subsection system. Ego is thus equipped with a closed calculus, an economical scheme of categories for managing all his social relations by reference to a small number of axiomatic rules of identification and allocation.

This is the institutional apparatus by means of which a person's jurally valid rights and duties, claims and privileges are defined and implemented. It presupposes a division of each person's social world into a kinship realm where moral relations (subject, for example, to the incest rule), jural relations (of marriage and affinal duties, for example), and religious relations (of totemic belief and ritual) prevail, and a non-kinship realm where such relations are impossible. The division is between the realm of conduct and values governed by what Hiatt (1965: 146) calls the "ethic of generosity,"[21] or, as I would prefer to call it, the rule of amity, and its contrary, the realm of the alien. Amity means consensus in accepting the value of mutual support in maintaining "a code of good conduct" for the realization of each person's "legitimate interests," as Hiatt puts it—in the last resort, even by acts of violence regarded as legitimate. Non-amity implies non-relationship. It is typified not only by the antinomy between in-group and out-group, but also by the person who outlaws himself by a breach of the incest or the marriage laws, or an act of sacrilege, and it is symbolized interestingly enough in some groups by the notion of sorcery (cf. Elkin, 1938: 205; Warner, 1937: 240–43).

If kinship is equated with amity, and non-kinship with its negation, the equivalent of a "rule of law" can obtain only within a domain mapped out by the kinship system. If we accept the proposition that Australian kinship systems are ultimately rooted in the structure of the parental family, we can say that their extension by the classificatory principle amounts to the generalization of the norms which hold within the familial domain to cover all licit social relationships. The jural domain and the familial domain are coterminous, unified by the common body of norms and the overriding ethic of generosity.

V

Yet even in this proverbially simple type of society there is a conceptual and institutional distinction between the inner core and the outward extension of what is in a formal sense an undifferentiated domain embracing all aspects of custom and conduct. The division is marked by the incest barrier. Since moral and jural relations are inconceivable except between persons defined as kin to one another, it necessarily follows that marriage, which entails crucial jural relations, is possible only between parties who are defined as kin. Hence the rule that "every marriage is

21. The significance of this principle is more fully discussed in chap. XII.

a marriage between kin."[22] But which degrees of kin are enjoined or permitted spouses depends on the incidence and range of the incest prohibition. It is this that underlies the rule restricting marriage to kin in (cross) cousin categories. More exactly, the incest rule defines the range of intra-familial (bilateral) kinship, which may prohibit marriage with genealogically primary, as opposed to classificatory, kin of permitted marriage categories—as with the classical Aranda type mother's mother's brother's daughter's daughter marriage.[23]

The conclusion emerges—and it could be further supported by examining the mobilization of kinship ties in *rites de passage* and totemic ceremonies and their representation in mythology and in metaphysical beliefs—that for ego his field of normal social relations is integrated from within, so to speak, by devices built into the kinship system and identified in the terminology.

The problem is more complex with the interlocking but disparate aggregation of the fields of kinship of a collectivity of persons, in the absence, as we have noted, of territorial boundaries or the constraining force of political authority or constituted jural machinery or even defensive necessity. Since every jurally autonomous person is entitled to assert his rights and claims by his own efforts, he might be tempted (and is indeed, on the empirical evidence, prone[24]) to exploit his own field of kinship relations arbitrarily for personal ends. Radcliffe-Brown formulated the problem from another angle when he said:

Thus though it is possible by means of a classificatory system of terminology to establish a kinship structure by which the social relations of individuals can be satisfactorily regulated within a community of limited size, the structure will remain unstable until it is supplemented by some segmentary organization which will group the individuals into permanent and recognizable groups (1930–31: 440).

It was by reference to this principle that he accounted for the moiety and section organization, as we have seen (Chap. IV). We do not have to accept his form of words in order to understand the significance of division by moieties and sections or subsections. It is noteworthy that sections and subsections have in the past, and still continue to, spread to tribal groups who were formerly without them.[25] This supports Warner's (1937: 122) and Elkin's (1938: 94–95) views that they are specially useful in relations between tribes with variant kinship systems. It is obviously much easier to articulate together variant kinship systems by means of a scheme of four or eight subdivisions than by equating a diversity of kinship categories. The fallacious supposition that sections and subsections are primarily concerned with regulating marriage was long ago disposed of by Radcliffe-Brown (1930–31: 436–37). All investigators confirm that it is the specific classificatory kinship relations of the parties, not their

22. Radcliffe-Brown, 1951: 55; but the principle is recognized by all authorities (cf. incidentally, Eggan, 1955: 532 for an enlightening parallel).

23. Cf. the Walbiri (Meggitt, 1962: 150–51, 163–64). Close kin in this context means within the limits of the inner core of the domain, bilaterally defined: classificatory kin are those who are affinally eligible and morally licit for marriage. I am using Meggitt's contrast between "intra-familial" and "extra-familial" kinship in a slightly different sense from his.

24. See, e.g., Meggitt's and Hiatt's case records.

25. Stanner drew attention to this in 1936, and others have since added confirmation, e.g., Meggitt, 1962: 168.

section and subsection membership which is ultimately decisive in marriage (cf. Elkin, 1938: 88; Meggitt, 1962: 169; Radcliffe-Brown, 1951: 436–37; Warner, 1937: 74–75). And what holds for this crucial jural transaction holds also for all other occasions which call for the exercise of mutual rights and duties, privileges and obligations, as for example Meggitt (1962: 173 ff.) and Hiatt (1965: chap. 5) show in their case records. This is consistent with the reliance on self-help in social control in Australian society.

The moiety division, Elkin suggests (1938: 84, 184–85), is mainly important for the allocation of reciprocal ceremonial and ritual statuses and duties, and for the incorporation of natural phenomena into the social order. The section and subsection scheme, on the other hand, is said to "systematise the kinship arrangements" (Radcliffe-Brown, 1930–31: 440), to "summarise" or "group" kinship relations "according to alternate generation lines and cross-cousin relationships" (Elkin, 1938: 89).

This description, however, leaves out the most important feature of the scheme. Moieties, sections, and subsections are fixed divisions or, rather, ascriptions. Assignment to them is permanent, immutable, and exclusive. Every person belongs to one only. Unlike kinship status, which varies in accordance with the relations of the parties, it is constant for all situations. The system is, moreover, closed and exhaustive. It is an arrangement of persons not of kinship categories and of all the persons embraced within a given range of interlocking kinship fields. It resembles the arrangement of persons by sex. Like the distinction between male and female, moiety, subsection, and section membership endows each person with an element of absolute social identity. It gives him a fixed position in the domain of kinship in his relations with others, especially in moral and jural situations and in intertribal intercourse. Placing a person by subsection is the readiest first step towards establishing an exact kinship relationship to him. It may suffice in itself for the initiation of social relations of generalized amity. And it is economical and conclusive because, from within, the section and subsection system is arranged on the simplest pattern of intersecting dichotomies derived from the elementary genealogical dichotomies recognized in the kinship system—between matrifiliation and patrifiliation, between consecutive generations, and consequently, between siblingship and cousinship. It is really by reason of these criteria of assignment to sections and subsections that the system can be described as summarizing or systematizing kinship categories, for each person's placement in the scheme is determined by a combination of the critical indices of his kinship statuses as laid down by these elementary dichotomies.

Here the famous rule of "throwing away the father" (cf. Elkin, 1938: 89–90; Warner, 1937: 119–20) is applied to ensure certainty and predicability of section and subsection membership.[26] It is, as Meggitt (1962: 185) comments, "an expression of the basic rule that the mother is an unequivocal point of reference in the kinship system". In my terminology, this is a striking example of the recognition of matrifiliation in social structure. Warner (1937: 120) and others call it matrilineal

---

26. The alternative rule of patrifiliation appears to be applied in the special circumstances of "wrong" marriages for patritotem alignment, as among the Murngin (Warner, 1937: 105–106).

descent. But his is an observer's construct. It is not hair splitting to prefer my term, for the ethnographic facts show that, for the actor, cognizance is taken only of the connection with the mother. That is to say, pedigrees stretching farther back are not utilized. Genealogical links with antecedent matrilineal kin such as the mother's mother or her mother or their brothers are not considered in the assignment of persons to sections and subsections.[27] Their placement is inferred from the secondary rule which allocates offspring to the proximate generation section to that of their mother, within the closed system of coupled sections and subsections.

In sum, the moiety, section, and subsection systems are strictly arrangements of persons, the only "absolute" arrangements, as some authorities put it, in the domain of kinship. It is comparable to the residential segregation of successive and the combination of alternate generations reported, for example, for the Ndembu.[28] It confers no rights of either an individual or a collective kind and entails no duties, other than those arising from their specific kinship statuses and their totemic associations, by which they are distinguished *inter se* (cf. Elkin, 1938: 129 ff.; Meggitt, 1962: 215–16).

The section and subsection scheme is built up on the same principles as those that underly the kinship system which organizes and circumscribes the individual's field of social relations. But it is, in a sense, outside kinship. It is a kinship device extruded, as it were, to make a quasi-external, quasi-topographical, fixed frame of coordinates within which the loosely aggregated kinship fields of a collectivity of persons are held together in a stable and integrated arrangement. Being only indirectly connected with the regulation of social relations, and including no offices of authority or of leadership, the section or subsection cannot be regarded as a political or jural organization comparable to an African unilineal descent group. It is not a corporate unit of social structure.[29] Its primary value is to serve as a set of structural compass points by which a person can initially orientate his social and ritual relations, kinship categories being used as a second-order selection frame to distinguish among section/subsection mates of the same sex. This is what is meant by the well-known saying that the section/subsection system keeps the kinship system straight.

VI

Are there, then, in Australia, no forms of descent grouping analogous to those with which we are familiar in Africa ? All the earlier authorities, including Radcliffe-Brown and Warner, regularly refer to patrilineal and matrilineal descent lines, groups, section, moieties, clans, and so forth. The Murngin subsection system is considered by both Radcliffe-Brown (1951: 50) and Warner to be made up of two sets of "matrilineal cycles."

27. At this stage it is sufficient to speak of descent in terms of the calculus of genealogical relationship recognized for purposes of assigning persons to status positions or group membership.
28. Cf. Turner, 1957: 79–80. This residential pattern is common in Central Africa.
29. "Subsections had no corporate functions in secular life" says Hiatt (1965: 50) echoing Meggitt. Cf. also Elkin's analysis, 1938: 86 ff.

I have already indicated why I regard it as a misnomer to ascribe the section/ subsection scheme to matrilineal *descent*. The same objections can be raised, for example, against interpreting the Murngin kinship sequences which Warner, Rad- cliffe-Brown, and others have called patrilineal and matrilineal "lines" to be descent lines. Insofar as they can be considered to be "lines," they are better thought of as representing successive degrees of kinship reckoned by steps of patri- and matri- filiation.[30] I take one example, Warner's brilliant analysis (1937: 99, 113–15) of the relationships in the "matrilineal" sequence from ego's *mari* (mother's mother's brother) to his *kutara* (sister's daughter's son). In fact, this analysis shows that what his notation presents as a "line" is actually a chain of discrete dyadic reciprocals.[31] This is evident in the opposed claims, prestations, loyalties, and identifications in which these relationships are expressed. It is difficult to believe, given the constitu- tion of Australian kinship systems on the basis of particulate dyadic elements, that *kutara* envisages his status in terms of matrilineal descent from ego's or ego's *maris* (his mother's mother's mother's mother's brother's) sister, the more so as *kutara* and *mari* are mutually assimilated by name-sharing, moiety membership, and common interests reflected in their close attachment.[32]

However, more substantial claims for the occurrence of descent lines and descent groups in Australian societies have been brought forward by Berndt (1955) and Meggitt (1962: 215).[33] They claim indeed to have discovered "corporate lineages" of the same form as in Africa and New Guinea, though of much smaller dimensions and of narrower political and jural significance. Their concern has been to show that contrary to the view I expressed in 1953, unilineal descent groups of a corporate nature do occur "among peoples who live in small groups, depend on a rudimentary technology and have little durable property" (Fortes, 1953b: 24, quoted in Meggitt, 1962: 211).

Meggitt (1962: 188–232) portrays the situation excellently and I paraphrase his analysis. The Walbiri kinship system, he notes, includes four (five, with that of the classificatory "mother's father" who is also wife's mother's mother's brother) "matrilines" of descent and, correlatively, five "patrilines."

Considering the "matriline" first, we learn that owing to the "shallow time depth" (three to five generations) of genealogical knowledge, due in part to reluctance about naming the dead, "matriline" connections are not strictly discriminated from the

30. Leach, 1951, has criticized the assumption that these are truly descent lines from an- other angle.

31. The "plus-minus" notation is a misleading shorthand unless it is taken in a purely metaphorical sense. Cf. the similar notation of Lévi-Strauss, referred to on p. 48, n. 8 above.

32. Most of the confusion that has built up in the celebrated Murngin controversy appears to have been due to the error of treating these alleged "lines" as if they were lineage-like descent groups and credited with a rule of exogamy. (Cf. Leach, 1951.) The warning given by Radcliffe-Brown in his trenchant review of the controversy (1951: 49) that "The use of the idea of lines of descent is *merely to facilitate accurate descriptive analysis*" (my italics) put the issue in a nutshell. Some of the blame for the misunderstanding must undoubtedly be attributed to ambiguities in Warner's ethnographic data but the main reason seems to have been a false conception of the significance of Murngin kinship terminology.

33. Hiatt speaks of "patrilineal descent groups" (1965: 18 ff.), yet he records that he "collected no genealogy in which all living members were descended from a man in the great-grandparental generation of the oldest living member" (p. 22).

wider network of "matrilineal" kin ties in the same community. When the "matri-line" does emerge as a "group" it is thought of as comprising the mother's mother's brothers, mother's mother, mother's mother's children, mother's mother's daughters, and mother's mother's daughter's daughter's children. But it seems that members of this "group" do not think of themselves, nor are they thought of by outsiders, as the totality of the uterine descendants of the mother's mother's mother, or even as a segment of such a group. Marriage disperses them and this prevents them from acting together regularly. The "matriline" is therefore not the "nucleus of a localized descent group." The effective unit for a mature man is his matrilateral family core of mother's mother's brother, mother's brothers, mother's sister's sons and brothers, numbering about ten people all told.

An important bond is the belief that members of a "matriline" share a common but unnamed matri-spirit transmitted from the mother after conception and dissipated at death. This is given as the reason for the incest ban prohibiting marriage with own mother's brother's daughter and mother's mother's brother's daughter's daughter. The "matriline" emerges most effectively in connection with the marriages and deaths of its members. A youth's mother's mother's brother has a decisive voice in his betrothal. For it is he who advises the boy's father and mother's brother on the choice of the circumciser, who will play a leading part in his initia-tion and would normally be a classificatory "father-in-law" who finds him a wife. A girl's "matriline," represented by her mother's mother's brother and mother's brother, though bound to have regard to her father's commitments, "actively give her in marriage and protect her rights thereafter." This, of course, is a grossly simplified version of a complex transaction in which a variety of kinship connections, both patrilateral and matrilateral, play a part. The main point, however, is that in marriage the "matriline" kin of both parties have an authoritative voice. Again, it is the men and women of a dying person's "matriline" and matri-moiety who perform the ritual actions which release his matrispirit.

Summing up, Meggitt states that the "matriline is in certain respects a corporate group, but it is organized on a contingent basis," acting corporately, that is, only irregularly and specifically in connection with marriage and death. It does not have the "single legal personality" of some African corporate lineages, nor are its male members "jurally equal" to outsiders. It appears, also, that the "matriline" has apparently no continuity beyond a sequence of living generations. "Matriline" is a cluster of persons linked to one another by congruent ties of intrafamilial uterine kinship, but it hardly qualifies to be regarded as a perpetual descent group.

The "patriline" appears to have more definite structural contours, though it also merges with the corresponding section and moiety arrangements of persons and of totemic allegiances. Patrimoiety ritual responsibilities and privileges embrace a number of interlinked "patrilines." A "patriline" is associated with the cult lodge in which are centered its particular "totemic dreamings." A boy is initiated into his father's lodge and thus shares the lodge-dreaming or patrispirit with his older brothers, his father, father's brothers, and father's father. A man calls his lodge-dreaming "father" and extends this term to the dreamings of parallel "father's father's patrilines" in his semi-patrimoiety, the half of the patrimoiety comprising his "mother's mother's brothers" patrilines and dreamings, and the opposite patrimoiety patrilines and dreamings designated as "mother's father" or "wife's brother." These usages are particularly revealing in showing, as they do, how the domains which we distinguish from the outside by such terms as religious and ritual are, for the Australians themselves, incorporated in the all-embracing universe of kinship. When a member dies, his share of the lodge spirit returns to the locality which is the dreaming site. Though women, being separated from the secret life of ritual, are not initiated into lodge membership, sisters and daughters share the patrispirit of their brothers and fathers who are its custodians on their behalf. This is reflected in the duties allocated to the elder sister, father's sister and father's father's sister in the ceremonies preceding the boy's circumcision. Unlike the dispersed persons of the "matriline," men of the "patriline" generally live in one community and gather regularly for ritual purposes connected with the lodge. The indestructible dreaming sites and the myths and dogmas create a belief that the "patrilines" by which they are preserved, though they are in reality of shallow genealogical depth, are perpetual. This is strengthened by the mutually complementary ritual functions of "patrilines" in maintaining the socio-religious framework. The "patriline" also has an "internal pattern of authority" in that the elders who control the transmission of the ritual knowledge direct "corporate lodge activities" and are its joint spokesmen. Another "corporate" feature of the "patriline" is its possession of non-material values such as "myths, songs and ceremonies as well as lasting material symbols of its identity such as bull roarers and incised boards." The "patriline" therefore acts as one of the basic units of participation in totemic ritual.

Finally, since lodge and community affiliation are related, "patriline" membership is indirectly associated with political status ("for what it is worth," adds Meggitt!). As it does not appear that this "group" normally acts as a unit, for instance in vengeance activities or in opposition to other like units in defense of its interests, its political attributes seem to be negligible.[34]

Meggitt concludes that the Walbiri "regard the patriline, or more particularly its associated lodge, as an enduring corporation that administers property which, although mainly intangible, nevertheless has great social value." Two other observations adduced by Meggitt and earlier stressed by Berndt deserve attention. Firstly, he notes that the recognition of a patriline as a "corporate unit" by outsiders is reinforced by the notion that its members are all "brothers" in spirit, though this does not imply that they think of themselves *inter se* or are regarded as jurally equal. In other words, the "patriline" does not participate in jural relations as an organized unity. Its unity in relation to outsiders is that of a spiritual or ritual "brotherhood." Secondly, he points out that the "matriline" spirit and the "patriline" spirit symbolize the two "groupings" of "social persons" which have "complementary secular and ritual functions"—the "groupings" established by the functional and ter-

---

34. Hiatt observes that though close agnates helped each other in disputes, "neither patrilineal groups nor land owning units ever opposed each other as corporate groups" (1965: 135). Nor were they "units in systems of wife exchange" of the kind assumed in Lévi-Strauss's model (p. 134), in actuality or by native ideals. The "patrilineal group" is obviously not a jural unit either.

minologically recognized bifurcation of patrilateral and matrilateral kinship categories in the bilateral framework. This is reflected in the notion of personality, well exemplified among the "Wulamba" (cf. Berndt, 1955: 89) in the complementary components believed to make up the physical and psychical constitution of the person (the flesh from the mother and the more sacred bones from the father). Meggitt (1962: 284) interprets analogous beliefs as "symbolic expressions of a principle of complementary filiation." Consistently and relevantly, the rites and ceremonies of circumcision and other initiation activities are managed for a youth by the close kin of his "patriline" and his "matriline," as well as his future wife's "matriline," and with the help of his patrimoiety. These ritual activities indeed dramatize, in part, the complementary responsibilities of his patrikin and his matrikin for his induction into the status of a jurally capable man.

We should not be far off the mark, I suggest, if we regard the matriline not as a unilineal descent group with corporate structure, but as a group of kinsfolk bound to one another by shared rights and responsibilities for particular persons which are characteristically derived from intrafamilial kinship relations and defined in kinship terms and which are vested in the maternal sibling group of the parental generation. Appropriately enough (cf. the Wulamba theory of the personality) these are the rites connected with marriage (in which matrilateral ties are critical and the disposal of a woman's sexuality and fertility is the issue) and correlatively the responsibility for ritual actions connected with the dissolution of the person and his body at death. The *ad hoc* and amorphous nature of this group is well symbolized in the notion of a shared but unnamed spiritual identity.

To say that the concept of descent is implied in matriline relations is, I believe, to stretch it too far. In fact it amounts to no more than a rule for the identification of ego's closest matrilateral kin primarily by the criterion of sibling connection and it is significant that their unity is focused in the bare fact of their genealogical connections, not in possessions, material or immaterial, or in enduring common interests.

The "patriline" would seem to be a more coherent unit with more definite descent attributes and some rudiments of corporate structure. Significantly and appropriately it is the bridge for the boy between the "profane" sphere of family and kinship relations and the "sacred" sphere of transcendental religious and mythological knowledge, ritual, and ceremonial which is the preserve of the men collectively and is regarded by them as the ultimate basis of their social and cosmic order. What is notable is that the corporate identity and continuity of the patriline is manifested in its status in the domain of religion and mythology, not in secular matters, and is symbolized in the concept of a common spiritual substance. If we accept that it is a corporate unit, can we regard it as also a descent group? The "patriline" seems to be visualized both by its members and by others as unilineally continuous, but it is in fact recruited by exclusive patrifiliation in every generation, not by a reference to a patrilineal pedigree going back three or more generations[35]—though never of course by other than kinship criteria. This is consistent with the rule of the merging of

35. Berndt (1955: 88) implies that the "Wulamba" patriline includes men and women of no remoter common ancestry than the third ascending generation; and see reference to Hiatt in footnote 33, p. 114, above.

alternate generations and the subsection system. If the notion of agnatic connections stretching back at least as far as the father's father is implicit in patriline structure, it seems to have only secondary relevance for the constitution and activities of the group compared with the immediate connection of father and son.[36]

If the patriline should be regarded as a unilineally ordered descent group in the formal sense, it is certainly only a minimal descent group in comparison with, for instance, a Nuer or Tallensi patrilineal lineage. But the idea that its members are bound to one another as if they were a single personality in the ritual sense is reminiscent of some African concepts of corporate personality.

VII

I know of no pithier characterization of Australian social structure than Meggitt's (1964: 172) remark that: "Even at the highest structural level or at the widest geographical extent, it is easy to believe that here we are dealing with nothing more than domestic or quasi-domestic affairs." This is a graphic image for what I have called the kinship polity. In such a polity the domain of kinship, which is constituted by the generalization and extrapolation of familial norms and institutions based on the irreducible elements of recognized genealogical relationship, not only provides a calculus of dyadic interpersonal relations, but constitutes *eo ipso* also the domain of political and jural relations. There is no structural differentiation of these domains, yet the jural aspect of the rights and duties, claims and capacities embedded in kinship relations is clearly distinguished, as in the definition of marriageable categories of relatives. A man has a right to marry a cross-cousin of the designated category and classificatory degree, though he may for contingent and practical reasons actually have to accept a woman of an alternative category.[37] There is even an element of contract in these arrangements, as Hiatt implies and as is illustrated, for instance, by the Walbiri procedure of appointing as circumciser a future father-in-law.

What makes this polity of particular interest to my inquiry is the way in which compliance with jural and moral norms is achieved in it. It depends upon individual action with the support of kinsfolk, both close and distant, and the approval of public opinion, in the assertion of rights and the honoring of obligations. This works because the kinship system arranges persons in relation to one another in a "matrix of interconnected statuses whose correlative roles define the norms to which observed social behavior more or less conforms" (Meggitt, 1962: 188)—subject, we should add, to the overriding axiom that consensual social relations cannot take place outside the universe of kinship.

The system requires that each kinship status should be precisely discriminable by terminological and customary indices in contrast to other statuses in the scheme. This is provided for by rules which relate persons by degrees of parentage in the first

---

36. This is evident from the part played by the alignment of persons in the structure of the "group" by kinship terminology (Hiatt, 1965: 50 ff., and Meggitt, 1962: chap. XII).
37. Hiatt, 1965: chap. 4, brings this out in detail.

instance, and then by classificatory assimilation in accordance with the rule of sibling equivalence. What it comes down to is counting steps of filiation and blocks of siblingship. Filiation as I have already pointed out has two sides: it implies the identification of parent and child but it necessarily also connotes their separation to the point of opposition as successive generations of siblings. Both elements are utilized in different structural contexts in Australian kinship systems—in the Walbiri "patriline," for example, on the one hand, and in subsection allocation, on the other. But the concepts of filiation and siblingship are central to the whole manner of operation of Australian kinship relations, as the rule of merging alternate generations exemplifies.

Filiation may bind proximate generations; it cannot ensure continuity of social identification through more than two generations. This is conducive to the dispersion of kinship ties in successive generations which we find in societies with cognatic kinship systems wherever they occur. Our own social system is an example; there are others, for example in South Asia and Africa. (I discuss specimens in the next chapter.) If there were no internal controls or external (i.e., non-kinship) boundary forces or constraints, there would be no limits to this dispersive drift.

Internal structural controls operate in the Australian kinship polity. They are built around the moral and jural regulation of marriage, on the one hand, and the all-embracing totemic cult system, on the other; and they take the form of a dichotomy in the kinship domain which aligns persons subject to the incest rule, in complementary matrimonial and ritual interdependence by patrifiliative connections, on one side, and matrifiliative connections, on the other. This pattern is so constant that all occasions involving rights over and responsibilities for persons require the collaboration of both the father and his implicated familial patrikin and the mother's brother and his implicated familial matrikin of the propositus. And this is what justifies Radcliffe-Brown's insistence on the familial basis of Australian social organization, though he overemphasized its total range. Symbolized in customs of cross-sibling and affinal avoidance, and elaborated in the organization and doctrines of the religious domain, this dichotomous form is ultimately derived from the complementary opposition of male and female in Australian thought and society. It is used also to fashion the quasi-external frame of association in the shape of the moiety and section/subsection system by which persons in a common field of social relations are grouped by filiation and generation into mutually exclusive categories. It is for maintaining this internal structure of complementary alignments that the reciprocities of services, gifts, and so-called matrimonial exchanges are deployed. These internal controls are supplemented by the powerful force of the system of totemic and mythological cult and beliefs.

It is principally in relation to this system that features of ostensibly corporate organization emerge in the kinship polity. Murngin moieties are an instance. They are presumed to be immutably and perpetually associated with distinctive natural objects, cosmic processes, myths, and institutions. Each is internally unified in opposition to the other by the prohibition of marriage and sexual relations between members of a moiety. They have what looks like corporate custody of totemic myths, sacra, rites and ceremonies in the sense that each moiety is responsible for and privileged to perform specific roles in initiation and totemic ceremonies. On a smaller scale, similar ostensibly corporate attributes belong to the "patriline" among the Walbiri. In both cases, and in parallel organizations among other tribes, recruitment is by entitlement through filiation and admission by initiation. Withal, "corporate" organization in these cases is weak. There is no structure of authority in the moiety. Ostensibly corporate action never mobilizes its entire membership. There is no concept of a unitary jural personality for the corporation. What it amounts to, in effect, is the assumption in tribal and intertribal ceremonies of their moiety-linked tasks and privileges by those members of the moiety who happen to be present. It is doubtful if they are considered to be acting in a representative capacity. Indeed, the corporate existence of a moiety seems for the most part to be diffusely exhibited in the norms, values, and beliefs by adherence to which members of one moiety distinguish themselves from the opposite one. The Walibiri patriline, as we have seen, has a more definite but still only minimal corporate structure; and this applies even more to its counterpart, the matriline.

What is chiefly significant about these inchoately corporate institutions is that they are media of intergenerational continuity and unity of interest amid the ever-shifting configurations of interpersonal kinship relations. It is to the point that they serve this purpose because they form structural bridges between the internally fluid kinship polity and the external, changeless domain of myth and totemic cult. They are the lawful and fixed channels of access by kinship-qualified persons to the stock of sacred knowledge and ritual capital by which the security and continuity of society and the cosmos are believed to be ruled. At the material level this is why the various component parts and elements of the social structure—communities, local groups, moieties, sections, and so on down to particular persons—are bound to localities by totemic allegiances, not by economic or political forces.

VIII

I have concentrated on the bare mechanics of Australian social organization. The facts of sentiment and attitude, on the one side, and of metaphysical and religious dogma and faith, on the other, have been largely ignored. My aim has been to examine an incontestable limiting case of a social structure wholly comprised within a framework of kinship institutions. Here we see the system of kinship institutions as the sole and sufficient apparatus of social order, though not of all the values and norms which this apparatus serves. We see how this apparatus is built up from irreducible structural elements by processes developed solely from, or modeled upon the basic relations of social reproduction. We see also how these same kinship institutions are classificatorily elaborated to provide controls and set structural bounds to the dispersive tendencies inherent in a bilateral kinship order. What I wish specifically to draw attention to is the rudimentary development of the descent concept and of corporate descent (or otherwise constituted) groups in this system. One could argue that this is connected with the absence, or at best marginal significance, of such political and economic variables as territory, office, rank, warfare, property, trade, ownership of natural resources, and technological specialization. It is the more noteworthy, therefore, that the rudimentary corporate organizations that are present in the kinship polity relate to certain rights over persons, and more conspicuously to the allocation of rights in and responsibilities for the resources of religious and metaphysical knowledge and belief. Stated summarily, the ostensibly corporate organization that emerges in this type of social structure is a function of the intersection of jural concepts and religious and metaphysical notions, not of control of material goods or productive resources.

CHAPTER VIII

Cognatic Systems
and the Politico-Jural Domain

I

THE AUSTRALIAN TYPE OF KINSHIP POLITY EXHIBITS SHARPLY A NUMBER OF STRUCTURAL concomitants characteristic of so-called bilateral kinship systems in societies in which the familial domain and the politico-jural domain are minimally differentiated. A conspicuous feature is the absence, or the relatively peripheral emergence within a politico-jural community demarcated by kinship boundaries, of exclusive structural units defined by rules of kinship and descent, outside the range of the domestic family. In the Australian systems this is consistent with the rudimentary recognition of descent as a principle of structural alignment and the correlative absence, or at best inchoate form, of corporate groups within the normal field of collective social relations.

Similar properties characterize the structures of societies built up on the variety of bilateral kinship system now commonly designated as cognatic. But there are also some striking differences. In these societies, kinship connections, whether taken in the narrow sense or in the wider connotation of including affinal relations, are potentially unlimited in range. Structural boundaries cannot be generated from within the kinship universe, and non-domestic corporate organizations delimited by kinship criteria, do not occur in such systems. Where cognatic connections are truly equilateral in value for economic, ritual, jural and political relations and activities, extra-familial closed associations usually emerge only insofar as they are contained by non-kinship institutions.

Freeman's analysis of the kindred (1961), which is the central field of extra-domestic kinship relations for a person in cognatic systems, shows this conclusively. Societies of the Iban type are often described as made up of "overlapping kindreds." This can be misleading for, as Freeman demonstrates, a kindred is an *ad hoc* constellation of people mobilized in particular situations within a variable range and relatively to a given person from among his kin on both sides of his parentage. Kindreds only "overlap" in the sense that where two or more propositi who are not full siblings are engaged in the same situation, their fields of kindred relations may include persons who are kindred to all the principals.

The Iban[1] are well aware that every person's cognatic connections extend indefinitely. When kindred emerge, any known cognatic connection, however remote by genealogical reckoning, is potentially available. In actual situations, the range is regulated by a combination of kinship and spatial propinquity. A person's effective kindred include accessible cognates within the limits, at most, of the bilateral progenies of his four sets of great-grandparents, that is, in his own generation, as far as second cousins. But these kin may be widely dispersed by reason of the high degree of family mobility customary among the Iban. Genealogically remote kinsfolk may be spatially or socially more accessible than closer kin, and therefore more readily mobilizable in kindred activities. And it is particularly relevant, as Freeman emphasizes, that such cognates are only recognizable on the basis of their classificatory kinship status. Though Iban pedigrees are seldom traced even to the great-grandparents, and track is thus easily lost of genealogical collaterals, the classificatory terminology keeps all of a person's kin potentially available to him in his field of kinship. It is the contemporary spread of his kindred relations that matters to each person, not their ancestral connections with him.

Taking the tribe as a whole, which might number 40,000 people occupying an area of 5,000 square miles, Freeman explains how it is "traversed" by a "network of kindreds." It has no overall political organization; politico-jural relations are coterminous with kinship relations. The "network of kindreds" thus maps out a tribal area "within which disputes could usually be settled . . . through the mechanisms of kinship" (1960: 77). This area is endogamous. Moreover, the members of it did not formerly take heads within it. Consistent with this, what ultimately binds kindred relatives to one another, Freeman concludes, is a bond of moral obligation to help and support one another and to settle disputes by negotiation. Acknowledgment of kinship, which in the narrowest sense means what Freeman describes as "membership of the same stock" (i.e., having demonstrable common ancestry), is the basis of this moral relationship. It is clearly the same thing as the ideal of kinship amity we observed in the Australian context. Outside of this circle of kinship amity there was formerly no means of dealing with disputes and endemic feud and headhunting prevailed (Freeman, 1953: 347).

From the angle of kinship, an Iban tribe is not internally partitioned into bounded

1. I base this discussion of Iban social structure on the admirable studies of Dr. J. D. Freeman (1953, 1955, 1958, 1960).

subdivisions. Some degree of localization for sections of the network of kindreds is provided by the long-house communities strung out at varying distances along the banks of the river. A long-house community consists of a number (averaging 14) of cognatically interrelated *bilek* families. It "is situated on a part of a specified tract of land" clearly marked off by natural features from neighboring long-house territories to which its constituent families have "either rights of access or ownership" in severality (Freeman, 1960: 69; cf. also his general account of Iban agriculture, 1955). The long-house holds neither property nor land in collective ownership and engages in no common economic activities. It is essentially a local aggregate with common ritual interests and obligations supervised by a ritual leader, the *tuai burong* (augur) and common jural interests safeguarded by a secular headman who has no powers of coercion but administers the customary law by consent (Freeman, 1960: 70). Consistent with the kinship structure and the free mobility of the *bilek* units, these are not hereditary offices. When vacant they are filled by choice of the long-house community as a whole from among close cognates of the deceased.

But what is more to the point is that the long-house is fixed only in its external relations, not in its internal composition. *Bilek* families—not, be it noted, individuals—move freely from one long-house to another. The *bilek* family created by monogamous marriage and parenthood—not a segment of a descent group—is the only ongoing and stable unit of social structure in this society. Freeman describes it as an autonomous and perpetual corporate unit—"the intrinsic and irreducible" unit of Iban society. The jural equality of men and women of homologous structural placement (i.e., siblings and spouses) which is a necessary condition for equilateral cognatic systems to exist is made manifest in the developmental cycle of the *bilek* (Freeman, 1958). Siblings normally split up when they marry, partition land, divide heritable family heirlooms equally, apportion the sacred rice and whetstones, and live utrolocally in husband's or wife's *bilek* in equal proportions. Furthermore, all the members of the *bilek* at a given time, whether they belong to it by birth, marriage, or adoption, have equal claims on its estate, but only while they are members of it. Thus outmarriage severs membership of the natal *bilek*. This is jurally registered by the cession to the outgoing member of his or her share of the estate. It means that he is no longer under the authority of the head of his natal *bilek*, and conversely owes no duties to the head, but siblingship and, consequently, cognation, remain. The preference for cousin marriage can be seen as a means of mitigating the disruptive effects of *bilek* fission, since it keeps outmarrying *bilek* members within the kindred circle.

Equality between siblings irrespective of sex, and opposition between the sibling bond and the monogamous conjugal bond, together constitute the core of the kinship structure. This is apparent in the fact that married siblings find it impossible to stay in the same *bilek*. It is also reflected in the terminology of reference. Father's siblings and mother's siblings rank equally and are designated by the same terms which distinguish them from parents, all cousins are equally eligible as marriage partners and are referred to by a single term which distinguishes them from siblings; nephews and nieces are all designated by the same terms whether they are fratri-lateral or sorori-lateral, and are distinguished terminologically from sons and daughters. Consecutive generations are strictly distinguished, with respect enjoined to the parental generation and joking permitted with grandparents. In address, kindred amity prevails and collateral cognates are assimilated to lineal kin, as when all cousins are addressed by the sibling term. And the affinal terminology follows the same lines.[2]

As I have noted, Freeman maintains that the *bilek* family is a "perennial corporation aggregate." Though some children of the family marry out and join or establish other families, one son or daughter always remains to ensure continuity of the *bilek* as a "jural entity" vested with a perpetual "estate" consisting of land, heirlooms and above all, the sacred rice and its taboos, held in common (Freeman, 1960: 66–67). I shall return later to the theoretical problem this example raises.

Here I wish only to note that this "corporate" entity is kept in being by the mechanisms of marriage and filiation—utrolateral filiation, as Freeman calls it, since a person can have membership in either his father's or his mother's *bilek* but not in both. A person attains membership of a *bilek* either by virtue of being the real or the adoptive child of one of his parents, or by being the spouse of such a filiative member. Unilineal pedigrees through either parent to earlier antecedents are not specifically recognized as entitlement to status capacities. They are not distinguished from mixed pedigrees when common ancestry to establish kinship relations is sought. In this sense it can be said that, though the facts of recent common "descent" are recognized, the principle of descent is not jurally effective in Iban social structure. Considered from the outside, cognatic systems of this kind can briefly be described as built up on the elementary relations of filiation and marriage, siblingship being regarded as the product of common filiation and kindred relations being considered as the product of cumulative and extended co-filiation. Looked at from within, it is a basic principle of such systems (in contrast to the complementarily organized Australian systems) that filiation to and through either parent counts equally in the social alignment of persons and establishes credentials of equal valency for residence, for jural status, and for consequential economic and ritual standing. This presumes the equality of the parents in family structure and in relation to society at large, and consequently, their joint possession of jural authority over children and the estate. This has implications which will be considered later.

The Iban model has wide validity, as Freeman shows by the comparisons he adduces from both ethnographical and historical sources (1960; cf. also Eggan, 1960; Frake, 1960). As I have remarked, these cognatic structures have no internal kinship partitions. In the Iban model, internal division into bounded units other than the conjugally based family is mutable and is regulated by locality and spatial contiguity, movement between units being canalized primarily by inter-*bilek* cognatic ties.

II

Consideration of locality and spatial contiguity, or more generally the territorial

2. Freeman, 1960:77–85. Note the observation (p. 71) that within the broad category of kith and kin three main distinctions are made, namely: (a) *kaban mandal*: cognatic kin; (b) *kaban tampil*: affinal kin; (c) *orang bukai*: other people.

principle, takes us back to the classical theories of Maine and Morgan of which Lowie declared "The soundness of Maine's and Morgan's position in drawing a sharp distinction between kinship (tribal) and territorial (political) organization is beyond cavil" (1920: 391).

For Maine and Morgan this distinction marked out not only the crucial difference between the social organization of early or primitive societies, on the one hand, and civilized or advanced societies, on the other; it also identified the crucial principle which transformed tribal society (Morgan's *societas*, Maine's "early commonwealths . . . founded on common lineage") into political society, or the state—Morgan's *civitas*. To be sure, Maine spoke of "local contiguity" as the revolutionary principle (1861, chap. V), whereas Morgan invoked territory and joined with it property as the foundation of the state (1877; 1878 ed.: 6 ff., 62–66). But both clearly had in mind what later writers—who include most of the leading social and political theorists of the past sixty or seventy years[3]—uncritically accepted as their views and have since taken as proven. What they had in mind was the modern nation state strictly defined and circumscribed as a whole and in its administrative subdivision by territorial boundaries in which, to paraphrase Maine, the individual and not the family is the unit of citizenship and citizenship is a status within the territorial limits of the state regardless of genealogical connection. In this extreme form, the territorial principle is held to exclude kinship as a determinant of citizenship in the political community. It is true that where there is an hereditary monarchy—whether or not there is also an hereditary nobility vested with political status and privileges—kinship regulates the succession, but this serves mainly to put the monarchy in a unique position within the politico-jural domain. In tribal society, as Lowie established in 1920, the two principles are frequently—some would say invariably[4]—conjoined in the constitution of the political community and in the regulation of social life.

Such a general formula, however, leaves much to be desired. It takes no account of the diversity of institutional forms and arrangements—the variety of "types"—comprised under the rubric of kinship organization. Nor does it allow for the equally varied manifestations of territorial and locality factors in social structure. The territorial anchorage of a Walbiri community is a tenuous tie compared with the local continuity of an Iban long-house, and both are indefinite compared with the territorial foundations of a Tswana chiefdom or an Ashanti *oman*. At this level, territorial relations have at best only diffuse and implicit politico-jural functions among such people as the Walbiri and the Iban. They do not, for example, engender civic status. Nor is there evidence that the territorial unity of the polity as a whole, for example, in an Iban tribe, is a source of politico-jural institutions and status. The main significance of territorial relations is that they serve partially to peg down kindred relations. To repeat what I said earlier, a cognatic kinship structure cannot generate discrete units of social structure which are mutually exclusive solely and strictly by kinship-derived criteria. In the absence of politico-jural mechanisms of internal partition, local fixation and delineation serve to group persons uniformly

---

3. Cf. Schapera, 1956: chap. I, for a critical review of this position.
4. Cf., e.g., Schapera, 1956, where reference is also made to other writers who share this view.

interlinked in the network of kindreds into quasi-discrete units of social structures. But it is indicative of the incompatibility of a thoroughgoing cognatic system with fixed kinship aggregates of any form that such local units as the long-house do not have a tied membership. They are temporary halting places for most of their occupants.

There can be no doubt that in this setting locality and kinship are mutually independent variables. But locality by itself offers only a minimal foundation for internally partitioning a cognatic collectivity. Mere co-residence in one locality, even if it is associated with the advantageous utilization of land and other natural resources, and is underpinned by interlinked kindred and affinal ties, is not enough to engender stable structural arrangements. It does not, of itself, make permanent structural units. Freeman (1955: 10) aptly compares the long-house to a "terrace of privately owned houses" in a modern city. What unity, continuity, and autonomy there is in a long-house springs from its common ritual interest and the modicum of politico-jural authority held by the head, not from its ostensible territorial unity.

What territorial relations by themselves cannot achieve, marriage does, in such systems. The Iban domestic family is a unit closely comparable to our own form of the elementary family, exclusive and discrete by virtue of segregating a married couple and their offspring from collateral kin. Freeman's claim that the *bilek* is a corporate organization must await comment until we can compare it with more commonly accepted forms of corporate organizations. I would stress however, that *bilek* exclusiveness hinges on its conjugal nucleus, not on the cognatic relationships of its members. It is true that filiation ensures its continuity, but it must be remembered that co-filiation links siblings in different *bileks*. Filiation cannot serve as a criterion of demarcation for the *bilek*. As to its presumed perpetuity, this is quite clearly vested in the office of the *bilek*-head which is perpetuated by "universal succession", à la Maine. Here, I believe, lies the key to the corporativeness the *bilek* possesses, inasmuch as the right to succeed is derived initially from co-parcenership in the *bilek*, to which filiation and marriage are equal entitlements; but it is distinctive of succession in the *bilek* that it cannot be fraternal, it must be inter-generational, and this means that it follows filiation, regardless of the sex of the parties.

III

We have been considering cognatic kinship structure in societies without—or with insignificantly—differentiated politico-jural institutions, that is to say where the familial domain and the politico-jural domain are fused into one. Kinship statuses regulate all social relations; civic status is unknown or, is at best, a dependent, nebulous capacity coterminous with kinship status. What happens when cognatic kinship is associated with clearly differentiated politico-jural institutions? Africa provides a number of examples of societies in which such an association is found.

Let us consider the Lozi of Zambia (formerly Northern Rhodesia). Their kinship organization sufficiently resembles the Iban type to make comparison useful, but their polity includes developed politico-jural institutions in marked contrast to the Iban type.

The Lozi, like the Iban, are a riverine people dwelling in relatively small village communities interlinked by an indefinitely spreading web of cognatic kinship ties. But they also have a traditional form of monarchical rule and tribal government comprising military, fiscal, judicial, legislative, and ritual institutions which fully justify the appellation of a nation state. More exactly, they are the ruling tribe of the Barotse nation, which is made up of some 25 tribal groups of diverse origins and ways of life. Politically dominant in this multi-tribal state, partly by right of conquest during a checkered history, the Lozi are also the geographically central community; though much intermarried with the other tribes, they are intensely conscious of their tribal identity and distinctness, symbolized in, for example, their facial tatoos and descent names, exhibited in their geographical cohesion and, above all, focused in their powerful and revered monarchy. This justifies considering them in their own right apart from their congener tribes in the nation.

I shall not attempt to summarize the notable series of studies in which Max Gluckman has depicted the economy, the social structure, the political organization, and legal system of the Lozi.[5] I select only those features that are here pertinent. The theoretically important point is that the Lozi social system embraces both a precisely differentiated politico-jural domain and a cognatically organized familial domain, the two being closely articulated through territorial arrangements adapted to a specialized ecological environment. As Gluckman phrases it, "Kingship is as ultimate as birth: subjection to the king and kinship by blood are the basic elements of all Lozi social relationships" (1951: 21).

The Lozi number about one-third of the 300,000 Barotse nation (a rough estimate based on Gluckman, 1951: 87–88). They live in the great flood plain along the upper Zambezi River. For about three months every year, the whole population, ceremonially led by the king, moves to the margins, returning again when the flood subsides. Traditionally, fishing, gardening, cattle-keeping, exploiting the resources of the bush, and trading such products as ivory for imported weapons and other wares, formed the basis of a varied and comparatively prosperous economy. Ultimate ownership of the whole land and its productive resources was vested in the kingship, which was sustained partly from royal estates and partly by tribute freely given by the people. In return, the king was obliged to redistribute much of this wealth among his councillors and to anyone in need. Kingship, the nation, and the land were identified with one another in the constitutional scheme, in the cult of the graves of former rulers, and in the attitudes and sentiments of the people. The resulting territorial and ideological unity of the state was emphasized in the centralization of government and judicial functions in the king's capital. There were no territorial subdivisions under subordinate chiefs, nor was there a territorial division corresponding to the dichotomy between the king's and the princess-chief's capitals.

Instead of territorial subdivisions, there was a remarkable system of multiple allegiances connecting all subjects with the kingship through royal and court

5. I draw in particular on the following publications by Gluckman: 1941, 1943, 1950, 1951, 1955, and 1963.

dignitaries. The latter, all normally commoners by extraction, were appointed by the king to titled offices which were by constitutional theory as perpetual as the kingship itself, but were not, like the latter, hereditary. Under the king's presidency, they formed an influential advisory and deliberative council responsible for representing the people before the king and, conversely, for supporting the kingship, of which they were integrally a part. They also constituted the highest court of law and the central administration of the state. And in these capacities the senior councillors were the heads of the sectors of the nation, as Gluckman calls them.

For administrative purposes, the nation was divided into a number (nine at the time of Gluckman's investigations) of sectors, each under the authority of a senior councillor at the capital. These were not territorial divisions. Every subject of the king belonged to a sector, but the members of any one sector were dispersed throughout the nation. Members of one village, even of one family often belonged to different sectors. The people were distributed in a similar manner in allegiance to the royal storehouses and to the successors to queens' titles, and this arrangement cut across the sector system, thus scattering the clients of a single sector head among several storehouse and queen-title groups.

Political and jural attachments were by this means distributively allocated. Litigants brought their cases to their sector heads and delivered their tributes to the king through them. Being widely dispersed and unconnected with one another, other than through their common sector allegiance, the members of a sector did not form a unitary organization comparable to southern Bantu age regiments or Tswana wards, even though they were assembled by sectors for war service and public works. Nor did they constitute a corporate group in any sense of the term. Indeed, it would not be stretching the parallel extravagantly to compare the sector scheme to an Australian section system.

What, however, this arrangement ensured was the unequivocal centrality and supremacy of the kingship as the fountain head of the entire politico-jural domain. Regional factions could not arise in rebellion against a king, nor could nationwide opposition led by dissident princes easily materialize. The king was unique and all political loyalties, however dispersed at the sector level, converged upon him. Thus every Lozi perceived and felt himself to be a subject of the king. This was the essence of the Lozi conception of citizenship, a status clearly recognized in law, custom and sentiment.

Citizenship, in the precise sense of status in the politico-jural domain, is an intrinsic element of Lozi social structure. Significantly enough it is not determined by territorial grouping; nor do property considerations enter into its definition, except insofar as every citizen has a right to some land and to access to other economic resources. It is a purely politico-jural status reflecting the automomy—the "ultimate" nature as Gluckman says—of this domain in the total social system of the Lozi. The contrast with both the Australian and the Iban types of society is patent. It confirms our observation that the absence of a concept of civic status is due, not to undeveloped territorial or property relations, but to the lack of differentiated politico-jural offices and institutions.

Yet it is important to note that Lozi citizenship is not unmediated, as for instance it is in our social system. A citizen holds his civic status by virtue of the "chain of administration" through his sector head which connects him with the kingship. But there is another and equally important link in the chain. This is the link through the village headman by which the politico-jural domain and the domain of kinship and family organization are articulated together.

Their transhumant mode of life obliges Lozi to have two homes, one on the plain in the dry season and another on the margin in the flood season. But the true home is in a village on the plain. These villages are situated on mounds scattered about the flood plain. The mounds form the most valuable garden land and are also places of vantage for exploiting the resources of the plain and of the river. Some mounds suffice only to support a family group, while others (mainly those belonging to the rulers) can accommodate several scores, and a few, several hundreds of people. They have been fixed places of residence from time immemorial. Commoner mound villages belong to their occupants, but the largest number are owned by the king and the princess-chief in their official capacity, and court dignitaries also have mounds.

Residence in a mound village confers what is to a Lozi his most precious right and a critical attribute of citizenship, a right to garden land. The king as the ultimate master of all the land and trustee for the nation is obliged to see that every citizen has land to cultivate and access to the other economic resources of the country in return for the allegiance, labor services, and tribute he receives. If a person has no other means of acquiring land, he has a claim on the king's bounty.

But the co-residents in a mound village are transient over time. They scatter among different margin villages in the flood season, and vice versa; and they do not generally remain in the same mound villages throughout life. People move frequently in order to acquire land, to escape quarrels and disputes, or to attach themselves to popular village heads, or under orders from the monarchy. In the past, ambitious men tried to attract dependents, for the larger their following was, the better were their chances of eventually attaining titled office.

This pattern of residential and economic mobility is at one level a function of the strength and unity of the political structure, ensured by the efficacy of the administrative and judicial institutions and buttressed by reverence for the kingship as the embodiment of the rule of law. The king's subjects are equally citizens of the state wherever they choose to live. A change of location might involve a change of sector attachment, it does not affect civic status.

At another level, however, the mobility of the Lozi is also determined by their kinship norms and institutions in ways reminiscent of the Iban situation. Gluckman characterizes the Lozi kinship system by contrast with that of the Zulu as marked by the absence of corporate unilineal descent groups (1950: 71).

It is a cognatic system with, as he puts it, an agnatic bias reflected in the belief that a child's "proper home" is with its father. However, in Lozi law the child belongs equally to both sides. He may be brought up by either parent and can choose to live in the village of either parent or of any of his parent's forebears by any pedigree which he can establish. Kinship thus traced gives title to dwell in a village and to farm and succeed to land and other property. Pedigrees are rarely traceable beyond the four pairs of great-grandparents and their progenies. By birth, Lozi acquire "descent names." In theory they have one from each great-grandparent, in practice they tend to know only their fathers' and mothers' paternal descent names. There are of course no descent-name groups analogous to unilineal clans. A common descent name, however, even when genealogical connection is not demonstrable, is taken as a sign of kinship. It is not a bar to marriage though. Marriage is prohibited only between persons who are found to have actual genealogical connections, which normally means within four generations of ascent. Since cousins of all degrees, however reckoned, are classed as siblings, they are presumed to be forbidden. But in practice, classificatory cognatic links are often disregarded and marriages are made in spite of them. Marriage is in any case very frequently terminated by divorce except when the partners are classificatory cousins. It is characteristic also that marriage confers only sexual rights, no rights of paternity. By Lozi law, a child's genitor, whether pre-marital, legally paternal or adulterine, is the pater. This is consistent with the more or less equal division of jural control over children, minimal as it is, between the parents, just as among the Iban. The small bride price is equally divided between them and shared with their respective close kin.

In the kinship terminology, father's siblings are all classified together as fathers and female fathers; mother's siblings as mothers and male mothers. Though opposite sex siblings are distinguished from like sex siblings, the children and grandchildren of siblings (own and classificatory) are all classified with own progeny. So also affines are assimilated to kin and all grandparents are lumped together under one term. Sister's son can take liberties with mother's brother's wife, and brother's son must behave with respect to father's sister, but otherwise there is very little difference in a person's relations with paternal and maternal kin respectively. All this suggests that for a Lozi his field of kinship relations is made up of more or less equally weighted elements, atoms of interindividual relationship, so to speak, which he can utilize in any combination that serves a particular purpose.

Any cognatic link—but not affinal ties—entitles a person to apply to the head of a mound village for an allocation of land and the rights of residence. This is what facilitates residential mobility. But kinship confers no right to land except by a way of residence. A man who moves loses any rights held in the village he leaves, regardless of his kinship connections in it. Entry into possession of the land and property of deceased kin is subject to the same rule.

Village membership is thus a *sine qua non* for getting land and livelihood. It is indispensable for full civic status. If a person cannot find a place in a village by virtue of kinship (affinal relationship does not count), he has a right to solicit a place and land in one of the royal or councillors' villages, many of which were originally settled by serfs and dependents of the king siezed or captured from neighboring tribes.

Considered from within, then, a mound village is at a given time normally occupied by a group of cognatically related kin and their spouses. Even the royal and councillors' villages, the inhabitants of which are bound together primarily by common allegiance to their master, in time assume this form. Now a village itself is permanent, but its inhabitants frequently change. Nor is their field of kinship and affinal relations limited by the village. People have ties of kinship, marriage, and also friendship in villages all over the country, especially those nearby. They assist one another in economic activities, support one another in the crises of illness and death, and of course shift residence on the strength of these ties. Intravillage kinship ties are therefore not exclusive. Considered from the outside, in its external relations, the village, says Gluckman, "is the basic unit, below the state, of the political structure as it exists territorially" (1951: 69). In this context it is, he avers, a corporate unit, and its identity as such is focused in the village headman. In commoner villages, the headman is normally related by kinship to all the inhabitants. Characteristically, there is no fixed rule of succession to this office. When a headman dies, "Men and women in all branches of the kindred meet to select an heir on the basis of his character" (Gluckman, 1950: 172). A son—any son—is preferred, but failing a suitable son, any kinsman of his own or a later generation, whether linked to him through male or female connections or by a mixed pedigree is eligible. But once selected, the headman must be ceremonially confirmed by the king and his council who have the right to dismiss him if he fails in duty and responsibility (Gluckman, 1955: 190–91). Thus his office straddles and interlocks the two domains of the state and of the local kin-community.

From the villagers' point of view, he is both a kinsman and representative of the state. Their relationship to him is, on one side, one of political allegiance to him and through him, and, on the other, one of kinship amity—reflected in what Gluckman designates as the "ethical code" of the "upright man" (1955: 197). Conflicts of loyalties are not unusual and expose him to charges of sorcery. As headman he controls the allocation of village land and other resources and presides over the internal affairs of the village. In external relations he is the leader and spokesman for the whole village. He escorts and speaks for litigants from his village when they bring or respond to suits at law. In all these ways the headman stands for the village as an enduring, corporate, politico-jural entity equivalent in status to all other villages in the land. This is demonstrated in land disputes, in sacrifices at the royal graves, and in public works, when each village acts as a unit in contradistinction to all others (Gluckman, 1951: 69).

But it is a corporate unit in the external politico-jural domain, not internally. In the internal life of the village, its members prosecute their personal and family interests in their own, several directions. It is not their mutual kinship bonds which also stretch far outside the village that make them a corporate group, but their politico-jural enclosure within the bounds of the village. Yet it is not territorial distinctness and permanence which establishes the village as a corporate unit, but as Gluckman's discussion makes plain (in both 1951 and 1955, *passim*), the political status accorded to it in the overall political system.

Like the Iban *bilek* system with which it can reasonably be compared, the Lozi village system does not lay down absolute structural boundaries within the total society. It is to be thought of rather as a system of fixed mooring points in the everchanging flow of cognatic relationships—"knots," in Gluckman's phrase, "which shape the network of kinship ties" (1951: 76).

To be sure, such knots provide a measure of stability for social relations in the familial domain. For the society at large the effective partitions are those laid down in the political organization, notably the sector system, but in this framework, too there is no constancy of association.

Just how fluid this cognatic system is at the kinship level, even in comparison with that of the Iban, is shown by the treatment of the dead, who are buried in common cemeteries. "At a funeral," Gluckman reports, "all kinsmen and neighbors and friends attend, and any men among them can act as gravediggers and under-takers—son or father, brother or nephew, grandchild or grandparent, brother-in-law or son-in-law or friend" (1951: 76). It is not surprising to learn that "ancestors have no fixed homes" and receive offerings of beer and meat indiscriminately from men and women. Naturally, also, male and female ancestors by any and every line of connection are equally and indiscriminately referred to in misfortune, for none has more mystical authority than any other. Such a confounding of kinship categories on vital religious occasions would horrify a Tallensi or an Ashanti.

IV

The Lozi provide a striking example of a social system ostensibly founded on kinship but in which the politico-jural domain is elaborately constituted and is the source of critical determinants of social structure. The two domains are precisely differentiated in relation to each other in their institutional make up as well as in their normative order. The principles on which they work are quite distinct, yet they are consistently interarticulated in a unitary structure by the village system. This is facilitated by the permeation of the entire social life by the ideology and the controls of the political system. These are focused in the kingship. Reverence for the kingship and for the authority consequently vested in royalty is the dominant value of Lozi society. It is, Gluckman reports, "implicit in every Lozi relationship . . . the parent is lord over his child and owns him; the husband over the wife," and conversely the king is spoken of as the parent of his subjects.

Gluckman considers the cognatic kinship system of the Lozi to be particularly well adapted to the transhumant way of life imposed on them by the ecology of their homeland and its diversified economy. One could also argue that it is eminently adapted to such a centralized, unitary state, and point in support to the absence of unilineal descent groups which might consolidate loyalties at the kinship level opposed to those of personal citizenship under the king and his deputies. It is, however, a line of reasoning dangerously close to circularity. Let it suffice to recognize the consistencies in the relations of all these components of the social system with one another.

It is nonetheless significant that succession to the kingship is described as strictly agnatic, by contrast with succession to all positions of authority lower in the scale of rank. Ideally a king should be a son of a king born "in the purple," but in fact any male descendent, through males, of a king may be chosen. The cognatic dimension, however, is influential in that all kinsfolk of royalty, including those born of marriages with commoners, share in the prestige of high rank. The rule of restricted succession to the kingship is the polar opposite of the rule of unspecified succession among commoners. This underlines the antithesis between the perpetuity and immutability of the kingship and the transiency characteristic of the tenure of status and of authority grounded in the kinship domain. We have seen how this ensues from its atomistic, bilaterally limitless constitution, as seen from the outside. The kinship terminology and such rules as the prohibition of marriage with genealogical cousins, because they are siblings by classificatory kinship, indicate that one factor is the extension of the principle of sibling equivalence outside the domestic group. By contrast, this principle appears to have a more restricted range among the Iban, hence their cousin terminology and preference for cousin marriage. But in both cases the cognatic network is associated with the dispersion of siblings, socially no less than physically.

Equivalence does not give the sibling group any unity. The kinship terminology and the institution of "descent names" imply that a concept of descent does enter into the regulation of social relations within the cognatic scheme of the Lozi. Gluckman frequently refers to "descent," but I follow him in this with reservations as we do not yet have enough descriptive and numerical evidence to consider the question rigorously. On the available information, genealogical cousins being classified with siblings and thus brought into the ambit of the incest ban by the criterion of common grandparental or great-grandparental ancestry, implies the reckoning of "descent." But it is, in fact, a reckoning of pedigrees by serial filiation through either parent to any antecedent. In the Iban system, it is not essential for ego to know that A. N. Other and he are grandchildren of common grandparents but not children of the same parents for ego to classify him as a cousin. It is enough if ego knows that one of his parents and one of A. N. Other's are siblings. In the Lozi system, ego must be able to distinguish his parents' co-filial (that is actual or lineal) siblings, from their collateral (classificatory) siblings in order to be in a position to determine whether a given opposite sex collateral sibling of his own is genealogically far enough for him to take a chance on marrying her. Reckoning by filiation to his parents is not enough for this.

In the case records expounded with such vivid effect in Gluckman's *Judicial Process among the Barotse* (1955), there is frequent allusion to siblings as "children of one womb."[6] In Ashanti usage, this expression would be just as likely to refer to a distant matrilateral ancestress as to the mother. With the Lozi, one cannot be certain. There is no case record in this book which is concerned with kinship connections going back beyond a grandparent, and no issue in which a link through a grandparent exclusively is critical. I conclude that the expression "children of one womb" signifies the understanding among the Lozi that common matrifiliation is the root of siblingship. It is not a statement about descent.

In short, insofar as descent is recognized at all among the Lozi, it would appear to be confined to the royal family. To be sure, among commoners the incest rule and kinship terminology imply that children succeed to their parents' siblingship, but

6. Compare, e.g., 1955: 40, where children of one womb are supposed not to take their disputes to court but to settle them among themselves.

frequency of marriage between collateral "siblings" shows how weak this link of succession is felt to be. It is swamped by a force of equilateral cognatic relationships which is, in this case, enhanced by the fragility of marriage. Bilateral filiation rather than descent is the guiding principle followed by ego in the registration of his field of kinship.

We have seen that the social system of the Lozi exhibits with special clarity the differentiation of the familial domain from the politico-jural domain. This emerges in its topographical arrangements, in its institutional forms, and, consistently also in its value system. It is, as we might expect, very explicitly represented in their legal procedures and ideas. I adverted to them in passing, in Chapter V, but some discussion of their relevance to the present context is here in order. (All cases referred to are from Gluckman, 1955.)

Most suits brought to the courts arise between kinsfolk, and then the fact that everybody is both a kinsman in one domain and a citizen in the other often becomes manifest. Many cases turn upon the conflict between political and kinship obligations (p. 197). For instance, the rule that residence in a village is a prerequisite for anyone who wants to cultivate in it is a political rule, and judges will enforce it if claims based solely on kinship are preferred. Judges have to determine "in what rôles the litigants are disputing"—whether as headmen with a village member, or parent with a child, and so on (p. 296). They have to distinguish kinship rules from those of village membership and from citizenship in the state.

The existence of constituted judicial agencies, by contrast with the Australian and Iban systems, means that authoritative decisions are taken separating norms of social relationship that are adjudicable and are enforcible by sanctions emanating from the politico-jural domain from norms that are purely ethical and moral. Lozi judges discriminate between "obligations [they] can compel people to observe, and [those they] can only urge . . . as right" (p. 173). Thus in one case (p. 172) a guilty husband is ordered to give his divorced wife half the crops she planted with him. This is her legal right. The husband is, however, also exhorted to act "like an upright man" and allow her to take some of the clothes and household equipment she acquired during her marriage. The order could be enforced, the plea not. The order concerns a right that pertains to a woman's status as lawful wife. It is a status validated in the extradomestic, politico-jural domain—hence adultery with a married woman is an actionable wrong against her husband. The plea concerns the intradomestic, interpersonal relationships of husband and wife governed by notions of decency, morality, and affection. How these are implemented depends on the individual's character and conscience, not on the law. The distinction is accentuated if we compare the obverse relationship of brother and sister and find that a man may not touch or be alone in a hut with his sister. This is a sin, not a breach of law; it exposes the culprit to charges of sorcery, not to a legal suit.

V

Let me try briefly to recapitulate the conclusions that emerge from this examination of cognatic forms of kinship structure in its politico-jural context. A key feature is that there is no differentiation between the status attributes and capacities that accrue to a person by reason of being his father's child and those for which filiation to and through his mother is the necessary credential. Filiation is equilaterally valid for status in all domains of social life. This differs from the bilateral Australian pattern, where patrifiliation and matrifiliation establish complementary status capacities. "Descent," in the commonsense interpretation of taking cognizance of personal pedigrees reckoned by steps of filiation to forbears antecedent to parents, is recognized though not beyond the range of normal memory, that is, to ascendants who could have been personally known to ego's parents, often to ego alone. But this recognition of "descent" does not align persons whose pedigrees converge in common ancestors into permanent and exclusive units of social structure, nor does it confer significant status capacities on the individual, or impose limitations (as, e.g., in the choice of spouse or of place of residence) on him.

Internal structural divisions in the framework of a cognatic system are ordered to non-kinship institutions. This principle is most explicitly observable in a society like the Lozi where the politico-jural domain is clearly marked off from the familial domain to such an extent that there is even a measure of opposition between them. But though filiation is primarily a kinship datum, it is also the irreducible and incontestable credential for membership in the territorially anchored politico-jural unit of the village, and through that for full status as a citizen. Though, topographically speaking, the internal composition of a village is based on the cognatic connections of its members, it is not this, but rather the villagers' place in the external scheme of politico-jural relations that gives it a discrete and unitary structure. The kinship factor in village organization is incidental, as we can see by comparing the commoner with the royal villages, which are externally like kinship villages but are internally made up of non-related captives and servants of the king. It is due to the fact that kinship is irreducible as a determinant of status in all domains of social life. It is an indefeasible credential for normal village membership and therefore for citizenship. And what this signifies can be seen from comparing it with the only other source of citizenship, that is a direct and initially quasi-servile subjection to the king. The entitlement to status in the politico-jural domain which comes from kinship is unique. Economic or residential or ritual association cannot, without being assimilated to kinship, confer this form of entitlement. This is well exemplified among the Iban, since adoption (and not mere co-residence), that is, the jurally licit fabrication of a filiative status for a non-kinsman, is necessary in order to provide a *bilek* family with a successor to the headship. It is in this sense that statuses and relations which fall descriptively under kinship and affinity signify statuses in both the familial domain and the politico-jural domain.

Though descent receives such limited recognition in these systems, forms of what our authorities assert to be corporate organization occur in them and raise the question of just what constitutes corporateness. In the Walbiri "patriline," it appears to consist essentially in the spiritual identity shared by successive generations of patrifilial kin; among the Iban, it is related to ideally perpetual succession to the headship of the *bilek*; among the Lozi, it is an aspect of the politico-jural autonomy of the village. The mode of recruitment to the corporate group is not critical, for the same filiative relationships, whether of first degree or by serial reckoning, that entitle members of a village to reside in it and hold land there, not only enable them also to leave it but link them with kin in other corporate villages. Again, filiation, siblingship, and marriage serve equally to recruit or retain *bilek* members, and as entitlement for them to opt out. The Iban long-house and the non-member status of affines in a Lozi village are evidence that mere co-residence does not establish corporate association.

As to the significance of property, the partibility of the *bilek* estate and the ownership of farm land by the household group, not by the village collectively, among the Lozi create the suspicion that it is a dependent variable in corporate organization and not the decisive factor. To all of these problems I return later.

This brings up the question of inheritance and succession. Analytical rigor requires treating the politico-jural domain as external to the domain of cognatic kinship, but in the actuality of social structure they are tightly interlaced. The headship of the *bilek*, like that of the Lozi village, is attained by virtue of kinship status in principle unaffected by jural consideration; but both positions have also politico-jural sanction and carry jural authority and control over persons and over resources. Their perpetuation by jurally regulated succession suggests that they represent some form of corporate organization, if only as "corporations sole."

Inheritance and succession reveal very clearly the intrusion of jural regulation into the domain of family and kinship relations. Even more revealing is the element of contract to which I drew attention in Australian marriage transactions. It shows how subtly jural constraints may be built into kinship relations, and it suggests, incidentally, how deceptive Maine's celebrated dictum about the movement of of progressive societies from status to contract is. Contract in a very broad sense of binding jural obligation to fulfil an agreement is present in some social transactions in all socieites, notably of course in marriage. The differences lie in the means available for its enforcement, whether by self-assertion, as in Australia, or through judicial machinery as in the state-like polity of the Lozi.

CHAPTER IX

The Ashanti: State and Citizenship

I

WE HAVE ARRIVED AT THE POINT WHERE IT BECOMES RELEVANT TO EXAMINE A SOCIAL system in which the concept of descent is precisely worked out and systematically applied in all domains of the social structure. With the Lozi, membership of a village depends on kinship, but its boundaries as a corporate unit arise from the conjunction of its external territorial and its politico-jural relations. I now turn to examine a system in which we find discrete and exclusive corporate groups demarcated not by such extrinsic boundaries, but strictly by rules intrinsic to the domain of kinship and descent.

The Akan-speaking peoples of Ghana (formerly the Gold Coast) are specially apt for this enquiry, the more so for the contrasts between them and the Lozi and for the parallels they evoke with Morgan's Iroquois.

As is well known, the Akan occupy almost the whole of southern Ghana.[1] They have long attracted attention, first for their conspicuously matrilineal kinship institutions, which have—ever since Bosman (1705: letter XII) ironically drew the parallel in the eighteenth century—been as well known as those of the Nayar, and secondly for their political genius and military prowess. The coastal Akan, collect-

1. And adjacent parts of the Côte d'Ivoire where they are known as the *Agni*, cf. Tauxier, 1932.

ively known as the Fanti group,[2] and those of the immediate hinterland, comprised some thirty-odd, relatively small, independent political communities before the colonial period. But in the interior, originally within the confines of the tropical rain forest, there grew up in the eighteenth and early nineteenth centuries the famous Akan state of Ashanti.[3] It was a state created by a successful war of liberation (c. A.D. 1700) and expanded by wars of conquest waged with an elaborately organized national militia armed with European flintlocks. By the middle of the nineteenth century, Ashanti suzerainty extended widely over formly independent Akan tribes. It was brought to an end only by the British conquest in 1896.

The social systems of the Akan peoples are of a singularly uniform pattern. I shall concentrate on the Ashanti but the principles I shall discuss apply to all the Akan. To steer the analysis, let me note in advance certain closely interlinked institutional features that are characteristic of Akan society.

First comes the constitution of the state. Regardless of size, it is in every case centered on a chief (ohene) elected from a group of candidates eligible by right of membership in a designated matrilineal descent group in which the office is vested. He is supported by a sister chief (ohemaa) from the same descent group and is guided by a council of mainly hereditary councillors, commonly known as elders (opanin). Chief and council exercise powers of legislation, form an executive, and, above all, function as a judicial tribunal.

Secondly, there is the rule of matrilineal descent operative throughout the social structure, in all domains.

Thirdly, there is the concept of office, which is likewise manifested in all domains of social life. The material symbol of every office is a stool (akonnua), hence the office is generically referred to by the term "stool," much as we use "the crown" metonymously for the monarchy. On the death of its holder, a stool of office is consecrated by animal sacrifices and added to a depository of ancestral stools which collectively form the sanctuary of the ancestral cult and bind office holders to their predecessors.

Rattray's splendid corpus of ethnographical and historical researches (1916, 1923, 1927, 1929) assembled within twenty years of the final defeat and banishment of the king and the annexation of Ashanti by the British in 1901, supplemented by the earlier records of travellers, missionaries, officials, political emissaries,[4] local scholars, and later research,[5] enables us to form a consistent and detailed picture

2. See Christensen, 1954, for a convenient summary of the ethnography of the Fanti.

3. A succinct modern account of the rise of the Ashanti state which incorporates the reliable conclusions of W. W. Claridge's classical *History of the Gold Coast and Ashanti* (1916) is given in Ward, 1948: chap. VII. The present Asantehene, Nana Sir Osei Agyeman Prempeh II derives the name "Asante" from the phrase osa-nti-fo—lit., "war-because of-people," which, he says, was adopted by the previously separate tribes when they united to fight the war of liberation against their overlord the Kind of Denkyira (cf. Rattray, 1929: chaps. IX–X).

4. Listed and extensively drawn upon in Ward, 1948.

5. My own researches were carried out in connection with the Ashanti Social Survey 1945–46. Publications of the survey relevant to the present discussion are the following: Fortes, 1948, 1949a, 1950, 1953c, 1954, 1963. Imprtant additions to the Rattray corpus are: Busia, 1951; Meyerowitz, 1951, 1952; Wilks, 1964; Kurankyi-Taylor, 1951. An invaluable source is the famous *Dictionary of the Asante and Fante Language Called Tshi (Twi)* by Christaller, 2nd ed., 1933.

of Ashanti society at its apogee. Indeed, such are the national pride and the social vitality of the Ashanti people that their most cherished traditional values and institutions were still vigorously maintained in 1945 when I was privileged to work among them. There had been some noticeable shifts of values in response to the new political, cultural, and economic forces released by the imposition of British sovereignty, the advent of schools and literacy, and the rapid development of gold mining, cocoa farming, transport, trade and urbanization,[6] but among the great majority of the people the basic principles of their traditional familial and also political ideology and patterns of organization stood firm.

II

Before the annexation, the Ashanti state, with a population of around a quarter of a million, was a confederation of nine originally autonomous founding chiefdoms and a number of subsequently incorporated communities.[7] At the hub was the wealthy and powerful chiefdom of Kumasi, whose hereditary ruler was acknowledged as the Asantehene, that is, the Head of the Nation, or king. However, his primacy as the focus of national cohesion and as the fountainhead of national institutions and of national policy gave him no authority in the internal affairs of the other founder-chiefdoms. In this respect all the major chiefdoms were of equal status,[8] a circumstance which conduced to occasional attempts at secession that had to be crushed by force of arms. But the king was supreme in the majesty of his office and by virtue of the military superiority of the Kumasi chiefdom.[9] The Ashanti state was created and maintained by war, and a military ideology remained a central feature of its structure to the end. Guns and gold were its twin foundations. As imported firearms spread among the populace, the chiefdom which could muster the largest supplies of guns and ammunition had every chance, if ably led, to triumph in the intertribal wars. For this, wealth was the first requisite and Kumasi had it. The victories of the Kumasi chiefdom and its eventual domination of the confederation were due to its economic preeminence no less than to the political astuteness of the founder-hero, Osai Tutu.

Spoils of war, tribute of slaves and of material goods from subject tribes, dues and duties levied on citizens and the constituent chiefdoms, trade on a substantial scale in gold, kola nuts, and slaves both to the interior and to the coast in return for textiles, flintlock guns, gunpowder, European liquor, tools, and many other com-

6. Modern political and economic changes up to the end of the colonial period are reviewed in Apter, 1955; Bourret, 1949; and Kimble, 1963.

7. When the confederacy was restored in 1935, a total of 21 constituent chiefdoms was recognized. They were then designated as "Divisions."

8. The generic term for chiefdom, "*oman*," reflects this. The National Union was the *Asante-man*, other chiefdoms were, e.g., the Juaben-man, Bekwai-man, etc.

9. The king's majesty was symbolically demonstrated in the ceremony, still followed in the forties, in which he received the allegiance of a newly installed regional chief. After swearing allegiance to the nation and the king, the chief knelt in front of the king who placed his bare right foot on the chief's bare head and pronounced the formula accepting him into his office.

modities, brought wealth to the courts of the king and of the regional chiefs. The bulk of the population derived their livelihood from subsistence farming,[10] and from hunting and exploiting forest resources, but skilled weavers, wood carvers, goldsmiths, and masons, drummers, musicians, and courtiers, testified to considerable occupational specialization and catered for the luxury and ostentation of the king's and the major chiefs' courts which nineteenth-century travelers were so much struck by. The foundation of this wealth, and of the political and military power it supported and displayed, was, of course, not the subsistence economy but the gold won in part from the soil, in part from tribute, and the kola nut for which the forest zone was famous.[11]

Though they lacked the art of writing,[12] the Ashanti achieved a sophisticated level of statecraft.[13] They had a complex machinery of government and administration based on the king's capital and linked to a nationwide system of judicial institutions that culminated in the sovereign authority of the king. A hierarchy of palace officials whose appointment was firmly controlled by the king conducted the fiscal affairs and the foreign commerce of the Kumasi chiefdom and thus, indirectly, of the nation, and supervised the intricate organization of the court and capital. Other high-ranking offices were connected with the military organization of the state, the maintenance of communication with the regional chiefdoms, and the implementation of the king's authority and prerogatives throughout the realm. These offices of the king's chiefdom, augmented when major issues of policy and war came up by the chiefs and councillors of the associated chiefdoms to form a national assembly, constituted the advisory and judicial councils without whose concurrence the king could not legitimately act in national affairs.

To diversification by rank, wealth, occupation, and locality was added the very important differentiation of status between the freeborn citizens and the subjects who were themselves, or were descended from, war captives, refugees, and others of slave or alien status. So powerful, however, was the ideology of common civic status

10. To judge by the descriptions of nineteenth-century travelers, Ashanti subsistence farming was of a high standard at that time. Bowdich remarks that: "The extent and order of the Ashantee plantations surprised us." But he adds cryptically, "yet I do not think they were adequate to the population", blaming this on their "military government" (Bowdich, 1819: 325). In the climatic conditions of the rain forest, ample and fertile land permitted of a form of shifting cultivation which yielded good crops of yams and guinea corn, as well as a variety of fruits and vegetables. Palm wine and oil, obtained from forest trees, seems to have been plentiful, and game and freshwater fish seem to have been regularly available.

11. Gold was, of course, found in other parts of the southern half of what later became the Gold Coast Colony as well as in Ashanti. A full study of the pre-colonial technology and economics of the gold industry in Southern Ghana has yet to be made. In Ashanti, a portion of all gold won had to be surrendered to the chief and the king. This was a major source of the finance used for the importation of firearms, ammunition and other European products (cf. Claridge, 1915: vol. I, pp. 160–62). The kola nut was traded north to the savannah zone where it was in great demand for chewing as a stimulant, and was exchanged for cloth, slaves, cattle, horses, etc. This trade was to a large extent under the control of the big chiefs and the king (cf. Rattray, 1929: 109–12).

12. Professor Wilks (1966) has recently found additional evidence that the kings made regular use of the services of immigrant Moslem scribes in their diplomatic exchanges with foreign powers.

13. As the nineteenth-century British emissaries to the Ashanti court found. (Cf. references in Ward, 1948.) This is vividly brought out in Bowdich's narrative.

that the incorporation of these alien elements into the descent groups of the freeborn was regarded as a binding moral as well as legal duty.[14]

Though the king was by status only the supreme chief among a group of brother chiefs, a number of whom were in fact linked to him by clanship,[15] his authority far outstripped theirs. This was implemented through his supremacy in military, judicial, and fiscal affairs. But his office also had an aura of mystical preeminence—of the majesty of supreme authority—because it was intrinsically bound up with the sacred Golden Stool. Believed to have been miraculously conjured down from heaven by the Priest Anotche, mentor of Osai Tutu the founder of the nation, the Golden Stool was and is revered by the whole people as the shrine of the "soul of the nation".[16] Personified in cult and belief (see below, p. 156), it symbolized the unity and identity of the nation as a sacred trust from its founders. It is not only the palladium of the nation; it is also the palladium of politico-jural office, the Stool of Stools, so to speak. Attributes of sacredness—of what I have called majesty—superior to those accompanying chiefship in general thus pertained to the kingship by virtue of this association, though the king was not a "divine king" in the accepted sense.

As to his secular powers, great though they were, a strict check on them was provided by a number of constitutional stipulations, disregard of which could lead to his deposition. Foremost among them was his obligation never to act without the concurrence of his elders and councillors. He was likewise not above the law.[17] He had meticulously to observe the religious prescriptions pertaining to his office and to conform to the legal and moral norms applicable to all.[18] When a new king was installed he swore loyalty to the associated chiefs and to his councillors as representing the nation, and promised obedience to the laws and customs by invoking the

14. The often quoted legal maxim that no person may reveal another's origins (cf. Fortes, 1950: 255) epitomizes this. This has the incidental effect of making public genealogical inquiries awkward and embarrassing to informants.

15. In addition to the Asantehene who is recognized as its highest dignitary, the chiefs of Juaben, Bekwai, Kokofu, Nsuta, and Juaso belong to the Oyoko clan. Other groups of chiefships are similarly linked by common clanship in one of the remaining clans.

16. The story of the concealment, desecration, and reconsecration of the Golden Stool, was made widely known by Edwin Smith's book, *The Golden Stool* (1926). Its origin and symbolic significance are described in Rattray, 1923: chap. XXIII. The Golden Stool (*Sika 'Gua*), personified by the addition of the day-name *Kofi* (Friday), had its own attendants and regalia, as if it were a king in its own right. In the *Odwira* and other state ceremonies it took precedence of the king himself (cf. Rattray, 1927: chap. XII). Anotche is said to have told Osai Tutu and the assembled people that "this stool contained the *sunsum* (soul or spirit) of the Ashanti nation, and that their power, their health, their bravery, their welfare were in this stool" (Rattray, 1923: 289). If it were captured or destroyed, the nation would sicken and fall to pieces. This explains the wave of horror and outrage which swept through the whole of Ashanti in September, 1921, when the desecration of the stool by some of their own people became known. (Rattray's spelling of Anotche and Osai are followed for ease of reference.)

17. Kurankyi-Taylor, 1951: 124–25, quotes the maxim "*Asem a esen Ohene wo ho*"—"There is something which is greater than the king"—in this connection. Three Ashanti kings and one queen mother are known to have been arraigned before the national assembly sitting as a court of law, and chiefs of all grades have been brought to trial before it and fined for offenses ranging from suspected treason and cowardice in war to actions disrespectful of the King (*ibid.*).

18. Thus one of the most heinous offences for which a king (like any chief) could be deposed was to "reveal the origins" of any of his subjects. Ci. n. 14 above.

same Great Oath in terms of which they swore allegiance to the nation and the kingship when they were elected. Like any newly installed chief (but at a much higher rate), the king had to make an *aseda* (see below, f.n. 22) payment for distribution among the chiefs which made his oath contractually as well as ritually binding. Last but not least, was the watchful eye kept on his activities by his co-adjutant, the queen mother, normally his lineage sister, who had the right to reprimand him if he offended against accepted rules of good conduct.

Yet exalted though it was, the kingship, together with the hierarchy of offices supporting it and the complex constitutional organization radiating from the capital, was only a magnified version of chiefship in all the other chiefdoms. The constitutional and ritual rules that governed his office held for theirs, too. Indeed the same pattern modified to scale prevailed right down to the village level. The principle of self-government in internal affairs held for the local communities which made up a major chiefdom[19] no less than for the whole chiefdom. The national military system, for example, had its counterpart in each chiefdom, and every chief, sitting with councillors, constituted a judicial tribunal.

The king's sovereignty was shown in certain constitutional formalities and reserved powers. Thus the king alone, with the concurrence of his council and the other chiefs, could organize war against external enemies or a rebellious subject, and to this end levy taxes on the whole nation. His tribunal was the final court of appeal to which all citizens had the right of transferring a suit by swearing the Great Oath or by seeking the sanctuary of the Golden Stool. And, most important of all, the ultimate power of life and death over all citizens lay formally with him. By law, he alone had the right of capital punishment (and its commutation for payment in gold dust or kind) for murder, treason, and certain other public delicts or acts of sacrilege, though in practice he could and did delegate to the major chiefs the power to act in some capital cases.

III

The existence of these prerogatives of the king emphasized the cardinal fact that citizenship of the nation was a recognized status, though it was derived, as we shall see, from primary citizenship of the chiefdom. In recognition of the king's status, every major chief, on election to his stool and after his installation in his own chiefdom, was obliged to attend on the king in Kumasi and there swear homage to him and the nation. To refuse this was a declaration of revolt, for the essence of the oath of homage was a promise to obey the king's call by night or by day to defend the nation. Similarly, minor chiefs on installment swore homage to their immediately superior chiefs and through them to the king (see Busia, 1951; Rattray, 1929: 102).

On the face of it, every chiefdom (*oman*) was a distinct territorial unit centered on the chief's capital village or town. In fact, it was thought of as an aggregate of people distributed in local communities and forming a political unit by reason of their common allegiance to or, as Ashanti put it, service of the chief. Boundaries

19. Or Division, in the terminology introduced with the restoration of the confederacy.

between the territories of adjacent chiefdoms were so inexact that litigation to determine them grew to epidemic proportions and absorbed huge sums of money in the colonial period, when mining rights, timber, and land for cocoa acquired large commercial value.[20] Furthermore, whereas in every chiefdom, some groups of peoples serve the chiefship—in Ashanti parlance, the chiefly stool—directly, the majority did so indirectly through one or other of his elders and councillors and the two kinds of villages or parts of villages were often haphazardly intermingled. Indeed, as a result of internal migration, of families fleeing during civil wars and of grants by the king of conquered villages to his captains and court dignitaries, people serving different chiefdoms lived side by side in some areas and villages.[21] Virilocal marriages between citizens of different chiefdoms, though not favored, contributed to disperse primary allegiances, too. This emphasizes the important consideration that primary allegiance is a relationship of political dependence on a chiefly stool—the complement of office, not an incident of territorial association. In a civil war (as in modern land litigation) neighbors might thus find themselves on opposite sides.

Nevertheless, though it had no fixed boundaries, an Ashanti chiefdom did have a definite territorial foundation. This was conceptualized in terms of jurisdiction over areas of habitation and surrounding tracts of forest and farm land vested in the chiefship from time immemorial by virtue of ancestral occupation and referred to as the "stool land." The right freely to take up a site for a house and virgin stool land for settlement and farming, and to transmit rights over land thus won to heirs and successors and, in the case of forests and rivers, the right freely to hunt, fish, and harvest their products (subject only to certain tithes owed to the stool), was a fundamental and exclusive attribute of primary citizenship of a chiefdom. A citizen had to get the chief's consent to take up unoccupied or abandoned land for farming and his usufruct was limited to the arable surface. The soil beneath remained inalienably and perpetually vested in the stool, which therefore retained all rights in minerals (e.g., gold) and in the deeply rooted timber trees. Non-citizens of the state

20. There is a formidable literature, both official and scholarly on the general subject of land tenure in the colonial period of Ghana's history and litigation over boundaries is examined at length from the legal, administrative, historical, and economic points of view in these publications. References and a review of the major issues can be found in Lord Hailey's *An African Survey* (1938, 1956 ed.: 737–39, 792–93), and his *Native Administration in the British African Territories*, 1951: pt. III. The traditional system of land tenure and its connection with citizenship is expertly clarified by Busia, 1951: chap. III, who also makes some trenchant observations on modern land litigation (pp. 205–209). I am also drawing on Dr. A. A. Y. Kyerematen's unpublished thesis, *Inter-State Boundary Litigation in Ashanti*, 1950, which is based on first-hand data obtained in the course of the Ashanti Social Survey. Among others, he describes a succession of boundary disputes between some minor chiefdoms which went on for thirty odd years, reached the Privy Council and cost one of the parties well over £30,000.

21. There were, in particular, many so-called "islands" of Kumasi subjects—that is, people owing allegiance to councillors and captains of the Kumasi chiefdom—in communities and among villages serving other chiefdoms. Some of these were the result of deliberate policy aimed at strengthening central control of the nation. Attempts to secede were made from time to time by one or other of the divisional chiefdoms and when these were crushed by the national militia the king would confiscate some of the rebel villages and give them into the custody of his Kumasi captains. After the wars of conquest Kumasi colonies were thus established in outlying areas of, at that period, uninhabited forest.

were obliged to pay annual dues for the use of farm land. An initial *asseda*[22] payment, when the land was allocated to them, was followed by an annual rental. But
what is particularly significant is that Ashanti subjects of other chiefdoms were
defined as non-citizens in this connection. Moreover, neither they themselves nor
their successors could ever become full citizens of the chiefdom merely by virtue of
long residence upon and the economic exploitation of its lands.

It is consistent with the structure of the nation state that the king had no authority
over the land and the soil of other chiefdoms than his own.[23] It is accepted, not only
as a point of constitutional principle but in deference to sentiment and to the idea of
historical right that a chiefly stool, its lands and its citizens form an inseparable and
perpetual unity. Thus when the Juaben rebellion of 1875 was suppressed, the then
Asantehene, to show his sense of justice restored the chiefship and its lands to the
lineage in which they were originally vested (Busia, 1951: 53). Likewise, the king had
no direct authority over the subjects of any of the major chiefdoms or even over the
subjects of any of his own palace officials, captains, or councillors. This principle
applied at all levels of the social structure, as Rattray brilliantly explained (1929:
chap. XXXVIII). As with every chief, his commands to and demands upon any of a
stool's subjects had to be transmitted through the appropriate hierarchy of chiefs,
councillors, headmen, and lineage elders in proper sequence, and a citizen's relations with his politico-jural superiors were mediated through the same series of steps.
Looked at from the outside, as Rattray commented, the system as a whole could be
seen as a series of concentric circles of authority and privilege. Conversely, considered from the point of view of the individual, citizenship was composed of a
series of layers, as it were, of rights and duties.

IV

What then were, formerly (and are still), the defining criteria of primary citizenship? In the paradigmatic case of the freeborn citizen, all our authorities agree and

22. Rattray gives an authoritative definition of this prestation (1929: s.v. *aseda* in the index).
Aseda (which is always paid by the beneficiary), he says, is a thank-offering intended "to
serve as a record for all concerned that such a gift or benefit has been conferred and accepted"
(p. 24). The "*tiri nsa*" paid in marriage is an *aseda*. In the 1920's many citizens of the Kumasi
division took up land for cocoa-farming in the Ahafo area to the northwest. As non-citizens of
these chiefdoms, they first paid an *aseda* of (as a rule) £2. 7. 0 (the traditional *osuaæ ne domma*)
to the local headman when he allocated land to them, and then paid annual dues varying with
the size of the crop and its market price. Farms established on these terms could be transmitted
to heirs and successors, but rental payments continued to be required of them as many cases
brought to my notice in 1945 confirmed. The constitutional principle here at issue was
reaffirmed by the Confederacy Council in 1935. *Aseda* is often compared to putting a stamp
or seal on a legal document. This points to its basic jural significance as an instrument which
makes a transaction binding in a contractual sense. Breach of an agreement entered into with
aseda is actionable in law. As mentioned, it is the *aseda* payment made by the incumbent of
high office at the time of his installation that confirms his accountability to his elders and
superiors for any dereliction of his duties and responsibilities.

23. Cf. Busia, 1951: 52, where a recent statement to this effect of the present Asantehene
is quoted.

my own researches in 1945 confirm[24] that the decisive criterion is membership, by right of birth, of one's mother's matrilineal lineage, it being understood that she is Ashanti by birth.[25] But this credential is not enough. As in the past, so now, a person is a primary citizen of the chiefdom whose stool his matrilineal lineage, in Asahnti parlance, "serves" (*som*) that is, owes allegiance to. This has the implication that he is a primary citizen of the chiefdom, in its territorial dimension, in which his lineage has legal domicile. But this is incidental. The domiciliary rights of a citizen follow from his lineage membership; they are not and were not in the past gained by the fact of residence in a village or even in the capital of a chiefdom, as our discussion of farming rights has shown. A man's wife and children, who are primary citizens by matrilineal descent of another chiefdom, do not become subjects (that is citizens) of his natal chiefdom merely by virtue of residing and farming or working with him in his lineage home. Such "strangers" as they are held to be, of course retain their citizenship in the nation wherever they might be living. They could, for instance, formerly,[26] if *sui iuris*,[27] invoke the Great Oath to transfer a suit in which they were a party to the king's court and they were, correspondingly, liable to suits for tort (e.g., for debt) and to prosecution for delicts (e.g., assault, adultery, etc.), or sacrilege (e.g., incest) at the local chief's court. But they had none of the rights and capacities of primary citizenship in the chiefdom and none of the duties that went with it, all of which were exercised through lineage membership.

Permanent settlement in the founding chiefdoms goes back at least to the establishment of the national union about the middle of the seventeenth century (for details see Ward, 1948). But this does not mean that all the lineages of citizens in these areas have been fixed in domicile since then.

I have adverted to this already, but some amplification is relevant here. On the one hand, lineages of outside origin accrued to a community and in due course acquired citizenship in it; and, on the other, branches of a lineage sprang up in other chiefdoms. In the past, this was often brought about by the flight, or the capture and enslavement, of families and individuals in war, by pawning persons away from their homes, by virilocal marriage of women to citizens of other chiefdoms—though most often of nearby villages—by migration of individuals and families in search of land or of opportunities for trade or the practice of a craft, or, not infrequently, to withdraw from political opponents after a destoolment case. I am speaking here of lineages of freeborn (*odehye*) Ashanti origin. Matrilineal descendants of women who were not primary citizens of the community acquired citizenship by becoming

24. Cf. Fortes, 1950, where references to Rattray *et al.* are listed. "The lineage principle" declares Kyerematen (1950: 28), drawing on his wide personal knowledge of Ashanti political and social institutions, "underlies citizenship. . . ."

25. In Ashanti law, an Ashanti (national) is a person whose mother is Ashanti. This principle was reaffirmed by the Confederacy Council in 1935. This definition, of course, covers not only free-born Ashanti but any person whose mother is Ashanti by adoption or incorporation in a lineage.

26. Until the dissolution of the Confederacy after the establishment of the independent state of Ghana in 1957.

27. A man became *sui iuris* in relation to the state organization when he was mature enough to bear arms, a woman when she had undergone the nubility ceremony and was therefore jurally marriageable (see below, p. 208).

attached to the local lineages of their clans and being permitted to assume the obligations of citizenship. Residence thus facilitated, but did not by itself confer citizenship;
and such attached lineages, though fully assimilated to the host lineage for all extra-
lineage economic, jural, and ceremonial relations of citizenship were not, as we shall
see, indistinguishably incorporated for the internal affairs of the host lineage. Matrilineal descendants of foreign slave-women—who, by Ashanti law, had an adoptive,
quasi-filial status in their owner's family—were defined as quasi-members, titular
matrilineal descendants, one might say, of their ancestress's owner's or husband's
lineage, and therefore citizens by adoption.

However, it is a fundamental principle of Ashanti law that lineage membership is
an inextinguishable jural capacity and the basic credential for citizenship. Religious
values and metaphysical beliefs emphasize this principle and sentiment echoes it.
Mere residential dispersal never deprives the members of a lineage of their status in
it. Many people fled from Juaben in Ashanti to the neighboring Akan State of Akim-
Abuakwa after the abortive war of secession staged by Juaben. Their descendants
never relinquished or were deprived of their lineage status and their citizenship
rights in their ancestral Ashanti communities. In 1945 they participated regularly in
the festivals, the funeral ceremonies, marriages, and politics of their ancestral
lineages and towns. They were eligible for and were elected to office in their
ancestral lineages and towns.[28] Lineage elders, both female and male residing in the
refugee settlements were, when they died, carried back to the ancestral home to be
buried in the lineage cemetery. And they discharged such corresponding obligations
as paying their shares of lineage debts and contributing the amounts due from
citizens to stool levies for public works or for defraying stool debts.

People thus circumstanced had, in theory, a choice of citizenship. Many did (in
fact) fulfill some citizen obligations in both communities,[29] for example by contributing to levies made for public works. But their right to resume full citizenship
in the chiefdom to which their lineage originally belonged was never extinguished.

This held in a modified form even for matrilineal descendants of a freeborn
woman sold into slavery. There are many cases of the ancestral lineages and chiefdoms of such people raising money to ransom them so that even if they did not all
wish to return to their ancestral homes at once, they would be free to do so at any
later time.[30] It should be borne in mind that, given the restrictions arising from the

28. The most influential senior councillor of the chiefdom of E—— was a case in point.
He had, as he put it, been summoned to take his ancestor's gun and succeed to the lineage
stool and he had felt it to be his solemn duty to his ancestors to acquiesce even though it
meant giving up a lucrative employment and leaving his comfortable home. Cf. Fortes, 1963,
for another case.

29. After the restoration of the Confederacy in 1935, a Committee of Privileges was set up
to determine the correct ranking and relationship of allegiance between the chiefs and headmen and lineage groups of Ashanti. Many cases occurred in which there was a clash of claims
to the allegiance of some groups of people based, on the one side, on the fact of their descent
from assimilated incomers who had accepted citizenship obligations in one chiefdom, and,
on the other, on their ancestral origins in another.

30. As the lineage is perpetual, the uterine descendants of a free woman who has been
enslaved remain perpetually redeemable. When peace was restored after the Juaben rebellion,
emissaries were sent to seek out the members of Juaben lineages who had been captured and
sold into slavery and persuade them to agree to being ransomed and brought back.

rules of primary citizenship, every freeborn Ashanti was free to live and gain his living in any chiefdom of the Confederacy. He had only to be acceptable to the head and council of the chiefdom in which he thus sought domicile. Liberty of movement to this extent was guaranteed by citizenship in the Confederacy—that is, as Ashanti would put it, in relation to the kingship.

V

Turning next to the attributes of primary citizenship, we have seen that it entitled a person—man or woman—freely to occupy and farm virgin land in his or her chiefdom of origin. Every citizen who was *sui iuris* had this right. Once cultivated, land was drawn into the pool of property subject to the rules governing the internal structure of lineage and kinship relations. A person's claim to use any part of it would then be an incident of his status within his lineage or be based upon inheritance, or gift. Much land in the older settlements was corporate lineage property, originally allocated to the founder of the lineage or later accrued to it by the normal process of matrilineal devolution of property. Use of parts of such land was, however, purely a matter of intra-lineage status, not of the citizenship mediated by this status, as the practice with regard to land held by "stranger" lineages implies. In the thirties and forties, leaders of a political faction worsted in an attempt to bring about the destoolment of a chief were often temporarily banished. They were never, however, deprived of their rights to their lineage land.

Primary citizenship entitled a person who was qualified by appropriate status in his or her lineage, to hold political office as a councillor or elder of the chiefly stool. The "young men"—that is, commoners of office holding lineages—had the right to participate in public discussion and decisions of political issues. This gave them an indirect but powerful influence on councillors and chiefs as a semi-formal "third estate."[31] Sojourners had none of these political rights and privileges, though they had of course, the same standing in law as citizens. They could for instance, sue citizens if they were wronged, arraigning them before the chief and councillors by swearing the chief's oath on them.

Citizens also had the freedom to exploit forest and river resources by hunting and fishing, as we have seen. Ashanti like quoting the example of snail gathering. Edible snails were and are much sought after as an alternative to meat and fish food. Citizens were free to collect snails in the forest areas of their chiefdom, subject only to

31. That the commoner-citizens, under the leadership of an informally elected leader played a big part in political affairs before the colonial period is now well attested (cf. Busia, 1951: chap. 1). Later, they often took the initiative in pressing for reforms of traditional government and for progressive policies towards new cultural and economic opportunities. They thus frequently found themselves opposed to their more cautious chiefs and elders, to the point of fomenting movements to depose them, often on what seemed to the colonial authorities frivolous or malicious grounds. Nevertheless, pressure from the organizations they made for themselves was an important factor in speeding the social changes of the thirties and forties reflected in such developments as the rapid extension of schooling, the opening up of new roads, the establishment of advisory and supervisory bodies attached to the traditional political authorities, and so forth (cf. Busia, 1951: chap. VI; Fortes, 1948).

handing over the tithe due to the chief. Strangers had to seek permission from the chief and were obliged to hand over up to half of their haul in tribute. Trespassing in search of snails was a frequent cause of quarrels and evidence of the exercise of snail-rights from time immemorial carried great weight with Ashanti courts adjudicating in boundary disputes. Citizen lineages celebrated the periodic *adae* festivals in association with the chief and the queen mother; stranger groups were merely spectators. In times of war, each lineage contingent received a share of the booty and of the captives proportionate to its rank; strangers would not fight in these contingents.

The obligations of citizens followed directly from their rights and privileges. Their liability to contribute to stool levies has already been mentioned. Levies were raised for specific purposes, to pay for a chief's funeral, to buy gunpowder and lead for war, or animals for sacrifices to the ancestral founders of the chiefdom, or regalia to add to the stool treasure, or to settle a stool debt. As Busia emphasizes (1951: 48–50), such levies could only be raised with the concurrence of the chief's council and the approval of the people. The amount required having been fixed, it was apportioned among the councillors, elders, and subordinate chiefs. Each then allotted a quota to each lineage in proportion to its rank and numbers. Strangers were exempt except in special circumstances when stool debts were incurred to provide services from which they could benefit (e.g., for school buildings nowadays). In this case they might pay half the sum demanded of a citizen. A citizen's liability to contribute to the revenues of the chiefdom by such payments did not cease till his death. By the right of *ayibuadie* (cf. Rattray, 1929: 107–109), the immediate superior to whom he owed allegiance by primary citizenship was entitled to a portion of any personally acquired movable property and wealth left by a deceased person. Councillors and elders received such death duties from their lineage dependents and were in turn liable for similar death duties to their superiors, and so on, up the hierarchy of ranks to the king himself.

It should be explained that only personal property and not lineage property was thus mulcted and furthermore the recipient of the death duties had the obligation of making a generous, customarily fixed contribution to the funeral of the deceased. The significance of this is clearer if we add that it was obligatory for lineage heads to report every death to their superiors and to the head of their chiefdom, for a citizen's death was regarded as a loss to the chiefdom as a whole. Citizens could be called upon to work on the farms attached to the chief's stool and to render tribute of first fruits for the annual *odwera* ceremony celebrated by the chief on behalf of the whole chiefdom. In return for such services, citizens received hospitality from the chief—who was bound to keep open house for his subjects. Strangers were not liable for these services though they could be called upon to contribute labor for public works which benefited them, as, for instance, road clearing.

However, the capital service owed by a citizen was his duty to bear arms in defence of his chiefdom. Every adult male owed this service and was therefore expected to have a gun of his own; and the normal practice was that he fought in his lineage contingent under the leadership of the head of his lineage.[32] The fighting

32. The attainment of adulthood by a youth was marked by his acquisition of a gun. When

forces of a chiefdom were made up of such lineage contingents grouped in companies, each under a captain who, in peacetime, served as a councillor, and the national army was similarly organized, with the forces of each chiefdom forming a unit assigned to a wing or division of the whole.

The duty of military service was regarded as the natural corollary of the two basic attributes of citizen status. Firstly, the right to land implied the duty of defending the state which guaranteed it; secondly, membership of the lineage implied commitment to the allegiance sworn to the chiefly stool on behalf of his lineage by every office holder, and the essence of this allegiance, as the oath declared, was a pledge to defend the chiefdom and support the chief in maintaining the laws and customs.

From the individual's point of view, then, his civic status had several layers, and placed him in a composite field of politico-jural relations. As a citizen of the nation at large, he had rights of free movement which permitted him to reside wherever he was acceptable to the local political authorities; he had the right to integrity of life and limb provided he conformed to law and custom and fulfilled his civic duties; he had, above all, the right of ultimate recourse to the king's tribunal for the redress of wrongs. Yet he could only implement these rights—and discharge the duties to which they were complementary—through the politico-jural agencies and institutions of the chiefdom in which he had primary citizenship. Primary citizenship, again, had two components. On the one hand, it presupposed, as an indispensable credential, membership of a lineage that was lawfully a constituent segment of the polity of the chiefdom; on the other, it had an aspect of personal franchise within the politico-jural domain. He could, for instance, acquire, hold, and dispose of personal wealth and property.

VI

In deference to strict accuracy, I have used the past tense in this all too schematic outline of the traditional political system of Ashanti. I must reiterate, however, that its essential institutions and norms were still operative in the 1940's and 1950's.

The restoration of the Confederacy in 1935 had undoubtedly helped to reinvigorate the kingship and the associated institutions of chiefship. But it must be added that despite the state's loss of sovereign autonomy to the colonial government and the mounting influence of the money economy, British colonial rule, Christianity, and urbanization, these institutions had never wholly fallen into desuetude. In the forties and fifties many of the leading public personalities and men of affairs, even in the "modern" sectors of Ashanti social life, had grown up in the pre-annexation

---

a successor is nowadays chosen for a deceased man, the formula is that he is chosen to receive the deceased's gun. Youths still too young to bear arms, and therefore often still in their fathers' care, might accompany their fathers to war but only in order to carry and care for his gear. Adult slaves might also attend on their masters in war as carriers, but the child of a slave, who would be an actual or adoptive member of his master's lineage, could bear arms and join his lineage in war. Details of the Ashanti military system and of their mode of conducting a war are given in Busia, 1951: 48; Rattray, 1929: chap. XV.

social order. The Asantehene's close advisers and court officials were as profoundly versed in the traditional judicial, ritual, and historical lore and customs as any of their predecessors, and their peers could be found in positions of influence in most of the regional capitals. At the same time, of course, the demands of the changing social and cultural order imposed a heavy strain on the traditional institutions, deepening cleavages, provoking chronic factionalism, squeezing out some established norms and values. The notorious insecurity of political office was reflected in the increasingly frequent and erratic destoolments of chiefs and councillors of all ranks.

But symptomatic as this was of what Busia has called the "disequilibrium of the Ashanti political structure to-day" (1951: 216),[33] it, at the same time, threw into relief the distinctive attributes and structural position of traditional political office. Destoolment was a constitutionally legal safeguard resorted to, however rarely in the past, even against kings.[34]

It is significant, for instance, that destoolment proceedings, whether promoted by a faction among chiefs, councillors, and elders or fomented by discontented commoners, were never aimed at wresting a stool from the lineage in which it was vested by the traditional politico-jural constitution. Indeed it was generally assumed that some member of the chiefly lineage, either a former rival candidate for the stool or else one newly covetous of the office, must be conniving with the "malcontents".[35] It would have been sacrilege and treason, an irreparable breach of their oath of allegiance, for the councillors to have permitted the election to a stool of a person who was not a member of the "royal lineage." The remotest branches of the lineage, including those that may have found their way to other parts of the country, would be explored, and if no suitable successor was found, the queen mother of the lineage might even be installed as a chief until such time as a male candidate became available.[36]

Similarly, the charges leveled against chiefs in destoolment proceedings, as in earlier times, included accusations of violating traditionally enjoined legal, moral and ritual norms. To the invariable charges of "misappropriating stool funds" for personal ends, extortion, and corruption, were commonly added accusations of acting autocratically without the advice of councillors and elders, of using abusive language to them, or of adultery with subjects' wives, of incest, of habitual drunkenness, of flouting moral and ritual prohibitions, and of concealing a physical infirmity—in short, acts not only prejudicial to a chief's dignity but offensive in law

33. Every Ashanti chief, with the exception only of the Asantehene himself, lived under the constant and not always covert threat of destoolment proceedings in the colonial period. The implications of and reasons for this are judiciously evaluated by Busia (1951: 214-17). As he notes, 12 of the 21 divisional chiefdoms had had a change of chiefs at least once, and two of the oldest established had had two destoolments in the period 1942-46.

34. E.g., Asantehene Osai Kwamina, whom Claridge described as "the most merciful of all the Ashanti Kings," was deposed, it was said, on the grounds that he had become converted to Mohammedanism (Claridge, 1915: vol. I, p. 224). Depositions of kings and senior chiefs became more frequent as the Ashanti central power declined, after the 1870's, in consequence of the wars with the British.

35. Cf. the resolutions of the Ashanti Confederacy Council in 1938 quoted by Busia, 1951: 215.

36. Cf. the case of Juaben referred to in Fortes, 1963.

and custom.[37] Though such charges were sometimes scandalously false, they were often justified. I cite them, however, to illustrate the persistence of the traditional norms of reputable chiefship.

The charges of financial misconduct, for instance, though calculated in part to win the support of the colonial administration, also bore on the traditional rule that a political office absorbed the whole person during his tenure of it, thus annulling his liberty to engage in gainful private enterprise. Once a chief, any property or valuables he might be instrumental in acquiring became part of the stool property. Hence, traditionally, a chief-elect would hand over any private wealth he might have accumulated to his mother, or a brother, or sister, either to be kept in trust for him as an insurance against the possibility of destoolment, or as a contribution to the "family" property.[38]

In the modern era, chiefs stood to lose much more if they were to divest themselves of cocoa farms and other commercial sources of income on election to a stool. Far from ceasing to take an interest in such property and sources of income, they often took advantage of their status to add to them, if only as an insurance against the much greater hazards of destoolment. Much stool litigation revolved about the claims of chiefs to be entitled to have private wealth and property, and about their alleged abuse of the traditional device of entrusting such possessions to close lineage kin while keeping the control in their own hands.

What is important, then, is that the factionalism, corruption, and intrigue so often associated with destoolment proceedings masked but did not destroy their true import. What was at issue was the principle of the quasi-contractual accountability (cf. Fortes, 1962b) of a chief to his elders and people fixed upon him by his installation and accepted by his payment of *aseda*; and this was becoming increasingly difficult to ensure by means of the traditional constitutional safeguards.[39]

As in the politico-jural domain, so in the religious domain, the traditional ceremonial and religious obligations and privileges of chiefship were reduced in extent but not in esteem in the thirties and forties. The *adae* and *afahye* (first-fruits) celebrations I was privileged to witness in 1945 had not noticeably changed in style or diminished in solemnity by comparison with those described by Rattray twenty years earlier (and as Rattray noted, the pattern was much the same as a century earlier, to judge by Bowdich's famous description). The reverence for the stool ancestors and awe of the gods (*abosom*) dramatized in the sacrifices, libations, and prayers offered on these occasions on behalf of chiefs and councillors bore eloquent witness to the vitality of the essential elements of the traditional religion.[40]

37. See Busia, 1951: 214, for some examples. Physical infirmities, such as blindness, lameness, or any mutilation, such as circumcision, were considered to be polluting in a ritual sense and therefore made a man ineligible to hold a stool.

38. Cf. Rattray, 1929: 331. Sundry examples of this practice, which was regarded as legitimate if it was openly done at the time of election, were brought to my notice in 1945.

39. Their emasculation by the combined influence of the overriding power of the colonial government and the disaffection of comments is too large a subject to discuss here. See Kimble, 1963 for relevant background.

40. Cf. Busia, 1951: 38: "Literates and illiterates, Christians and pagans have participated in ritual *Adae* ceremonies, and shared the sentiments they expressed or symbolized. I have questioned literate and Christian young men who have been privileged to attend the pouring

The principle repeatedly emphasized by Rattray and Busia that, in the latter's words, "Chiefship in Ashanti is a sacred office" (1951: 36) by virtue of legitimate succession to and representation of the ancestor-founders was constantly affirmed by chiefs and elders, as well as by commoners, both youthful and literate, and elderly and illiterate. Particular chiefs could be stigmatized; the institution itself was still held in deep respect.[41]

This ideology of the sacred, or more concretely, of ritual validation, infused all Ashanti politico-jural and moral institutions. At one end of the scale, the nation, as we have seen, had its mystical focus in the Golden Stool, and its ritual affirmation in the annual *odwera*; and every political division had corresponding ritual symbols of its differentiation and identity.[42] At the other end of the scale, the elementary relations of kinship, descent, and locality had mystical projection in ancestral stools, lineage gods, deities associated with rivers and forests, and local taboos, as well as in metaphysical beliefs concerning the physical and psychical constitution of the person (see below p. 197–8). Breach of oath was at one and the same time a politico-jural delict and an act of sacrilege, and so it was with many other institutions.

What I have said of the persistence of traditional Ashanti politico-jural and ritual institutions applies more emphatically to the familial domain. In turning in the next chapter to examine this domain, I shall therefore follow the customary practice of using the ethnographical present.

41. An ex-catechist chief movingly described the agony of conscience he had suffered when he was elected and had to choose, as he put it, between his church and his ancestors. He accepted the stool, he explained, because to do otherwise would be to dishonor his ancestors. This was not because he feared retribution, he added, as pagans with their belief in "ill-luck" (*musuo*) of mystical origin might do. It was simply unthinkable. Cf. a similar case cited in Fortes, 1963.
42. Cf. the list of taboos for the chiefdom of Mampong in Rattray, 1929: 314–15. And, more mundanely, the ritually obligatory weekly day of rest (Thursday) from farm work dedicated to Asaase, the Earth, and regularly observed by pagan Ashanti and many Christians in the forties.

---

of libations to ancestors, or have witnessed the sacrifices at *Adae* and similar ceremonies. Their answers were in many instances, 'I felt its reality' or 'I was deeply moved'. The Ashanti expression often used 'ɛtɔɔ *me so*' describes a very exalted feeling of awe." I can testify to the accuracy of this observation from my own field experience.

CHAPTER X

The Lineage in Ashanti

I

To UNDERSTAND THE SIGNIFICANCE OF KINSHIP AND DESCENT, IN ASHANTI (AND AKAN generally) social structure, it is essential to bear in mind how they fit into the politico-jural system. As I have explained, the state was not a territorial polity in the determinate sense postulated by Morgan and Maine, either at the national level or at the level of the constituent chiefdoms.[1] It was primarily a constellation of stools—a union of political communities bound to one another by chains of interlocked allegiances to eminent office within a framework of law and of fiscal, religious, and military organization, reinforced by a network of clanship, dynastic kinship, and marriage ties.

1. An indication of this which supports the ethnographic evidence brought forward earlier is the historical fact that external wars were not fought by the Ashanti in defense of territorial boundaries or with the aim of extending them. They were fought to gain tributaries, who were otherwise left to govern themselves in their own way, or to secure safe trade routes and trading posts, or, above all, to assert the dignity and honor of the realm as personified in the Golden Stool and vested in the king. The successive wars against the British and their coastal allies from 1806 to the 1900 rising provoked by Governor Hodgson's egregious demand for the surrender of the Golden Stool, all arose in this way. One cannot read the record of these wars in Ward and Claridge without blushing for the ineptitude displayed time and again by the British colonial officials in dealing with the kings of Ashanti. To the offense thus frequently caused, the only answer could be war.

Here lies one of the main contrasts between the more centralized Lozi state and the Ashanti union. Without pretending that the equivalence is exact, we can say that what the village represents in the Lozi polity, the lineage does in Ashanti. More generally what the substratum of locality represents among the Lozi, the kinship substratum, in the broadest sense, does for Ashanti.

In Ashanti, polity and kinship interpenetrate; so much is already clear. The point of consequence here is that their interrelationship hinges on the concomitant demarcation—in some respects, indeed, opposition—of their respective domains by conceptual, by institutional and by topographic criteria. *Oman*, the body politic, is conceptually counterposed to *fie*, the household and family sphere. The former has its institutional focus in the chiefship (*ohene*), the latter in lineage and household headship. To this corresponds a distinction between things of law (*mera*)—that is, matters (*asem*) that must or can be brought to a chief's court for adjudication—and *amammre*, commonly translated by literates as "custom," but signifying conformity to approved norms of virtue, honor and propriety, and to ritual prescriptions sanctioned primarily by conscience and public opinion. Naturally, the distinction refers not to concrete acts but rather to their contexts and implications. Disrespect shown to one's lineage elders is a breach of *amammre*; shown to a chief, it is actionable in law. Incest is both a heinous transgression of *amammre* and a criminal sin punishable in law. These distinctions lie at the heart of the elaborate system of Ashanti public and private law that prevailed before and through the colonial period.[2] It was first described in detail by Rattray and was still substantially in force in 1945 where its procedures and norms were not in conflict with colonial law.[3]

The feature that is of immediate relevance is the distinction made between the two broad categories of wrongs rubricated by Rattray as "Sins or Tribal Taboos" (*Oman Akyiwadie*) and "Household Cases" (*Efiesem*), respectively. The former, which Kurankyi-Taylor glosses as "public wrongs" or "things hateful to the legal [in my terminology, politico-jural] unit," fall directly and compulsorily under the jurisdiction of the political authorities, both at the level of the chiefdom and at the national level. These wrongs formerly included a wide range: murder, dishonorable suicide, incest and other sexual offenses, abuse, assault, invoking a curse on any holder of high office, treason or cowardice in war, withcraft, and violation of taboos enjoined on the whole community. Particularly heinous were violations of the

2. The stability and continuity of Ashanti judicial organisation, legal procedures and substantive law is well attested in the records of the nineteenth century observers from Bowdich (1819: 252–60) to Perregaux (1906: 139–58). Perregaux's description of the institution of the oath, for example (147–48) tallies closely with accounts given to me by litigants in 1945.

3. Rattray, 1929: chaps. XXV–XXVIII. Both Busia and Kurankyi-Taylor pay tribute to the accuracy and perspicacity of Rattray's analysis and accept it with minor qualifications. Kurankyi-Taylor (1951: 35–51) clarifies Rattray's discussion in some important respects. Essentially, however, in the spheres of family and property law, in constitutional law within the framework of indirect rule, and in regard to religious concepts and values, the traditional system prevailed, especially outside the modern cities, in the forties. I should add that administrative and judicial records going back to the beginning of this century which I was permitted to examine in the then Chief Commissioner's Office, amply confirmed the account given by Rattray.

sanctitity of the Golden Stool and offenses against the majesty of the king.[4] All of these offenses were punishable by the death penalty or some extremely drastic alternative, such as forfeiture of property, or expulsion from the community or even the clan, and thus from the nation

What these "tribal sins" had in common, and what brought them within the purview of the state, was that they struck at the very roots of the whole social system. They were sins from the angle of moral values, sacrilegious in religious terms and *lése majesté* in the political sphere. They were described as violations of "Komfo Anotche's laws"—that is to say, of the fundamental principles of the social order believed to be coeval with Ashanti society.[5] To leave them unpunished by the state would be to risk the alienation of the ancestors and the gods and, in the last resort, lead to the disintegration of society. So deeply ingrained was this conception, that in 1941 the Confederacy Council issued an order designating these *oman akyiwadie*, or their modern counterparts which the colonial government had left under their jurisdiction, as criminal offenses.[6]

The sexual transgressions formerly and still regarded as crimes against society are of special interest. For instance, adultery with the wife of a commoner, even one's own brother's wife, was defined as a private wrong classed with theft. But if she was the wife of the king or of a high-ranking chief, it was an "outrage not only upon the semi-divine person of the King, but also upon the departed spirits" (Rattray, 1929: 307) and punishable by death. Again, incest (*mogya die* or *mogya fra*—pollution of the blood) or the seduction of a pre-nubile girl[7] fall descriptively within the realm of

4. Among the taboos of the Golden Stool listed by Kurankyi-Taylor (1951: 44–45) are the prohibition of its being allowed to touch the earth and of its name being mentioned in light talk. These and other ritual injunctions concerning the Golden Stool symbolize its equivalence to a high-ranking chief, ultimately the king himself. A chief may not step barefoot upon the earth. By enstoolment he is raised above the earth and the culminating rites of deposition of a chief consist in "bumping his buttocks on the ground, or taking his sandals off his feet, or by mutilating his body" (Busia, 1951: 37), and thus making him sacrilegious by force. Offenses against the king included adultery with one of his wives and insulting him or his forbears.

5. Kurankyi-Taylor comments (1951: 69) that no exact and complete account of these laws is obtainable but they embrace such "fundamental principles" of the political constitution as the taboos of the Golden Stool and the ban on treason, as well as such basic principles of social organization as the rule of clan exogamy. In my own experience, Komfo Anotche was also invoked as the author of taboos on polluting the earth (e.g., by sexual intercourse or child-birth "in the bush"), on menstruant women, and on "things hateful" to a village or town, such as the keeping of forbidden animals in it.

6. Their list differs little from Rattray's. Murder and suicide are of course excluded. But among other items, the following are specified: incestuous intercourse between members of the same clan or of close patrilateral kinship; the impregnation of a girl before her nubility ceremony; menstrual pollution of a stool house or a divinity; wanton invocation of an oath; insult and assault of an office holder or his close kin; a refusal to render lawfully obligatory services to the Asantehene or a chief; and other offenses which are also enumerated by Rattray among the sins that were "hateful to the tribe."

7. *Kyiribra*, the crime of sexual intercourse with a girl before her public nubility ceremony, was traditionally classified as murder, unless she had concealed the onset of her menses. In that case, the culprits underwent a public ceremony of purification and humiliation, followed by their expulsion to the forest until the child was born (cf. Rattray, 1929: 298; Busia, 1951: 72). I heard many allegations in 1945 that it had become common owing to the sexual laxity of young people in schools and towns (cf. Fortes, 1954: 268–69). In actuality, I came across only one definite case and reached the conclusion that these allegations were symptomatic of

household and clan morality and would among many peoples be left to the arbitrament of mystical powers. But in Ashanti they were and are grave public delicts, as
well as sins, nowadays incurring heavy fines and requiring the provision of sheep for
sacrifices to purify the ancestral stool of the chiefdom.

In short, the politico-jural authorities—in other words, the executive agencies of
the state—maintained a strict surveillance not only over the political conduct of the
citizens but also over their moral and religious conduct in relation to the familial and
ritual institutions presupposed in the structure of the total polity. The machinery of
enforcement is an incidental matter in the present context. It is enough to say that
palace and court servants and officials, as well as lineage heads and village headmen,
and indeed all reputable citizens, could and were in duty bound to ensure the
prosecution of wrongdoers. Fear of the mystical disasters they would bring on the
whole community—let alone the likelihood of being found out and punished by a
chief—made concealment out of the question.

The significance of "Household Cases" (efiesem) was quite different. In substance,
these were cases concerning marriage and divorce, lineage and personal property, inheritance of kinship statuses, sale, gift or pawning of land, chattels and persons,
theft and trespass, insult and assault—in short, cases relating to the laws of persons
and property. Correctly speaking these were "household cases" if the parties
belonged to the same parental family or lineage. If they were not so connected, the
dispute became "mansosem" (Kurankyi-Taylor, 1951 : 49), that is, open litigation. In
either event, the procedure resorted to was arbitration by lineage heads and elders,
redress was by conciliation and the payment of a pacification fee (mpata), or
compensation to the injured party, who might use it to make a libation to his birth-
soul (Kra) in order to assuage its anger. (See p. 198, below.)

There were no penal sanctions at the disposal of the arbitrators. Their decisions
were accepted by the parties because they were regarded as equitable "according to
custom," because of the support of public opinion, because of the authority the
elders held in their lineage by virtue of office or seniority, because of the dependence
of lineage members on their elders in corporate jural and ritual situations. There was,
for instance, an accepted scale of mulcts for adultery or illicit familiarity regarded as
its equivalent, with the wife of a kinsman or fellow-citizen.

Nevertheless, the internal regulation of private and lineage rights was not completely dissociated from the external jural control of the state. If the wrong lay
between members of different lineages or communities and their elders failed to
agree or to bring about a settlement, the recalcitrant party could swear the chief's
oath against his opponent, in extreme cases even the Great Oath. This compelled

---

the fear of parents and not based on facts. So great, it seemed to me, was still the horror of
pre-nubile pregnancy that girls took special pains to resist sexual temptations before their
nubility ceremony or, among Christians, the confirmation which had begun to take its place.
In the case I came across, the chief and queen mother were informed as was obligatory but,
instead of the customary ceremony of purification, a private settlement was made which
included the provision of a sheep for a piacular sacrifice to cleanse the chiefly stools and the
community of defilement. The parents of the girl were deeply ashamed and angry and
expressed real anxiety lest the girl's sin should bring bad luck (musuo) on themselves and the
community, though all the parties concerned were church members.

those concerned to take the case—now turned into a public litigation (*mansosem*)—to the appropriate chief's court where it would be judicially dealt with.[8] It should be understood that the oath had this force because false or wanton invocation of any oath was a sin, and in the case of the Great Oath subject to the capital penalty. The basis of this procedure was of course, the status of the parties as citizens of the chiefdom and the nation. And this points to the most important feature of the politico-jural constraint that inheres in the familial domain.

The internal relations of kinsfolk and affines among themselves are regulated, on one level, by the norms of kinship morality and propriety. Thus it is not now and never was possible to prosecute a person before a chief's court for failing to provide adequately for his or her children. It is a matter purely of conscience, sentiment, and self interest, buttressed by religious notions and moral principles. But at another level these relations of kinship and affinity had and have critical jural determinants. This applies above all to the structure of the lineage. As the fount of citizenship, the lineage belongs to the politico-jural domain. It is both internally and externally subject to the jural regulation of the state, and all relations of kinship and affinity are affected by this circumstance.

The lineage derives it status in the politico-jural domain from its corporate structure, and a fundamental determinant of this relationship is the systematic and consistent structural demarcation of the politico-jural domain from the familial domain to which I have alluded. The three institutions of office, the oath, and descent are of crucial importance in this connection, since it is through them that the two domains are interarticulated.

II

This brings us to the question of what the corporate structure of the lineage consists in. Ashanti and other Akan kinship institutions have been extensively described and analyzed in the publications already frequently cited,[9] and the crucial features can readily be picked out.

The fundamental principle of Ashanti kinship structure is summed up in the concept of *abusua*. The popular maxim, "*Abusua bako mogya bako* (one *abusua*, one blood),"[10] declares its essential significance, and the definition of sexual relations between *abusua* relatives of any degree as incest sums up its moral basis.

The term *abusua* is a substantive denoting a named and exclusive group of persons of both sexes who are known, by Ashanti criteria of genealogical connection, to be of commonly matrilineal ancestry. In a more abstract usage, it connotes matrilineal descent as a principle of social alignment. In the most extensive topographical sense, considered in the context of the nation or, more precisely, of the Ashanti as a people,

8. Cf. Rattray, 1927: chap. XXII. As Rattray puts it, the oath had the implication of a taboo "deliberately broken in order to remove a dispute from a purely private domain and carry it *in judicium*" (p. 208).

9. See in particular Rattray, Fortes, Christensen, Busia, Sarbah, as cited.

10. See Rattray, 1923: 35. Christaller gives the translation, "*family, kindred, relatives*, esp. *the relations of the mother's side*," etc. (1881: 54), but this is inadequate.

abusua denotes a dispersed, named clan made up of localized sections, all of which are believed to be connected by common matrilineal ancestry. There are only eight[11] such clans in Ashanti, and it is noteworthy that the same small number of clans bearing the same or equivalent names is duplicated among all the Akan-speaking peoples. This is often adduced in confirmation of their remote common origins (see Christensen, 1954). There is evidence that traditionally each clan had specific "totemic" animal avoidances. These appear to have been associated with the hereditary offices held in the clan, and have largely lapsed in modern times.[12] What now remains distinctive of each clan is the strict recognition of its structural autonomy, founded on the dogma of common matrilineal descent, and expressed in politico-jural terms, that is, the rules of clan exogamy and of claims to office, and conversely, in the ideals of amity and fraternity within the clan.

The clans are believed to have come into existence by the miraculous emergence from the earth or descent from heaven at one, now sacred, place of their founding ancestresses and other forbears,[13] and to have spread through the whole country by fission and migration. Thus they are thought of as having been in existence continuously from time immemorial,[14] indeed from the very beginning of the race. By contrast, the nation is known to be an historical entity brought into being at a definite time by the genius of an heroic leader. The known genealogical and dynastic sequence of the kings and high-ranking chiefs provides a relative chronology of its historical development which is further and richly documented in artifacts of value, in institutional forms, and in oral traditions.[15] It is the ideological generaliza-

11. According to my own inquiries, which confirm Rattray's conclusion (Fortes, 1950: 259). But some authorities claim that there are only seven clans—cf. the tabulation and discussion in Christensen, 1954: 23–25. In 1942 Captain Warrington, then District Commissioner in Kumasi, compiled an outline entitled *Notes on Ashanti Customs* in consultation with a Committee of Chiefs and elders appointed by the Confederacy Council. This (unpublished) authoritative statement lists seven clans. The issue is confused by the prevalence of alternate and plural names for most clans. It does not, however, matter in principle. What is significant is that the number is small and fixed at *seven* or *eight*.

12. It was forbidden to kill or to eat the flesh of these animal species. In accordance with a common West African pattern (cf., e.g., Fortes, 1945: chap. VIII), it was believed that a clan's totem animal or animals revealed itself to an ancestress by saving the life or conferring some benefit on her or her clansmen. The totem species were believed to protect the clans that respected them and also to reflect, in their peculiarities of nature, the character distinctive of each clan. Cf. Meyerowitz, 1951: 29–31; Rattray, 1929: 65 ff.

13. Cf. Rattray, 1923: chap. X; 1929: *passim*. The sacred birthsite of the clans is at Asantemanso. Rattray (1923) gives a moving account of the "reverence and awe" with which his Ashanti sponsors approached this, to them, holy place. His description of the sacrifices offered at the grave and of the taboos which marked it as a sanctuary and guard it from the pollution of blood and death, brings out the central value of the founding of the clans in the Ashanti social system. It suggests that the sacred birthsite of the people has a ritual status equal and complementary to that of the Golden Stool. I was prevented by illness from making a pilgrimage to Santemanso in 1945, but authoritative informants assured me that Rattray's account is accurate though incomplete.

14. *Efiri tetee* is the Ashanti phrase (cf. Christaller, 1881: s.v. *tete*, p. 505. It is used especially of ritual custom and can be aptly translated by the Bractonian formula, "of which the memory of man knoweth not the origins."

15. Every king and high-ranking chief is expected to add to the stool regalia and stool treasures which came into his custody when he was elected. Thus the state umbrellas, the stools, gold ornaments, ceremonial swords, certain drums and horns, and all the other numerous and varied paraphernalia that are employed on ceremonial and ritual occasions, as

tion relative to the widest context of the social system of the polarity of polity and
family, law and custom, public delict and private wrong.

Thus, on the one side, along one axis of the total social structure, as it were, lie
the sempiternal clans, embodying the morally universal, indefeasible, office-
centered and ancestrally oriented principle of matrilineal kinship, and, on the other
side, along the other axis, is the temporally conceptualized, militarily organized and
quasi-historically sanctioned state based on the rule of judicially administered law
and the majesty of kingship.

I have quoted the rule that a person is deemed to be an Ashanti if his mother is an
Ashanti. This suggests that tribal identity is conferred solely by matrifiliation, but
this is correct only in contraposition to non-Ashanti of independent political status.
Within Ashanti, there is no such status; the critical feature is membership of a clan.
Every freeborn Ashanti is by matrifiliation made a member of one and only one clan.
In the Ashanti formula, he is a "royal," a true scion (odehye) of the clan. This
emphasizes the structurally critical implication that he is, in theory, eligible for
election to any of the offices vested in any branch of the clan. A clanless person is, by
definition, of slave or alien maternal origin,[16] and therefore not eligible for such
offices. The cloak of clanship conferred by adoption never wholly legitimizes its
beneficiaries.

It is, I believe, not fortuitous that there are only seven or eight clans. The Ashanti
clans either have paired names (e.g., Oyoko and Daako), or alternative names in
different areas (e.g., Aduana and Atwea). Rattray[17] interpreted this as a survival of a
superseded system of intermarrying moieties. What I was given to understand was
that these names indicate amalgamations of what were formerly independent clans.
Be this as it may, the inference is that this restricted number of clans fits the
Ashanti social system better than if they had been allowed to proliferate. The limitation is, I believe, associated with the nucleus of the key offices which form an
integral extension of the eminent office of chiefship. The military organization,
which was the basis of the titled offices held by the councillors of a chiefdom,

16. It must be remembered that a freeborn Ashanti could not be enslaved in Ashanti.
This would have been both illegal and sinful. A freeborn person could be pawned away from
his or her own community or, if unredeemed, a woman-pawn could originate a lineage group
in a chiefdom different from her own. Such a lineage would be freeborn in the context of
clanship, but would remain hereditary pawns unless and until redeemed.

17. Rattray, 1927: 326–28. I speak of Ashanti here, but what I am suggesting probably
applies to the Akan type of social system in general.

well as in the daily life of high-ranking office holders, are precisely associated with their
predecessors who had them made and with the events they commemorate. (Cf. Kyerematen,
1964; Rattray, 1927: chaps. XXIV–XXVIII, for example.) It was the custom for every king
to create one or more new offices of state to add luster to his reign, and these remain as
permanent testimony to their founder. All oaths likewise commemorate historical events,
though in this case it is the disasters and misfortunes of a reign that are perpetuated. Last but
not least, the oral traditions are preserved and recounted in the drum and horn recitals that
accompany all occasions of ceremony and ritual. This pattern, it goes almost without saying,
is repeated on a less elaborate scale in every chiefdom. (Rattray, 1929: passim, gives many
examples.) There is now also, of course, the historical literature on Ashanti, originally derived
from records of European travelers, officials and traders, which I have several times referred
to, and now being added to by Ghanaian scholars, such as Busia, Kyerematen, and others.

required seven—and only seven—primary positions of command apart from the chief's.[18] Together, these councillor-officers formed the balance wheel of the political organization of a chiefdom. Authority and responsibility were so distributed among them that each had a function independent of those of the others and all were necessary for the defense and for the normal government of the chiefdom. Their only bond with one another on the political level was their common allegiance to the chiefly stool, in relation to which they held a collective watching brief. And the most common structural arrangement which held this constellation in place was the allocation of each office to one clan-lineage in exclusive corporate possession. There was also a complementary principle that, ideally, every lineage primarily domiciled in a chiefdom should be represented by an elder in the chief's council. Converging with the constitution of the officer-council, this rule could best be satisfied by limiting the number of descent-autonomous groups in any chiefdom to about seven or eight. The chief's (and the linked queen mother's) office reflects the principle of *primus inter pares*. They are perpetually vested in one of the lineages, which also has a councillor representative, in accordance with the principle that the chief belongs to the whole state, not to a lineage, once he is installed. Once again we observe how the institutions of chiefship, of political office, and of descent are inter-locked.

The clans are so dispersed that every clan is likely to be represented among the people of every chiefdom.[19] Thus, from the collective point of view, a clan is made up of politically discrete regional sections. A clan never emerges as an all-inclusive unit of political or ritual action. Indeed, regionally distinct sections of the same clan were often and inevitably opposed to one another in the political contests which in the pre-colonial period sometimes turned into civil wars when high-ranking chiefs fell out with one another or attempted to secede.

Yet clan solidarity and an ideal of clan corporateness are effective forces in the social relations of all ranks of peoples. *Abusua* implies amity. "We are brothers" is the way Kumasi Oyoko explain their clanship with the Juaben, the Kokofu, and other Oyoko, and this is typical.[20] More significant is the statement, "We are one blood, we have one mother," offered to account for common clanship. The implication is that the clan is the lineage writ large, though it is accepted that this is not genealogically demonstrable. It is neither possible nor considered relevant to establish exact genealogical connections of co-descent among the territorially dis-

18. The details are set out in Rattray, 1929: chap. XI. These were the councillors who, together with the queen mother, had the decisive voice in the election of a chief—and conversely, in the destoolment process. In actuality, there was usually, of course, a number of other offices associated with chiefship, in the case of the king a large and diverse hierarchy of offices. But apart from the special case of the Gyasehene who was controller of the king's (or chief's) household, these offices were purely administrative and carried no political or military authority. By contrast with the major lineage-held offices of state, many of these were in the king's (or chief's) gift or were filled by selection from among a late holder's sons (see below, p. 201).

19. Surveys carried out in a number of Ashanti chiefdoms in 1945 confirmed this. (Cf. for example, Fortes, 1954: 294, no. 40.)

20. So say the Asona of Offinso of Asona lineages elsewhere, and so say people of all the other clans. Chiefs and elders of the same clan in different chiefdoms address and refer to one another by fraternal kinship terms (cf. Fortes, 1950).

persed sections of a clan. Nevertheless, clanship is equated with brotherhood. A stranger clansman arriving either for a short stay or as a would-be immigrant finds food, lodging, protection and sponsorship with the local lineage of his clan.

The corporate characteristics projected on to the clan fit the image. As I have mentioned, sexual relations, and therefore marriage, between clans-folk are forbidden. It would be incestuous, exactly as with members of the same lineage, and likewise punishable by death. The belief in the immortality and sempiternity of the clan system is the basic premise. A clan has no common property, no unity of administrative leadership or of an estate. But the stools of office severally vested in the regionally discrete sections of the clan are regarded as a common prerogative, and the highest ranking of these offices is thought of as the titular head of the clan. The notion that every true member of a clan is eligible to succeed to any of the offices vested in its branches is understood to be a fiction. It would indeed be an outrage offensive to the ancestors for a person to lay claim to an office vested in another branch of his clan than his own, even within his chiefdom, while true successors in that branch were available. In the troubled history of Mampong (the chiefdom next in rank to the king's), rebellion against the ruling chief was more than once led by his senior subchiefs of other branches of his own clan. Yet never was an attempt made to replace a defeated head chief by a member of any other branch of the clan.

This is not to say that lineage-vested office has never been transferred. There are well-authenticated cases in most chiefdoms of lineages becoming extinct or being disfranchised for treason, and offices held by them being awarded by the chief to a member of a collateral lineage or even to a son of the last holder and thus to a different lineage. The principle is not thereby invalidated. It rests on the postulate, as I shall presently explain, that lineage-vested office is tied to the sanctified ancestral stools and that a person who is not eligible by demonstrable descent to offer sacrifice and libation to them in his own right cannot have ancestral sanction for occupying the office bequeathed by them.

III

Abusua as clan delimits a diffuse field of amity, wide in extent but of minimal structural specificity. Ashanti think of it as the amity innate in the ties of siblingship extended to the farthest limits of putative co-descent. By contrast, *abusua* as lineage is the structurally specific field of descent relations. It is descent translated into specific jural, political, and ritual rights and duties, commitments and privileges.

Let us look first, at what I have elsewhere defined as the maximal lineage, that is the most inclusive unit of common matrilineal descent found in any particular community.[21] Considered from the outside, such a lineage can be regarded as a

21. I have described Ashanti lineage structure in some detail (in Fortes, 1950). Sarbah, writing as a jurist in 1897 (*Fanti Customary Laws*, p. 71), listed what he called the "ordinary incidents" of the Akan lineage as follows: (1) A common penin (i.e., lineage head). (2) Common liability to pay debts. (3) Common funeral rites. (4) Common residence. (5) Common burial place. This list (so reminiscent of Morgan's enumeration of the distinguishing features of the Iroquois gens), though far from complete, remains applicable to the Ashanti lineage.

localized division or, more aptly, chapter of a clan. Though its members may, at any given time, through circumstances I have previously referred to, be scattered, every maximal lineage has a fixed home in a particular chiefdom of primary citizenship. In the past, it occupied its own quarter or ward in the capital township of the chiefdom. This tendency towards local concentration was reflected in the domestic residence arrangements (see Fortes, 1949a).

The most common pattern in the forties was the dwelling group made up of the uterine descendants of both sexes of a common grandmother or great-grandmother, as frequently under a woman head as under a male head, in effect therefore a domestic segment of the maximal lineage. Though wives with young children often resided virilocally, it was normal for spouses to live in their respective maternal dwelling groups in the earliest years of marriage and again when their children were grown up.[22] A marked preference for marriage within the closest permissible local and structural range[23] enabled conjugal, affinal and patrifilial relationships to be maintained without inconvenience.[24] Corresponding to this spatial localization of the living, every maximal lineage still had its own cemetery where both male and female members were buried, and where their ghosts were believed to be present, especially when the annual harvest festival was celebrated.[25] The lineage cemetery was thought of as consecrated to the ancestors. Unwarranted trespass on the cemetery of a lineage by non-members was and is still resented and treated as a public wrong actionable in the chief's court.

Seen from the outside, as a segment of the external politico-jural organization, a maximal lineage is defined as a unit controlled and represented by its male head (*abusua panin*) with the assistance of the senior woman (*obaapanin*) of the lineage. The lineage head is normally a member of the chief's council of elders, either as the holder of a titled public office vested in his lineage or simply in his representative capacity. It is a basic constitutional principle that every maximal lineage of established domicile in a chiefdom must be so represented. Hence, as I have already indicated, the chief's lineage, which cannot be represented by him since he "belongs to the whole people," has a lineage head apart from him.

All transactions of a political or juridical nature between a chief and the members of a lineage owing allegiance to his stool are conducted through the lineage head; and though he is not responsible for the crimes, sins or torts of individual members of his lineage, he is in duty bound to attend or to send a deputy to plead for any of them who is brought to court.[26] The lineage head as councillor must be vigilant in

22. In 1945 I found that from 60–70 per cent of the total population of relatively stable townships and villages resided in such matrilineal dwelling groups. The members of such domestic groups are brothers and sisters, mothers' brothers, mothers' mothers' brothers, sisters and sisters' children, grandmothers, mothers and daughters to one another. The 30–40 per cent of virilocal domestic groups were characterized by the predominance among them of pre-adult children of the head and his wife.

23. Figures obtained in 1945 show that in 75–80 per cent of extant marriages in rural areas, the partners came from the same or adjacent communities (cf. Fortes, 1954).

24. Cf. Fortes, 1962a, for some discussion of the principle of structural propinquity in marriage here exemplified.

25. Christian members are nowadays buried in the cemetery of their denomination.

26. I have records of cases (e.g., in adultery, debt, inheritance, and land suits) in which a

safeguarding his constituency's interests, for example in the apportionment of levies and in rights to take up virgin farm land and house sites. He must consult the lineage elders, but he does not have to act under instructions from them. He is free to follow his own judgment and the dictates of his conscience. This is typical of all relationships in which members of a maximal lineage engage collectively, or severally, with outsiders. The authority of the lineage head is invariably involved. Even in so informal a situation as the entertainment of a visiting clansman or stranger, he will be apprised, as a matter of courtesy.

It is, however, in the jural relationships entered into by lineage members with outsiders that the *abusua panin's* status is of decisive significance. Marriage is a crucial case, since, by the incest rule, it is obligatorily exogamous. Until the *tiri nsa*[27] has been formally presented by the husband's lineage head, on his behalf, to the wife's lineage head, and accepted, there is no marriage, however long and harmoniously the couple may have been cohabiting. This prestation, which Ashanti regard as creating a form of contract, confers on the husband the exclusive sexual rights and the legitimate claims on the domestic services of his wife which, with the reciprocal rights of the wife to sexual and procreative satisfaction and economic support for herself and her children, constitute the essentials of marriage for them. Conversely, it is only by refunding the *tiri nsa* through the husband's and wife's lineage heads that a divorce is made certain in law. Breaches of marital rights, such as infidelity or neglect, must be submitted to them for arbitration.

A particularly instructive instance of the lineage head's jural primacy is the rule relating to gifts *inter vivos*. A man has the right to transfer by gift a part of his privately gained wealth or property (e.g., nowadays a cocoa farm) to a son or daughter —that is, to a member of a different lineage. But such a gift is not valid unless it is made with the consent of the donor's *abusua* and has been confirmed by an *aseda* payment from the beneficiary to them. The lineage members immediately concerned are those who are required to waive their primary rights of inheritance, but their consent must be signified (if only formally) to the lineage head. The point in issue is instructive. A male person in the bodily sense and in his politico-jural capacity belongs to, is indeed "owned by," his lineage. His productive (but not reproductive) capacity is, strictly speaking, "owned by" the lineage. His self-acquired wealth should therefore accrue to the lineage patrimony. It is an equitable concession to his paternal commitments and interests, to permit him to implement them (as he does daily with, e.g., food and shelter) with gifts of property. But these must be within reasonable limits and with the consent of the corporate unit which thus emerges as the ultimate donor and arbiter.[28]

27. For further details of Ashanti marriage and divorce law and procedures, see Fortes, 1950, 1953c, 1954.

28. An aspect sometimes emphasized is that the donor's ghost (*saman*) will, after his death, continue to "care for" his children and yielding some of his personal property to them is an anticipatory acknowledgment of this and a sign of respect for the ghost. Death-bed gifts ("things set aside by the ghost") (*samansie*) made in the presence of witnesses must be particularly respected, since one cannot dispute with a ghost.

lineage head has pleaded with the court to refer the dispute back to him and a fellow lineage head for settlement by arbitration and negotiation.

In all such transactions, the lineage head acts in the name of the lineage as a whole, as the representative of its corporate interests. Though he does have a power of veto by virtue of his office and of the respect he commands, he can act with authority only with the concurrence of the lineage elders and of those members most immediately concerned. He cannot, for example, accept the espousal prestation of *tiri nsa* without the prior consent of the woman's mother and senior mother's brother. (And her father, too, for the reasons which will be mentioned later.) Loans, mortgages, and sales of property for common purposes—for example, in order to redeem pawned lineage kin or, nowadays, meet the costs of stool litigation or pay a member's debts—are subject to the same rules. In general, the lineage head's authorization—always with the explicit concurrence of the body corporate—is required for any transaction in which rights and obligations determined by status in the lineage are assigned or transferred. It is characteristic of the manner in which law pervades the social structure that all such assignments and transfers must be ratified in the contractual form of an *aseda* payment, even between kinsfolk. Disputes over such transactions can therefore in the last resort be brought to court by swearing an oath. The watchful presence of the state is thus acknowledged within the structurally private domain of the lineage.

IV

These prerogatives of the lineage head stem from the domestic facet of his office, that is, his status in the internal structure of the lineage. It is a fixed principle that every office vested in a lineage, from the kingship downwards, is filled by election from among all the genealogically qualified persons of the lineage,[29] irrespective of age or generation. There are no pre-designated successors defined by generation, or age, or birth order. An office is the possession of the lineage entrusted into the keeping, for the time being, of one of its members. This is not metaphor. Office, as I have previously noted, is tangibly and materially embodied in the sacred blackened stools of its deceased holders. Personal relics though these are, they are also, by virtue of the office they symbolize, the collective habitation of all the lineage ancestors. Election to office means in the first place being entrusted and charged with the custody of the stools and the ritual duties towards the ancestors this entails. It is, strictly speaking, by virtue of election to this incumbency that the executive powers and duties of office within the lineage and in the politico-jural domain accrue to its holder.

The final choice of an incumbent of any office is made in a public assembly.[30] For

29. It should be remembered that there are female stools (e.g., of queen mothers of all grades of chiefs) as well as male stools. The rule here stated applies to both sexes. "Genealogically qualified" here may mean membership of a designated branch of a lineage—as will be explained later. It refers, of course, to the Ashanti conceptualization of the criterion. From the observer's point of view it would be formally more accurate to speak of "qualified by acknowledged descent."

30. In the case of a chief there are three stages. First a candidate is selected by the queen mother and elders of the lineage which has the chiefship from among those who are eligible. Then the assent of the councillors and the elders is sought, and finally there is a public

the election of a lineage head, all adult members, both male and female, should be present and children of all ages are free to attend as well. The elders of both sexes have a powerful influence but not the last word. The candidate they favor must be approved by the consensus of the whole assembly and this will depend on the confidence he commands. Tact and wisdom, intelligence and probity, knowledge of affairs and skill in leadership are the qualities looked for. In 1945 it was common to find relatively young men with some experience of the world outside—in commerce, or in educational or government service—selected as heads of important lineages.[31] Literacy was particularly valued in candidates for chiefship.

Every maximal lineage has a house (the *abusua fie*) in a consecrated room of which the blackened stools are permanently kept, together with any ceremonial paraphernalia that belong to the office. This is where lineage meetings are held and the lineage head may reside there if he wishes. Every lineage also has its own *abosom* deity, which may be separately housed in the care of a priest or priestess of the lineage. Apart from these buildings, the stools, and the paraphernalia (and its cemetery, if we wish so to regard it), a maximal lineage has no common material property. The head succeeds to a position of custodianship, not to that of a trustee for an estate of productive utility.[32] Formerly, the traditional residential locality of the lineage was not owned by it but formed part of the stool land vested in the chiefship. House sites could not be mortgaged, leased, or sold but were freely occupied by accredited citizens. A maximal lineage might have an exclusive user-right in land for food farming before the era of cocoa. This entitled every member of the lineage to take up an unoccupied portion of it for food farming, subject to confirming with the lineage head and chief that there were no prior claimants to it. Once cultivated, the right to farm such a parcel of land could be passed on by inheritance from a woman to a sister, a daughter or other uterine cognate and in a man's case to a sibling or sister's child, or it could be loaned to a spouse or a child. It could not be alienated by gift or sale. It is usually claimed, as has already been noted, that such land was originally cleared from virgin forest by the founders of the lineage and became perpetually vested in the lineage as corporate property by the normal process of corporate inheritance and succession. Many maximal lineages did not in the past and do not now have common farm land, however; and no Ashanti considers the common ownership of farm land to be a critical feature of lineage unity.

31. That is, lineages that provide the senior councillors of a chiefdom or are specially influential on account of their large or wealthy membership or long-established settlement in the community.

32. There is little doubt that traditionally, and certainly in the forties, private wealth played a part in elections to chiefships. It was notorious that candidates for high-ranking chiefships were not above resorting to bribery aimed at winning the support of councillors and the leaders of the commoners. Electors to a stool encumbered with heavy debts were prone to favor a prosperous candidate who might be expected to pay off some or all of the debt. But these considerations did not decisively affect the choice of lineage head, except to the extent that economic achievement was taken to be a sign of enterprise and intelligence and to promise generosity in lineage affairs.

ceremony at which the selected candidate is presented to the assembled people and enstooled. He is then conducted to the house in which the ancestral stools are kept and presented to them. Opposition may occur at any stage and alternative candidates considered.

What is crucial in traditional Ashanti law, moral values, ritual practice, and personal sentiment is the notion that the *abusua* as lineage is "one person", *nipa koro*. This, again, is no metaphor. It is another way of expressing the fact—for such it is to Ashanti—that a lineage is of "one blood," *mogya koro*, transmitted matrilineally from a single common ancestress. That descent, thus visualized, is a matter of fact, not of assumption, for its members is demonstrated by the lineage genealogy. Considered from within, the maximal lineage differs from the clan in that it has a precise genealogy which links every living sibling group by a known pedigree to the founding ancestress and by exactly computable degrees to all collateral sibling groups. The genealogies I collected in 1945 go back to founding ancestresses from ten to fourteen generations antecedent to the youngest living generation.[33]

The genealogical charter is indispensable for the conduct of lineage affairs at all levels of the internal structure, and a knowledge of personal genealogical relationships—geneonymy, as I have called it elsewhere (1965: 122–24)—is essential for the individual in the conduct of his social relations within his personal field of kinship.

A lineage is conceptually "one person" when it faces the world at large, but in the internal relations of its members it is strictly stratified by generation and segmented by descent. The genealogy is the charter for this. It also has the force of a jural instrument in the regulation of inheritance, succession, and the distribution of rights

---

33. These genealogies vary greatly in span, some having no more than two major branches which are stated to have diverged four to six generations prior to the latest current generation, whereas the most extensive in my collection has nine branches of a rank order equivalent to this and two major branches which bifurcated thirteen generations previously. This genealogy (of the Asona maximal lineage of Agogo), which was assembled by one of its members, my field assistant Mr. T. E. Kyei, embraces thirteen generations inclusive of the latest current generation. It records the matrimonial and matrilineal connections of 755 persons of all ages, of whom 614 belonged to the lineage. These included 324 living and 290 dead members. This genealogy was constructed in lengthy consultations with the elders of the lineage, in particular the female elders who are the acknowledged genealogical authorities. Our informants were unanimous about the major modes of segmentation in the genealogy, and highly consistent in regard to the more proximate connections of existing collateral branches. As with all orally transmitted genealogical knowledge, none of the elders had a knowledge of the whole genealogy, though one or two came pretty near to this. One Agogo elder of a different clan was able to enumerate 252 persons, living and dead, with whom he had matrilineal, patrilateral, and affinal connections stretching across eight generations. In general, persons of mature years know thoroughly their genealogical connections within four to six generations and the main steps in their pedigree back to the founding ancestress. Elders have a wider range, depending on the part they are accustomed to take in lineage affairs. Whenever there is a death in the lineage, or a marriage, or some other notable event, genealogical connections come under discussion and thus get known. At festival times, when the lineage head performs libations and sacrifices in the ancestral stool house, he will invoke his predecessors by name; and I have often heard a parent explain to a child how they are related to someone whom he or she has addressed by a kinship term. The genealogical charter of every lineage thus undergoes public revision from time to time but there is, at any given time, an accepted version backed by the authority of the elders. Ashanti naturally regard their genealogies as exact and complete records, but close examination shows that they in fact conform to the now well-known pattern of orally transmitted genealogies. They represent accurately current alignments of persons by filiation and descent, but the further back they go, the more obviously are successive generations telescoped, and persons without surviving lineal descendants dropped out unless they were notable for some office or rank achieved, for famous exploits, or for memorable qualities of personality. Such persons are likely to be commemorated in the personal names of living lineage members.

over persons. It is most dramatically brought into play when rival candidates for office vested in the lineage are under consideration. A candidate must have the proper credentials. This means that he must produce a pedigree that links him by named matrilineal forbears in each generation to a previous incumbent of the office, and this pedigree must be accepted as correct by the lineage assembly.[34] It is at such times that genealogies are most minutely scrutinized, inconsistencies ironed out, and lacunae patched.

The importance of this procedure derives from the frequent admixture of alien and servile descent elements in most maximal lineages. Since the descent principle defines the matrilineal descendents of a woman in perpetuity as of "one blood," and since matrifiliation allocates a person unequivocally to a line of descent, an adopted or alien slave woman's matrilineal descendants remain perpetually of quasi-servile status within the lineage. They can never become the custodians of the lineage stools or consequently, occupy the office associated with them.[35] Likewise, many maximal lineages contain assimilated segments descended from immigrants of the same clan who were incorporated in the lineage. These, too, cannot hold lineage office vested in the authentic line. As, however, attached lineage-kin, whatever their origin may be, are in most other respects on a footing of equality with the authentic members, they are not above aspiring to lineage office. It is an indication of the genealogical vigilance exercised in matters of this sort that a common charge laid (often without justification) against chiefs whose destoolment was sought was that they were not true descendants of the founder of the stool.[36] Disputes arising out of contested claims to authentic membership of office-holding lineages were frequently brought to court in the 1940's.[37]

34. Until I met with instances of this, I was puzzled as to why lineage genealogies were so elaborate and so meticulously preserved in oral tradition. One could imagine that membership by matrifiliation in the named, locally unitary, and politically discrete collectivity which constitutes a lineage from the outside, would suffice to align persons in clans. The significance of the genealogy is internal to a lineage and clan. Thus, adherence to lineage-bound totemic observances could, in the past, have had some evidential value. A claimant to office must be able to show and be acknowledged to have lineage status by demonstrable descent from the founding ancestress; and since every authentic member is in theory entitled to lay claim to office, this means that everybody must be able to produce his pedigree.

35. In principle; but as I mention later, slaves could inherit as a last resource, and lineage office has undoubtedly in some cases passed to a "house person" (*fie nipa*)—i.e., slave's offspring, by this process. Such questions are of strictly domestic concern to the lineage outside the bounds of which it is, of course, a wrong to divulge a person's origins.

36. In spite of the ever-present hazard of destoolment and the steady whittling away of the political powers of chiefs, the office was still passionately competed for in the 1940's, as much by the younger, educated men as by their illiterate brethren. To be sure, in prosperous cocoa areas and the big towns, opportunities to take advantage of their position in order to make money did come the way of chiefs. But the main incentives were not economic. Pride of ancestry, ambition for public esteem, local patriotism, and last but by no means least, a sense of obligation to forbears and to uphold traditional cultural values were most important. Kurankyi-Taylor observes that "status is still prized very highly in Ashanti . . . and connections with a stool-owning [that is, chiefly] lineage is emphasized whenever, for any reason a man has to explain who he is" (1951: 340).

37. Kurankyi-Taylor (1951: 340–42) reports that more than half of the cases which came before divisional councils in the 1950's were disputes which concerned rank or status depending on membership of a particular lineage. I came across several cases of this sort in 1945.

V

Where, however, genealogical exactitude is of most importance is in delimiting the segments of a maximal lineage. These are designated either by the term *fie*, house, when the emphasis is on its jural status, or as *yafunu koro*, one womb, when its descent constitution is emphasized in contraposition to the lineage as a whole.

The *yafunu* segment consists of the uterine descendants of a common ancestress three or four (in special cases up to six) generations antecedent to its latest generation of members. They are most commonly a group of people whose mothers' mothers (*nana*) and mothers' mothers' brothers (*nana*) grew up together as siblings of the same maternal parentage in the same household and they think of themselves as, and often act as if they still are, one household even though they may live in different family dwellings. Each married adult in such a group earns his or her own living, whether as a farmer or trader or craftsman or in other ways, and there is no common exchequer for the group. But this is the widest unit in which material property and personal status pass by inheritance and thus become a corporate possession. This is the unit in which jural control of persons and property is primarily vested.[38] There is an acknowledged "head of the house" (*fie panin*) who is normally the most senior male in the status of brother (*nua*) and mother's brother (*wofa*). But as with office in the strict sense, if he is not considered to be competent for the task another man may be selected. The selection is made whenever a successor is appointed to the position of a deceased "house-head." The same rules apply also to the coadjutant position of senior woman (*obaa panin*) of the lineage.

In the context of the uterine (*yafunu*) group or stirp, the senior male vested with jural authority is defined as a *wofa*, mother's brother, not as a lineage head. He is the immediate guardian having jural control over dependent and especially filial members of the group. Thus *tiri nsa* cannot be offered, accepted, or refunded for a marriage without the concurrence of the respective mother's brothers. The cross-cousin marriages which older Ashanti still favor are arranged by mothers' brothers asserting their jural authority over one of the parties, and their paternal claims upon the other.[39] And, most significantly, a mother's brother could in earlier times pawn a sister's child in order to settle a debt incurred for the sake of the child's close maternal kin or for the common benefit of the *yafunu*.[40] It is worth noting that these powers[41] are akin to rights of disposal over property such as land or chattels or

38. This is the unit to which Rattray usually applies the term "family," e.g., when he remarks that "the family was a corporation; action and even thought were corporate affairs" (1929: 62 and *passim*).

39. See below, p. 213, for further comment on this form of "cousin" marriage.

40. For example, to ransom a captured brother or sister or to "buy the head" of a member convicted of a capital offense. But note that the father had to be given the first refusal to pay the debt. If he accepted, his child could thus become legally his pawn. If he refused, his consent for the pawning away of the child was necessary (cf. Rattray, 1929: chap. III). The payment *tiri sika* for a wife to her matrikin, by her husband, is analogous. She thus becomes his quasi-pawn (cf. Fortes, 1950: 281).

41. See Rattray's penetrating discussion (1929: chap. III). But neither the mother's brother nor the lineage head, nor, for that matter, the lineage acting as a corporate body, had any *jus vitae necisque*. This right was vested solely in the king. Even expulsion from the lineage required the king's consent (see below, p. 185). Thus citizenship in the nation put a limit to the degree to which a person could be regarded as "owned by" his lineage.

livestock or slaves but with the important difference that they are constrained by the coincident moral rights of the parents as well as by the reciprocal rights of the filial parties, notably the indefeasible right to inherit.

These rights exist in the domain of the lineage and their jural character is patent in the sanctions pertaining to them. Disputes arising out of actual or threatened infringements upon them can be brought to the chief's court. A typical case is where a widow attempts to retain possession of one of her late husband's farms on the grounds that she had loyally worked with him throughout a long marriage and had assisted him in making this particular farm. In the cases of which I have records, the court has invariably ruled in favor of the legitimate matrilineal heir—but with an exhortation, on the grounds of equity and common decency, for some concession to be made by the heir to the dispossessed wife. Similar suits arise over gifts claimed by sons.[42]

VI

The *yafunu* group—the uterine stirp—is the nuclear and paradigmatic descent unit within the maximal lineage. The *yafunu* group is defined and delimited by the rule of matrilineal descent. It is both a segment of the greater lineage and a greater lineage writ small, in process of becoming one. It is jurally corporate in the way the maximal lineage is corporate, as participating in that corporateness. Its parts, on the other hand, are sibling groups, defined by matrifiliation, and axiomatically corporate.

These distinctions are made explicit in the laws of property (Rattray, 1929: 330 ff.). Rattray established that the Ashanti laws of property, in conformity with the common Akan pattern earlier described by Sarbah[43] distinguished three classes of property irrespective of its kind. He lists them as (a) stool property; (b) family property; and (c) private property. More accurately, this should read, (a) property vested in office; (b) property vested in a lineage segment; (c) self-acquired property. In other words, property is classified by reference to the status of the owner and its mode of acquisition, not in terms of such characteristics as its durability or movability, realty, or personalty.[44]

Prima facie, these classes of property are mutually exclusive, as is evident from the litigation previously referred to over claims of chiefs to dissociate their private wealth and resources from the stool property in their official custody. But they are in fact interconnected by a rule of one-way transformability arising from their status-fixture. Taking into account such relatively durable personal possessions as clothes, jewelry, tools, weapons, utensils, and furniture, as well as consumables such as

42. I have analyzed elsewhere the clash between jural principles and equitable norms that are at issue in such cases (1963).

43. Sarbah, 1897: 47 ff., systematized information available from his own legal practice, personal experience as a Fanti, and records of court cases, government commissions, etc. Bosman and Bowdich have observations that show how deeply rooted these laws are in Akan thought and social structure.

44. This is, of course, a common pattern in African societies with unilineal descent groups. Cf., e.g., Lloyd, 1962.

livestock, food crops, and cash, every person who was willing to exert himself or herself could, in the past—and can much more easily nowadays—accumulate private property. Farms, houses, slaves could be thus acquired. Nowdays a person can also acquire buildings, vehicles, cash savings, and cocoa farms by his own efforts. Even slaves could do so (cf. Rattray, 1929: 41). But only a free citizen, *sui iuris*, could lawfully dispose of his private property at will. (A slave's property—since he was not a citizen, *sui iuris*—was deemed to be ultimately owned by his master.) However, as we have seen, his citizenship is contingent upon his lineage membership, and as with an office holder, the prerogative rights of the latter take precedence of and are absorbed in the former in the field of intralineage relations. This emerges particularly in regard to aspects of his status, and to material goods associated with them, which are heritable—which, in Ashanti jural theory, must be perpetuated by devolution post mortem on an heir and successor. Self-acquired property which has not been consumed, or disposed of by gift, or by a death-bed declaration complying with the proper formalities of dispensation by the lineage, becomes automatically heritable; and property once inherited is converted into a corporate possession which must forever afterwards thus be preserved.[45] Property originally acquired by a particular ancestor thus becomes the corporate possession of a lineage segment of greater and greater span in each generation and eventually gets vested in the lineage head's office as if it were stool property. This is how the lineage "ownership" of land previously mentioned has come about.

But before looking more closely at this process, I should like to return for a moment to the *yafanu* group. Considered from within, Ashanti visualize the structure of the lineage as an expanded and extended *yafunu* group. And the core and paradigm of its constitution, as they see it, consists of a woman, her brother, and her children of both sexes. All the elementary relationships through the combination and expansion of which the structure of the lineage is generated are given in this constellation—the relations of matrifiliation, siblingship, generational succession, fraternal and avuncular authority. And what unifies this constellation and makes it uniquely binding in an absolute sense is its genesis in "one womb," its focus in "one mother." *Abusua*, lineage, or more abstractly, matrilineal descent, in essence signifies to spring from one mother, as the pathetic proverb, "when your mother is dead that is the end of your *abusua*,"[46] implies. The lineage is this constellation perpetuated. Thus, when any group of Ashanti describe themselves as the offspring of one mother they might be referring to their own mother; but they might, just as likely, be referring to a genealogically remote common ancestress. Having a common mother means having the same blood and this is tantamount to replicating her in the next and all successive generations. *Mogya, wom popa*—"The blood, you cannot extinguish it," says the proverb. That is why the matrilineal descendants of a slave woman remain forever jurally unfree. Thus when Ashanti define the lineage as

45. The Ashanti concept *di* signifies both to inherit (*di ade*, to inherit things, i.e., material goods and property) and to succeed (*di ohene*, to succeed as chief). As Christaller rightly observes (1881: 77), *di* is a word of manifold meanings, but the root meaning seems to be connected with the idea of "eating" in the sense of appropriating, or incorporating, as is the case in many other African, and particularly West African, languages.

46. *Wo ni wu a, wo abusua asa* (cf. Rattray, 1916: 38–39).

being "one person" they are thinking of it as if the founding ancestress were etern-
ally present in her descendants, multiplied and replicated but still one and the same,
much as a tree (to which a lineage is often compared) is the same tree however many
branches it proliferates. And the mechanism on which this depends, which ensures
the perpetual transmission of the blood and the consecutive replication of the
person, is the succession of uterine generations. This is the root of the concept of
abusua. For a given generation it means a status derived from the fact of being born
of one mother; in the continuity of the generations it means the status derived by
the successive replacement by jural right of each generation by the next. Filiation
thus merges into descent.

Thus the basic building block of structural continuity in the lineage is the sibling
group born of one mother,[47] not a "line of descent" reckoned from person to
person, let alone the individual. The lineage—otherwise, the expanded *yafunu*
group—is not to be thought of as a collectivity of individuals bound together by the
common matrilineal descent documented in their convergent matrilineal pedigrees.
At the level we are here concerned with, its constituent units are the uterine sibling
groups. The often-quoted proverb "The lineage is like an army but your own
mother's child is your true sibling [i.e., your closest kinsman]"[48] expresses pithily
the Ashanti ideal of siblingship. The unity of the sibling group is exemplified in the
norms of residence; their solidarity is stressed in the assumption that absolute
loyalty and unrestricted confidence and intimacy distinguish the relations of
siblings, irrespective of sex, by contrast with the conjugal relationship,[49] and their
jural equivalence is shown in the rules governing inheritance and succession.

Siblingship uniquely segregates those united by it in contradistinction to other
intragenerational ties. Internally to the sibling group, that is, among themselves,
true siblings feel bound not only by mutual affection and identification, but by a
bond of inescapable moral obligation to support one another against outsiders
regardless of idiosyncrasies of personality and character; and so tight are these
affective and moral bonds felt to be that they are carried over into the next and next
but one or even two generations. This is the pragmatic basis of the *yafunu* group's
unity and solidarity which, conceptually and dogmatically, is referred to its single
maternal origin. Thus to speak of the uterine grandchildren or great-grandchildren
of one woman through different daughters or daughters' daughters as "classificatory"
siblings is to imply a formality of relationship which does scant justice to the way
Ashanti feel about it.[50]

But by the fourth and fifth generation, as a rule—depending upon the number of
distinct matricentric branches comprised within its span—a *yafunu* group is in
process of fission into its component sibling groups. At this point, in terms of the
developmental cycle, or, from the observer's angle, with this collocation, the jural

47. As Radcliffe-Brown perceived—cf. p. 76 above.
48. *Abusua ye dom, na wo na oba ne wo nua* (cf. Rattray, 1916, no. 472, p. 125).
49. The concomitant tensions that result in suspicions of witchcraft are adverted to later.
50. The assimilation of mother's sister to mother, mother's sister's children to own
mother's children, sister's children, to own children, etc., gave rise to some awkward problems
in the demographic study I made in 1945 (cf. Fortes, 1954: *loc. cit*). But see below, p. 176,
reference to the autonomy of the matricentric group.

norms that govern the sibling group's external relations with other such groups in the maximal lineage, and with the maximal lineage as a unit, come into operation. The crucial test lies in the regulation of inheritance and succession.

VII

It is a fixed principle of Ashanti social structure that every citizen at death must have an heir and successor, be it no more than a nominal one.[51] What is primarily at issue is a person's status as lineage member, as parent or spouse, and as citizen. The correspondence with office this implies is explicitly understood (cf. Fortes, 1963). And just as office is identified by a title and anchored in a palpable, physically durable, and transmissible stool, so personal jural status is anchored in a person, labeled by kinship terms, and represented in material possessions which can be passed on. Though a person may have no other possessions than a piece of clothing, Ashanti declare, this is enough to serve as the material focus for the procedure of appointing his successor. The important consideration is that his position in society shall not be extinguished finally with his death. Merged with his successor's status, it can lapse with the next shift in the sequence of succession. An heir is appointed (according to my information) in characteristic Ashanti fashion on either the eighth day or the fortieth day after the burial, when the whole lineage, together with patrilateral relatives, many affines, and other fellow citizens, assembles under the presidency of the lineage head to balance the accounts of the expenditure incurred. In the case of a man, the senior males of the *yafunu* segment confer and announce to the lineage assembly, through the head, the name of the person they deem to be the proper heir. If the head and the lineage elders approve, the heir is forthwith appointed to "take his predecessor's gun" and he signifies his acquiescence by the customary procedure of making an *aseda* payment to those present. If the deceased is a woman, the appointment is proposed by the senior women and the same procedure is followed.[52]

Thus a personal heir is appointed by a procedure similar to that followed with

51. The parallel with the widespread Central African custom of positional succession needs no emphasis. This applies most directly to anyone who has jural authority over others as a household head, parent or senior member of a matrilineal group such as the *yafunu*. However, every citizen (for that matter, formally speaking, even a child and even a quasi-citizen such as a female slave's offspring) has that modicum of personal identity and of jural autonomy which permits him to acquire private property and to swear an oath; he has also, in any case, status in his lineage, and by patrifiliation, and possibly as spouse or parent. Thus every adult is deemed to have a sufficiently definitive identity and position in the social structure to necessitate the termination of his status incumbency by replacing him with a successor, *post mortem*. I have discussed some of the implications of assimilating jural status in general to office in Fortes, 1962b, where I allude, also to the parallel with Maine's concept of the "corporation sole."

52. It is interesting that a woman's successor is said to "take her predecessor's hoe." The stereotype of a man is that he is a hunter and a soldier, always ready to take up arms at the chief's command; a woman, in contrast, is thought of as a housewife and provider of food, hence the symbolism of the hoe. Since women are jurally autonomous as citizens and capable of owning property, incurring debts, and holding any of the offices allocated to women, their successors have a parallel status to those of men.

succession to office; but the selection is in this case more precisely restricted. The presumptive heir is the deceased's oldest surviving sibling of the same sex.[53] Next in line is a sibling descended from a common maternal great grandmother. Failing a sibling, the right devolves on the next sibling generation in the uterine line, that is, the deceased's own sister's children, in order of their mothers' respective ages. Failing any of these, in the case of a man's status and estate, the choice lies between own sisters' daughters' sons and collateral sisters' (mother's sisters' daughter's) sons. Age and personal qualities will be the deciding factors. Failing these, the material estate passes to own sister or own sister's daughter or even daughter's daughter (that is, a sororal stirp), or, next in order, to the collateral sister of the same grandmother and her stirp. Specifically male elements of a dead man's status (as husband and father) may, in such circumstances, be devolved upon a collateral brother or sister's son within the *yafunu* group of more distant connection. Succession to a woman's estate and status follows the same schedule, with the sex reversed.

The lawful heir is thus precisely specified, but, as with office in general, it is accepted that if he or she is considered to be incapacitated by age, sickness, or infirmity of character, the next in line may be selected. For it is not merely the deceased's material assets and correlated debts but also his jural and moral responsibilities that have to be taken over, among the most important for a man being the husbandhood of a deceased brother's widow and the proxy-paternity of his children. Kinship usages imply recognition of this rule. Thus it is, Ashanti say, because a man's brothers and his sisters' sons are the prescribed successors to his paternal status that his children address them proleptically, as it were, by the kinship term for father (*agya*), especially if they are older and therefore entitled to deference in any case.

I must reiterate that these rules have the force of law as well as the sanctions of moral values and religious obligation. Anyone acting in contempt of them risks not only ostracism by his lineage but an action in the chief's court. This is because an estate that is heritable is not in the exclusive possession of its holder at a given time. He cannot even appropriate to his exclusive use such parts of it as a house or a parcel of land as were personally acquired by his predecessors and merged in the heritable estate. The dominium, as the Roman lawyers might have said—that is, full ownership—vests always in the entire body of the uterine descendants of the estate's originator. A heritable estate is, in this sense, a corporate possession.[54] What the holder has at any given time is the custody of it. Thus he cannot mortgage, sell, or give away any item of the estate except by the common consent of the co-parceners. All that his trusteeship and *de facto* control entitle him to is some private benefit from the estate, provided this does not diminish its heritable value

---

53. Formerly, in the sibling group comprising the children of full sisters—that is, having a common maternal grandmother. Nowadays, own mother's child often takes precedence of older mother's sister's child.

54. Cf. Rattray, 1929: chap. III. Emphasizing this point, Sarbah (1897: 85) observes that "there is no such thing as succession in the proper English meaning in a family owning ancestral property. The whole family, consisting of males and females, constitutes a sort of corporation." Discussing this, he adds, "partition being extremely rare, the idea of heirship scarcely presents itself to the mind of any member of the family. . . ."

or deprive his co-parceners of their rights in it. He can, as it were, use the income from it, especially if he incurs costs in connection with it, such as contributing to the funeral expenses, paying his predecessor's debts, or supporting the widow and children; but he may not expend the capital. Nowadays, he can freely dispose of the cocoa he harvests from an inherited cocoa farm, but the farm itself belongs to the heritable property of the corporate group and he is under an obligation to assist from the proceeds other members of the group who may be in need. It is likewise with semi-durable inherited articles such as fine clothes and household furniture, and with valuables such as trinkets of gold. He has the custody and the use of these things but any member of the group has the right to borrow them. If, as is rare with ordinary folk, any cash savings come to him, these should be applied to such common purposes as the education of the children, both of his predecessor and of his co-parceners. All the co-parceners and their children have rights in an inherited house and, in my experience, frequently exercise them.

VIII

However, the most significant feature of these rules of inheritance is their limited range. The accepted principle is that property should not be allowed to pass out of the sibling group beyond the range of the descendants of a common grandmother. Rather than allow this to happen, women are appointed as heirs to property normally transmitted and held by men;[55] and, formerly, in the last resort, even a slave[56] of the house in preference to a collateral stirp. If, as is inevitable for demographic reasons, property does pass to distant lineage collaterals, it ceases to be heritable by universal succession. It now takes on the character of "stool" property attached to office and is administered for the corporate group by its head.

This restriction in principle of the ownership and inheritance of material property to a close uterine stirp is an enforceable right. It has two roots. Firstly it reflects the jural and moral singularity of matrifiliation, as opposed to matrilineal descent in the wider sense, though it is the irreducible credential for the latter. Full matri-siblings are "one person," "of one womb," a corporate unit in the narrowest sense, and sibling succession expresses the recognition of this indivisible corporate identity of the sibling group in opposition to the total lineage. Furthermore, the discrimination in this way of the unique character of matrifiliation also testifies to the assumption that every woman is a potential originator of a distinct uterine stirp. A reflection of this premise is the rule, strictly enforced by lineage elders, that two matri-sisters, even if they are genealogically distant sisters of the same lineage, may not be married to the same husband or to lineage brothers. Ashanti say it would be like incest, a confounding of the blood. As sisters, they say, the women are one person; as mothers, each is the origin of what will in due course become a separate *yafunu*

---

55. Though women can and do own land and houses, it is often said that such types of fixed property should be controlled by men.

56. This would normally have been a person of servile descent who had quasi-filial status in the house (hence *fie-nipa*).

group. These must have separate father-lineages to originate separate maternal branches,[57] a proviso the significance of which will be clearer presently. So important is this application of the criterion of complementary filiation to distinguish matrifilial sibling groups[58] that the converse, that is, the marriage of a man's sister of the same lineage to his wife's lineage brother, is also prohibited. Ashanti say this would be like buying and selling women in the market. Yet a brother can, by fraternal succession, inherit a deceased brother's wife and have children by her. The point is that the heir assumes his deceased brother's status which would otherwise lapse. He, in a sense, becomes his brother and is not competing with him. For behind these restrictions lies the assumption that siblings as autonomous persons are rivals beneath the surface of their amity—not on account of property and office but on account of conflicting claims upon offspring and on the power to produce offspring; and a symptom of this is the ideology of witchcraft, as we shall presently see. Restricted sibling succession marks off each matricentric uterine stirp from collateral units of the same order in the lineage, both from within and externally by a calculable and objective jural criterion.

But there is also a second root to be considered. This is the right of the individual as citizen to acquire and dispose of personal property in his lifetime. It is jurally and morally rightful for property so gained to remain with those who directly replace him in overall status (by universal succession) in the succession of generations. Hence the right of a man to make gifts of such property in his lifetime to his children, in particular his sons, who perpetuate his patrifilial status and spiritual essence. He may on the same principle also allocate some of this property, which would by normal inheritance accrue to the pool of the corporate property of the lineage, to siblings and sisters' children severally, and, in the case of a woman, own children. Such property then becomes exclusively heritable in the uterine stirp of the donee. A scrupulous heir should have regard for this ideal, and if no pre-mortem allocation is made, he or she should, in equity, hand over some of the deceased's personal possessions and private property to the deceased's own children and own sisters' children.

This emphasis on the identification of siblings with one another spills over to lineage offices and positions for which the jural rule is that all authentic members of the lineage are equally eligible. When a chiefship or councillorship falls vacant it is customary to give first consideration to brothers of close genealogical proximity

57. This is epitomized in a maxim complementary to that which asserts one lineage to be of one blood: *Agya, wonye no abien*—[As for] father, you do not have two of him."

58. As I have said elsewhere (Fortes, 1949a: 72) the matricentric group consisting of a woman and her children "seek[s] to assert its autonomy wherever possible, and to maintain its unity as long as the social relations created within it survive." Full autonomy is reached when the mother is able to establish herself as head of her own household made up of her uterine issue. Such a unit often remains co-resident and undivided for jural purposes until the fourth generation, as has already been implied. This is the unit which the concept *fie*, house, in the narrowest sense—applied, that is, without qualification—identifies. In the fourth generation the matrifilial sibling groups who make up the founding house (mother's daughters' daughter's children) are apt to move apart residentially and structurally, to establish coordinate sister-households, that is, stirps within the *yafunu* range. This developmental cycle is mirrored in the kinship terminology, as I shall later explain.

to the latest incumbent. There is a marked tendency, thus, for such offices to be retained within a *yafunu* group as long as suitable successors can be found in it.[59] Collateral *yafunu* groups of the same descent consequently get squeezed out, and in the thirties and forties claims for the recognition of their eligibility for ancestral chiefships were frequently brought before the Asantehene's court by such seemingly disfranchised uterine groups.

Lineage headship[60] like the chiefship, is by this practice, apt to be restricted to one major branch of a maximal lineage as long as suitable candidates come forward, though other branches are lawfully entitled to hold it, too, and from time to time succeed in doing so.

IX

What, then, of the constantly quoted rule that sisters' sons are the lawful successors of their mothers' brothers? The Ashanti maxim "If the brothers (*nua*) are not yet finished, nephews (*wofase*) or uncles (*wofa*) do not succeed",[61] is the clue to its proper significance. It is not the case that every man's designated successor is his sister's son. What the rule signifies is that the generation of nephews is ineluctably destined to replace by right the generation of their mothers' brothers in the structure of the nuclear stirp, and the lineage. This is the obverse of the jural dependence of sisters' children on mothers' brothers. And it is the kernel of the belief voiced in the saying, "Your nephew is your enemy," waiting for you to die so that he may inherit your property and status (cf. Fortes, 1950: 272).

This does not mean that nephews are believed to or normally do openly "hate" their uncles. On the contrary. They often reside together, since nephews are expected to and commonly do move from their fathers' to their uncles' dwelling groups after adolescence.[62] In any case, post-adolescent males come under the jural authority of their mothers' brothers and often cooperate with them in economic activities. Nephews are, moreover, required to behave with marked respect towards their mothers' brothers and other senior matrilineal kin. And in the background of their relationship there are always, also, the bonds of lineage solidarity which impose a common front against non-members.

What the maxim reflects is the ambivalence in their relationship that springs from the opposition of consecutive generations. A symptom of this is the watchfulness of nephews—and, for that matter, of younger brothers, too—lest uncles (or older brothers) show excessive favoritism to their own children or abuse their trusteeship by squandering corporate property, or abuse their jural authority by

59. The genealogies recorded by Rattray, 1929: *passim*, show this, and those collected during the course of the Ashanti Social Survey confirm his data.

60. The duty and privilege of supplying a priest or priestess for a lineage divinity and other custodial offices vested in a lineage are similarly restricted in practice.

61. *Nnuanom nsae a, wofase* (or *wofa*) *nni adie*. Cf. Rattray, 1929: 333.

62. See Fortes, 1949a. In the 1940's, in the more traditional rural areas, I found that among post-adolescent males living in households with male heads approximately 50 per cent resided with their fathers and the remaining 50 per cent with their mothers' brothers.

oppressing sibling and nepotal dependents. But the real issue, even with uncles and nephews living together in amity, is the underlying rivalry due to their inescapable jural and moral relationship. It is not a question of economics. In modern times nephews can be much better off than uncles by reason of personally acquired wealth. It is a question primarily of the irresistible claims and rights *in personam* of each upon the other; and the potential clash of these claims is sharpened by the knowledge of the inevitability of the mothers' brothers' supersession by the nephews' generation. Rights in property and office are objective foci for the deployment of this relationship, but they are not the force that makes it what it is.

Siblings do not have an overtly ambivalent relationship. Their jural equality within the corporate unit predicates equality of sharing (differences of seniority being allowed for) in jural authority and responsibility, and consequently in property and status. This may not always be realized in practice, but it is emphatically asserted as the norm in sentiment. However, important elements of ambivalence do enter into siblingship. Younger brothers, as has been mentioned, sometimes feel like nephews. It is most obvious, though, in the cross-sibling relationship. Ideally (and commonly in practice) it is a relationship of the closest intimacy and trust. But every woman, as wife and mother, is at times torn between her loyalties to husband and children on the one hand and to her siblings and uterine kin on the other. She can leave her husband if he neglects her or her children; she cannot opt out of the corporate sibling group even if she suspects her brother's intentions with regard to her beloved sons. A brother has jural authority over his sister's children because he is her male cofiliate in the corporate stirp and because men take jural precedence over women in the politico-jural domain and, therefore, in the management of the corporate group. A sister has jural (as well as moral) claims on her brother because she is his female equivalent and co-parcener by right of matrifiliation, but most of all because she is the sole source of the continuity and perpetuity of their branch of the lineage and, therefore, of his status. This is the core of the tension which under-lies their relationship even when they are living together in ostensible harmony. This is the intragenerational coefficient of the ambivalence that lies behind the relations of consecutive generations in the lineage.

We perceive from this that matrifiliation has two dimensions. In the language of our conventional notation, there is the primary, "lineal" dimension of filiation in the exact sense, that is, the customarily defined and recognized connection of offspring with parent; and there is the secondary, "lateral", dimension of uterine cofiliation which establishes siblingship. As the elementary credential for alignment by descent, matrifiliation *senso strictu* implements siblingship, but the structural cleavage between successive generations introduces an antinomy between these two equally binding connections.

X

The ambivalences generated by these contrary pulls and pressures of jural norms, moral claims and personal attachments in the uterine stirp find customary outlet in a way familiar to us from other African societies. They emerge in beliefs and conduct that postulate the notion of witchcraft. In the Ashanti social system, the witchcraft syndrome has a special structural implication. By throwing into dramatic relief the strains that are peculiar to uterine kinship relations, it makes conspicuously evident the structural opposition that exists between patrilateral ties, on the one side, and matrilateral ties, on the other, within the total field of a person's kinship relations.

The Ashanti notion of witchcraft (*bayi*) corresponds broadly to a pattern that is widespread in Africa.[63]

The critical feature for my present argument, in the generally accepted ideology of witchcraft, is the belief that it operates only within the lineage and more specifically within close uterine range—that is to say, within the primary field of the incest taboo.[64] Ashanti often speak as if it is by reason of their potentiality for committing witchcraft upon one another that close matrikin know and feel themselves to be "one person." Spouses and patrikin are believed to be immune. The cases I met with, and those quoted by Field, Debrunner, and Ward, conform with few (and doubtful) exceptions to this expectation and my own informants were unanimous about this.[65] The stereotype of the witch is an old woman (*aberewa*) consumed with malice and envy. This means, in effect, an aged grandmother or mother. The term *aberewa* is normally used in address and reference as an expression of deep respect—

63. The parallels are especially close, as one might expect, with other African societies that have corporate matrilineal descent groups in which witchcraft is believed to operate. (Cf. Marwick, 1965; Mitchell, 1956.)

64. Our best source for the pre-colonial picture of the syndrome is Rattray. There are brief references to the subject at various places in the Rattray corpus, but even the lengthier discussions (1927: 28–31, 1929: 313–16) provide only an outline of information. The inquiries that mainly occupied my attention in 1945 left time only for some incidental observations on this topic. More recently, Dr. M. J. Field's important study (1960) of mental illness in Ashanti and its treatment by diviner-healers has provided a wealth of pertinent observations. Interesting and relevant material is also to be found in H. Debrunner's compilation (1959), despite its generally biased and tendentious tone, and its heavy reliance on Field and other writers. Barbara E. Ward's paper, "Some Observations on Religious Cults in Ashanti" (1956) has some admirable material on conditions in the forties. (See also Goody, 1957.) These observers agree in general that there was a considerable proliferation in the thirties and forties of cult centers especially devoted, among other things, to exposing and purging alleged witches and protecting their adherents against mystical injury by witchcraft. This suggests that there was indeed during this period, as Ashanti public opinion maintained, a notable increase in fear and suspicion of witchcraft. They agree, also, in attributing this trend to increasingly acquisitive and competitive economic habits, and to the social stresses due to the new political, educational, and cultural developments of this period. My own informants frequently asserted this. However, the social pathology, of which the spread of witch-finding cults is inferred to be symptomatic, is not relevant to my present discussion. What is relevant is the observations of these authors on the patterns of belief, and on the structural locus of witchcraft charges revealed in the confessions of alleged witches and in the opinions of informants. The interesting point is that they corroborate Rattray's account in essentials. It may well be that the suppression of the traditional poison and other ordeals and public measures for detecting and eliminating supposed witches gave an impetus to the growth of cults that now achieve the same end by extorting public confessions, fines, and penance from purported witches in order to purge them and thus enable them to be readmitted to normal community life.

65. Cf. Rattray, 1927: 28: "a witch is powerless . . . over any one outside the witches' clan" (*sc.* lineage, in my terminology).

but one with an admixture of affectionate regard—for elderly female kin.[66] Observation confirms that it is in fact grandmothers, mothers, sisters, brothers, and mothers' brothers of all ages, within close uterine range—though predominantly women relatives—of purported victims of witchcraft who incur suspicion and exposure.

Characteristically, witches are supposed to inflict injury by mystically "eating" the flesh and "drinking" the blood of (cannibalistically incorporating) their victims— the very flesh and blood they share with them by the dogma of lineage descent. This vice is of the essence of witchcraft. It is a kind of incest, a perversion and a sin and doubly abominable, therefore. To be initiated into the mystical college of witches, a witch must begin her nefarious career by "killing" and offering for the common witch-meal a close uterine relative. A presumed witch's confession often begins with the admission that she thus "slew" and offered up her own child. Witchcraft is believed to be an inherent, basically hereditary[67] propensity arising by matrifilial transmission either at birth or by action analogous to the passing on of female property from mother to daughter. Thus it is sometimes alleged to have been acquired from a witch-mother or grandmother through the medium of a medicine or other mystically contaminated substance or object. Any misfortune could, in the forties, be attributed to witchcraft. But the commonest acts of witchcraft claimed in the public confessions of suspected witches at cult centers were causing the death of relatives or destroying, by "eating" or "stealing" it, the health or the economic skill or, above all, the sexual potency of male kin and the fertility ("the womb") of female kin. Furthermore as Dr. Field's case records of self-accusation vividly illustrate, witchcraft can turn punitively inwards and cause its possessor to fall physically or mentally ill or succumb to economic misfortune through ineptitude. The fantasies of nudity, cannibalism, flying, walking upside-down, harboring snakes in the body, metamorphosing into animals, and so forth, brought out in confessions by supposed witches, aptly portray propensities most antithetic and abhorrent to the ideals of fidelity, propriety, and moral responsibility, especially in the intralineage relations focused in the incest taboo, that are regarded as the hallmarks of normal humanity. It is these propensities that are symbolically projected in the notion of witchcraft;[68] real cannibalism or perversion would, of course, be legally punished.

66. Cf. Christaller, 1881: 18 (2nd ed. 1933): " 'm'aberewa' is even more respectful than 'me na' " (that is, mother). *Opanin* (elder), the corresponding term for males, has more formal overtones since it connotes a status of authority. English colloquialisms such as "my old man" = "my father" or "my husband"; "my old lady " = "my mother," "my wife," exemplify a similar usage. Christaller, incidentally, has an excellent note on witchcraft, s.v. *bayi*.

67. Cf. Christaller, 1881: 11, s.v. *bayi*: "bayi yε abusuade," which he translates as: *"witchcraft is inborn, innate, hereditary,"* but which I would translate, *"bayi* is a thing (that is, property) of the lineage."

68. This aspect of the Ashanti ideology of witchcraft is ably analyzed by M. D. McLeod in a comprehensive study of the syndrome submitted as a dissertation for the B. Litt. degree at Oxford (1965). I am indebted to Mr. McLeod for the opportunity of consulting his dissertation, which I have found helpful in clarifying my presentation of the subject. The sexual aggression and moral depravity symbolically expressed in these fantasies are patent. They indicate what is felt to be the most characteristic and abominable trait of witchcraft, that is,

In the context of interpersonal relations, *bayi* is seen as morbid lust, hatred, and aggression; in the wider ethical context, it is thought of as evil incarnate—as the association with the *sasabonsam* indicates. It is peculiarly dangerous just because it is an involuntary, unconscious proclivity inherent in the very fabric of the social relations which are, for Ashanti, the fount of their existence as a society and of their whole moral order. For *bayi* comes ultimately from the mother, the source of the individual's flesh and blood which fixes his rights to his place in society through the corporate existence of the lineage and imposes the incest rule on him. It is the person, both as a physical entity and as a right- and duty-bearing unit trans-mitting the blood which forms the lineage and the norms that bind it to society, that *bayi* destroys. One can easily see the symbolic aptness of the notion that a witch slays and injures by consuming the blood and flesh of its victim.

Seen from the outside, *bayi* is the eruption of unacknowledged lust and hostility behind the ineluctable bonds of matrikinship. It is the hidden canker at the heart of the solidarity demanded by law and morality and symbolized in the incest rule in the relations of mother and child, brother and sister. Ashanti regard the affective attachments of uterine kin as laid down by the fact of birth (in what Malinowski described as the "Initial Situation of Kinship") and as absolutely bind-ing. *Bayi* is the negation of this. On the one side, there is no licit escape from the jural obligations and moral prescriptions coterminous with matrikinship; on the other, there is, equally, no customarily legitimate expression, direct or symbolical, for the potential rivalries of siblings and successive generations rooted in the unalterable genealogical distinctions of sex, birth order, and generation. It is the brother's or son's potential duplicity in his alternative capacity as husband and father; the daughter's or sister's potential disloyalty to her mother and brother when she puts the children of her own womb before them; the mother's ambiguous position as the source of both the bonds and the rivalries; the mother's brothers' invidious status as the lawful holder of authority and the proper target of jealous claims; it is these ambivalent statuses within the unbreakable ring of matrikinship that attract

---

its menace to the sexuality and fertility of the victims, and therefore of the lineage. The connection with the incest rule is again evident in this. Witchcraft does not "pollute" (*fra*) the blood; it consumes (*di*) the blood. Following long-standing convention, I translate *bayi* as witchcraft. Like most Ashanti mystical and metaphysical concepts it is only diffusely defined in speech and custom (cf. Ward, 1956). The information I was able to gather is in line with Dr. Field's analysis (1960: 36–37, *et passim*). *Bayi* is spoken of as if it were an evil power, "implanted" as she phrases it, by birth or by contact. It is thought of as taking posses-sion of and entering into a person as if it were an alien object or creature. The fantasies of witches having snakes in their body or, significantly, concealed in the vagina (Debrunner, 1959: 52–60) symbolize these notions graphically. Thus objectified, *bayi* is sometimes spoken of as if it were a particular and personal incarnation of the imaginary pseudo-human forest monster *sasabonsam*, often designated in the literature by the word "devil" (cf. Rattray, 1916: 47; 1927: 28; and Christaller, 1881: 429 (2nd ed. 1933), s.v. *sasabonsam*). He is a spectral personification of the abhorrence, disgust, and terror evoked by any acts of repudiation of the moral and civic standards and habits that are assumed to distinguish humanity from the non-human. Appropriately enough, *sasabonsam* is imagined as having grotesquely exaggerated and partly back-to-front human bodily features, as living in the forest outside the pale of human society, and as abandoned to the hate, malice, and deceit that is destructive of amity and mutuality.

apprehensions of secret malignity in situations of stress and ill-luck which seem to threaten the personal existence, or the precious faculty of reproduction owed to the mother and the lineage. The envy and malice to which Ashanti summarily ascribe the maleficence of witches cannot, as they emphasize, arise between patrikin, or spouses, since they are not "one person" bound by jural duress or the moral imperative focused in the clan incest rule.

It is understandable why *bayi* is pictured as an evil power that can even take on a material form and possess a person from the outside, as it were, but is carried in the very blood which it destroys. For as elsewhere in Africa, a witch is not conscious of her wicked powers or known to have them until a misfortune occurs and she is exposed.[69] And it is significant that nowadays once she has confessed, made amends, and been ritually cleansed, she is said to be accepted by the very kin whom she was supposed to have injured, as if nothing had happened to mar the harmony of their relationships.

A saved witch must become an adherent of the deity at whose cult center she was made aware of her evil propensity. Like voluntary adherents who join for protection or to gain benefits, she thus binds herself to abide faithfully by its ritual and moral rules. And it is noteworthy that what these rules generally enjoin is obedience to the conventional norms of marital fidelity, honesty, faithful kinship, and neighborly amity and ritual observance—in short, to the norms of morality, propriety, and amity in kinship and community relations outraged by witchcraft. The end result of every such crisis is therefore to reaffirm the ideals of unity and amity within the uterine group focused upon its good, life-giving progenetrix, and the concomitant norms of good citizenship.

It is always an individual who is revealed as a witch, but the whole uterine group and, consequently, the whole local lineage in its corporate character, is implicated. Since the witchcraft syndrome expresses the repudiation of the fundamental norms of lineage structure, it is a threat to the very existence of society. The lineage at fault must not only regain its internal unity and cohesion; it must, also, purge itself in relation to society at large as in a case of overt incest. This is one reason why the lineage is not permitted to dispose of a witchcraft crisis privately, as a domestic case. Another is the fact that in pre-colonial conditions a citizen's life was at stake in a witchcraft trial.[70] Left to the private arbitrament of the lineage, suspicion of witchcraft could easily precipitate wanton accusations and persecution. It is understandable, therefore, why the commission of witchcraft was traditionally classified as a public delict and sin.[71] A charge of witchcraft had therefore to be proven by due process of public trial. It was a suspect's right which he could implement by swearing the chief's oath. Traditionally the trial was by ordeal regulated by jural

---

69. "According to witchcraft dogma, a person can possess an *obayi* without awareness of it, and can furthermore use it harmfully without knowing of it" (Field, 1960: 36). I use feminine pronouns for the sake of brevity in writing of witches here, but it must be emphasized that men can also be witches.

70. Cf. analogous ideas discussed in Middleton and Winter, 1963, "Introduction".

71. This principle applies in most African societies to the social control of witchcraft and sorcery; cf. Middleton and Winter, 1963: *passim*, and Marwick, 1965, and cf. again the notion of incest.

and ritual precepts and carried out with the consent and under the surveillance of chiefs and elders.[72]

The principle still held in the forties. Witch-finding cults could not be established in a community without the concurrence of the chiefs and elders.[73] They not only kept a watch on the activities of the priests and servitors, they often also had a stake in these centers. The costs of establishing them were heavy and the persons who procured the cult medicines and the rights to use them were often subsidized by chiefs and elders in return for a share in the profits.[74] Nevertheless, this represented, in the idiom of the new economic and social structure, an element of politico-jural control aimed at preventing wanton accusations and blatant extortion. The essential point that a suspect must be enabled to prove his or her innocence (and atone for his or her guilt) in a public trial—which had, by the very nature of the beliefs involved, to be of a ritual character—was preserved. People could and did deny guilt successfully.[75] Abuse of the principle by unscrupulous cult-priests lost them adherents. But this did not invalidate the principle that irrational and anarchic threats (as they appear to be to Ashanti) to the corporate identity and integrity of the lineage are of concern to the whole body-politic. It is comparable to the requirement for a lineage to have the king's assent if it wished to expel a sacriligeous or contumacious member, and to the subjection of incest and murder to politico-jural penalties. As has already been emphasized, beliefs about witchcraft and incest are linked. They are spoken of as if they were two sides of the same syndrome of immorality and wickedness, one being the perverse and secret, the other the public repudiation of the primary norms of matrikinship.

XI

What then, to sum up so far, is the lineage in its maximal span? Viewed from the outside, the lineage can properly be described as a corporation aggregate, in Maine's sense. It is a locally anchored association but not locally or territorially bounded. As such, it is a single politico-jural entity, a jural person, participating, as an indivisible segment of the political structure, in the government and ceremonial of the chiefdom through the office vested in its representative head. As such, likewise, it establishes and exclusively mediates the individual's citizenship in the state; and

72. Cf. Rattray, 1929, *op. cit.*, pp. 392 ff. The usual form of trial was by the *odom*, "poison drink ordeal." In this case the lineage head and kin supported the accused by their presence and prayers and were permitted to "buy her head" if she was convicted. The other form of ordeal was by carrying the corpse (Rattray, 1927: 167 ff.). The persistence of this custom to more recent times is referred to by Field, 1960: 77. Both the form of witchcraft trial and the corpse carrying were described to me by informants who had witnessed these practices in the early years of this century.

73. It is significant that they were (and are) mostly of non-Ashanti, especially Northern, origin. (Cf. Ward, B., 1956).

74. Quite modest centers could require a capital expenditure of £200–300. Famous centers to which petitioners came from all over the country were notorious as money-making enterprises on a substantial scale, as both Field and Debrunner confirm.

75. Field dicusses some instances.

as citizens, all members of a lineage are on a par with one another (sex and age being allowed for), entitled to the same rights and privileges, subject to the same duties and claims.

In this context, the significant requirements are that lineages shall be demarcated from one another by unequivocal structural boundaries, have continuity through time, and be unambiguously represented in the office of lineage head. These conditions are met by the recognition of matrilineal descent as the sole and exclusive rule for the assignment of persons to the politico-jural divisions of the community. But the same purpose could have been fulfilled by some other rule of exclusive politico-jural assignment—a locality rule, for example, as at the village level among the Lozi or, better still, the ward level among the Tswana.[76] Whether or not the lineage has an estate is irrelevant in this context.

So much for the corporate status of the lineage in the external politico-jural domain. The corporate *continuity* of the lineage depends, however, upon its internal structure and mechanisms of social reproduction; and here the rule of matrilineal descent operates in a different plane—as the central *internally* unifying organizing principle. Firstly, it uniquely and absolutely regulates the incorporation into the lineage of persons qualified by birth or adoption. Secondly, it is the basis of the structural framework within which the succession of matrifilial generations through time, and the consequential differentiation of uterine segments at a given time, are held together in exclusive, unitary, and perpetual association. It fulfills this task by virtue of being embodied in an accepted genealogical charter which validates both the unity of the lineage, as a whole, at a given time, and its internal differentiation by generation and stirp conceptualized as extended over a stretch of time. And thirdly, it is the institutional medium through which the metaphysical dogma of the perpetuity and unity of the lineage blood is translated into jural and moral process. The concept and rule of matrilineal descent serves, thus, as the crucial institutional bridge between the internal structure of the lineage and its external relations in the politico-jural domain. Lineage headship—the other, conceptually distinct, bridge institution—is, from the internal point of view, partly an administrative office and partly a priestly office, contingent upon the requirements for the orderly management of lineage affairs and for the implementation of its internal corporate unity.

Descriptively and for the actor, the lineage is a genealogically demarcated association of persons of both sexes and all ages and generations. It is an exclusive and rigorously closed association. A free person can belong to one and only one lineage. He belongs to it from birth to death and even after death. He can in no circumstances transfer his membership from his natal to any other lineage.[77] This is a politico-jural requirement for the unequivocal determination of citizenship. Thus the lineage can be properly described as a descent group in composition. Its freeborn members are without exception in it by indefeasible right of matrifiliation and

76. Cf. p. 242, below, and references in Schapera, 1955.

77. When a branch of a lineage becomes attached to a maximal lineage of the same clan in a community other than that of its original domicile, its members do not transfer membership but become incorporated in the host lineage as a secondary corporate unit—that is, as if their natal lineage-branch were a branch of the host lineage.

matrilineal descent. Conversely, a person cannot be a member of a specified lineage if he lacks the appropriate entitlement by matrifiliation and descent.[78]

From the point of view of the individual, what is crucial is that his jural status and capacities, both as citizen and as kinsman, are fixed unequivocally and *a priori* by his matrilineal descent. Within the lineage, his relative status is exactly specified by the generational and stirpal position he occupies vis-à-vis other members, while his parity with them is expressed in his formally equal eligibility with them for lineage office.

Externally, his lineage membership binds him so irrevocably that he could not in the pre-colonial period renounce it and remain in the society as a free citizen.[79] Even today, when many jural capacities and attributes of civic status are derived from the modern state structure, it is unthinkable for an Ashanti to renounce his lineage membership. To do so would be deleterious not only to his personal life but to his public activities as well. Formerly, it could however be forfeited, as I have mentioned. A person could be expelled from the lineage for outrageous misconduct or sacrilege, for example, incest or witchcraft, inimical to the norms of lineage morality and solidarity. This was tantamount to outlawry and like capital punishment, to which it was virtually equivalent, required the assent of the king.[80]

It is thus primarily as seen from within that the lineage constitutes a matrilineal descent group; and it is a corporate group by virtue of its structure and ideology, not by reason of corporate ownership of material property or corporate rights in a non-material estate. As Ashanti see it, the structural differentiation and relative internal autonomy of uterine segments within the total field of lineage relations is a matter of degree. The temporal extension mirrored in the genealogical calculus of lineage structure stretches back through preceding generations to a fixed origin, but it also stretches forward, proleptically, to the coming generations, in principle *ad infinitum*. The sibling group of today is assumed to be in process of expanding into a uterine stirp which in turn is potentially a main branch of an *abusua* (as maximal lineage). Present process reproduces past growth and presupposes future continuity within the same structural framework. The lineage is "one person," a single politico-jural personality, in time as well as at a given time.

This premise operates not only in the external politico-jural and ritual relations of the lineage, but also in its internal structure and administration. Hence all jural

78. To be pedantically exact, a person is a member of his lineage by *incorporation* to which he is entitled by *matrifiliation*, provided his mother is an *Ashanti* and is demonstrably connected by an exclusively matrilineal *pedigree* to the founding ancestress of the lineage. Each of the italicized words represents a requirement non-compliance with which can be invoked in litigation to disqualify a claimant. The incorporation of adoptive members is, as has been explained before, never absolute.

79. A person of servile origin would, of course, never be in a position even to contemplate such an action.

80. Cf. Rattray, 1929: 19, 71, 139. According to Rattray, a person expelled from his lineage was commonly "handed over to the chief for execution or enslavement" after the ritual act of "splitting" (*pae*) him off (*ibid.*, p. 19). To judge by the remarks of informants in the forties, this measure must have been regarded with such abhorrence that it was rarely resorted to. But unsubstantiated stories were told of distant branches of chiefly lineages which were alleged to have sprung from persons thus disinherited and sold into slavery. Sarbah refers to the same custom among the Fanti.

transactions and arrangements within the lineage require the concurrence of the whole lineage assembly, even if they directly concern only a minor segment of its membership. Without such concurrence, the limitation of the uterine range of inheritance and succession would be invalid. The lineage as a whole, as a body corporate, is the source of all rights and duties that ensue from matrilineal status. Characteristically, there is no fixed hierarchy of authority and responsibility within a lineage corresponding to its segmentation by sororal stirpes, precisely though these are distinguished in the genealogical calculus and by structural criteria.

As Ashanti see it, the corporate structure of the lineage is a continuum bounded at one end by its totality vis-à-vis the political community and at the other by the matrisibling group. The lineage as a whole is the maximal extension of the nuclear corporation constituted by the sibling group. The domain of lineage relations and interests lies between these two poles. Their polarity is, from one point of view, as represented in the lineage genealogy and as expressed in the distribution of mutual rights and duties, claims and privileges, sentiment and attitude, purely a matter of degree. The variable middle range of the *yafunu* group which is seen as marking, in some contexts, the furthest extension of co-filial sibling relations, in others, the limit at which lineage relations subsume siblingship, is evidence of this. Yet from another point of view, the polarity implies a divergence, if not an opposition, of interests. This is epitomized in the conceptual and custodial dissociation of material property and inheritance from ancestral stools and office.

Property in the physical sense is thought to appertain primarily and distinctively to the minimally corporate sibling group vis-à-vis the lineage; ancestral stools to the maximally corporate lineage vis-à-vis the political community. But this does not mean that Ashanti think of physical property as the constitutve basis, the *raison d'être*, of the unity and corporate character of the sibling group. On the contrary. Property is the vehicle of the unity and solidarity of the sibling group and its projection in the intergenerational continuity of the uterine stirp, just as the stool is of the lineage and, at the political level of the chiefdom. One might as well argue that a man is a man *because* he has a gun and a woman is a woman *because* she owns a hoe. These are but the material foci of the social status of the sexes. Common interests in heritable property follow from, they do not determine the recognition and differentiation of, matrilineal connections by degrees of kinship. Common interests in material possessions flow from mutual and corporate rights and duties *in personam*, not from shared interests in their utility for productive or exchange purposes in an economic sense; they do not eliminate the competitive cleavages which lead to the differentiation of matrifilial sibling groups with the passage of generations; nor does their absence promote fission in a uterine stirp. Property does not create the social relations of kinship and descent; it is an instrument by means of which they are given tangibility, as gifts and bequests from fathers most convincingly show.

There is other evidence that a material estate is not a determining factor of the corporate constitution of the sibling group or, above all, of the lineage. If Ashanti are asked what *shows* a lineage to be "one person"—as contrasted with the unity and perpetuity of the blood that *makes* it one person—considering the distinctions of age, sex, generation, genealogical distance, and, nowadays, occupation, wealth, and religious affiliation that necessarily obtain among its members, they never refer to material possessions, be it land or a house or any other utilitarian goods. They cite, firstly, the ancestral stools and, secondly, the identification of the lineage, as a unit, with its members, collectively and severally, in life and in death.[81]

As to the latter, the crucial instance always brought forward in evidence is the responsibility of the lineage for disposing of the death of a member. It is phrased in terms of solemn and inescapable obligation on the part of the lineage and of un-questionable right for the deceased. In explanation, informants speak of a person as "belonging" to his lineage almost like an item of physical property.[82] The lineage not only *is* the totality of its members; as I have already noted, it owns them; they constitute severally and collectively the primary "social value" for the group as a whole, as Radcliffe-Brown would have put it.[83]

When a member of the lineage dies, whether he is of the blood or incorporated by adoption or attachment, it is the lineage head's duty to take charge of the mortuary arrangements and observances and to preside over the eighth day, fortieth day, and anniversary obsequies. He must send the customary prestation to inform the chief. He must in particular provide a burial cloth to add to the mortuary apparel given by the close kin and spouse of the dead. And exceptional weight is placed on this duty. It is meant to demonstrate that the dead "belongs" primarily to him, as represen-tative and responsible head of the whole lineage, and not to the immediate kin. It is the lineage that has been bereaved; the grief of the immediate relatives is absorbed in the common grief. The whole lineage is in full mourning for the first one or two weeks and again on the obsequial days.[84] The immediate matrikin—mother, brother,

81. Note that this concerns the internal "self-image" of the lineage, not its responsibilities for its members in external politico-jural relations. Traditionally, totemic animal avoidances would also be cited.

82. This rule was repeatedly emphasized. It was brought home to me when my friend John O.'s father died in 1945 in the distant forest village where he was farming. John was, for his age, a well-educated man, a civil servant by profession, and a Methodist, at least nomin-ally. In accordance with custom, his father's body had to be brought home for burial in his own lineage cemetery. But for various reasons the elders of the lineage were not able to arrange transport quickly. John therefore took it upon himself to fetch the body. However, as he carefully explained to me, this was not properly his duty. He was doing this because, he said, it was a question of conscience. It was out of respect and affection for his father. But the body belonged to the lineage. They would receive it and perform the necessary rites and ceremonies in which he would participate only as a *mma-mma* (see p. 188).

83. I confine myself to a few of the structurally relevant features of the funeral ceremonies for commoners, which, even nowadays, are still elaborate and long drawn out, though some of the more harrowing customs observed by Rattray in the twenties and by earlier writers (cf. Rattray, 1927: chap. XIV), such as the treatment of widows, are obsolete.

84. Mourning consists in "fasting" (that is, refraining from eating the traditional staple foods of yam and plantain), wearing the dark-colored mourning cloths, and daubing red clay on the arms and face. Drinking alcohol often to the point of somber intoxication is permitted. These customs continue to be observed, even among Christians. The elaboration and, even today, abandon of Ashanti mourning customs deserve a consideration that cannot here be given to them. They show how death was regarded as a catastrophic threat to the whole social order. The notorious "human sacrifices" that accompanied the funerals of members of the king's or of high-ranking chiefs' families (cf. Rattray, 1927: chap. XI and references there to Bowdich and other earlier eyewitnesses), the drinking of alcoholic beverages to excess in order, it is said, to drown sorrow, the drumming and costly display, the elements of public

sister, nephew (father and son of course have no right to act)—of the deceased can take no action over the funeral without the formal concurrence of the lineage head and his elders.

Most significant is the distribution of obligations to meet the expenses, which can be heavy if the deceased is a person of standing.[85] Some costs, notably the provision of the coffin, fall upon the "sons of the lineage" (the *mma mma.*) Affines, friends, and sympathizers make voluntary donations. But the largest share falls upon the lineage. It is their collective obligation to meet the specific expense of providing such items as the beverages[86] and the sheep[87] which are prescribed by custom for the libations and sacrifices that may be required, and for the reception of the affinal and patrilateral relatives, the fellow citizens, the chiefdom dignitaries, and the friends, who come to condole, and with whom custom requires that drink and food be shared. When the accounts are made up, the appointed heir may be expected to contribute up to a third of the costs from the estate of the deceased. The balance is apportioned exactly on the lines of a stool levy for communal purposes, per capita, among the adult members of the lineage, the men usually paying twice the rate of the women. Ashanti link this with the obligation of the lineage to help a member who is in debt or extreme distress. A lineage could not and cannot be held responsible for the private debts of any of its members. But it is incumbent on the head to take action to save a member from being driven to desperation by debt or misfortune. The money needed is then collected by a capital levy on all the adult members.

XII

Let me turn back now to the lineage stools. The consecrated stools deposited generation after generation in the stool sanctuary of the lineage are thought of as replications of the stool of the founder which forms the material symbol of the headship. A rule of cardinal significance is that only lineage heads (and in chiefly lineages, their female coadjutants) who die in office have stools consecrated to them and receive sacrifices and libations in the stool sanctuary. No other antecessors are thus perpetuated.

85. In the mid-forties, newspaper editorials in the Gold Coast press constantly inveighed against the extravagant expenditure incurred at funerals and people at large complained vociferously. Yet the expenditure went on and according to information I have recently had still remains high. At the time of this writing, the funeral of a revered senior-woman of a lineage well known to me cost well over £400. Funerals I attended, in 1945, in a relatively poor village, cost around £100.

86. Traditionally, palm wine; in modern times, bottled soft drinks, beer, gin, and tea. To drink to the point of intoxication was formerly an accepted accompaniment to the display of mourning grief, as I have already noted.

87. One or more, depending on the esteem in which the deceased was held and the pride of the lineage, or equivalent comestibles and offerings.

---

frenzy, and most of all the preservation of kingly skeletons in the extremely holy royal sanctuary—all this eloquently testified to this attitude to death. It was and is connected with the danger that is felt to arise if office, especially high office, is left vacant (cf. Fortes, 1962b).

Ashanti offer libation and invoke their antecessors by name in many situations, both informal as well as formal. Whenever I met with elders of a lineage to discuss genealogies, the most senior began proceedings by pouring a little gin or whiskey (presented by me, as custom required) on the ground and calling upon the departed, some by name and others in a general formula, to come and receive the drink, to permit the inquiry to go forward, and to grant health and well-being to all of us. This is typical. Any individual, man or woman, can appeal to his antecessors in this way to bless an occasion or a person. But only deceased lineage heads are enshrined and receive ritual offerings and prayers from their successors, either on behalf of the whole lineage on ceremonial occasions, or on behalf of individuals or segments of the lineage. No branch of a lineage has its own consecrated stools. The antecessors who link it to the lineage founders and distinguish it from other branches are not specifically enshrined for worship, as in such patrilineal segmentary systems as that of the Tallensi. In religious as in jural terms, the lineage is a single entity subject to the perpetual ritual authority of those who held supreme jural authority in it at the time of their death.[88] This transmutation of pre-mortem jural authority and office into the post mortem religious authority and status of ancestorhood is the basis of Ashanti ancestor worship (cf. Fortes, 1965). But the point of immediate relevance is that it signifies the retention, within the ideological framework of the lineage structure, of the transmuted lineage heads. The lineage stool, in its generalized representation, is the keystone of the lineage's continuity, both on the plane of religious ideology and *ipso facto* on that of jural relations. It is by reason of this that chiefs and lineage heads combine in their office jural authority over the living and priestly service of the ancestors.

The lineage ancestors, incidentally (and consistently with the jural concept of the lineage as an indivisible corporation), are not visualized as mystically persecutory agencies, but rather as just and watchful arbiters and protectors of the social order. Their principal concern is with the corporate existence of the lineage as a whole, not with its individual members. Hence they are rarely offered worship and sacrifice except in the communal ritual festivals of the *adae* and *afahye*, or to purge sacrilege. It is the lineage as a whole, even the political community as a whole, not only the wrongdoers, that will suffer disaster due to the anger of the ancestors if anyone commits an act of sacrilege such as incest or false swearing of an oath or transgression of a rule of ritual pollution. The stool ancestors, therefore, are not appealed to for the protection of individuals or lineages against witchcraft, or to confer health, wealth or fertility on individuals. Before the advent of modern cults, the *obosom* gods were the religious agents from whom such benefits were sought (cf. Rattray, 1927: *passim*). "The ancestors," says Busia (1951: 24 ff.), "are believed to be the custodians of the laws and customs of the tribe." They are thought, he continues, to be constantly watching the moral conduct of their descendants. At death a person is said to rejoin his lineage forbears in the spirit world and is supposed to be made to give an account of his conduct in life, especially towards his kinsfolk.

---

88. Deposed or abdicated office holders revert to commoner status and do not, at death, have stools consecrated to them.

FIG. 1–STOOL SEGMENT OF THE ASONA LINEAGE, AGOGO ASHANTI

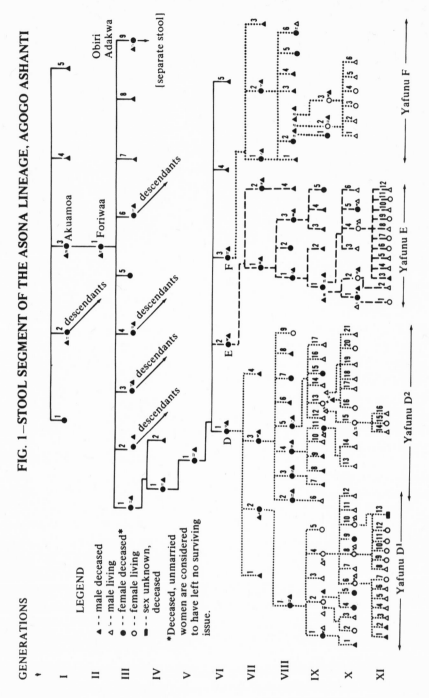

GENERATIONS

LEGEND

▲ - - male deceased
△ - - male living
● - - female deceased*
○ - - female living
■ - - sex unknown, deceased

*Deceased, unmarried women are considered to have left no surviving issue.

Extracted from a genealogical census of the Lineage compiled by T. E. Kyei (Dip. Ed. Oxon.), in 1945 with the aid and consent of the then Lineage Head and Elders. I am greatly indebted to Mr. Kyei and to the Lineage Elders for permission to reproduce this chart.

CHAPTER XI

Ashanti Patrilateral Kinship
and its Values

I

THE LINEAGE FRAME OF ORGANIZATION, THEN, REGULATES THE POLITICO-JURAL statuses and relations of matrilineal kin to one another and to others. But it does not regulate all the social relations that are founded upon kinship and genealogical connections. There are intrinsic affective and moral components in the inter-personal relations of lineage kin. The nodal bond of mother and child implies self-sacrificing love and support on the one side, and lifelong trust and devotion on the other. The values mirrored in this relationship have their roots in the parental care bestowed on children, not in jural imperatives. Their observance is dictated by conscience,[1] not legality. The bonds of intimacy and solidarity between matri-siblings have the same foundation. And the ambivalence in these nuclear relation-ships which erupts, under the stress of moral prescriptions and jural demands, in suspicions of witchcraft, likewise and understandably, are fed from the same spring. Yet such is the overriding force of the lineage concept and structure that these inter-personal relations are themselves felt to be sanctioned by and contained within the lineage ambit. It is as if a mother's love for her child was authorized by her lineage status and commitments.

1. The Ashanti concept *ti-boa* (lit. "head-creature") corresponds precisely to our concept of conscience.

191

It is, perhaps just because the structural parameters of the political constitution, of matrilineal descent, and, as we shall see, of patrilateral kinship, are so well defined, and also because the political order is so pervasive, that Ashanti rules of customary behavior in dyadic kinship relations have little specificity. The basic premise of amity holds for kinship relations in general. The concepts *mogya*, blood, and *mogyafoo*, people of the blood, refer strictly to matrikin. But there is a derivative term, *bogyaa*, which can rightly be translated by our word kinship, or by Morgan's term, consanguinity. A kinsman, whether matrilateral or patrilateral, will be described as *mbogyaani* in contrast to a friend (*adamfo*) or comrade (*oyongko*) who is not a relative. And *bogyaa* predicates amity in the diffuse sense.

Though Radcliffe-Brown's tetrad is applicable, it is not conspicuously diagnostic, in the lineage context. Through the influence of the political paradigm, seniority of generation, age, rank or office, and superiority of status, authority, or influence, all command respect, whereas equality of generation or status permits familiarity. There are no customarily prescribed joking relationships. The nearest thing to this is the condescension, tinged with mild banter, with which a superior sometimes receives an inferior by rank or kinship (particularly grandchild) status. A mild avoidance rule is the attitude to affines recommended in the maxim "mother-in-law's house—we (i.e., men) keep away from." In actuality, as a man's wife is often living in her mother's (and mother's brothers') house, he is quite free to visit her and his children there. She, of course, regularly comes to his house, where he may be residing with his mother and mother's brother, both by day and to sleep with him at night. The maxim is really a reminder that a wife's mother and other matrikin have great influence over her and will support her if she wants to leave a negligent or disrespectful husband. A more significant avoidance is that laid down for great-grandparent and great-grandchild, to which I shall return again in a moment.[2]

The interpersonal affective relations of lineage kin thus depend on predilection and temperament, within the limits of their customary expression in a blend of familiarity and respect. One can be on easy terms with one's mother's brothers or mother's mother's brothers but always behind a screen of deference in address and posture. For, as with siblings, the potentiality of bitter rivalry is always present. Kinship and rank terms are obligatory in addressing, and in formal reference to persons of a senior generation or status, though they may use personal names in return and the kinship terms only in reference. For ego (male), all males of his lineage are *nana* (mother's mother's brother), *wofa* (mother's brother), *wofase* (sister's child with a masculine suffix), *nua* (sibling with the masculine suffix, *barima* for brother), and *nana* (sister's daughter's child); all females are *nana* (mother's mother), *ena* (mother), *nua* (with feminine suffix, *baa*, sister), *wofase* (with suffix *baa*—sister's daughter), and *nana* (sister's daughter's daughter). For ego female, the terms for males are *nana*, *wofa*, *ba* (child—with sex suffix), *nua*, and *nana*; for females they are *nana*, *ena*, *nua*, *baa*, and *nana*.[3] All these terms are used in reference, and those for

2. The obligatory seclusion of menstruant women lest they contaminate the realm of male activities by contact is a form of ritual avoidance, not an affinal avoidance.

3. The traditional terminology is exhaustively and accurately tabulated by Rattray (1923: chap. I). This terminology is unchanged, but in addition the borrowings *maami*, and *papa*

the parental and grandparental generations also and obligatorily in address. There is no sex discrimination, except for parental statuses, in the root-terms of this terminology. This is consistent with the marked jural equality of the sexes. The critical feature of the system is the separation of consecutive generations. Its usage follows the usual Crow-type rules of classificatory generalization. Thus all males and females of ego's own generation are siblings in reference, though they are addressed by personal names, and so on, systematically. Genealogical specification ensures the precise placing of every person relative to every other both in jural situations and in everyday intercourse. This, incidentally, makes it easy to extend kinship terms metaphorically, honorifically, or by courtesy even to strangers.[4]

The term for grandparent, *nana*—that is, to be genealogically exact, mother's mother and her siblings of both sexes who are identified with one another by the rule of the corporate unity of the sibling group—is significant. It is commonly used to designate all ascendants including those antecedent to the grandparental kin and can in this sense be translated as antecessor, or, as literate Ashanti do, ancestor. On this view, a grandparent is the first ancestor in one's lineage pedigree. The term is used to express reverence in prayers addressed to ancestors and gods. It is also used in designating and addressing chiefs and other holders of political office to signify respect for their rank and authority. Consistently with these usages, the self-reciprocal term *nana* is used to designate and, when necessary, formally address post-filial kin of any generation beyond and including that of the grandchildren's generation. However, there are also specific terms for referring to great-grandparental kin (*nana payin*—lit. "senior grandparent") and great-grandchild (*nana n'ka wo aso*— "grandchild who must not touch your ear"). The grandparent-grandchild reciprocal *nana-nana* is the customary terminology of address however. The term for great-grandchild enshrines the belief that if a person's grandchild's child touches his or her ear it will cause his or her death.[5]

The lineage principle unites successive generations without distinction, for external politico-jural purposes; but in its internal structure they fall into an ordered sequence in which generation differences are critical. This is bound up with the differentiation of the uterine stirpes derived from sibling groups. But behind this lies the constellation of familial relations generated by matrifiliation and encap-

4. It is customary to respond to a salutation either with the correct *ntoro* sobriquet (see p. 198) for the person who offers the greeting, or with a kinship term appropriate to his or her generation, age, and status, whether or even if he or she is not a relative or an affine. "Oh mother," "oh father," "oh sibling" are common. I have never heard *ya wofa*, "oh uncle" used in this way except to a lineage kinsman. This might be because the term and its reciprocal have such strict jural connotations that it is thought improper to use it outside the proper lineage context.

5. Cf. Rattray, 1923: 39. To save circumlocution, I am using "grandparent" and "grandchild" in the generational sense to include mother's mother's brother and sister's child's child, as well as the exact lineal relatives. This corresponds, of course, to Ashanti usage. I was told that the avoidance relates to own, i.e., lineal, great-grandchildren, not to collaterals, but it would be consistent with Ashanti kinship ideas to include siblings of lineal kin in the category without further specification.

---

have become common terms of address and reference for mother and father, especially with pre-adolescent children. The variants *ena, eno, eni* for mother are euphonic.

sulated in the descent structure. The kinship terminology applied within the lineage categorizes the dyadic relations, in the classificatory as well as in the primary sense, in which these inter-generational and intra-generational differentiations come into action. Together with the complementary and partially overlapping categories pertaining to patrifilial and patrilateral connections, they map out the total field of familial kinship in contraposition to the field of lineage relations. The distinction is seen in the contrast between the familially generated ambivalence liable to emerge within and between generations, as for instance in the jealousies and rivalries of siblings, on the one hand, and the obligatory solidarity of the lineage in its external orientation, on the other.

Special significance attaches to the relations of alternate generations, in this context. Though not merged, as in Australian systems, they are coupled together in a way that is common in Africa, as can be inferred from the reciprocal terminology. There is a bond of freely given, mutual affection and trust between grandparent and grandchild which Ashanti say is due to the benevolent care lavished by grandparents on grandchildren on both sides, and which they contrast with the constraint that underlies relations with parental kin, however great the affection and devotion felt for them may be. This is connected with the idea that grandchildren are the true replacement of grandparents in the cycle of familial and lineage development. Ashanti of both sexes feel that their life is well fulfilled if they live to have grandchildren.

It is consistent with these values that the kinship terminology recognizes a total span of only seven generations. In fact this comprises four generations of ascendant lineal kin inclusive of ego and the converse of four generations of descendant lineal kin inclusive of ego. What the nomenclature thus represents is a double cycle of social reproduction each consisting of three consecutive generations and a terminal fourth generation. Grandchildren replace grandparents and a new cycle begins with the next generation and this is structurally defined by the avoidance enjoined between the founders of successive cycles. This terminological configuration and the developmental cycle represented in it characterizes both the matrilateral and the patrilateral sections of ego's kinship field.

It is relevant to add that it is rare in Ashanti (as in other African societies) for a person to live long enough to have contact with, let alone to play a part in bringing up, a great-grandchild, and, conversely, for anyone to have personal acquaintance with a lineal great-grandparent. Until the advent of photography and literacy, people had mainly hearsay knowledge about their great-grandparents, passed on to them by their parental and grandparental kin. This ineluctable fact of demography in the pre-literate community certainly plays a part in the developmental cycle of family structure in Ashanti, but primarily, I would surmise, as a contributory factor rather than as a determinant.

What is more to the point is the consistency of the terminological configuration, and the usages it enjoins, with the collocation of residential relationships in the domestic group. Thus the four-generation span is normally the maximum genealogical span of co-residence for the uterine issue of one woman, as we have previously seen. It is also the normal range of ideally indivisible corporate unity within which control over property and succession to personal status are primarily vested, within which direct jural authority over filial dependants operates, and within which, finally, witchcraft suspicions germinate. Stirpal fission is rarely delayed up to or beyond the fifth generation of successive filiation in the matrilineage. Seen from the individual's point of view, these structural alignments fall into place consistently with his life experience. He sees the grandparent under whose oversight he has grown up as, from one side, his parent's parent and thus his most remote family ascendant, and, from another side, as his nearest lineage ascendant, linking him with the great-grandparent by reference to whose genealogical position he is accorded his status in the lineage, as opposed to his status in his domestic stirp. As we have already found, people of the same generation with a common maternal grandmother definitely think of themselves as co-filial siblings; those who are connected by convergent pedigrees to a common great-grandmother may still, in some situations, regard themselves in this way, but more often think of themselves as lineage siblings.

Ashanti define all these terms as immanent in and originating from the relationships of matrifiliation and siblingship in the three-generation, nuclear domestic group—that is, the uterine stirp consisting of a woman and her daughters and their children. What we describe as their classificatory extensions are thought to follow naturally from the concept of the lineage as one corporate person. The mechanics of these extensions are explained straightforwardly: a woman whom my mother refers to by the term for sibling is *eno* (mother) to me, a man she describes as a sibling is *wofa* (uncle) and so on. And matrifilial kin within the nuclear uterine group are distinguished when necessary by suffixes or descriptive phrases from more distant kin. The brother of my mother-who-bore-me will be addressed as *wofa* but described, if necessary, as *wofa animpong*, my true *wofa*, or by some equivalent phrase. A lineage brother of my mother will be addressed as *wofa* but referred to as *wofa* so-and-so where specification of the relationship is relevant. There are many situations of extra-lineage activity where specification is not relevant and even immediate kin may be referred to simply as *abusuani*—my lineage-fellow—or *mogyani*—my blood kinsman. In short, from the observer's point of view, the terminology follows normally from the application of the rules of the unity of the sibling group and of the corporate lineage.[6]

However, among all these terms there is in fact only one terminological couple which is exclusive to the lineage context.[7] This, understandably, is the couple *wofa* and its reciprocal *wofase*, mother's brother, sister's child; for, as Ashanti see it, it is the relationship thus isolated that uniquely and categorically distinguishes the field of matrilineal kinship and descent from every other field of social relations. It is the jural principle of "nephew inheritance," as they put it, which they nowadays

6. Note that there is only a single common term for sibling and it is often used without the sex suffix. The jural identification of siblings regardless of sex, which is basic to the Ashanti concept of the corporate matrilineal descent group, is thus registered in the kinship terminology.

7. The term for mother is applied, also, as a mark of courtesy and respect, not in recognition of parenthood, to a father's wife other than own mother, and, also, as has already been noted, to women of one's mother's generation who are not relatives.

select as the critical feature of their social organization, by contrast with the patri-lineal and cognatic forms they are familiar with through contact with foreign immigrants and acquaintance with Western concepts of family organization, in-heritance, and succession.

II

We have moved from considering the structural features and institutional forms in Chapter IX that characterize the lineage as a corporate body in the politico-jural domain, in respect both to its external relations and to its internal constitution, to a consideration of what lineage membership signifies for the individual in his personal field of social relations. The full import of this becomes apparent only when the patrilateral dimension of this field is taken into account. In the Ashanti social structure, legitimate patrifiliation is the necessary complement to matrifiliation in the definition of normal social personality. Formally, lineage membership by right of matrifiliation confers full citizenship status and all the moral, jural, and ritual capacities that accompany it, on a freeborn Ashanti, regardless of his natural paternity. A slave woman's uterine descendants, even when begotten by freeborn fathers, remain perpetually in a quasi-servile status, as we have previously recorded. Formally, therefore, the condition of bastardy is not recognized in Ashanti law and custom. But jural sufficiency does not make the whole person; he must be morally and spiritually complete as well. For this, a freeborn person must have a known, freeborn pater. If he cannot name a father who has acknowledged him, this is tanta-mount to admitting either slave-paternity or a condition akin to bastardy.[8] These are blemishes that impede eligibility for high office. Just as marriage of the mother is not a necessary jural antecedent for legitimate matrifiliation,[9] so it is not a pre-requisite for legitimate paternity.[10] However, the genitor must make public acknowledgement of his paternity, notably by exercising his paternal prerogative of naming his child. The rule that a child born in wedlock is its mother's lawful husband's child, even if it is suspected to be adulterine, rests upon his exclusive marital right to her sexual services. The maxim *okromfo ni ba* ("A thief has no child")

---

8. Cf. Rattray, 1923: 39: "An illegitimate child to an Ashanti is one who does not know the father's *ntoro*—an illegitimate child (by a free woman) will of course always have its mother's *abusua*, and hence may inherit *almost* equally with a legitimate child." (My italics—note the implication.)

9. Provided the mother has undergone the public nubility ceremony (discussed below, p. 208 ff) which releases her adult sexuality and childbearing capacity and thus eliminates the danger of mystical pollution for the whole community which prenubile pregnancy (*kyiribra*, see p. 156 n. 7) is believed to cause (cf. Fortes, 1953c).

10. As I have explained elsewhere (Fortes, 1950; 1953c) *mpena aware* (public and continu-ous living together of a man and a woman without the formalities of marriage but generally with the consent of the woman's guardian) is, and always was, common. Children of such unions acknowledged by their fathers are in every respect on a par with those born in proper wedlock. And this is true also for the offspring of an unmarried mother resulting from a short-lived liaison. A man acknowledges paternity by maintaining his lover during pregnancy and making certain customary gifts to her at the time of the delivery, as well as by naming his child.

expresses this pithily, for, as we have seen (p. 156), adultery is defined as a kind of theft.

Just as legitimate paternity is a *sine qua non* for entirety of moral and jural filial status, so it is considered to be indispensable for the fulfillment of manhood. A man of appropriate age who is not a father after lengthy marriage is defective in the same way as one who has suffered a bodily mutilation or is physically infirm, and is thus debarred from election to office.[11] He is an incomplete person and people expect him to be psychologically disturbed—sullen, suspicious, and unhappy. There are pragmatic benefits to be considered as well. A man's closest and most disinterested allies and supporters are his sons. Unlike his matri-brothers and nephews, they have much to lose and nothing to gain by his death. This means that a man's standing in society and his self-esteem require him not only to beget children but to rear them to adulthood; and herein lies a major incentive to marriage for men.

In any case, the paradox mentioned in an earlier chapter, holds: as the necessary structural complement to matrifiliation, patrifiliation is jurally underwritten, as it were, by contraposition with the lineage. Acknowledgement of paternity cannot, as can recognition of avuncular or nepotal status or marital rights, be enforced by jural process. It depends entirely on metaphysical beliefs, on moral ideals and on pressures that spring from the affective relations of the parents with each other and with their children. Thus, legitimate paternity confers no politico-jural capacities on either parent or offspring. It creates only moral and sentimental loyalties, claims, and privileges. But these are not wholly at the mercy of personal whims and self-interest; they are defined and sanctioned by custom, by public opinion, and above all by religious beliefs and moral values. However, given the structure of society in which ultimate authority resides in the state, more explicit politico-jural validation of patri-filial claims and privileges is effective in the background. In default of the judicial sanctions at the disposal of a chief's court, they are supported by appeal to complementary principles of equity which have great force (cf. Fortes, 1963).

Ashanti account for the critical value attributed to paternity by their theory of the conception and formation, physical and psychical, of the human person. Blood, *mogya*, which stands for the whole material substance of the body, is contributed by the mother; but it must be quickened by the spiritual essence transmitted in the semen of the father for the embryo to be formed and developed. For a freeborn Ashanti, this blood is the blood that has come down by matrilineal descent from the founding ancestress of his lineage and makes him one with all who share it. It incorporates the lineage in him and him in the lineage. The male essence, on the other hand, has been passed on from father to son in the continuity of successive generations of patrifiliation. It implants the father and his paternal forebears in his offspring.

Just as blood and lineage are symbolically focused in the cult of ancestors who have held supreme office in the lineage, so the male essence is symbolically focused in the

---

11. Cf. the treatment of a man who dies barren, referred to below p. 199, n. 16. In recent history, sterility, or chronic disease, or such bodily mutilations as circumcision have been alleged by malcontents seeking the disqualification of unpopular candidates for cheifly office.

ntoro divinity common to persons of the same paternity[12] but transmitted only through father and son. To the consecrated stool that enshrines lineage ancestry, correspond, on the male side appropriately enough, consecrated ceremonial swords in the possession of the king and of important chiefs on which the oath of allegiance is sworn by chiefs and subjects to the king and his oath of office by the king.[13] Blood and patrispirit are thought of as complementary elements in the constitution of the person both as a physical and social being. They make explicit the understanding that a person is a complete person only by reason of his filio-parental connections on both sides. Apart from his unique identity as a human creature, conceptualized in the notion of his birthday soul and destiny (the *kra*), he is a matri-person endowed with politico-jural status by incorporation in his lineage, and a patri-person endowed with personal moral and affective claims and privileges by patrifiliation. With these go qualities of mind and of personality, intelligence and will, that are regarded as in

12. A daughter is born with her father's *ntoro* spirit and ritual allegiance, but cannot transmit it. When she marries she must observe both her father's and her husband's (for the sake of her children) *ntoro* taboos. As I have explained elsewhere (Fortes, 1950), the traditional beliefs and ritual practices associated with the *ntoro* concept were falling into obsolescence in the nineteen-forties among the younger people. The idea of a patrifilially transmitted spiritual essence which guarded a child's well-being and shaped its character still prevailed, however. But it was referred to the *sunsum* which, for many informants, seemed to have a psychological meaning devoid of the traditional ritual aura. (See n. 14, below.) On the other hand, the *ntoro concept* retained its older significance for holders of high office. No chief of superior rank, let alone the king, could have held office if his *ntoro* were not known. It testified to free and worthy, often eminent, paternal ancestry, which might be expected to show itself in his character and ability. High-ranking chiefs and, of course, the Asantehene, punctiliously carried out the ritual observances of their *ntoro* divinity, notably the "soul washing" rites. The notion of the *ntoro* is one of a cluster of metaphysical and ritual concepts that depict the Ashanti theory of the human personality, its formation and structure, and its connection with their world view, their kinship and descent system, their political order, and especially their religious doctrines and cults. Since Rattray first sketched its main elements (1923: chap. II), this theory has received attention from a number of scholars. Meyerowitz (1951: chap. VII), quoting at length from the unpublished study by the erudite Akan scholar the late Dr. J. B. Danquah, amplifies Rattray's account in important particulars and offers some valuable interpretations. My own inquiries and those of Professor K. A. Busia (personal communications, 1947) led to the same conclusions as Rattray's except in one respect. Both of us found that membership of the same *ntoro* division is not a bar to marriage in the absence of demonstrable patrilateral connection.

13. The Asantehene's most sacred ceremonial sword is known as the Bosommuru sword. It is dedicated to the Bosommuru *ntoro*, to which the Founder of the Nation, Osai Tutu, and no less than nine of his successors belonged, and is the focus of an elaborate cult of considerable political importance. It figured prominently in the traditional *Odwera* (National New Year) festival (cf. Meyerowitz, 1951: 174). It is on this sword that the Asantehene takes the oath of office, when he is installed, promising to observe all the laws and customs of the nation. The sword next in rank among his regalia is dedicated to the Bosompra *ntoro*. Chiefs swear allegiance to the king on the Mponponsuo sword, which is not an *ntoro* sword. Other *ntoro* are enshrined in swords in the possession of the leading divisional chiefs (personal communication, A. A. Y. Kyerematen). To take the oath of political office on a sword must seem peculiarly appropriate for the military obligations of high office in the Ashanti state system. The symbolical association with paternity is also apt. Patrilateral connections often, in the past, promoted alliances between heads of different chiefdoms based on mutual trust rather than expediency. But more important is the consideration that patrilateral relationships, not being bound to localities or offices or contained within genealogical boundaries, could be regarded as standing for the detachment from sectional lineage-tied loyalties and the universal benevolence required of holders of high office. This is what the common saying that a chief must be the father of his people is meant to convey.

part hereditary concomitants of his *ntoro* nativity and in part induced by the guardianship of his father's *sunsum* or individual soul.[14] It is by the father's ritual act of naming his children and so distinguishing them from other children of the same lineage that patrifiliation is formally validated.[15] It is significant that this personal name is not given until the eighth day after the child's birth. Until that day it is not regarded as fully human. If it dies unnamed, the body is not given proper burial, no funeral is held, and the parents dress and behave as if rejoicing. It is said to have been a ghost child, not a being of flesh and blood.[16] The naming rite follows on the rite of "out-dooring" the child in which it is accepted by its maternal grandmother as its mother's true offspring and is thus incorporated into the family, the *yafunu* group, and the lineage. In short, a person is not incorporated as a member of his lineage until his matrifilial status is ritually recognized and legitimized by the bestowal of complementary patrifiliation.

Once named, a child comes under the protection of its father's *sunsum*, and it is believed that an infant who is deprived of this spiritual surveillance cannot thrive.[17] In their own theory of kinship and descent, therefore, Ashanti represent paternity as the source of a distinctive and inborn spiritual bond between father and child. Upon this bond there is built up, in the course of a child's upbringing, a relationship of mutual trust, affection, and respect which is at bottom subject only to the internal moral sanctions of individual conscience, not to politico-jural constraints. It is felt to be a created relationship, but one that is an indispensable complement to the *a priori*, jurally binding relationships of matrifiliation, in forming the total social person.

14. The concept of the *sunsum* corresponds roughly to what we mean when we speak of personality in such phrases as "a strong (or weak) personality," "an attractive personality," etc. Its basis is the hereditary *ntoro* essence derived from the father—or, as we might put it, a constitutional disposition. His personality is likely, therefore, to bear the stamp of the character type associated with his *ntoro*. But *sunsum* also embraces the individual gifts and capabilities which enable a person to realize his inborn potentialities. Thus a man may be described as having a "weighty" or "forceful" or "gentle" or "weak" *sunsum*. It is thought of as watching over his life, guiding his conduct, guarding his interests. These are the ideas behind the description of the Golden Stool as the "sunsum of the Nation." The concepts of *mogya*, *kra*, *ntoro*, and *sunsum* do not exhaust the Ashanti metaphysical theory of the constitution of the person. They are, however, the most important elements of it for my purpose. The crucial point is that, broadly speaking, what appertains to a person in his capacity as a relatively autonomous individual falls under the aegis of paternity, and what appertains to him in his capacity as actor in the politico-jural domain comes from his mother's side.

15. The father's father, if alive, or his sister or brother normally performs this rite and the name selected (which is the child's personal name, not his day name) is commonly that of a paternal antecedent unless the mother's kin especially request that the name given should commemorate a famous or beloved maternal antecedent. For the naming ceremony, see Rattray, 1927: 61 ff. Ashanti nowadays commonly use their father's name or their own personal name as their surname for modern legal and social purposes. The lineage name would obviously not be discriminative.

16. A slave, likewise, was not buried in the lineage cemetery or given a proper funeral. Similarly, convicted witches, murderers (in the wide Ashanti sense), and barren men and women were not given burial in the lineage cemetery or accorded the proper funeral ceremonies. Clearly all of these were regarded as outside the jural and moral community of the lineage, either because they were never fully incorporated in it, or because they were alienated.

17. Cf. Fortes, 1950. This may happen if the father deserts the mother or, being known, refuses to acknowledge his paternity. It is invoked, as I found in several cases in 1945, when attempts are made to reconcile estranged spouses or put pressure on a man to acknowledge fathering a child.

The metaphysical representation of this antithesis is, one must concede, profound and apposite. But the structural aspect that is most significant relates to the constitution of the *ntoro* division. Ashanti are inclined to harp on the contrast between the inescapable constraint in matrilineal relations and the free and voluntary nature of patrilateral relations. This corresponds to the contrast between lineage and clan structure, and the *ntoro* grouping. Unlike the former, a *ntoro* division is not an association of persons of known or even putative common descent. Though the *ntoro* divisions are as limited in number as the clans, and are nationwide in distribution, they are more like the scattered and otherwise unrelated collection of the devotees who have vowed ritual allegiance to an *abosom* deity than like a clan. There are no local *ntoro* chapters corresponding to lineages.[18]

People who serve the same *ntoro* divinity never, on that account, assemble to perform the rituals connected with it and do not claim to have common patrilineal ancestry. Kinship connections with the father's kin are recognized both by nomenclature, customary norms of amity, and in marriage prohibitions. But compared with the connections generated by matrifiliation, they have a limited range. It is rare for anyone[19] to be acquainted with his father's paternal ascendants either by direct

18. Rattray's view (1923. chap. II; 1927: chap. XXIX) that the *ntoro* divisions are eaxctly parallel to the clans is not acceptable, in the light of later research (cf. Fortes, 1950, and n. 27, below). The parallel holds on the plane of metaphysical and ritual doctrine and belief but not in terms of descent structure. The Ashanti system is not a double unilineal one in the strict sense (cf. Goody, 1961). It is true that, as with the clans, only a limited number of *ntoro* divisions (from seven to twelve have been reported in different parts of the country) are recognized and that each is distributed throughout the nation and indeed among all the Akan-speaking peoples (cf., e.g., Christensen, 1954). Likewise, the myths of origin that account for the inception of the *ntoro* divisions have the same character as those relating to the clans. Each is under the aegis of a divinity (*obosom*) associated with a stretch of water (river or lake) after which the *ntoro* is generally named and this is reminiscent of the way lineages come under the mystical authority of stool ancestors and lineage divinities. Again, the belief that semen and saliva are the fluid media through which the *ntoro* spirit passes from a man to his children obviously parallels and complements the association of the blood with matriliny (and no doubt with the menstrual taboos on women). Each *ntoro* division also has distinctive totemic taboos, primarily upon the killing and eating of specified totem animal species, a set of distinctive names ("Osai" is a famous and common name given to members of the Bosommuru *ntoro*), and a special response with which a greeting proffered by a member is answered. Finally, it is believed that each *ntoro* carries with it distinct traits of character and innate disposition, and these are supposed to reflect the nature of the *ntoro's* main totemic animals. The illustrious Bosommuru *ntoro*, for instance, has the python as its main "forbidden animal" (*tweneboa*) and those who belong to it are supposed to be as elusive, predatory, and dangerous as pythons are believed to be (Busia, personal communication; see also Rattray, 1923: 48–49). Similar ideas have been reported about clan totems, and character types (cf. Meyerowitz, 1951: 30). Yet the fundamental distinction remains. Patriliny has no function in the politico-jural domain comparable to that of matrilineal descent. A *ntoro* division is a category of, in principle, ritually defined persons, not an identifiable segment of the total society. The essential significance of the institution lies in the counterpoise it forms to the imperative force of matrilineal descent. My surmise is that the *ntoro* principle is institutionally elaborated in a way that closely resembles the clan system, the better to emphasize the "equal but different" relationship, and the essential complementary of patrifiliation and matrifiliation (semen vs. blood; divinity vs. ancestors; individual names vs. common clan name; diffuse ramification [like the rivers characteristically associated with *ntoro* grouping] vs. lineage concentration; and the common roots in parenthood and genealogy symbolized in similarity of totemic prescriptions).

19. Other than those connected with *mma mma* (quasi-patrilineal) offices which I discuss

contact or by geneonymy, even though he may bear the name of one of them, for more than three generations antecedent to himself.[20] His mother's paternal ascendants other than her father are normally of no interest to him. As I have demonstrated elsewhere (Fortes, 1950), there is no patrilineal corporate group corresponding to the matrilineage. But the parental family, even though it is not very commonly based on a lifelong conjugal partnership and does not always form a domestic unit under one roof, is a distinct and fundamental entity in the social structure. Hence the developmental cycle I have previously described in fact embraces the patrifilial as well as the matrifilial side. Patrilateral connections are, as a rule, recognized among the offspring of men whose own fathers were the sons of one man, that is, among the children of parallel cousins, but rarely beyond that range. This corresponds to the genealogical constitution of the property-controlling uterine group. But on the paternal side it represents the maximum range of successive generations over which patrilateral ties are normally maintained. There being no corporate organization to absorb and unify under a descent rule mor edistant patrilateral connections, the beginning of a new developmental cycle generally puts an end to the recognition of these connections.

Thus by the fifth generation—that is, among third cousins—the common patrilineal ancestor is normally no longer significant even if he is geneonymically identified by those of his descendants who are expert in these matters, and this is generally because of adventitious status considerations. For example, if he was an important office-holder, or a man of outstanding personality and achievement, his name would be perpetuated. Patrifiliation did not formerly and does not entitle a person, as of right, to inherit property or succeed to office or claim citizenship.[21] The sons' stools provide a crucial test.

From time to time, and right down to recent years, Ashanti kings created offices

20. Partly, of course, by reason of the demographic limitations referred to in the earlier discussion of the matrifilial developmental cycle, but chiefly for structural reasons presently to be considered.

21. However, a person who has grown up in his or her father's care in the father's chiefdom of domicile and continues to reside there—by reason, for example, of marrying a local citizen or merely out of personal choice—can acquire quasi-citizenship there. To be granted this status, he must undertake such distinctive political obligations as paying his share of any levies imposed by the chiefdom and, formerly, serving in its fighting forces in defense of the chiefdom. The acquisition of quasi-citizenship in this manner is not comparable to naturalization, as we understand it. An alien can in no circumstances acquire quasi-citizenship—let alone full citizenship—in an Ashanti chiefdom. The foreign African merchants and Moslem ("Moorish") residents encountered by Bowdich and other nineteenth-century travellers in Kumasi were not recognized as Ashanti citizens. In the 1940's there was no large village or town in Ashanti without its foreign quarter, the *zongo*. But however long a foreigner might have resided in a community he was never recognized as a citizen or quasi-citizen. In the case of a citizen's son or daughter, it is on the strength of the moral claims created by patrifiliation that quasi-citizenship is sought and granted. It is of course impossible for a quasi-citizen to succeed to any office vested in his father's lineage, even if it was held by his father. Nor can a quasi-citizen transmit to his or her offspring the status of citizen or even of quasi-citizen in the community, by right of filiation or descent. The status is in fact exactly parallel to a gift of property made by a father to his child *inter vivos*, terminating with the grantee.

---

above. The patrilateral ancestry of the kings and high-ranking chiefs, is apt to be held in special honor and is therefore more fully commemorated than in the case of commoners.

designed specially to supply an administrative and military elite or to commemorate notable events and occasions. These offices, which included minor palace functionaries at one end and high-ranking officers of state at the other, were not vested in lineages; they were *mma mma dwa*, sons' sons' stools which passed *de facto* to patrifilial brothers and then to sons, not matrilineally. But as Professor Wilks shows (1966) brilliantly confirming Rattray's brief allusions to this institution, this was not by right of patrilineal succession, but by appointment or at least confirmation by the king.[22] They became "contingently patrilineal" as Wilks puts it because, as with all crafts, sons and sons' sons acquired and developed the skills required for these offices and tended to keep them within a patrilineally limited range, commonly of first-cousinship. A number of important offices closely connected with the royal court and army were also traditionally bestowed on kings' sons (*ohenema*) and sons' sons (*ohene nana*). This reflected the assumption that the disinterested loyalty of sons and sons' sons could be relied upon as counterweight to the jealousy and hostility of the king's lineage kin and the latent opposition of his councillors and captains. Sons and son's sons were permitted direct access to a king or a high-ranking chief, whereas all his lineage brothers and nephews were strictly excluded from the palace in the belief that their jealousy with regard to the office might incite them to seek the ruler's injury by physical or magical means.

III

Thus, apart from the immediate filio-parental relationship created by it, what patrifiliation generates is a nexus of patrilateral connections in the individual's personal field of kinship that is complementary to his matrilineage ties. It must be emphasized that we are concerned with the structure of the personal field of kinship. Patrilateral and matrilateral kinship ties are complementary for ego's organization of his social space. They do not represent complementary principles of equal force in the total social structure as seen from the outside. I must emphasize that, unlike complementary matrifiliation in such patrilineal segmentary lineage systems as that of the Tallensi, for example, patrifiliation in Ashanti social structure does not serve as a focus of segmentation within matrilineal sibling groups. Nor by the same token does the recognition of patrilineal descent make the Ashanti system a double descent system.[23] Its sphere of operation is wholly outside the lineage structure.

What matrifiliation and patrifiliation serve for in ego's social space is to polarize his kinship alignments and the commitments and sentiments, the jural and moral rights and obligations entailed by them along complementary lines. It is this polarity that is symbolized in the opposition of blood and spirit in the makeup and

22. Rattray emphasizes the significance of "generations of continuity in office," the son leaning from and succeeding father, as the basis of the administrative knowledge and efficacy of these officials (1929: 92, 118). This is the same pattern as is found among ordinary people, where fathers are expected to train their sons in craft skills and knowledge of affairs (see below, p. 203). The various "stool servants" of chiefs and the king learned their duties and special knowledge in this way and thus these servitor offices were normally passed on from father to son.

23. Cf. above, n. 18, p. 200.

naming of the person. Ashanti see it as experienced constantly on the one side in the conflicting claims of marital bonds and siblingship, fatherhood and avuncular duty, filial attachment and nepotal obligation; and on the other in the contrast between the adventitious privileges of paternal gifts and the lawful rights of matrilineal inheritance. On the one side, there is affective and moral commitment; on the other, jural compulsion. To show disrespect to one's father is a sin against his outraged *sunsum*. A father can punish or, if the offence is grave, even curse an incorrigibly contumacious son and this spells mystical disaster (*musuo*) for him if he does not make proper amends; an uncle can only censure an offending nephew or, in a grave case, submit his grievance to the arbitration of the lineage elders.

This polar division is reflected in the life cycle of each person. Ideally, a son should be, and in the majority of cases he is, in his father's charge during his formative years. He moves to his mother's brother's control and, often, house after adolescence and the attainment of jural majority.[24] A daughter, likewise, should be in her father's care until her marriage. It is from his father, Ashanti say, that a boy learns craft and economic skills, etiquette, and the values and habits that characterize the good citizen. Sons of officeholders and court dignitaries and functionaries acquire the knowledge of public affairs, stool histories, and political procedures and law, which is the basis of the institution of *mma-mma* stools, by attending on their fathers. A boy's misconduct is laid at his father's door.[25] Girls learn feminine skills and virtues from their mothers, but a girl's delinquency is blamed as much upon the negligence of her father as of her mother.

In all of this there is, in Ashanti thought, a weighty element of moral obligation. It is a father's duty as well as his pride to bring up his children worthily and endow them for life; it is a child's duty, as well as his privilege and desire, to honor and obey his father. The most conspicuous expression of the latter is the obligation of a man's children to provide his coffin and to perform certain special services at his funeral. This obligation is extended to the whole of a father's lineage, since his bodily existence and jural status are so bound up with its corporate constitution. The *mma-mma*, that is the children of the lineage sons, should attend the funeral of any member of their fathers' lineage, contribute to the cost of the coffin, and bring donations. But most important of all is their duty to prepare the body for burial and

---

24. The complexity of Ashanti residence patterns might seem to stand in the way of realizing this ideal but, as I have shown elsewhere (Fortes, 1949a), it is, in fact, substantially implemented. Where parents live in the same house in virilocal marriage, the children spend their early years in the care of both. Hitherto unpublished investigations made by me in 1945 show that this applies to about 50–60 per cent of children of both sexes under the age of about 17. The parents of the other 40–50 per cent live in their respective matrikin houses. In these cases it was found that nearly all the girls lived with their mothers but took meals, from time to time, in their fathers' houses. Boys under the age of about 12 also lived with their mothers and more frequently took meals with their fathers. Of the boys over 12, rather more than half lived with their fathers and the rest very often had meals with their fathers. These figures indicate that fathers care for pre-adolescent children to a very marked extent even when they live separately from their wives. However, whether their children reside or eat with them, or do not do so, they are always at hand to exercise paternal responsibility and administer paternal discipline.

25. Hence the traditional rule that if an unmarried young man seduced another man's wife, the culprit's father had to pay the fine.

attend to all the menial tasks of fetching and carrying that are called for in big gatherings. They "do all the work," as it is sometimes put. In this respect their role parallels that of joking partner or half-brother lineages in other African societies, though those present (for not all the *mma-mma* will normally attend) constitute only an *ad hoc* team in the particular situation. Ashanti do not associate these services with ideas of mystical pollution or joking or avoidance relations. They are thought of as reciprocation for the paternal care and devotion received by children. They are related also to the idea that a death is an injury to the whole body corporate of the lineage and the lineage cannot, therefore, as it were, bind up its own wounds. The sons' sons and daughters, bound to it only by ties of affection, gratitude, and mystical dependence, are the right people to perform this service for them. Coming as comforters, not bereaved, they wear the white clay that symbolizes rejoicing not the red clay of mourning.

The significance of these usages is registered in the kinship terminology. Patrilateral kin are *bogyafoo*, cognates. Father is designated by the term *agya* (in address) or *ose* (in reference); father's sister is *sewa*, "female father." All members of the father's lineage, regardless of generation or sex, are designated by these terms in any situation where ego's patrifilial status is operative. This is accounted for in principle by the argument that they are all "one person," specifically, by the laws of inheritance and succession. Formally, every lineage brother or sister's son, or even sister, of the father is eligible to be chosen as his heir and successor; and he conversely is eligible to inherit and succeed to the status of any of his lineage siblings or mother's brothers. Since an heir and successor is bound by the rule of the levirate[26] to assume his predecessor's conjugal and, consequently, parental status and obligations, this makes every member of the father's lineage a potential father or father's brother or sister. It is of interest that a father's sister is regarded with special respect untinged with the intimacy that tempers the deference due to the father himself. Ashanti say this is because she is the mother of a man who will eventually and by right take the father's place. She is "one" with the father and can act for him in such ritual situations as the naming of his child. Marriage with a father's sister is unthinkable. It would be incest.

Paternal half-siblings are assimilated to matri-siblings and are designated as brothers and sisters (*nua*) and this term is extended in appropriate circumstances (e.g., at a funeral) to all *mma-mma* (son's children) of the father's lineage. There are distinctions of degree, however, which are most precisely expressed in the incidence of the prohibition of marriage between siblings. It is deemed to be incestuous and, just because it has moral but no jural sanction, more reprehensible than for matri-siblings, for patrisiblings (actual or classificatory) who, as Ashanti put it, have the same known paternal great-grandfather, to marry or have sexual relations. Beyond that range of patrilineal connection where, that is to say, pedigrees are not normally preserved, marriage may and does occur.[27] This limit is related both to the probability

26. If only notionally, for, increasingly in recent times, leviratic marriage is not *de facto* obligatory for either a widow or the husband's heir (see Fortes, 1950).
27. Marriages within these limits, e.g., with a father's paternal parallel male cousin's daughter, are known to occur. They are criticized but if the fathers cannot or will not prevent them nothing can be done except to leave them to the workings of providence.

that the fathers of the parties personally knew and had regular contact with their common grandfather, and to the general structure of the kinship system. They have no jurally sanctioned rights or obligations toward one another. Their relations resemble those of close patrisiblings.

However, the situation is different with paternal great-grandparent and great-grandchild. They are designated by the same kinship terms as are the maternal kinsfolk of these categories and the same rules apply. "Grandchild do not touch my ear" (*nana nka aso*) must, as the terminology implies, avoid close contact with the great-grandparent whom his touch on the ear "would cause to die." There are, however, as I have already noted, not many people in Ashanti who live long enough to be contemporary with a great-grandchild, and there is even less chance of such contact occurring between patrilateral kin of these classes than among matrikin. As with the latter, it signifies the completion of a cycle of successive generations constituting one filiative sequence and the inception of a new cycle. It is within the limits of such a cycle that patrilateral generation equals are regarded as siblings and prohibited from marrying.

Patrilateral cross cousins are assimilated to matrilateral cross cousins as preferred spouses and are designated by the corresponding term *sewa-ba*, literally, female father's child or, alternatively, *agya-wofase*, father's nephew or niece.[28] But in some situations the sibling term is used to emphasize their quasi-siblingship; and in others the affinal term (*akonta*, self reciprocally, for same-sex siblings-in-law) is considered appropriate, whether or not an actual marriage exists between members of the two sibling groups, to emphasize their ideal and potential marriageability. Personal names are used in informal address, as among matrisiblings.

IV

Viewed in this context of kinship and descent relations, it is not surprising that a constant theme emphasized by Ashanti in the evaluation they make of kinship relations is how to balance up the obligations and rights that arise from their matrilateral and sororal connection, on the one hand, and the claims, privileges, and commitments that spring from paternal and patrilateral bonds, on the other. A conscientious father is believed to shape his children's mind and character by heredity as well as by his parental care, and the essence of this process is considered to be equipping them with the means and the capacities for normal adult life. He cannot pass on to them, as of right, property, rank, office, or citizenship. But he can, as we know, by gift, lawfully make material provision for them; and he can equip them with such non-material assets as economic and craft skills and, nowadays, schooling. (I have discussed this at greater length in Fortes, 1963.) In particular, he is entitled and expected to ensure that they are suitably married, as is indispensable for

28. In some parts of Ashanti it is still the custom for cross-cousins of either the bride-to-be or the bridegroom-to-be, in a forthcoming marriage, to demand and receive a gift in compensation for the presumptive right of marriage they have been ousted from, if the marriage is with a person who cannot be placed in the cross-cousin category (see further reference below, p. 214).

the attainment of full adult status. But as we have seen a father cannot be compelled to fulfill these ideals. He acts from a sense of moral responsibility tempered with personal solicitude and pride of name and status. And he must not overdo it. He has the avuncular duty of helping his sisters to equip their children for adult life, too, especially if (as can easily happen in the circumstances of Ashanti family structure) by reason of divorce,[29] or lack of means, or some other impediment, the children's fathers are negligent.

The relative weights in the individual's kinship field of patrifilial and matrifilial connections, as reflected in paternal solicitude and responsibility, on the one hand, and avuncular right and duty, on the other, can be estimated from some of the data I assembled in 1945. The transmission of productive property gives one indication.

My field staff recorded the current ownership of a large number of cocoa farms, the most valuable of rural productive resources at that time, in several areas. The area of Asokore and Efiduasi, about twenty miles northeast of Kumasi, can be taken as representative of conditions in an area of falling productivity much influenced by urban social and economic forces. Of 262 farms listed, 4 were pledged for loans, 182 were still owned by the men and women who had first established them, and 75 had passed by transmission from a previous generation of owners. Of these 42 (56 per cent) had passed by matrilineal inheritance from brothers, mother's brothers, and, in a few cases, mothers, whereas 33 (44 per cent) had come to their owners by gift from their fathers. For the more traditional Ashanti-Akim district, which is 45 miles southeast of Kumasi and was in 1945 still on the margin of urban influences, the figures were as follows:

Total farms listed	228
Owned by those who established them	141
Pledged	15
Matrilineally inherited	45
By gift from fathers	15

Thus in this area, of the sixty farms which had passed from a previous generation, 75 per cent had passed by matrilineal inheritance and 25 per cent by gift from fathers. None of the other areas sampled yielded figures showing such a marked matrilineal bias as these or so large a proportion of farms obtained by gift from fathers as in the Asokore-Efiduasi area. My estimate for Ashanti as a whole is that, in the mid-forties, in the transmission of the kind of heritable productive property typified by coca farms, matrilateral rights and patrilateral claims were weighted in the ratio of about 2:1. For the individual[30] this suggests that where heritable material property is in question his lineage obligations weigh twice as heavily with him as his

29. In the marriage inquiry I made in 1945, it was found that in one sample of 500 ever-married women of all ages, 43 per cent were divorced or widowed, and among the still-married 57 per cent, approximately one in four, was in fact carrying on her life and bringing up her children with little or no regular support from her husband, at that date (see n. 31 below).

30. I am speaking here of men. The choice does not confront a woman. Any productive property she may leave goes automatically to her children.

paternal responsibility. It is difficult to assess the corresponding expectations of offspring. In the mid-forties it was still taken for granted that a man's sons would have far less chance than his brothers and nephews of becoming the owners of cocoa farms and other productive resources in his possession, even if the sons had helped their father to exploit and maintain these resources.

If we look next at the non-material and non-heritable investment in offspring, the picture is different. With the great importance attached in the forties to school education, a useful index of parental responsibility for the preparation of children for adult life was the payment of the costs of maintaining children at school. As I have reported elsewhere (Fortes, 1963), it appeared that fathers and the close maternal kin (mother's brothers, mothers, and older brothers together) taken as a unit shared the responsibility more or less equally, except that (as is consistent with the norms of residence) fathers took rather more responsibility for younger children than the matrilineal kin, who took rather more for older children. In the most rural and traditional area sampled, fathers fell slightly behind the nuclear matrikin in providing schooling for their children, but were significantly ahead in the more urbanized areas. Further broken down, the data suggest that fathers in general provide for children's education twice as frequently as mother's brothers and nearly four times as frequently as mothers and other matrikin.[31]

The interpretation of these data is complicated by the relatively high incidence of divorce and the changes in residential alignments in the developmental cycle of the family. Nevertheless, taken at their face value, they reflect with gratifying fidelity the distribution of authority in Ashanti domestic structure and the ideals of paternal and avuncular conduct. The father stands alone; the nuclear matrikin, who constitute a corporate inheritance group, distribute the burden among themselves. From the individual's point of view, a man's affective and moral bonds with his children and his jural and moral ties with his nuclear uterine kin have equal claims on him. He can keep a balance between them, though not without risk of friction and grievance, by reason of the structural cleavage which segregates his paternal and marital relations from his matrisibling and avuncular relations within his field of kinship and marriage. We see this pattern of segregation in the residential arrangements and their correlation with the opposition between matrisibling and conjugal relations and between the stage of jural infancy and the stage of jural majority in the individual life cycle, as well as in the institutional contraposition between law in the regulation of lineage relations, and equity in the adjustment of patrifilial relations. We see it in the symbolism of the religious cults and beliefs directed toward lineage ancestors, on the one hand, and patrilateral divinities and spiritual essences, on the other.

However, there is another side to this configuration. Responsibility and obligation predicate correlative rights, whether in law or in equity. The respective rights and claims of matrikin and patrikin are well exemplified in the arrangement of marriages. They are dramatically adumbrated in the traditional nubility ceremony for girls. This was, in rural areas, still regarded as an obligatory prelude to marriage for

31. It should be realized that absentee or divorced fathers often contributed towards children's schooling.

non-Christian girls in the forties and though, according to Sarpong,[32] now rapidly obsolescent, it still survives, albeit in a simplified form, in conservative families.[33]

The nubility ceremony follows the attainment of physiological maturity. At this stage a girl is, to all intents, fully grown. She is proficient in the skills required of a housewife and is able to make an adult's contribution to the family economy by her work in the gardens and farms, by her marketing activities, or by plying some craft. She might already be receiving suitors and be promised, though it is forbidden for her to be given, in marriage. To seduce her at this stage is the crime and sin of *kyiribra*, that is, pollution of the menarche, which I have already referred to. But these physical and economic attainments do not qualify her for jural adulthood: the ceremony does this. Before she undergoes it, she is a child—a jural infant without citizenship in her own right, a moral infant sexually, and, consequently, matri- monially taboo, a ritual infant in relation to the gods and ancestors. Her lineage membership, though still jurally and morally potential rather than operative, of course entitles her to move to full adult status. But meanwhile she is the responsi- bility of her parents, being able to act only as one who is in their care and under their authority and protection.[34] After the ceremony she becomes a full citizen, both bound by lineage obligations and liable to chiefdom levies. She is expected to marry and, in particular, to enter upon the proper and ideal role of a woman, that is, the bearing and rearing of children.[35] As a fully enfranchised member of her lineage, she now comes under the authority of her mother's brother and the lineage elders in her politico-jural capacity. She can, for instance, be suspected of witchcraft now.[36] As a married woman and potential mother of offspring, she is bound to her husband in a conjugal relationship of obligatory sexual fidelity and domestic duty. But she is more likely to reside with her mother, just as before, than with her husband. And this indicates where the critical change in her status as daughter has occurred. It is in

32. The most thorough study of this institution known to me is the unpublished disserta- tion, Girls' Nubility Rites in Ashanti, submitted for the B. Litt. degree at Oxford by Fr. Peter Sarpong, 1965. Himself an Ashanti, Father Sarpong bases his work on personal observa- tion and inquiry in his native land. I am indebted to him for allowing me to draw on his thesis. I witnessed the ceremony only once, but the circumstances were such that I had to refrain from detailed inquiries. Rattray's description of the institution is the most complete as yet published, but it gives only a bare outline (1927: chap. VII). The details of the customary practices and beliefs associated with the ceremony are expounded with subtle insight by Sarpong. However, it is only the general principles which he brings out that are here relevant. I might add that his analysis bears out a valuable eyewitness description of the ceremony made in 1945 by my field assistant, Mr. T. E. Kyei (unpublished) and kindly placed at my disposal by him.

33. So strong, however, was the feeling of the importance of this ceremony, that Christian parents commonly celebrated a daughter's nubility without the traditional ritual but with emphasis on the social and convivial elements. It was also becoming customary in certain denominations for confirmation at the menarche to be substituted for the traditional ritual (cf. Fortes. 1954: 268, 297).

34. If a pre-nubile girl dies, she should, by traditional custom, be buried and mourned as a child. After the ceremony she is buried and mourned as an adult.

35. As Robert Lystad expresses it (1958: 297).

36. As I have previously noted, a non-adult is deemed to be incapable of witchcraft activity since he or she, not being *sui iuris*, cannot personally be answerable for wrongs—or, conversely, assert rights. More exactly a person becomes capable of witchcraft when he or she becomes capable of legitimate procreation, the central target of witchcraft conflict.

relation to her father. She is no longer in his direct care and protection; he is no longer responsible for her physical well-being and moral purity and, thus, through her mother, for any social or ritual transgressions she may commit. Attaining adulthood for a woman means relinquishing her childish dependency on her father, not only in the material sense but also in the spiritual and moral sense symbolized in the dogma that a child cannot thrive if its father's patri-soul (*ntoro*) and personal essence (*sunsum*) do not watch over it. The obverse of this is that she reaches jural autonomy within the limits set by her lineage membership and thus wins freedom to act, and to be answerable for her actions, in sexual, reproductive, and economic relations as wife and mother. She is henceforth mistress of her own sexuality and of her working powers, but—significantly enough—not of her body, which, alive and reproductive or dead, belongs to her lineage. And this has an important implication. Though ideally and properly a woman's emancipation into adulthood is sealed by her marriage, an Ashanti woman need not be married in order to have legitimate children. Once sexually liberated, she is free, as we have already seen, to produce offspring for her lineage, provided she does not violate the incest prohibitions, which is one reason why she must be able to cite a licit genitor.

The nubility ceremony marks, legitimizes, and publicizes this change. We can understand why it was and is eagerly and hopefully looked forward to by Ashanti girls. It is incumbent on parents, as a duty phrased in terms of ritual sanctions, to have the ceremony performed at the earliest convenient date after the onset of a girl's menses.[37]

But the ceremony, which normally lasts eight days, is a public, not solely a family and lineage, event. From the outset, it is the change in the girl's jural and moral status, not her physiological maturity that is celebrated. A sign of this is that permission has to be given by the queen mother of the community for the ceremony to take place. Likewise, the chief and the priests of important divinities have to be notified. The conduct of the rites is in the hands of the elderly women—the "grandmothers"—of the community, not only those of the girl's lineage; and pre-nubile girls from all the lineages attend on the initiand. Gifts come to her from well-wishers throughout the community as well as from her patrikin and lineage kin, and if she is already promised in marriage, specially valuable gifts symbolic of his anticipated conjugal relationship with her are brought to her by her fiancé. Women of the whole community escort her when she goes out, drumming, dancing, and singing, and young and old join in the festivities.

The organization of the ritual acts is instructive; the inaugural rite is eloquent. The maid's head is ritually shaved and this must be done by a father's sister on behalf of the father.[38] The parallel with the eighth-day naming ceremony for a baby

37. Cf. Fortes. 1954: 296 ff. The modal age for this is 16 years. Marriage, in the forties, followed soon after in rural areas, except for school girls. Since the nubility ceremony entailed considerable expense both for the parents and the girl's fiancé (if she was already betrothed), it was often delayed for some months until such time as the parties could afford it.

38. Or by a patrilateral substitute. If the father (or his successor) repudiates this obligation, he thereby renounces his paternity and his spiritual connection with the girl. As long as her father is alive, a girl's head may not be shaved before her nubility ceremony, even when, as is the custom, a close relative dies. It would imply denial of his paternity and "wishing him ill," and the perpetrator can be sued at court by the swearing of the chief's oath.

is plain, as Ashanti themselves point out.[39] A gift of money or treasure from the father must accompany this rite, supposedly in payment for the infantile hair that is removed. However small, this gift is regarded as the nucleus of the private wealth to which every woman aspires and is legally free to accumulate; and it is believed that if she dissipates her father's gift, she will never succeed in this. This is how the father, by structurally appropriate female proxy, ritually emancipates his daughter from her childish status of dependency and sexual immaturity, legitimizing her marriageability and setting her on the road to the economic independence which reflects her jural autonomy. Released from under his wing, she is able to realize her personal destiny which, for a woman, manifests itself primarily in her reproductive achievement.

This accomplished, the young woman is taken in hand by the lineage and village "grandmothers." They conduct her to the river or stream which, in this well-watered country, is generally within easy reach of every village and is associated with its chiefdom deities and taboos. She is carried into the river on a "grandmother's" back as if she were a baby and undergoes a ritual ablution amid the cheerful congratulations of her younger attendants. Then, clad in a new cloth, she undergoes the rite which is, from her lineage's point of view, the crucial one. It is called "*ano ka*," mouth-touching. The young woman is seated in a humble posture, and the officiating "grandmother" touches her lips first with a number of magically symbolical objects and then with morsels of the staple foodstuffs ready cooked. The magical objects include such items as a species of fish, a piece of elephant skin and an egg; and with each touching, the "grandmother" pronounces a blessing invoking prolific and easy childbearing for the girl, and health and well-being for her kin. Thus is the vesting in her of her fecundity by her lineage reaffirmed by an act of magical transmission performed by the old women whose fertility has kept the community in being and has now been entrusted to their newly nubile descendant.[40] And this is

39. Cf. Rattray, 1927: chap. VI, and reference above, p. 000. There is no need for me to expatiate on the characteristic Van-Gennepian form of this passage rite. In Ashanti, as in many other African societies, shaving the head is a common rite to mark the relinquishment of one status and translation to another, in particular a ritually cleaner or socially superior one. A newly elected chief's head is shaved when he is installed and a widow's or orphan's is shaved to remove the pollution of mourning. In this case we might say that it is the pollution—or the sexual innocence—of infancy that is ablated. The traditional blessing pronounced by the father's sister, as recorded by Mr. Kyei, states exactly what the rite signifies. It goes: "Your father it was who begot you and looked after you as a child. Now you are grown up. He has given me this money with which to take off your hair. Your father's sister am I, and I am taking this money to remove your hair. May you menstruate well. Do not have a cursed puberty and let no bad thing happen. May your father be successful in gaining money so that he can have it to care for you."

40. There is much more to the symbolism of these rites, as Sarpong shows at length, but this is not the place to go into great detail. The touching of the initiand's mouth symbolizes incorporation by her of the fecundity and fertility conveyed by the magical items and of the housewife's role represented in the cooked food. The "sympathetic" significance of the egg (fecundity), the fish (prolific fertility), and the elephant skin (quick pregnancy) is well understood by all the participants. The two forms of ritual purification, by shaving the head and by lustration, here separated to represent the complementary opposition of patrifiliation and matrilineal descent, are conjoined in such rites as the termination of a widow's mourning. In this case, the patient has to be both purified of the pollution of her conjugal connection with the deceased spouse's ghost, and restored to a normal marriageable woman's status in her lineage. When a chief is thus purified on being installed, it is both to rid him of his commoner status as an individual and to separate him from his lineage. Lustration at a river-

fitting, since it is they who are the source of the "blood" she will perpetuate in her offspring.

It is worth adding that the ceremony as a whole is joyous and even ribald in tone.[41] And compared with the mother's mothers, mothers, and sisters, the males of the lineage, despite the jural authority vested in them, play but a secondary part. They offer libations and sacrifices to the ancestral stools with prayers for the maid's fertility and well-being to mark her acceptance as a full-grown member of the lineage, with potential genetrical status in it. But these are acts of ritual and jural acquiescence, for she is a member of the lineage by right of birth, she is not being incorporated in it.

No such ceremonies mark a boy's attainment of adulthood. He does not undergo a change of status or of social personality comparable to his sister's. If he moves to reside with his mother's brother, this is no more than implementing a right and accepting duties that were already potentially his by virtue of his membership of the *yafunu* group and lineage. His productive capacity and his duties and rights as a citizen accrue to his status as lineage member by simple growth and ripening. This is associated with the fact that males are the privileged sex in the politico-jural domain.

But the crucial fact is that his distinctive relationship with his father is not severed. He does not, like his sister, have to be endowed with capacities that make adult lineage membership and citizenship a contrast and break with childhood. Like his sister, he remains bound to his father by the spiritual bond of the hereditary *sunsum* and *ntoro*; but, unlike her, he can transmit it to his offspring and thus link his father and his paternal antecedents to his children. He remains the carrier of the patrifilial connection and the perpetuator of its distinctive spiritual and moral attributes, its associated names, and its ritual observances. Traditionally, what a father did in sign of terminating the childhood dependence of a son who reached physical maturity was to present him with the gun every adult male should possess, or with the tools of his craft, and seek at once, for a wife for him. Nowadays, as I said earlier, supporting the son to the end of his school years fulfills this purpose of setting him up for adult life.

The moral rights of a father symbolized in these acts are reflected in the privileges he exercises in the arrangement of his children's marriages. Though jural control in marriage transactions rests with the mother's brothers and the lineage elders of the

41. The special songs sung by the women during the week of celebration are erotic in content to such a degree that educated young men described them to me as "vulgar" and "lascivious." This, incidentally, as one might expect of a licensed occasion celebrating sexual maturity, is the very opposite of the reticence and periphrasis with which sexual topics are treated in normal social intercourse. It is as if a girl's adult sexuality is thus publicly acclaimed and approved. Many of these songs, Mr. Malcolm McLeod informs me, are concerned with the relations of husbands and wives, and others exalt—or lampoon—public personalities, as if asserting that the occasion is specially privileged.

---

side is also the normal way of purifying the shrines of deities during *adae* and first fruits ceremonies. It is the way, finally, in which a man purifies himself by "washing" to establish communion with his *ntoro*, the male-transmitted spiritual essence that is associated with rivers and, in a more symbolic sense, with the fertilising water of the body, the seminal fluid. The bathing of the newly nubile girl implies both purification and symbolic fertilization.

two parties, the consent of their parents was traditionally and still is necessary for the marriage to take place.[42] This is especially significant in the case of the father. Since it is by ritual dispensation on behalf of her father that a woman's procreative sexuality is recognized and placed at the service of her lineage, it is understandable that her father will have a legitimate interest in how her uxorial capacities are disposed of, and he has, in fact, a critical voice in the choice of a husband for her. Because her fertility belongs to the lineage, and a man's does not, a woman is more subject to jural control in her marriage than is a man. She can be "given" in marriage, whereas a man may be commanded, or persuaded, or restrained, but has much more freedom to take the initiative on his own.

The requirement of the father's consent relates to the *sunsum* and *ntoro* he passes on to his offspring. If he withholds consent, it signifies a disagreement so great as to offend the *ntoro* divinity—that is, a repudiation of the moral bonds of patrifiliation, and sickness or back luck could follow from this.[43]

These values ascribed to patrifiliation are symbolically asserted in the traditional marriage prestations from the bridegroom to the bride and her kin. Before the *tiri nsa* ("head wine") is handed over, he must distribute small (but fixed) gifts of money to each of her kinsfolk who have rights in or claims upon her—her mother's brother and her father (equal amounts), her mother (the same or a little less), her close uterine sisters collectively (about half the mother's share), and her close uterine brothers, collectively (the same amount).[44] A very generous gift must be made also to the bride herself. But the most important prestation comes after the marriage has been jurally ratified. This is the *Nyame-dwang*, "God's sheep," given by the newly-wed husband to his wife's father.[45] This sheep (or its equivalent in money) is to be used by the father to offer a libation and sacrifice to his *ntoro* divinity and his *sunsum* soul. It is given to him in gratitude for the care and guidance devoted by him to his daughter during her childhood. Failure to make this prestation can lead to divorce; but, unlike the *tiri nsa*, it is not returned if the marriage breaks up. A man's daughter's transition to sexual maturity, wifehood, and motherhood is final and irreversible, and once he acquiesces in it by offering the "God's sheep" to his personal divinity, he cannot retract.

The formalities of contracting a marriage indicate that the interests, and the rights and claims of the father, on the one hand, and of the nuclear uterine corporation, on the other, over filial dependants are pretty evenly balanced. This conclusion is

42. To avoid frequent qualification, I should add that the argument applies primarily to first marriage. In Ashanti, as elsewhere in Africa (cf. Fortes. 1962c: 1–13), first marriage confers an irreversible element of status, so that subsequent marriages do not necessarily have to conform to the non-jural customs of first marriage.

43. The ghosts (*saman*) of the recent dead were believed to be able to bring sickness and death on successors who failed in kinship duties or offended against customary moral norms (cf. Busia, 1951: 24–25). A father's ghost was regarded with special awe in this connection.

44. As I have mentioned earlier, the bridegroom has also, according to traditional custom, to give gifts (generally at the time when his bride is escorted to his house) to the bride's male cross-cousins in acknowledgement of the theoretically prior rights of the cross-cousins to her hand. The cross-cousins stand in his way and demand, partly in jest, to be bought off. But the custom is indicative of the value ideally attached to cross-cousin marriage.

45. The acknowledged genitor has first claim, but failing him or his successor, the mother's husband receives the sheep.

borne out strikingly when their respective influence in the bestowal of girls in marriage is examined. Ashanti emphasize the parents' prerogatives in this and claim that the father's goodwill is more important than the mother's brother's. In 1945 in recording details of 561 marriages contracted by 262 men over the preceding forty to fifty years, I found that fathers were stated to have had about the same degree of authority as the nuclear matrikin (mother and mother's brother in particular) in the bestowal of wives,[46] though one must bear in mind the fact that all parental kin have rights and interests in the married partners, and therefore have a voice in the match. The consistency between the distribution of paternal prerogative and avuncular jural authority in marriage and the distribution of responsibility for bringing up and educating children is worth noting.[47] They are the two sides of the same underlying configuration; a closeup of the essential features of this configuration is provided by the institution of cross-cousin marriage, which was, in the forties, still regarded as the ideal form of marriage by middle-aged people.[48] Cross-cousin marriage properly speaking is marriage between the children of actual matrisiblings of opposite sex, but it is readily extended to apply to matrisiblings within the *yafunu* group.

Mother's brothers' daughter (*wofa-ba*) marriage is regarded as the most desirable form; and it appears, from the 1945 marriage inquiry previously cited, to have been about twice as frequent as father's sister's daughter marriage. This conforms to the distribution of paternal control and avuncular jural authority in the familial domain which we have already encountered. A man can as father command his daughter,

46. The data related to the first marriages of the respondents, who ranged in age from about 20 to about 70. I leave aside marriages subject to special rules of selection, that is, with cross-cousins, or brother's widows, and with girls betrothed before their nubility ceremony, and consider only those stated to have followed upon normal courtship and solicitation of the girl's guardians. Of the 369 first marriages reported as falling into this category, the girls' fathers were said to have had the decisive voice in their bestowal in 165 cases (44.7 per cent), the mothers in 64 (17.3 per cent), the mother's brothers in 118 (32 per cent), and other matrikin (e.g., older brothers) in 22 (5.7 per cent). In addition there were, in the total sample, 44 marriages declared to have been entered into primarily because the parties were cross-cousins, and 75 cases in which the principal reason for the marriage was said to be betrothal to the girl before the nubility ceremony. Since child betrothal was often with a cross-cousin, and the commonest form of cross-cousin marriage, that is, with the mother's brother's daughter, generally came about by the girl's father bestowing her on his sister's son, these cases strengthen the claim to priority of paternal over avuncular authority in the arrangement of marriages. I must emphasize that parental and avuncular assent is just as important on the bridegroom's side in a first marriage, but it would only be withheld if the bride he has chosen is regarded as notoriously unfitted for him—if, for example, she is reputed to be of loose morals or the child of a witch.

47. Comparison of the two sets of numerical data brings this out.

48. Cross-cousin (in the classificatory sense) marriage appears to have been relatively common up till the 1930's but was falling into disfavor among the young people by the 1940's (cf. Fortes. 1950: 282). But the figures given there, which are derived from the marriage inquiry referred to above in fact represent a low estimate. Since many marriages, as is noted in n. 46, above, attributed by respondents to other factors or motives than cross-cousinship are, also, in fact, with cross-cousins (in the classificatory sense), I estimate the incidence of *de facto* cross-cousin marriage to have been of the order of 15 per cent among the first marriages contracted in the years between about 1900 and 1925, and of the order of 5–7 per cent among those entered into between about 1935 and 1945. These figures reflect the increasing insistence among young people on choosing spouses for themselves. Being no more than rough estimates, their main value is to provide evidence of a trend often stressed by informants.

and as uncle, his sister's son, who is his potential heir, to marry for the benefit of both families; he can only persuade his own son to fall in with his wishes to marry his sister's daughter, and must be careful to avoid a clash of authority with the latter's father. As Ashanti phrase it, the reason why cross-cousin marriage is so desirable is that it reconciles the potentially conflicting interests and divergent loyalties that confront the individual—especially a man—in his personal field of kinship and descent relations. We must remember that it is for him a bipolar field, though constituted, in its external structural setting, by the complementary norms and mechanisms generated by matrifiliation and patrifiliation respectively.

By this reckoning, father's sister's daughter (*sewaba*) marriage ensures, first, that father's son's son (*nana*) is reputably fathered. He will bear father's name (or one of the other names distinctive of his paternal forbears) and share his *ntoro* spirit, thus perpetuating his patri-personality and status.[49] What is more, he will also incorporate father's matripersonal status and inherit his lineage property as heir to his sister's son. Thus the circle will be completed. It will be as if father were himself resurrected as a total social person. Father's father and son's son thus related are closely identified. Indeed Ashanti sometimes speak of a dead father's father as being reborn in his son's son.[50] But on a more mundane level, such a marriage reconciles the care and expense a man has devoted to preparing his son for life with the obligation to provide also for his matrifilial dependants, that is, his sisters' and sisters' daughters' children. The training he has given his son benefits his *yafunu* in the end. His fatherly wish and duty to ensure that his son is properly married is identified with his avuncular duty and right to steer his niece towards a good and secure marriage.

The more popular mother's brother's daughter (*wofa ba*) marriage is commended by the same general line of argument. A man desires his daughter to be reputably married and well cared for in marriage. He desires her and her children to benefit from the property he must needs leave to his nephew and his *yafunu*. He is concerned that his nephew and heir should marry a well-trained and respectable girl. He desires to fuse the two sides of his parental commitments and obligations. Thus, whichever of the two forms of cross-cousin marriage proves most convenient or feasible in a given case, it is initiated by parents and uncles and permits them to fulfill a major paternal duty without doing violence to avuncular obligation.

Women also take the initiative in their double capacity as mothers and sisters. A woman is concerned that her children should take spouses of reliable heredity, good character, and industrious and faithful disposition. Women say that cross-cousin marriages are more secure than other marriages because the kin of the spouses and the spouses themselves are already bound to one another by mutual kinship amity. They emphasize also the material advantages of, for instance, the fact that the gifts a

49. Cf. Fortes. 1950: 282; Rattray. 1927: chap. XXIX, where cross-cousin marriage is described and analyzed at length. I am, however, here restating the explanation Ashanti elders gave me twenty years after Rattray's field investigations. As is evident, they are fully consistent with the rationalizations he was given.

50. Such a child may be addressed as "grandfather" (*nana*) by his parents and siblings, though there is no implication of his being a "positional" successor of his grandfather in the Central African style.

brother might make to his children at the expense of their children in the end turn out to the benefit of their grandchildren.

Why then, considering the advantages imputed to the institution and the continued primacy of matrilineal descent in the politico-jural domain, was cross-cousin marriage becoming increasingly unpopular in the forties ? Older Ashanti attributed this to a variety of causes—to the much enlarged freedom of movement and of choice of occupation open to young people, to education and Christianity, to new economic opportunities for acquiring private wealth with which to endow one's children, to the diminished authority of parents, uncles, and chiefs—in short, to the ferment of change alleged to be undermining the whole traditional order of society. Young people accounted for their reluctance to marry cross-cousins on two grounds: firstly, that nowadays people must be free to choose their spouses for themselves; and, secondly, that cross-cousins were felt to be too near by kinship and too familiar to be attractive as spouses.

In structural terms, what this change seemed to me, as an observer, to be associated with, was a noticeable tendency for polarization of matrilateral and patrilateral alignments in the total kinship field to become sharper. Men were endeavoring more deliberately than in the past to segregate their conjugal and parental from their fraternal and lineage commitments and responsibilities. The ideal of preferential marriage as a means of bringing about a fusion of the divergent interests and obligations generated by matrifiliation and patrifiliation, was becoming incompatible with this widening split in the structure of the kinship field (Fortes, 1950).

V

In presenting the traditional social and political system of the Ashanti at such length, I have had in mind, in particular, its exceptional paradigmatic relevance for my inquiry. But it is hardly necessary to add that Ashanti social structure is by no means unique, either phenotypically or, more significantly, in regard to the principles implemented in it. I am not thinking here of its comparability with other systems founded on the primacy of matrilineal descent. Basehart's analysis (from which, incidentally, I have greatly profited) in the volume edited by Schneider and Gough, and Gough's comparative survey, elucidate this comprehensively.[51] I am thinking, rather, of the representation in the Ashanti social system of principles that operate in a wide range of polities of this type, those that are patrilineally as well as matrilineally based and irrespective of differences from Ashanti and from one another in such exogenous features as their natural environments and their technology and economy, as well as in many institutional forms. An example that comes to mind is the patrilineal Mossi of the Haute Volta (cf. Skinner, 1964). If we consider the regulation of civic status, the hierarchy of legal tribunals, the kingship and the military organization—even the interrelations of successive generations—among the Mossi, they could easily be placed side by side with their Ashanti counterpart in

51. Schneider and Gough, 1961; 450–56; "Ashanti" by Harry W. Basehart, pp. 270–97; and note especially chaps. 12 and 13 by Gough.

the same analytical frame. Yet the Mossi agrarian economy and their general mode of life are as different from the Ashanti way of life as the open, semi-arid savanna zone in which they live is from the tropical rain forest of Ashanti. Nor are these parallels confined to kingdoms and other centralized states. At the familial level, as Goody has shown (1961), principles operative in Ashanti social structure are discernible in numerous societies that are inexactly described as having double descent systems.

A more impressive confirmation comes, however, from the other side of Africa. On the face of it the ethnically mixed, Nilotic Alur of Uganda are as different from the Ashanti in their language and culture, their economy and mode of life, and their familial and political institutions as they are distant from them geographically. Their patrilineal clan and lineage system and their decentralized political system, associated though it is with a form of chiefship, have much in common with what are usually thought of as acephalous segmentary social systems. But Southall's analysis (1956: 40, 61–69, 122 ff., and *passim*; fortunately, from my present point of view, developed within a framework of structural theory very close to the one I am applying) shows that the general principles of social and political structure represented in the Ashanti system also operate among the Alur. The political system is based on localized, corporate, and jurally unitary lineages loosely interlinked in dispersed clans that are vaguely demarcated but supposed to be of common origin and to pre-suppose a bond of amity. There is a notion of a lineage as being "people of one person" by descent. Chiefship is patrilineally hereditary and vested with political authority primarily by right of descent but also in virtue of the chief's ritual status in the ancestor cult and in the possession of rain magic. And, most interesting of all, the quite clear-cut distinctions between the sphere of familial authority and the sphere of political authority to which I drew attention earlier, operate to maintain a complementary pattern in the regulation of jural relations and in the dispensation of justice that closely parallels the Ashanti system. There is provision, for instance, as in Ashanti, for disputes that arise or wrongs that are committed in the familial or local group to be transferred for adjudication to the chiefs' tribunals.

Many other examples could, of course, be cited. But these must suffice to emphasize my point that (as Radcliffe-Brown's thesis of 1935 implies) the principles of social structure represented in the Ashanti paradigm can *mutatis mutandis* readily be shown to have more general validity in patrilineally as well as matrilineally based systems.

But the chief interest of these examples for our present inquiry lies in the demonstration they afford of the indissoluble interconnection between the domain of kinship and descent institutions and values, on the one hand, and the politico-jural domain, on the other. It would be no distortion to say, of the Ashanti, that full civic capacity and the ritual status that is part and parcel of it presupposes essentially the same elements of status as are comprised in the Roman formula of *Libertas*, *Civitas* and *Familia* (cf. Buckland; 36). This means, ideally, freeborn parentage, legitimate membership of a lineage of authentic Ashanti clanship, and citizenship in a chiefdom and the nation. Though never inflexibly applied in practise, either in Ashanti or in any of the other polities cited, these rules reflect criteria of wide, if not general validity.

PART III

SOME ISSUES
IN STRUCTURAL THEORY

CHAPTER XII

Kinship and the Axiom of Amity

I

THE INQUIRY I HAVE BEEN PURSUING IS CONCERNED WITH THE PROBLEM THAT LAY AT the heart of Morgan's researches and speculations and remains the central one for us today. Stripped of its historicist pretensions and restated in structural terms, it is the problem of how kinship and polity are interconnected in tribal society. Modern field research has shown that "*civitas*" does not identify a specific "type" or "stage" of advanced society by contrast with a conjecturally "primitive" or historically antecedent form of society founded exclusively upon ties of "blood." "Status," in the sense of Maine's juristic equivalent for Morgan's "*societas*," does not characterize primitive or archaic forms or stages of society in contradistinction to the principle of "contract" which is supposed to be the hallmark of "progressive" societies. The evidence is indisputable that these antinomies and others that have been linked with them do not identify different forms of social and politico-jural organization. They represent correlative and interdependent institutional complexes that work together in all social systems. Our paradigmatic specimens exemplify this over a wide range of phenotypically diverse societies. It is true that variations in demographic scale, economic complexity, and politico-jural differentiation regulate the ways in which these complexes are manifested and interlinked. It is evident, likewise, that variations in the kinds of symbolic representation and in the schemes of philosophical apprehension available in different cultures shape the ways in which their nature and their interconnections are conceptualized and handled. But their occurrence is not contingent upon any of these factors. Where there is society, there is both kinship and polity, both status and contract. What is distinctive is their relative elaboration and differentiation, their relative weight and scope in different sectors of social life.

These findings reflect the radical shift in our methods and frame of analysis from the earlier pseudo-historical orientation to the synchronic mode established by the application of functionalist theory. But the conceptual and theoretical problems we have met with in this inquiry go back, as we have seen, to Morgan's day, and I would like, now, to reconsider some of them. So far I have considered them only incidentally as they have emerged in the presentation of the historical background and the paradigmatic ethnographic specimens. Now a more direct approach is in order.

II

Before turning to these questions specifically, however, I want to dispose of a more general matter. I adverted to it earlier in citing the controversy between Gellner, Needham and others. It is symptomatic of a point of view that has obtruded itself on studies of kinship and social organization from the beginning. I refer to the assumption that what we designate as the relations and institutions of kinship, descent, and affinity are in reality merely artifacts, or expressions of more fundamental, more lasting, and more solidly real data of social life. It is not quite the same thing as, for instance, Tylor's recourse to residence patterns to explain matriliny and later elaborations of this hypothesis, nor is it just Morgan's theory of property as the prime mover in the evolution of the family that is being reasserted. For though Morgan at the end of his peroration on the Monogamian Family declared that the family "is the creature of the social system, and will reflect its culture" (1877: 491 [1878 ed.]), he did not regard family and kinship relations as mere by-products of the technological or economic factors he made so much of. He gave the credit for the establishment of certainty of paternity to the advent of monogamy, but repeatedly insisted that at least the relationships of mother and child, brother and sister were always certain and founded on the facts of nature (1877: 393). The assumption I refer to is far more specific, and its interest for the present inquiry lies in its continual reappearance in modern ethnographical researches. I cite two examples in illustration.

I take first Worsley's reanalysis (1956) of Tallensi kinship and social structure as presented in my books and papers. It is an incisive study which justifiably draws attention to loose ends in my analysis. But it gravely misinterprets many of my data, owing to Worsley's determination to find the hidden hand of economic compulsion everwhere. "As we have seen," he proclaims, "kinship is the form which the essential relations arising from the needs of agriculture, the inheritance of property, etc., take, and as these latter relations change, so kinship changes. Far from being basic it is secondary." Explaining, he adds: "The particular forms which kinship relations will take—corporate unilineal descent-groups, cognatic systems without lineages, double unilineal systems, etc.—are largely determined by economic and historical forces" (1956: 62–63).

There is, I fear, no way of refuting Worsley without going over the ethnographic data in detail.[1] It is characteristic of the naive determinism he espouses that its arguments are circular and based on such a nebulous and sweeping concept of economics that every social activity one can think of is included. Yet he himself remarks that "in Taleland co-operation between more people than are contained in the elementary family is necessary for survival: one co-operates in economic activities with people to whom one is already related by blood or marriage" (1956: 68). Here surely lies the crux. How does one get related by blood (to use Worsley's technically slipshod term) or marriage—and not only among the Tallensi? Marriage, parenthood, filiation, siblingship and other relations of kinship occur in similar arrangements in societies very different from the Tallensi in their modes of production of food, shelter, and services, in their property relations and in the other items cited by Worsley as "economic." They even occur—in forms that Tallensi would spontaneously recognize as analogous to their own—in modern Lancashire. Or does Dr. Worsley consider these relations in Lancashire to be "basically" determined by the modern industrial economy of the area?

He particularly objects to my conclusion that the kinship system is

. . . the primary mechanism through through which the basic moral axioms of the type represented by the Tallensi are translated into the . . . give and take of social life (1949c:346, cited by Worsley, 1956:63).

But he offers no *economic* explanation of such moral institutions as the incest taboo. He rejects my thesis that the kinship system, the economic system, and the religious system of the Tallensi are analytically distinct from one another and irreducible one to another, yet so closely interdependent that they cannot be understood in isolation from one another. He must have a single-track mechanistic explanation which, contrary to the evidence he himself cites, reduces kinship to a secondary by-product of agricultural needs and property relations.

There would have been no object in thus cursorily discussing Worsley's fallacies if it were not for the fact that the point of view represented in it continually recurs in kinship studies. It is advocated with characteristic rhetorical vigor in my second example, Leach's previously cited (1961a) study of the village of Pul Eliya in the Dry Zone of Ceylon. The special relevance of this study lies in the fact that the field data, which are presented in scrupulous detail, unequivocally contradict the polemical stance (as Cohn [1962: 105] and Oliver [1962: 622] have pointed out).

What Leach purports to demonstrate is proclaimed in the following statement

1. I revisited the Tallensi in 1963 and was greatly struck by the evidence of the stability and continuity of their lineage, family and residence patterns which had not appreciably changed since 1937. My earlier maps and genealogies were still completely valid. The demographic, economic, political and cultural changes of the past thirty years had had obvious and marked influences but had brought about no radical changes in the social structure or the religious system. (Cf. Fortes and Mayer, 1966). So far, then predictions ventured by Worsley of structural changes he believed would follow from economic changes he forecast for the Tallensi have been falsified.

Kinship as we meet it in this book is not a "thing in itself." The concepts of descent and affinity are expressions of property relations which endure through time. Marriage unifies; inheritance separates; property endures (1961a: 11).

Anthropologists are given to epigrammatic flourishes and one must not take this *au pied de la lettre*. But the implication is clear: Property constitutes the enduring, the basic stuff of social life; the "concepts" (as entertained by the actor or by the observer? Leach is never explicit on this point) relating to the universe of kinship are "expressions"—that is, secondary to, derivatives of, this permanent reality. This echoes an earlier pronouncement:

It is in this sense that I want to insist that the student of social structure must never forget that the constraints of economics are prior to the constraints of morality and law (1961a: 9).

Applied specifically to kinship, the argument continues:

Social anthropologists are prone to make a specialism of kinship and to treat it as a separate dimension. Such presentation can be very misleading. Kin groups do not exist as things in themselves without regard to the rights and interests which centre in them. Membership of such a group is not established by genealogy alone. Properly speaking, two individuals can only be said to be of the same kinship group when they share some common interest—economic, legal, political, religious as the case may be—and *justify that sharing* by reference to a kinship nexus. The anthropological problems that then arise are: What are these common interests? What individuals share them? What is the nature of the nexus? Why is kinship rather than some other *principle of incorporation* used to provide the sanction of legitimacy? (1961a: 65–66; my italics).

Here I find myself in deep water. The social anthropologists at whose door these ambiguous charges are laid are not named. Certainly none of those cited by Dr. Leach in the course of his study has ever presented *kin groups* as "things in themselves" (whatever this may mean) and "without regard to the rights and interests which centre in them." It may indeed be that genealogy alone is not sufficient to establish membership of such a group, depending of course on how the group is defined. On the other hand, without genealogy, there can, in certain politico-jural systems, be no title to membership. The Lozi village and indeed the Pul Eliya *gedara* are instances. By the same token, to go back one step, marriage presupposes at least an incest rule that prohibits siblings from thus uniting and may prescribe partners, as in Pul Eliya, by genealogically framed criteria. Similarly, inheritance, if intestate, presumes laws that define next-of-kin-right by criteria of kinship and genealogical specification. And, lastly, property, in the purely material sense of lands, buildings, tools, or what you will, is, surely, dead as a dodo if it is not owned and utilized by living human groups in accordance with law and morality.

However, there is no point in pursuing these minutiae further. As I have remarked, we should not, perhaps, take Leach's polemical declarations too literally. For the real problem we are all concerned with is well formulated by Leach himself in the last sentence of the preceding quotation. To paraphrase Worsley, it is the problem presented by the fact that relationship by kinship or marriage appears to be the necessary and prior condition for economic and property relations in this community as in others of the kind we are concerned with.

To take some of the more general features first, it must be realized the Pul Eliya is a village of under 150 souls, all of whom are members by birth or incorporation of one endogamous subcaste (*variga*) of the widely dispersed Goyigama caste. Thus, in village theory, all members of the *variga* are kin.

There is a *variga* court which deals with breaches of the rule of endogamy either by a fine (which is "tantamount to a *variga* admission fee" [1961a: 72]) or by expulsion from the subcaste. Two cases are quoted. In the first a fine and admission into the *variga* is the outcome; in the second the parties are expelled. Leach's interpretation is characteristic:

The principle involved is clear. Where the "sinner" is a desirable relative, his offence is purged with a fine; where he is undesirable he and his accomplice are cut out of the *variga* altogether (1961a: 73).

But in fact the data show that the "desirable relative" was a member of the same caste as the Pul Eliya *variga* (Goyigama), though apparently not of the same subcaste; whereas in the second case, the man had grown up in the village as a gardener's son but was not of the Goyigama caste. Thus this case was a definite offense against caste endogamy, while the first case could be interpreted as tolerance of a breach of subcaste endogamy which yet kept within the bounds of the wider and prior endogamy of the whole caste. It is not simply a case of ulterior or mercenary motives being the main criterion.

The probability that the rule of caste morality was the paramount consideration here is strengthened by further observations reported by Leach. He notes, for example, that men who take women from a wrong subcaste of the same caste to live with them are tolerated, whereas he "did not meet with any case where a man had set up house with a woman of wrong caste" (1961a: 74)—though there must surely have been circumstances in which such a ménage would have been economically advantageous. Now Leach maintains that "it is land rights and place of residence rather than descent which provide the ultimate basis for *variga* status" (1961a: 79), but the case of the gardener's son throws doubt on this generalization. Though long resident, he was not permitted to marry a woman of the Goyigama *variga* and thus cannot be said to have acquired *variga* status by virtue of his place of residence. Confirmation is found in the following statement:

The primary economic requirement for a villager is not that he should be the owner of land, but that he should be a member of the village with rights to a share in the water in the tank. All members of the village (provided they do not transgress against caste rules) transmit to all their children this first essential right to membership of the village. Pul Eliya villagers do not use *gedara* names or detailed genealogies to specify this membership transmission, they simply employ the much vaguer notion that house compounds are continuing units (1961a: 98).

Recruitment to them is "primarily through pedigree" (Leach, 1961a: 106). But pedigree alone provides only a latent right which is asserted through the fact of common residence. An example of such a house unit elicits the comment:

The exact details of the pedigree are uncertain, but because the descent is admitted all these individuals are "members of the village" . . . Pul Eliya people, even though some of them live outside the main *gamgoda* area (1961a: 98–99).

The bias introduced by describing as an "*economic* requirement" a "right" transmitted (presumably automatically) to children by "pedigree," provided their "descent is admitted" and their caste-membership certain, is glaring here. But calculation of pedigree and descent is not essential in prescriptively endogamous groups for the establishment of primary entitlement to membership. It is enough to have recognized, that is, legitimate, filiation to parents who are known to have legitimate membership of the group to have the entitlement (cf. Fortes, 1959a).

Leach makes a special point of presenting the *pavula* (kindred) combinations within the subcaste, as emerging as "political factions," and sums up:

Let me repeat: although recruitment to a *pavula* is based in kinship alone, a *pavula* is in essence a political faction. . . . The whole sytem thus presupposes the existence of the overall *variga* organisation by which everyone in the village is necessarily a kinsman of everyone else" [which includes affines, as they too are "kin in a very general sense"] (1961a: 123).

In short—and there is not the space here to go into further detail—turn where we will, as far as this community is concerned, a person cannot be in it and of it, a full member, if he does not have the right kinship credential. And he cannot exercise the economic self-interest or indulge in the political maneuvers for prestige or power *within the community* except as a legitimate member of it. The boundary between the internal system of the *variga* village and its external social and political environment is laid down by the criterion of kinship—and kinship here merges into caste with all its moral and jural rules.

The most important property in the village is the land in the Old Field, tenure of which confers rights in the water of the irrigation tank. Individual holdings, says Leach (1961a: 173), are acquired by inheritance, by gift and by purchase. Here lies a crucial test of his thesis. Inheritance of plots obviously presupposes a kinship right, by filiation to either parent, since testamentary disposition does not appear to be common. Gifts of land *inter vivos* (1961a: 132–37) are made to either an adopted child, or the giver's potential heirs, normally his children, or as dowry to a daughter. Here, too, it would seem that the determining factors fall within the domain of family and kinship. One could of course argue that such gifts are motivated purely by economic or political self-interest, with men and women (for the sexes are on an equal footing in respect of their land rights) making them in return for undertakings to support them in old age or assist them in other utilitarian ways. But then one would expect frequent cases to occur of capable and reliable young men being chosen for such gifts without concern for the filiative or affinal connections with them. Is there no factor of "morality" or "law" in this?

But let us turn to mortgage and purchase. Can a mortgagor or purchaser of land by virtue of this economic transaction become a citizen of the village or even, as a literal interpretation of Leach's thesis would entail, a member of the *variga*? We discover that he cannot, for:

out of the 107 numbered plots [in the Old Field] no less than 45 have changed hands by sale at least once between 1890 and 1954. . . .

But this deviation from theory does not imply a breakdown of traditional custom. The essence of traditional custom is, . . . that all land should be retained in the hands of members of the local *variga*. In 1890 only one of the recorded plot-holders was an " outsider" in this sense; he owned, according to the record, $7\frac{1}{2}$ acres. In 1954 it was likewise the case that only one of the recorded plot-holders was an outsider; he owned $3\frac{1}{2}$ acres. From the *variga* point of view the 1954 situation was a great improvement on the 1890 position (1961a: 173).

There are Tamil and Moslem traders in the village from whom money is borrowed on the security of a plot of land. But it is impossible for these traders to become members of the *variga*. They cannot buy themselves in; for they are of course of different castes. We are told (1961a: 174) that, as a rule, land that is sold away to an outsider is within a short while bought back again by some other member of the local *variga*. And now follows a pregnant remark: "When this happens the close network of kinship existing between all local *variga* members can be used to obscure the sale transaction," thus restoring the plot to the pool of land held by members of the *variga* under the rubric of traditional title (*paraveni*). Thus here, too, the irreducible constraint of *variga* membership, which depends in the last resort upon entitlement by kinship, is at work. An outsider by kinship cannot simply by right of purchase, and thus of owning, a piece of property in land, become a full citizen in Pul Eliya. For, says Leach:

To be a full member of the community, a man of Pul Eliya (*Pul Eliya miniha*) it is necessary (a) to be of the right *variga*, (b) to have a holding of land in the Old Field, and (c) to have rights in a compound in the Pul Eliya *gamgoda* . . . those who reside in the village but do not own land there are *not* Pul Eliya *minissu* (1961a: 193).

But the significant fact is that all the non-citizens referred to by Leach are lacking in the one essential qualification for citizenship, that is, membership by kinship right in the *variga*.

One further datum deserves to be noted. Summarizing "the general principles of labour-group formation" Dr. Leach says:

Kinship alone does not *determine* who shall join in a common work team. People work together because of economic relationships, that is, because of debt obligations of the *ukas* and *andē* types or because of obligations of reciprocity. Nevertheless we find, on actual inspection, that the people who work together are bodies of kinsmen linked together by *pavula* ties such as have been described in earlier chapters (1961a: 280).

Now Leach puts special emphasis on free choice by individuals in *pavula* alignments and other collective arrangements ostensibly regulated by kinship. This is a cardinal point of theory for him, since he maintains that structure, so-called, results not from the operation of jural and/or moral rules or kinship principles but as a statistical outcome of the free choices of individuals.

It is all the more interesting therefore to consider one of the institutions in which free choice would seem to be at a maximum. This is the siting of threshing floors. Dr. Leach declares that:

Since choice was free, each individual teamed up with his closest bond friend to share in the construction of a threshing floor and in the building of *kola* stacks (1961a: 271).

But when the results are looked at, we find that:

those who reside in the main village and have well-established hereditary [i.e., kinship] status there—have all sited their *kamata* in the Ihala elapta and have further roughly sorted themselves out according to their compound group filiation. This accounts for thirteen of the twenty *kamata* (1961a: 271–74).

The principal owners of two of the other seven *kamata* are all, in one way or another, "outsiders"; and in the diagram showing the relative position of these threshing floors, the "outsiders" are all at the other end of the area from the "insiders." If choice is indeed free in these circumstances, and is motivated entirely by economic considerations or self-interest wholly uncontaminated by notions of caste or kinship obligation, one might have expected the threshing floors of "insiders" and "outsiders" to be indiscriminately mixed. At least one would not have expected a distribution of a purely utilitarian facility to conform so well to the cleavage between those who have correct *variga* status and those who have wrong *variga* status.

    This point does not escape Dr. Leach, for he concludes:

My point is that the positioning of individual stacks is the outcome of a combination of "accidental" circumstances, but the total pattern which emerged at the end was a significant arrangement which represented the social structure in a quite valid way and in a manner which was consistent with the behaviour of the same individuals in much more formal situations such as village festivals and family festivals (that is, girls' puberty and marriage) (1961a: 283).

In other words, the arrangement conformed to patterns of behavior in which *pavula* membership and kinship considerations are critical.

    There is one particular section of double-talk in Dr. Leach's analysis which is too revealing to overlook. It concerns the relations of brothers in contrast to brothers-in-law (who are, of course, classificatory cross-cousins). I must content myself with one short citation:

"Brothers" are always in elder-brother/younger-brother relationship. It is a relationship of inequality and polite respect. In contrast, "brothers-in-law" (*massina*) are in a standing of equality and may joke together.

    The reason for this difference in expected behaviours is plain. Brothers are expected to be co-resident; brothers-in-law are not. Co-residence implies joint-heirship to a common estate; joint-heirship is a relationship of restrained rivalry. Although brothers in this society are often seen to be rivals this does not derive from any intrinsic principle of kinship; the rivalry is manifest only in so far as they are competitors for managerial control of the same piece of parental property. It is only because brothers are expected to reside virilocally (*diga*) that personal relations between them are expected to be difficult.

Brothers-in-law do not ordinarily have managerial interest in the same piece of land, and it is for this reason that they are able to co-operate on a basis of equality without strain (1961a: 118).

What is here suggested is, clearly, that brothers are rivals, not because they have prior rights in relation to each other that spring intrinsically from the fact of their being the children of the same parent(s), but because they have competing economic interests. However, the land alleged to be the incentive to their rivalry is "parental property"—that is, land inherited or inheritable by right of filiation, not land held by right of, say, purchase or otherwise economically acquired. The hard and irreducible fact is that, in order to have the right to compete in this specifically brotherly way, men have to be brothers and sons first; and that is what distinguishes them from affines. The jural equivalence of siblings may well be exaggerated in expression in cognatic systems, as I have previously indicated; it never precludes rivalry. Brothers-in-law, by contrast, are in quasi-contractual partnership terminable at will. Their joking relationship is of classical pattern, implying ambivalence of attitude, rather than amity.[2]

The last shot in Dr. Leach's locker is a brief discussion of shifting cultivation. *Variga* membership, village citizenship, and kinship affiliations are quite irrelevant in this connection, since none of these constitutes entitlement to land or to special consideration. It is an economic facility supposedly provided for landless peasants, though now exploited also for more purely commercial ends. Each individual works his own *chena* land. There is no cooperative labor and no sharing of economic rewards and responsibilities. Whether or not the individual uses the produce for his own private purposes, and not in order to discharge any of his duties and responsibilities as parent or husband, or kinsman, or member of his *variga*, we do not know.

2. Since the above was written, an important addition to the economic ethnography of the Dry Zone villages of Ceylon has been made by Dr. S. J. Tambiah (1965). Dr. Tambiah aligns himself grandiloquently with Leach in the following declaration of principle (p. 133): "Anthropologists who study the phenomena of kinship roughly divide into those who think of kinship as 'a thing in itself', which can be 'explained' only by reference to other kinship phenomena, and those who think of kinship as a kind of epiphenomenon of the hard practical facts of land use and property allocation," and he describes his study as belonging to the latter kind. Dr. Tambiah is, however, too good a scholar to be drugged by his own rhetoric. So he tells us (p. 157): "Kin relationships and groupings . . . comprise the core of the social structure in a Kandyan village," and introduces us (p. 158) to the concept of "*urumai*," which anyone who examines the data impartially will see is correctly translated as "kinship right," e.g., the "right" an eldest son has to receive more than his brothers, the reciprocal "rights" of mother's brother and sister's son. Noting that it is the relationships of older brother and younger brother, on the one hand, and those of cross-cousins, on the other, that "constitute the critical sets" (p. 159), he examines the same statement of Leach's that I have quoted above. He seems to agree with this statement, but adds, cautiously (p. 160): "But I should like to introduce certain nuances, expressive of underlying shifts in the economic context and certain attitudes *expressive of kinship* relations *per se*, [my italics— ? as "things in themselves"] which may require a re-examination and reformulation of Leach's thesis". This he proceeds to do. And he comes out with a thoroughly orthodox description of the relations of brothers irrespective of the economic aspect—e.g. (p. 160): "Brothers should help each other in their fields. If one brother's child is getting married, the other brothers must join in and spend money." Likewise with cross-cousins, having examined some of his data, he remarks (p. 161): "This calls into question the general applicability of Leach's hypothesis, and thereby complicates the issue as to how these *massinā* can co-operate despite competitive interest in land," which he has shown they have.

But even if this were so it would not be altogether unusual. There is no social system in the world in which kinship rules and relationships regulate *every* human activity, or in which scope for the individual to acquire and privately use some material goods is rigidly excluded. It is notable, however, that no "outsiders" have plots in the traditional "wheel" *chena*.

The Pul Eliya Goyigama *variga* is described by Dr. Leach as being in some ways a corporate organization. But unlike a joint stock company in our society, it is impossible for an individual to belong to the corporation, to have a voice in its affairs, to exercise rights that are vested in it, simply by virtue of holding property, as we can hold stocks and shares acquired by purchase. Nor can he do so by virtue of any other purely economic role. *Variga* membership, and the consequential rights, duties, privileges, and claims that follow from it, can only be attained by virtue of a kinship credential. The common and normal way is to acquire this credential by filiation. But it can also be acquired by a form of adoption into an appropriate kinship status, with the consent of the *variga* council. One must first be a kinsman, then, and consequentially, a member of the subcaste, and on this basis a village citizen, before one can have access to its economic resources or play a part in its internal politics. There is nothing in Dr. Leach's book to suggest that a landless member of the *variga* (whose father or grandfather may well have been, according to his data, one of the wealthiest men in the community) is therefore, through being propertyless and poor, deprived of his *variga* membership. In the case of a joint stock company, if I sell my shares, I thereby cease to belong to the "corporation." Again, a foreigner coming to England, who receives the necessary work permit, may engage in trade or follow any legitimate occupation or profession to earn his living. He does not have to be a citizen for this to be permitted; and, on the other side, he cannot acquire citizenship merely on the grounds of his economic pursuits or achievements. He cannot *buy* citizenship of the United Kingdom. He can, however, after a certain period of residence in England, provided he has not fallen foul of the law or proved undesirable in any other way, apply for naturalization; and he can be granted citizenship by the appropriate department of state, namely the Home Office. In short, admission to citizenship is governed by legal and moral rules laid down by the state and controlled by administrative organs of the state. The same principles apply in the United States of America and in most modern European and American societies. And this is one of the most significant contrasts between our type of social system and the types represented in our paradigmatic samples. Pul Eliya belongs among the latter. Membership of the community which carries the full rights of citizenship is not marketable. It cannot be acquired by purchase, or by right of occupational specialization, of property ownership, or even by residence only. The indispensable credential is a recognized kinship status within the village subcaste. And if this is not irreducibly a function of "law" and "morality"—as admission to the status of citizen is everywhere—but rather a by-product of "economic" relations and institutions, then our current dictionaries of the English language need drastic revision.

III

I have discussed the studies by Worsley and Leach at some length because they represent an extreme position in the denial of structural autonomy *sui generis* to kinship relations and institutions. There are others who have seemed to lean in the same direction; but—keeping closer to the ethnographic facts—they have emphasized what functionalist anthropology has always stressed, that is, the concomitant variation and mutual dependence in tribal societies of economic systems and kinship and descent institutions (cf. Evans-Pritchard, 1940; Firth, 1929, 1939; Richards, 1939; the subject is reviewed in Herskovits, 1940). Firth's statement of the "general proposition that the economic organisation of any community is very closely bound up with the social structure in such manner that each serves to reinforce the other" (1959: 140) is still valid. Systems of production, consumption, and exchange, the distribution of wealth, the forms and degrees of occupational specialization, and other components of what are often loosely lumped together under the rubric of economics, certainly act as external constraints and as media for the deployment of kinship institutions, norms, and relationships. They have never been incontrovertibly shown to be the ultimate *raison d'être* of such institutions, norms, and relationships regarded as an internal system. No one has so far succeeded in showing that the system of kinship terminology, customary in any society, or the structure of kinship and descent relations operative in it, or indeed even the occurrence of some particular norm of kinship can be deduced from a knowledge of the economy or of any strictly economic process, practice, or institution. The point is almost too banal to emphasize, for every textbook account of kinship systems gives examples of identical systems occurring in technological, economic, and ecological contexts of the greatest diversity. Nowhere in the world can economic man whether as capitalist, as trader, or as artisan, as pastoralist, fisherman, or subsistence farmer, as entrepreneur, or plantation owner, or bond slave, as consumer of goods and services, and so on and so forth, fulfill his economic functions if he is devoid of politico-jural status in the community, be it only that of a foreigner subject to the laws of the country. In tribal societies a person must very frequently be a kinsman, or a member of a descent group, by politico-jural status, in order to be permitted to have access to economic resources, to ply a craft, to exercise economic power, to make economic demands and have economic claims.[3]

This is not to deny that technological changes such as a shift from hoe culture to plough culture, or structural changes such as a shift from a subsistence economy to a cash and market economy may influence the form and operation of kinship

3. There is no point in citing an array of ethnographic witnesses to this far too obvious generalization, but I would like to mention one recent work in which it is well represented. This is the collection of essays edited by Gray and Gulliver (1964). The editors conclude that among the peoples represented in the book the family stands out "as the nexus of various processes—ecological, economic, and ritual processes, and the processes of human mating, reproduction and descent" (p. 32). But earlier they emphasize the requirement revealed in all the studies in the book that, for example, in order to have access to lineage land a person must first be a member of the lineage. Outsiders, they point out, can only be granted land if they are assimilated into the lineage system in some recognized status (p. 25).

institutions. But an exclusive causal connection has never as yet been established, if only because concomitant political, legal, sociogeographical, and cultural changes are also directly involved.[4] In this connection, there is a widespread assumption that corporate descent groups break down, as it is said, when they are drawn into a modern market and cash economy, or when their members enter modern commercial and industrial occupations. The Ashanti case does not bear this out. Better still is the evidence of Dr. Polly Hill's researches on the early history of cocoa farming and marketing in Southern Ghana (1963).[5] She shows conclusively how the lineage organization of the Akan cocoa entrepreneurs, far from breaking down, was and is utilized to exploit the economic opportunities afforded by the advent and promotion of cocoa as a cash crop. Considering how vulnerable matrilineal descent systems are usually supposed to be to modern economic and social changes, this finding is important. And it is confirmed by the thorough comparative study of matrilineal systems made by Kathleen Gough.[6] Biased as this study is toward detecting disintegration in matrilineal systems caught up in modern economic and social change, and toward ascribing the primary causal efficacy to economic factors, the general picture that emerges from it of the tenacity and adaptability of matrilineal ideology and norms is all the more persuasive.

The history of the Israeli kibbutz movement during the past thirty to forty years illustrates my point dramatically, from the angle of our own familial system. The agricultural kibbutz described by Spiro[7] is typical in that it began as a communal productive organization in which all the land was owned and managed by the community, and the cooperative labor was rewarded on a strictly egalitarian basis without regard to the occupational differences among the workers. In settlements of this type, conjugal, parental, and familial relations, as they exist in the West European societies from which the settlers came, were, at the outset, barred or, at

4. Raymond Firth's masterly study (1959) demonstrates this *in extenso*.

5. It is especially interesting to note that side by side with the Akan lineage groups that took part in the movement described by Dr. Hill, non-Akan locally based companies not united by descent also took part, and also retained their distinctive forms of kinship organization throughout. I discuss these observations at greater length later.

6. Schneider and Gough, 1961. Dr. Gough's contribution (parts II and III of the volume, pp. 443–652) devotes a special chapter (chap. 16, pp. 631–52) to "The Modern Disintegration of Matrilineal Descent Groups," in which she reviews the mass of data assembled for the whole study. The extreme example quoted by her of "the collapse of the descent group" (p. 645) is that of the poorest, landless Tiyyar among whom, however, it is clear that even before the advent of the modern economy, the descent group was but rudimentarily developed, being generally of no more than two or three generations in depth. But her conclusion is "The Tiyyar and also the low-caste Mappilla descent group has thus in most cases become no more than [remains?] a scattered exogamous unit, whose members may or may not congregate for life-crisis rites" (p. 646). Throughout her analysis, however, she takes care to draw attention to the concomitant effects of political and other social changes in the total picture. On the Nayar, cf. also the interesting short study by Nakane (1962) "The Nayar Family in a Disintegrating Matrilineal System". In the *tarwad* she studied, the men were all professional and salaried workers who took personal paternal responsibility for such things as the education of their children. Nevertheless, as she records: "In spite of the final partition of the *tarwad* property, and the establishment of elementary family households which made the *tarwad* functionless, the idealogy of the *tarwad* (matrilineal system) still persists" (p. 25).

7. Cf. Spiro, 1958. The most authoritative analyses of the problems I here touch upon are to be found in the series of studies published in various periodicals during the last dozen years or so by the late Dr. Yonina Talmon. See for instance her 1965 paper.

least, regarded with scorn, as being contrary to the Marxist ideals of their founders. In particular, the rearing and education of children was vested in communal institutions, not in the domestic association permitted to parents and children. With the lapse of nearly two generations, however, the internal economic organization of most of these settlements has become highly differentiated and modernized. But the pattern of collective or communal economic organization has remained. Thus there is no room in this economy for the parental or any other form of family to serve as a housekeeping unit, let alone as a productive or marketing or saving group. With these economic limitations reinforced as they are by an ideology hostile to the mating, child-rearing, and domestic institutions believed to be characteristic of "bourgeois" society, it might have been expected that traditional family forms rooted in domestic continuity would by now be obsolete, for there are now many kibbutz-born members incorporated into the economic structure and social organisation of these communities. However, in the event, the very opposite has happened. Conjugal relationships very like those of traditional faithful marriage are becoming the norm. The parental family with a "home" of its own and domestic continuity is becoming the rule. Women are tending to move into occupational roles that enable them to keep close to the "home"; husbands and wives are apt to spend their free time privately together instead of in the public kibbutz activities open to them; parents devote their leisure to their children, in their own homes; sibling ties are being stressed in contrast to the diffuse quasi-siblingship of the kibbutz age group; and to crown it all, kinship ties with collateral kin outside as well as within the kibbutz are being widely reasserted in ways that are traditional and usual in most areas of West Europe.[8] Like the lineage systems of the Akan and the Nayar, the traditional West European family form is holding its own in the face of very determined economic and ideological pressures deliberately calculated to eliminate it.

Familial and kinship norms, relationships, and institutions are not reducible to economic factors; they are not reducible, either, to political, or religious, or juridical, or any other non-kinship basis. Granted, then, that we are concerned with what is from both actor's and the observer's point of view a quite specific, relatively autonomous domain of social life, what are its distinctive features? There is the question of the mechanisms and processes by which a person acquires the irreducible and indispensable credentials that make him a kinsman—as opposed to a stranger, a slave, a paid supplier of goods or services, a client, and so forth. But once he is a kinsman, what does this bind him to that is not reducible to economic, or political, or other externally derived relations and values?

IV

Our paradigmatic specimens confirm what is well known, that kinship concepts, institutions, and relations classify, identify, and categorize persons and groups. They

8. For details, see Talmon, 1965. One of the most extraordinary developments that has aroused the comments and speculations of all students of these communities, has been the emergence of spontaneous kibbutz exogamy among the kibbutz-bred young people (cf. Spiro, 1958: 347–48, and Talmon, 1965: 281–82).

show, likewise, that this is associated with rules of conduct whose efficacy comes, in the last resort, from a general principle of kinship morality that is rooted in the familial domain and is assumed everywhere to be axiomatically binding. This is the rule of prescriptive altruism which I have referred to as the principle of kinship amity and which Hiatt calls the ethic of generosity.

In societies of the type we are dealing with, the actor in his status as a kinsman perceives his social universe as divided, in the first instance, into two opposed spheres of moral alignment. On one side is the sphere of kinship and the familial domain; on the other, the sphere of non-kinship. In the extreme case, this specifies all that is alien and strange and outside the nexus of normal social relations. We have seen how, in the kinship polity of the Australian type, status assignment within a field of kinship is the necessary condition for social relations in conformity with moral and jural norms to take place at all. Nor is this by any means unusual. Wherever citizenship in the politico-jural community is mediated by a status based on a kinship credential, analogous procedures of incorporation are followed. This is exemplified in all our paradigmatic specimens. In such polities, kinship may not mark out a fixed and bounded collectivity. It always, however, serves as the focal premise by reference to which the actor's social universe is polarized into a field in which the rule of amity prevails, and into its contrary, ultimately perceived as the outside world, in which it does not.

We find this pattern conspicuously in societies with cognatic kinship systems that lack a differentiated politico-jural structure. The range of persons actually drawn into the orbit of kinship—as opposed to the sphere of strangerhood that merges with enmity—then varies with circumstances. Barton (1949: 82–83), for example, describes how among the Kalinga, inveterate killers though they are, war-scattered cognates may invoke previously neglected or unknown kinship ties to stop fighting between local communities. Kin and non-kin do not, in cognatic systems of this type, constitute defined "groups," but rather an *ad hoc* structural polarization of allegiances for the actor. Cognation among the Iban operates in the same way, as we have seen. In systems of this type, kinship establishes for the actor an internal field of moral relations that are also politico-jural relations, as against the outside world at large, on the principle of amity within and enmity without; and there are no rules or criteria by reference to which an outside observer can determine unequivocally where the boundaries of the field lie.

The Kandyan *pavula* appears to be a variant of the cognatic kindred as it occurs among peoples like the Iban and the Kalinga.[9] But consideration of the *pavula* introduces a further dimension. In this case, kinship operates on two levels: first, to establish membership in the externally bounded and distinguishable subcaste;

9. Cf. Leach, 1961a. The structural elasticity of the *pavula* is specially emphasized by Nur Yalman (1962), who, confirming Leach, notes that "those who consider themselves kinsmen at the moment may, for unforeseen reasons, become enemies" (p. 560). He draws attention, also, to the importance of the practice whereby non-kinsfolk are incorporated into the kinship scheme by the assignment to them, by what he thinks of as kinship fiction, of kinship status. Among the multitude of parallels that could be adduced, an especially interesting example which shows graphically how economic, locality, and ceremonial variables influence the range of kindred relations recognized in particular circumstances, is provided in Marshall Sahlin's brilliant study (1962).

and, secondly, to segregate for the actor *ad hoc* fields of consensus and solidarity that are internally opposed to those of other actors, though externally aligned with them. It is in this context that economic and political interests and motives, as well as deviant tendencies, come secondarily into play.

A distinctive refinement in specifying the range of kinship morality is indicated by the rule of prescriptive cousin marriage within internally cognatic groups. In these circumstances, kinsfolk who are specified as "consanguines," demonstrable or presumed by classificatory rules, are segregated by the actor in contraposition to those who are or become affines.[10] In the internal relations of the group, the ambit of kinship amity is then contracted. It holds where relationships are interpreted as determined by kinship, not where they are regarded as affinal. Externally, however, the principle of amity applies to all cognates in contraposition to outsiders.

An interesting variant of this structural arrangement is provided by the northern Ojibwa. Within the band, "kinsfolk" bound by the principle of amity are, primarily, patrilateral relatives and, secondarily, matrilateral relatives (i.e., mothers' sisters and their children). Other cognates—as well as affines—are classified as "non-kinsfolk." Persons defined as kinsfolk are not marriageable; those defined as "non-kinsfolk" for a given ego are classified as "cousins," if they are of his own generation, in contraposition to his collateral siblings in that generation, and are therefore marriageable for him. Ojibwa of other bands are termed "strangers" (Dunning, 1959, who notes ". . . these categories are explicitly conceptualized [p. 73; cf. also pp. 72–74, 109]).

Corresponding modulations in the locus and the range of efficacy of the rule of kinship amity are common. Ashanti regard patrikinship and close affinal relationship as falling within the familial domain and being therefore subject to the rule of amity; but "real kinship" which binds unequivocally is associated with the *yafunu* segment of the matrilineage, and by extension with the localized lineage. Beattie (1957), to take another instance at random, records[11] a similar attitude for the Banyoro of East Africa, among whom clanship is the focus of the ethic of generosity in contraposition to the rest of society. Tallensi make the same distinctions between the claims and obligations that follow from lineage and clan membership and those of familial provenance that also predicate kinship amity.

These examples are characteristic. The actor segregates a field of moral obligation

---

10. E.g., by selection of a relationship permitting marriage when alternative identifications are genealogically or classificatorily permissible. Firth's analysis (1930) of how the Tikopian kinship calculus is manipulated to this end has been amplified and confirmed in many later studies, e.g., Yalman, 1962. A recent example is provided by Sahlins, 1962: 160–62, who shows how Moalans "resuscitate" a "path of kinship" which makes non-cousins into cross-cousins, and therefore marriageable.

11. "Clan membership, then," Beattie writes, "dichotomizes the whole universe of persons whom a Munyoro is (or was in traditional times) likely to meet in the course of his life. Everybody he encounters is either a member of his own patrilineal clan, or he is not." Continuing, he observes that clan membership "in its broad sense . . . determines . . . whom a person may not marry," and goes on: "There are strong obligations of hospitality and mutual aid between members of the same clan, even if they are strangers to one another and unaware of any kind of genealogical connexion. Fellow clansmen are 'brothers,' 'fathers,' or 'sons' "; "Banyoro believe that a man should be friendly with his fellow clansmen and co-operate with them just as he would with his 'real' brothers, fathers, and sons" (p. 321). Cf. also Southall, 1956: 63.

that is quite precisely circumscribed by a rule of kinship or descent, is often anchored in locality, and is cognizable, by outsiders as well as from within, in contraposition to other like divisions of the total politico-jural structure. But it must be stressed that the ethic of generosity is not confined to the descent group. Its roots are in the familial domain and it embraces the bilateral kinship linkages of this domain. Kin by complementary filiation are also embraced within the orbit of kinship amity. Indeed, it is by emphasising the filiative component of descent relationships, and thus assimilating them to familial relationships, that the actor projects on to them the ethic of the familial domain. And there are structural contexts in which these values spill over to relations with persons who are in the same politico-jural or religious or local organization but who are not relatives by any form of genealogical or affinal reckoning and are not accorded kinship status.

Before returning to this, I want to draw attention to some features that are distinctive of the contraposition of kinship and non-kinship spheres of social relations in terms of the rule of kinship amity. Two of the commonest discriminating indices are the locus of prohibited or prescribed marriage, and the control of strife that might cause bloodshed. Kinship, amity, the regulation of marriage and the restriction of serious fighting form a syndrome. Where kinship is demonstrable or assumed, regardless of its grounds, there amity must prevail and this posits prescription, more commonly proscription, of marriage and a ban on serious strife. Conversely where amity is the rule in the relations of clans or tribes or communities, there kinship, or quasi-kinship by myth or ritual allegiance or by such institutions as the East African joking relationships, is invoked and the kind of fighting that smacks of war is outlawed. By contrast, non-kin, whether or not they are territorially close or distant, and regardless of the social and cultural affinities of the parties, are very commonly identified as being outside the range of prescriptive altruism and therefore marriageable as well as potentially hostile to the point of serious fighting (or, nowadays, litigation) in a dispute. It is as if marriage and warfare are thought of as two aspects of a single constellation the direct contrary of which is kinship and amity.

The Tallensi saying "we marry those whom we fight" exemplifies the connection and epitomises a scheme of values and of customary practices that is widely distributed.[12] Like most peoples of the world, they distinguish degrees of gravity in fighting, in accordance, partly, with its manner and, partly, with the structural distance between the contestants. How punctiliously this is worked out by the Tiv will be considered presently. For the Tallensi, one end of the scale is marked by the quarreling and wrangling which they say, tolerantly, is inevitable among kin and especially among members of the same family. Such quarrels may be serious. Blows

12. Cf. Fortes, 1962c: 1–13 and *passim*. This sentiment is met with in tribal society all over the world. It has been reported from New Guinea, among the Siane (Salisbury, 1962), and the Mae Enga (Meggitt, 1958), both of whom say that they marry those whom they fight. Courtship, betrothal, and wedding customs often reflect this assumption. A striking instance is the Gusii practice of "privileged obstruction" in marriage ceremonies (Mayer, 1950). The Gusii, too, have the saying, "Those whom we marry are those whom we fight" (p. 123), and Dr. Mayer interprets these practices as a means of emotional release in explosive ambivalent situations. Cf. also Beattie, 1958. Describing the behavior of a suitor, Beattie says: "The suitor feels himself to be, as it were, on enemy ground" (p. 13). See also reference to La Fontaine and Harris, below.

may even be exchanged; but this does not necessarily, as they put it, "spoil" kinship. Estrangement in one generation is commonly repaired in the next, if only in submission to the wrath of the ancestors. Kinsfolk, paradoxically, can fight with impunity. "We quarrel but we stick together" is the common saying. However, there is the other end of the scale, when bows and arrows are seized and fighting amounts to warfare. For this to happen between kin of any degree, by any reckoning, is a heinous sin. But it can and formerly did happen between lineages that may intermarry. Disputes over bride-price, or even over more trivial affairs, could provoke such fighting. Where, nowadays, kin quarrel, affines litigate.

What, then, is the premise behind this structural and normative contrast? It is neatly expressed in the Chinese saying that the bond between brothers and sisters comes from Heaven, whereas the bond between husband and wife is created by man. Relations of kinship and social relations assimilated to kinship by the extension to them of the rule of amity, are presumed to be *a priori*, ascribed, as Linton said, or ordained and not achieved, whereas matrimonial and affinal relations are intentionally created by jural transactions of a contractual nature; and this presupposes a divergence of primary loyalties which may verge on hostility. To overcome this requires at least a minimum of moral and jural consensus. Enemies who marry can do so only if, in the last resort, they accept some common norms of morality and jurality, together with the corresponding procedures and sanctions for implementing them. Failing this, the rights and obligations engendered by marriage and affinal relations could not be maintained. Enemies thus turned affines become legitimate opponents within a common politico-jural framework. Against the rest of the world, however, they may become allies to whom the norms of kinship amity then apply. The regulation of blood vengeance, wherever it is institutionalized as among the Nuer, the Somali, the Beduin of Cyrenaica, and the culturally and structurally very different Kalinga, testifies to this (cf. Barton, 1949; Evans-Pritchard, 1940; Lewis, 1961; Peters, 1960). For in all such cases, composition could not be effectively negotiated if either party were outside the law in relation to the other. Tallensi norms of inter-clan warfare (Fortes, 1945: 238–39) and the regulation of fighting among the Tiv, illustrate the principle from another angle.

V

The opposition of kinship and affinity is most conspicuous in structural arrangements, as well as in moral and jural norms, in societies with exogamous unilineal descent groups. It is clear-cut in the Tallensi contraposition of *dogham*, kinship, and *deen*, in-law-ship (cf. Fortes, 1949c: 16–17). The Gisu maxim, "In affinity there is no kinship," even if the parties belong to distantly connected patrilineal descent groups, sums up a common African point of view (cf. La Fontaine, 1962: 94 and Grace Harris, 1962).

Though on the surface it may seem blurred where marriage with cognates (cousin marriage) is the rule, the opposition of values and norms expressed in the Gisu proverb is, as is well known, made conspicuously manifest in many customary practices. The residential segregation of married siblings among the Iban reflects it,[13] and the celebrated customs of marriage by capture and affinal avoidance, familiar to us from many societies and not only Australian aborigines, typify it.

The opposition is frequently expressed in eating customs. As in many other African societies, husband and wife never eat together among the Tallensi and other Voltaic peoples. Visiting affines, whether the occasion is mundane or ceremonial, are regaled in privacy or, at any rate, strictly separately from the host family or lineage.[14] Evans-Pritchard (1951b: 55) notes that Nuer men and women "unless they are close kin, avoid each other in the matter of food. ... A man may mention food but not sexual matters before kinswomen, and he may mention sexual matters but not food before unrelated girls" whom he may court in marriage. A nice example from Oceania comes from the Siuai. Oliver (1955: 363) tells us: "Everyday eating ... is nearly always done in the privacy of the household" and food plays a central part "in rituals formalizing kinship relations and life crisis episodes." But the observation pertinent here is that "avoidance between a man and his mother-in-law is manifested in the prohibition against food-sharing."

To eat together signifies amity; to refuse, or to be prohibited from doing so, signifies its absence. Studies of caste systems bring this out, but the principle is widely exhibited in the institution of sacrifice, as Robertson Smith showed long ago. A characteristic norm of Tallensi ancestor worship is that kinsfolk sacrifice together (Fortes, 1945: chap. VII), and the critical element in this is that those who do so can and must all partake of the meat and drink of the sacrifice. In contrast, affines may not sacrifice together. It is an offense against the ancestors even to give an affine a portion of the uncooked meat of a sacrificed animal. But what is much more important is that open enmity prohibits even people who are entitled to do so from joining together in sacrifice. Kin who are irreconcilably at loggerheads must not sacrifice together to common ancestors. That would be sacrilege, the penalty of which is ancestral wrath and possible death. Non-kin, other than those who are bound together in the quasi-kinship of common allegiance to the same External Boghar, have no basis at all for sacrificing together, in the sense of jointly contributing to the offerings made and, especially, partaking equally in the sacramental consumption of the offerings.

13. It hardly needs to be said that this dichotomy and the contraposition between kinship and affinity is not confined to Africa. It plays a decisive part in South Indian systems of marriage and kinship, for instance, as has been described in the important theoretical study by Dumont previously quoted (1957). Its wider implications figure prominently in Lévi-Strauss's theory of cross-cousin marriage (1949). But it is such a fundamental topic in kinship theory that it is really superfluous to cite the literature. The Iban conceptualization of their kinship universe is particularly revealing, in this connection. As I have previously noted (p. 125, n. 2), they distinguish between cognates, affines, and others. But it is significant that they group cognates and affines together as kinds of kin in opposition to the rest of the world. This is just what one might expect in a widely anastomosing cognatic system. But cf. Barton, 1949: 81: "Marriage is antithetical to kinship solidarity, for the reason, partly, that it introduces a different kind of tie into the group, also second cousins may marry, so that in this respect the group is narrowed to the first cousins."

14. Cf. Fortes, 1949c. 122. The implications of food distribution and consumption patterns for familial and kinship relations among the Voltaic peoples are excellently brought out in Jack Goody's paper, 1958b.

These indications must suffice to remind us how pervasive the opposition of kinship and affinity is in tribal society. I adduce them only to emphasize the central premise in question, for I want to conclude this discussion with a glance at the Tiv to whom I have several times referred. The association between marriage and fighting on the one hand and the structural opposition of kinship and affinity, on the other, is explicitly worked out by them (Bohannan and Bohannan, 1953: 25–27). The basis is a graduated scale of weaponry and violence that is permitted in fighting. Close brother segments of a minimal lineage may use only clubs and stones in a fight; more distantly connected segments may use bows and arrows but must avoid killing; very distantly connected lineages fight with poison arrows and Dane guns, and aim to kill. Fighting with non-Tiv is war without restriction on weapons, but, add the Bohannans, whereas it "provokes no magical consequences" (Bohannan and Bohannan, 1953: 26) to kill a non-Tiv (that is, an alien), to kill any Tiv does, since he is, by definition, a member of the great lineage that is supposed to include all Tiv, and by that token, a kind of kinsman. What is relevant here is that this scale corresponds closely to the scale of exogamic values observed in marriage. The marriages of greatest prestige are those that occur between members of major exogamous lineages—those that are by genealogical projection distant enough from one another to be liable to go to war. But the barrier which at the limit segregates Tiv from the alien is affirmed in the marriage rules. There is a ban on Tiv women marrying non-Tiv. Thus marriage and regulated interclan fighting in defense of corporate rights are both contained within the politico-jural and ideological community of the total Tiv system.

VI

Though the structural connotation which the notion of kinship carries varies widely, the central value premise associated with it is uniform. Kinship predicates the axiom of amity, the prescriptive altruism exhibited in the ethic of generosity. Some of the most definitive examples come from studies of tribal law. Gluckman, as I have earlier noted, describes how Lozi judges explicitly recognize the distinction between legal right enforceable by the courts, and moral right, the implementation of which is left to the pressure of public opinion, individual conscience, and social reciprocity. Lozi judges invoke these where a dispute is between persons in their capacity as kinsmen and affines. When they litigate as fellow villagers or citizens of the kingdom, the legal sanctions of the politico-jural domain are applicable. Kinsfolk are expected to be loving, just, and generous to one another and not to demand strictly equivalent returns of one another. Since fellow villagers are mostly also kinsfolk, the legal claims based on politico-jural relations often clash with the ethic of generosity prescribed for the familial domain (Gluckman, 1955: 46–48 and *passim*).

We must not, however, misunderstand the ideal that kinsfolk should love one another. Many ties of close kinship (notoriously, siblingship), we must remember, subsume rivalries and latent hostilities that are as intrinsically built into the relationships as are the externally oriented amity and solidarity they present.[15] This appears in competition for hereditary office[16] and in the now well-documented antagonism, patent or customarily regulated, between the "holder" of an estate and his pre-designated successor (cf. Goody, 1966: 1–56). The character and incidence of witchcraft and sorcery suspicions and accusations, as we have seen, betray more dramatically these underlying conflicts in the nuclear units of kinship structure, where the dogma of amity is supposed most stringently to prevail.[17]

What the rule posits is that "kinsfolk" have irresistible claims on one another's support and consideration in contradistinction to "non-kinsmen," simply by reason of the fact that they are kin. Kinsfolk must ideally share—hence the frequent invocation of brotherhood as the model of generalized kinship; and they must, ideally, do so without putting a price on what they give. Reciprocal giving between kinsfolk is supposed to be done freely and not in submission to coercive sanctions or in response to contractual obligations. This is the Tallensi ideal of proper kinship behavior. An example from more recent ethnography refers to the Plateau Tonga. In hunger years, says Colson, they "still walk many miles to beg from kinsmen. . . . These may grumble, but so long as anything remains in their granaries . . ., they are likely to divide with their indigent relatives."[18]

Kinsmen must have concern for one another and therefore refrain from wantonly injuring one another or heedlessly infringing one another's rights. And above all, one may not kill an innocent kinsman as one may a complete alien. It need hardly be added that no society, anywhere, expects these general and diffuse moral pre-scriptions to be invariably adhered to. Tallensi always used to point out to me that there are criminal characters who do not shrink from offending against the norms,

15. It is a safe generalization, as modern ethnographic research has repeatedly shown, that wherever kinsfolk are united and identified with one another in respect to common interests, rights, and duties vis à vis outsiders, but are differentiated *inter se* by genealogical and structural criteria such as sex, age, generation, etc., entitling them to particular rights, duties etc., their externally oriented solidarity will be balanced by internal rivalries, actual or potential. Hence the rivalries of siblings and of persons of successive generations by descent.

16. This fact is so well known that it hardly needs amplification here. I want to point out, however, that I am not referring to cases where the competition is overt and organized when an office is vacant, e.g., among the Ankole (cf. Oberg, 1940) but where it is ostensibly ruled out by legal provision, as, e.g., among the Tswana (cf. Schapera, 1938: 62; 1957).

17. Gluckman (1955: 154) quotes a Lozi song which makes the point poignantly: "He who kills me, who will it be but my kinsman/He who succours me, who will it be but my kins-man." The "Sin of Cain" to which I referred in my observations on the principle of sibling equivalence (p. 79) springs immediately to mind.

18. Colson, 1958: 21. One of the most interesting of many similar statements relating to tribal peoples dependent primarily on some form of subsistence economy is the following on the institution of the *kerekere* among the Fijian Maola: "Kinship between donor and recipient is an indicative characteristic of *kerekere*. Most requests are made to kinsmen within the home community, but in any case the person putting the request and the potential donor should be kinsmen. This does not in fact restrict the sphere of *kerekere* in any way because kinship can always be widely extended through classificatory devices . . . . The significance of kinship for *kerekere* is that kin ethics, the obligation to give support, aid and comfort, dominate the transaction" (Sahlins, 1962: 203–204). It is perhaps hardly necessary to be reminded of the extensive discussions of the obligation to share food, in particular, among kinsfolk that figure in the literature of Australian aboriginal society and other hunting and gathering societies. The theme recurs in such classical studies of kinship and social organization as those of Evans-Pritchard, Firth, Richards, Eggan, etc., already frequently cited.

sinners who fail in kinship duties, selfish, foolish, dishonest, hypocritical people, and others of weak character, who flout the ideals and may even deserve punishment for this. But these, they emphasized, are the exceptions. By and large, people conform; parents, elders, and officeholders continually reaffirm the axiom of amity; and on ritual occasions such as funerals and sacrifices to ancestors, it is made apparent that mystical retribution sooner or later catches up with offenders.

These considerations apply everywhere. Gluckman's case records, already referred to, afford many illustrations. Turner's "Social Dramas" (1957: 116–30) demonstrate how the norms governing proper conduct among the Ndembu are in the last resort always upheld, however powerful the underlying conflicts and tensions may appear to be.

As to the nature of these norms, they follow from the fact that:

People live together because they are matrilineally related . . . the dogma of kinship asserts that matrilineal kin participate in one another's existence . . . the norms of kinship state that matrilineal kin must at all times help one another, [so] open physical violence between them seldom takes place (Turner, 1957: 129).

Turner's study shows up brilliantly the nature and course of the ritual and other redressive action taken to restore amity among close kin after the eruption of underlying conflicts. To the observer in the field, however, the most convincing evidence is not the conduct and sentiments displayed among close kin, but rather the acknowledgement of kinship amity in what seem to be situations where kinship is so tenuous as to be only nominal, as when persons seek out remote clansfolk or classificatory cognates and without further ado claim and receive hospitality and protection.

VII

The Greeks and the Romans doubtless had terms for the moral principle I am discussing. The notion of Christian charity in its earlier, more etymological sense, would, I suppose, come near to it.[19] But the most vivid expression for it known to

19. It is not within my competence or my proper subject matter to follow this up but I cannot refrain from citing one reference that came my way in the course of a desultory search. The following passage occurs in the Ethicorum Aristotelis ad Nicomachum Expositio, of St. Thomas Aquinas (bk. VIII, lesson vii): ". . . amicitia est quaedam unio sive societas amicorum, quae non potest esse inter multum distantes, sed oportet quod ad aequalitatem accedant. Unde ad amicitiam pertinet aequalitate jam constituta aequaliter uti; sed ad justitiam pertinet inaequalia ad aequalitatem reducere. Aequalitate autem existente, stat justitiae opus. Et ideo aequalitas est ultimum in justitia, sed principium in amicitia." The passage is translated as follows by Litzinger (1964:) ". . . friendship is a kind of union or association of friends that cannot exist between widely separated persons; but they must approach equality. Hence it pertains to friendship to use an equality already uniformly established, but it pertains to justice to reduce unequal things to an equality. When equality exists the work of justice is done. For that reason equality is the goal of justice and the starting point of friendship." The notion of "amicitia," here translated as "friendship," corresponds closely to what I mean by "amity" in the kinship context. This is indicated by the stress on the requirement that "friends" should be close and equal. It is to the point to note that in feudal France, from the thirteenth to the fifteenth century the formula "kinsmen and friends" (parens et amis) regularly appears in documents relating to wergild. (Cf. Phillpotts, 1913: 188–89).

me was brought to my notice a dozen years ago by Dr. Peter Lawrence.[20] It came
to light in the course of his field work among the Garia, a small aggregate of about
2,500 people who live in the mountainous region west-southwest of Madang in
New Guinea, an area in which the clusters of villagers forming a language group
are politically acephalous and do not have institutionalized offices or other forms of
political authority with powers of social control. The Garia are a unit only in that
they are attached to a common territory, speak the same language, and have certain
deities in common. Kinship and affinal connections ramify bilaterally and are
buttressed by connections established between individuals and groups by the
ceremonial exchanges of pigs. The concept of citizenship as a status in a politico-
jural community is totally lacking. What guarantees a person's rights is the support
of his "security circle." This embraces a group of persons centered upon a "patriline" made up of the descendants of a common patrifilial grandfather and including
close matrilateral and affinal relatives as well. Everybody with whom a person can
trace close genealogical connection belongs to his "security circle." Marriage
between members of the "security circle" is forbidden; so is the eating of pigs, dogs,
and fowls domesticated by any of its members; and so is physical violence or resort
to sorcery. A special bond of moral obligation is created with close matrikin by gifts
of pigs, and prestations of pigs wins a man a wife and draws her kindred into his
"security circle." Ceremonial pig exchange adds a further dimension, linking unrelated or distantly related persons by a network of quasi-contractual ties of
political expediency and economic reciprocity that stretches across tribal boundaries
and, in certain respects, mimics kinship. In the past, a serious wrong was quite
likely to lead to violent reprisals, though settlement by negotiation might be
attempted by the supporters—in effect, the security circles—of the parties.

What then, are the sanctions for the solidarity, cohesion, and mutual support

20. In his unpublished thesis for the degree of Ph.D. at Cambridge. He has since then
published some of his field data in (a) 1955, and (b) 1965–66. The Garia appear to be representative of a number of similar "tribelets" in the Madang area, and the moral concepts reported
by Dr. Lawrence have close parallels in some of these. The Tangu of this area, for example (cf.
Burridge, 1960), have a cluster of interrelated moral concepts centered on what Dr. Burridge
designates as "the notion of amity" (p. 81). "Amity," he states, "exists within its own moral
right: it is the critical norm by which all relationships are judged, and with which all relationships should coincide or approximate. . . . The breach of amity immediately sets in motion
procedures designed to ensure a return to amity." Pursuing this theme, Burridge explains that:
"Amity is itself most significantly manifested in the idea of equivalence" as expressed especially
in food exchanges that must be of exact equivalence. Perfect moral equivalence between
households is designated by a special term and this state is demonstrated by their neither
exchanging nor co-operating. The structural background to this notion of amity (so reminiscent,
strangely enough, of the definition I quoted in n. 19 from Aquinas) is the interconnection of all
households in a community with one another by actual or putative kinship or by institutionalized friendship (Burridge, 1960: 58, and *passim*). Furthermore, it appears that the model
relationship in which exchange is the norm is that of affinally related households, i.e., where
the husband in one is brother (actual or classificatory) of the wife in the other, and, by contrast,
where cooperation is the norm, the households are related by like sex siblingship, i.e., where
wives are sisters or the husbands are brothers. Restoring ruptured amity thus comes down to
restoring cooperative relations of brotherhood or the reciprocal relations of cross-siblings
(Burridge, 1960: 105 ff.) and the mechanism for this is the remarkable custom of the *br'ngun'-
guni*, the oratorical contests and disputations in which grievances and claims are vented
(Burridge, 1960: 75–76 and *passim*).

that prevail within the "security circle"? Their essence is conveyed by the Garia concept of *nanunanu*. It means, says Dr. Lawrence (1965: 381–82), to "think on," to have concern for, "to have a proper attitude toward a person," and thus "to fulfill all the obligations due to him." A bad man lacks or has bad *nanunanu*. But the significant point is that *nanunanu*, strictly and ideally speaking, refers only to conduct towards other members of one's security circle; it may be extended however, to include associates or farming neighbors to whom one is not by kinship reckoning under any moral obligation but to whom one is bound by common interests and propinquity.

Here then we meet the dogma of kinship amity vividly conceptualized. Commenting on the biblical Israelite family institutions and ideas, Pedersen (1926: 59) remarks: "Wherever there is social unity, we have brotherhood. Through the pact of amity David became the brother of Jonathan . . . the pact may extend beyond the limits of the community of the people." We have already had some evidence that the model relationship of kinship amity is fraternity, that is sibling unity, equality, and solidarity, but here we are given a case of artificial brotherhood not, as the Chinese would have said, made in Heaven.

Artificially created ties of kinship throw much light on the nature of kinship amity. A *pact* of amity implies an artificial relationship. It connotes a relationship deliberately created by the mutual agreement of the parties, not one imposed by the chance of birth. It calls to mind the institutional blood-brotherhood to which Robertson Smith (1903) attached so much importance as evidence for his contention that in early Arab societies "relationship cannot originally have been reckoned by counting degrees from a common ancestor, but was something common to a whole group" (p. 71)—the group being united by the bond of blood which was "the only effective bond" (p. 69). This thesis, and the views of others who took up the problem, are discussed in Evans-Pritchard's classical paper (1933) on Zande blood-brotherhood.

Later research, notably the comprehensive and learned monograph of Harry Tegnaeus (1952) has, in general, confirmed Evans-Pritchard's conclusion that blood-brotherhood does not change the status of the parties to that of clansmen or kinsmen in the exact sense. Zande blood-brothers may marry one another's sisters or daughters; unlike true kin they perform funeral services for one another; their mutual obligations are not subject to "the compulsive nature of family and kin sentiments" (Evans-Pritchard, 1933: 399; 1962 ed.: 160). "Blood-brotherhood," concludes Evans-Pritchard, "is a legal contract entered into by two men of their own accord. Real brotherhood is a circumstance into which men are born without any act of their own" (1933: 400; 1962 ed.: 160). Yet one feature stands out in his description and in the material assembled by Tegnaeus: Blood-brotherhood imitates true brotherhood in order to bind those who enter into the pact to unquestioning amity, mutual protection, and goodwill—to *nanunanu*. More rigorously than true kinship, it prohibits the suppressed jealousy and competitiveness that seem to be inherent in the most intimate, and therefore inescapably binding, degrees of actual consanguinity, as we have already noted.

There is no point in piling up more evidence on this theme, but it is as well to be reminded that the Euro-American kinship institutions and values of Anglo-Saxon origin are imbued with the same notion of the binding force of kinship amity. Take for example the following testimony from the Bethnal Green study by Young and Willmott (1957) that has become justly celebrated. It refers to the marked and life-long attachment of women to their mothers, revealed in the study:

Though they [mother and daughter] both derive benefit from the relationship, it is far more than a mere arrangement for mutual convenience. The attachment between them is supported by a powerful moral code. . . in most of these families. . . duty and affection seem to co-exist and, indeed, reinforce each other. . . Parents do not choose their children, nor children their parents; the relationship exists whether or not either has the qualities which might arouse affection. Both are usually accepted despite their faults. . . and what applies to parents and children applies in some measure to other relatives as well. Secure in the knowledge that they are valued because they are members of the family, not because they have this or that quality or achievement to their credit, they respond with affection which then becomes as reciprocal as duty. Affection, for its part, helps to make duty not so much the nicely balanced correlative of rights as a more or less unlimited liability beyond the bounds of self-interest and rational calculation (pp. 161–62).

I have recorded sentiments that are exactly the same among the Tallensi and the Ashanti, and their parallels can be found in any of the classical monographs on kinship in tribal society.

VIII

The facts I have here described have long been familiar and have commonly been designated by such terms as kinship solidarity (cf. Phillpotts, 1913: 2–3). What I wish to stress is the basic premise: kinship is binding; it creates inescapable moral claims and obligations. Diffuse as these claims and obligations appear to be, they are, nevertheless, correlated to morphological and institutional distinctions which put kinship proper on one side, and the complementary or coordinate spheres, notably those of affinity, locality, and polity on the other.

An interesting test is found in the spillover I alluded to in passing which often leads to a fusion of kinship and locality in neighborhood relations. They may appear to blend inextricably, but it is always possible to separate them out. In an Ashanti *brono* (town quarter), neighbors who are not lineage kin, patrikin, or affines, but merely fellow citizens of a deceased, condole and mourn with the bereaved but are not under an obligation to contribute to the funeral expenses, nor have they a right to or a voice in the selection of an heir. Tallensi explain many ties of clanship between genealogically independent lineages, and especially ties of ritual collaboration, by invoking long lasting association through, "dwelling together in the same place," and the ensuing common interests in peace and in the maintenance of the social and ritual activities upon which the common well-being is believed to depend (cf. Fortes, 1945: *passim*). Allegiance to common Earth shrines, intermarriage, and the resulting web of collateral kinship ties and sharing in one another's joys and sorrows contribute to knit kinship, clanship, and neighborhood relations into a unity. Nevertheless, the lines of differentiation are precise. Neighbor lineages of different descent have distinctive totemistic observances and funeral customs; they will intermarry, and being, therefore, affinally connected cannot merely, by virtue of being neighbors, share in one another's domestic sacrifices to ancestors, nor can they, on these grounds, exercise any of the rights or perform any of the duties that normally fall on clansmen, members of the same lineage, or cognatic kinsmen. If neighboring independent lineages have a dispute over bride-price payments, they might, in former times, have come into armed conflict (nowadays such disputes are likely to end in the chief's court), whereas if members of the same lineage have a dispute, this is normally submitted to their own lineage elders for settlement. The same pattern appears with even greater clarity among the LoDagaba, described by Goody (1957b). Though there is an implication that long neighborly association conduces to amity as if people were kin, this is not inevitable.

The Tswana ward is a neighborhood unit that, in a certain sense, closely resembles a Lozi village. In its external relations with other wards of the tribe and with the chiefdom as a whole, a ward is an administrative unit under an hereditary headman vested with judicial and executive powers and subject only to the chief's superior authority. But considered from within, a ward is the home of a collection of families, a majority, if not all of whom are connected with one another by ties of kinship and marriage in the same way as occupants of a Lozi village. Like the Lozi, too, most ward dwellers have kinsfolk and affines in other wards and even in other tribes. A person's closest kin, especially on the jurally dominant paternal side—"from whom", writes Schapera (1950: 143), "he expects immediate support and protection" and to whom he is bound by such fundamental rights and duties as those of inheritance and succession, of linked siblingship and of economic collaboration—are normally in his own ward (cf. also pp. 19–24, 118–19, and *passim*).

Yet ward membership, Schapera emphasizes, is not a kinship status. A ward may include people of extra-tribal origin; for citizenship in a chiefdom "is defined, not in terms of birth, but of allegiance to the Chief" (1950: 118), and strangers can be thus incorporated in a chiefdom. Ward membership, fundamentally, is an aspect of the politico-jural status of the citizen which every adult male has in his own right and women through their fathers and husbands. The age regiments organized for public service reflect this; and the possibility of appealing to the chief's court from judgments first given in a ward head's court are further evidence of this.

We can go a step further with the Nyakyusa (Wilson, 1950, 1951), and other Central African peoples such as the Ndembu (Turner, 1957: 67–68). The "age village" shows us neighborhoods physically segregated as well as demarcated by genealogical reckoning. In theses cases the two frames of social and political alignment—by kinship and by locality—appear to stand in a complementary rela-tionship to each other. A Nyakyusa village is eventually occupied by an age group of men and their wives and young children. Thus, within a village the only familial ties that may occur between the members are between half-brothers and affines; kinship by patrilineal descent or matrilateral connection runs, essentially, between villages, spreading widely in a chiefdom and beyond. All the same, the village is not a random aggregation of persons drawn and held together by the facts of co-residence in a locality. Villages are in fact grouped in three successive generation strata. The village is a political unit under a headman in a tribe-wide association of coeval villages. But even more important is the fact that it is, internally, a quasi-fraternal subdivision of a generation unit established in compliance with a criterion of selection that is involuntary and arbitrary, and that belongs essentially to the domain of kinship since it reflects the compulsory stratification of and avoidance between successive generations. It is governed by moral norms of a kind which in many societies belong more strictly to the domain of kinship and familial relations than to that of local relations in the political sense—that is to say, norms which conform to the general principle of the ethic of generosity. This emerges in the Nyakyusa ideal of "good company," conceived of as "mutual aid and sympathy" and expressed significantly in "eating and drinking together"; and it is consistent with the general pattern of the structural location of witchcraft and sorcery tensions that their expected social context is the village, not the dispersed lineage or kindred.

I have used the concept of neighborhood to indicate a peculiar intermeshing of norms and patterns of collocation by kinship and affinity, on the one hand, and by ostensibly local contiguity, on the other. The examples I have quoted show how varied this intermeshing can be in its descriptive manifestations. Further examples could be quoted from East Africa (the classical example being the Nuer local community as described by Evans-Pritchard, 1940: 210–11, and 1951b: chap. I; cf. also the Lugbara as described by Middleton, 1958: 203–29), West Africa (Gibbs, 1963), Melanesia (Burridge, 1960), Ceylon, etc. But the principles in question are already apparent. To clinch the argument, however, I add one specially relevant example. I take it from Dr. R. Abrahams' study (1967) of the political system of the Nyamwezi of Tanganyika, now Tanzania.[21] In this system, neighborhood relations, kinship and affinity, domestic (that is, commensal) grouping, chiefdom, citizenship, and secret society membership are explicitly distinguished from one another in nomenclature and in institutional forms. Nyamwezi move about a good deal. They live in dispersed homesteads which fall into clusters that make up loosely grouped villages. Kinsfolk, even siblings, tend to be widely dispersed, and the true residential neighborhood clusters are heterogeneous, including people over half of whom may normally have no kin or affines in the vicinity. Often such neighborhoods include members of non-Nyamwezi tribes. Now every adult is a citizen in his chiefdom, wherever he may live within its boundaries. His relations with his neighbors as neighbors are quite distinct from those he has with them either as kin, if they are relatives, or as fellow citizens. In comparison with true kinsfolk, the distinction is phrased in terms that between neighbors debt can occur—that is, equivalent returns must be made for goods or services given—whereas kinsfolk help one another freely when they can. It is from kin, primarily, that assistance is sought in ritual matters connected with births, marriages, and deaths, or in times of food shortage or other personal disaster. Kinsfolk, however distantly related, may not in theory marry or

21. A close parallel is found among the Taita; cf. Harris and Harris 1964.

have sexual relations, though kin who are not easily accessible to one another are liable to drift apart. Neighbors may marry if they are not kin. They also assist one another in ceremonial and ritual affairs but the emphasis is much more on mutual aid in practical matters, notably in the millet threshing groups in harvest time. These are apt to include only close neighbors but the concept of neighborhood generally extends to the whole of the village and may even embrace adjacent villages.

The special interest of the Nyamwezi situation lies in the precise demarcation of neighborhood relations from chiefdom relations in politico-jural terms. The mature men of the neighborhood constitute an informal tribunal which meets *ad hoc* to take corrective measures against anyone who offends against the prescribed norms of good neighborliness. Their only sanction is to ostracize a recalcitrant offender; and it is significant that a headman, who holds his office in the framework of the chiefdom may, as villager, participate in the decision to ostracize an offender but may also, in his official capacity, visit the offender *qua* citizen. The offenses of which a neighborhood court takes cognizance are precisely distinguished from the wrongs which must be adjudicated at the chief's court. The former include offenses such as failure to help neighbors in communal tasks, disrespect for a neighbor in mourning, unseemly behavior at a communal ritual ceremony, abuse or assault of a neighbor. The penalty is always a fine in kind which is consumed by the whole neighborhood group including the offender and thus restores mutual trust and harmony. The chiefdom courts, by contrast, deal with suits arising from wrongs against state laws (e.g., concerning taxes), serious offenses against persons, and civil dispute over such matters as inheritance, succession, divorce, damages, etc. The cleavage is reminiscent of the differentiation in Ashanti of *"efiesem,"* that is, disputes in the sphere of lineage and domestic law, from *"mansosem,"* that is, litigation in the sphere of the public law of the state. It confirms a conclusion implied in my earlier remark about the intermeshing of kinship and locality norms and patterns.

Superficially, the concept of neighborhood signifies social relations arising out of local contiguity. In fact, it has a narrower connotation. It pinpoints a field of social relations in which local association is suffused with the ideology and values of kinship and is thus drawn into the familial domain. This is in part due to the overlap of neighborly relations with kinship relations, but it is not entirely and solely due to this structural convergence. At bottom it is a question of the ethic of generosity, the axiom of amity, basically derived as it is from the domain of kinship and family structure, here spilling over into the area of neighborliness. Our examples make one aspect of this very clear, however. The intermeshing of kinship and locality in the neighborhood, and the extension of the axiom of amity are features of internal structure. Facing outwards, in the external system of the state, the chiefdom, the system of interclan and interlineage politico-jural and politico-ritual relations, every man is a citizen, vis-à-vis his neighbor, either immediately, as with the Lozi and the Nyamwezi, or mediately, as with Tallensi and Ashanti. Locality, like kinship, is redefined in relation to the external politico-jural system to confer elements of status that are distinct from, in some ways opposed to, those associated with it in the internal system.

IX

Mention has been made in passing of the obverse of the prescriptive altruism deemed to be inherent in kinship. This is often comprised in the notion of debt. Kinsfolk cannot, as kinsmen, contract debts with one another, for ideally they are bound to share freely. One of the contrasts often emphasized by Tallensi is that kinsfolk cannot have "debts," whereas affines are bound to one another by the perpetual indebtedness of the wife-receivers to the daughter-givers. If land or tools or livestock or even food is loaned, or services are rendered to kinsfolk they should reciprocate equitably, if not equally, but there are no sanctions for enforcing this; the returns are expected to be made out of mutual amity. With actual or potential affines, by contrast there occurs what I formerly described as a sort of bookkeeping. There is an element of deliberate calculation in the reciprocities of affines (cf. Fortes, 1949c: 122, 214–15).

The same ethic is conspicuous among Ashanti. In the 1940's, salaried employees, especially those in government or local authority employment, constantly complained of the demands made upon them by kinsfolk. Teachers and clerks preferred to be posted far from their natal communities to escape these irresistible demands. Men of means said that it was inadvisable to lend money on a mortgage to a member of one's own lineage, as recovery was doubtful. The principle of corporate identity of the lineage might be invoked by the recipient to interpret a loan as rightful sharing, and though this would not necessarily be accepted in a chief's court, it would cause ill-feeling. With patrikin, mutual help in crisis was not obligatory but was assimilated to the ideal of the freely rendered gift. With non-kin, legal redress for non-repayment of loans was possible and often resorted to. Since a spouse falls into the category of non-kin, loans made by one spouse to another placed the recipient in debt and were liable to be subject to suits at court, especially in cases of divorce.

The Tikopia evidently hold similar notions. Thus Firth (1963) remarks that Tikopia prefer exchanges of gifts that are connected with the initiation of boys to pass between people living in different villages or, better still, districts, rather than between close neighbors. Exchange between members of the same family is particularly reprobated as a sign of meanness. Close kin share freely and happily; non-kin who include affines, exchange, often as a result of coercive solicitation (Firth, 1936: 460–61; 1939: 316).[22] The particular interest of this instance, as I have previously noted, lies in the fact that, owing to the intricate mesh of intermarriage over many generations within what is *de facto* an endogamous community, all Tikopia are potentially recognizable as kin to one another by some reckoning or another. Firth's analysis of how persons who are, from one point of view, kin can be redefined to be marriageable non-kin, has already been referred to (Firth, 1930). In the present context, we see how the opposition is made explicit in the idiom of sharing among kin *versus* affinal indebtedness.

22. Similar ideas are current among the Moalan Fijians (Sahlins, 1962), the Siuai (Oliver, 1955), and the Tangu (Burridge, 1960).

The principle underlying this type of structural discrimination is so common as to need no further exemplification. It is common wherever prescriptive cross-cousin marriage is the rule. But I cannot resist quoting one African example that has much in common with the Tikopian. Among the Taita of Kenya, marriage is permitted between distantly connected members of territorially based large patrilineal lineages. The effectively exogamous lineage segment is one of four generations depth, and this is the lineage within which inheritance of land and livestock usually falls. Beyond its limits, exact genealogical links do not have to be precisely known. Commenting on this, Alfred and Grace Harris remark:

Observation confirms that in fact the small lineage is for most Taita the limit of precise genealogical knowledge (or agreement). It is also the limit of strongly enjoined mutual aid, within which bringing suit for repayment of a "gift" (thus turning it into a debt) is considered in dubious taste (1964: 122).

In transactions with complete outsiders, the concept of debt merges into that of sale and purchase. The Tiv notion of a "market" reflects this. "Market" signifies buying and selling. It is opposed to gift exchange which implies "a relationship . . . of a permanence and warmth not known in a 'market' ", for "market behavior and kinship behavior are incompatible" (Bohannan, 1955: 60).

The Tallensi have similar notions. It comes out in a striking way in their attitudes towards payment for labor or special services. In the 1930's, youths from the neighboring Gorni communities would sometimes come over to offer their labor during the height of the farming season. This was a boon to a sick family head. If they were employed, they were paid in money—threepence to sixpence a day—and in food. But if the same work were undertaken for a sick clansman, matrilateral kinsman, affine, or neighbor by a Tallensi, he would be offended if he were offered monetary payment for it.[23]

In the last resort, debt justifies retaliatory or redressive action which may provoke war, and is therefore the negation of kinship morality. Tallensi raids by one lineage or another in former times were generally described as "cancelling a debt" and they were, indeed, often precipitated by failure to pay a bride-price. Even among the Kalingas, ready as they are to wound or kill on the slightest provocation, there is, says Barton (1949: 218 ff.) greater forbearance among kindred than toward non-kin.

Finally, there is one further extension of the ideology and morality of kinship amity that deserves mention, however briefly. The most revolutionary change in the social landscape of Africa, from Cairo to the Cape and from Senegal to Ethiopia, has been the establishment of ever-expanding urban agglomerations centered on institutions, activities, interests, and values primarily of West European provenance.

---

23. In 1963, when I revisited the Tallensi, I found that the style of building rectangular instead of circular rooms was being adopted by a few people. This requires special skills and only a few men possessed them. By this date the traditional economy was much overlaid by the national money economy. Yet the best new-style builder in Tongo, who was paid by the day when he undertook to build for outsiders, accepted only the traditional form of recompense in food and drink from neighbors and kinsfolk who sought his services.

How these administrative, industrial, commercial, missionary, and other urban centers came into being, some going back to the sixteenth and seventeenth centuries, under the colonial rule of European powers, is not relevant here. What is relevant is that most of them have grown with explosive rapidity in the past fifty years and have sucked in large numbers of immigrants from far-flung tribal areas. All modern African towns thus come to be inhabited by a multiracial, polyglot population of very diverse geographical, cultural, and political origin, including Europeans and Asians, as well as members of many indigenous ethnic and tribal groups; and the diversity can be just as great whether they are made up predominantly of immigrants from within the confines of a successor state to a colonial territory, as in Nigeria, or whether they include many of foreign origin, as in Ghana or the Republic of South Africa.

Summarizing many years of research in the heterogeneous urban agglomerations of the Far East, J. S. Furnivall (1948) called them "plural societies" unified only by geography, by subordination to an overriding political power, and, above all, by the convergent but usually fiercely competitive economic interests of the constituent ethnic and social groups. Furnivall's thesis has been criticized and challenged, but its essential point remains valid. In African cities this is reflected in the tendency for immigrant groups to create for themselves voluntary associations, commonly on a tribal or regional basis, more rarely on an occupational or status basis, for mutual aid, protection, and cultural self-vindication in the alien and competitive urban environment. The range and variety of these associations, their diverse functions— extending from the organization of recreation to insurance against sickness or unemployment and provision for decent and ritually proper burial—is remarkable. There is now a large body of knowledge relating to these associations as they emerge and operate in West African towns, which we owe to the authoritative researches of Kenneth Little (1965) and his colleagues. They show that hope of economic advantage or support, desire for material protection in a harsh and often exploitative social environment, sometimes political factionalism, and often just the wish for associating with one's "own" people play important parts in the rise of these associations. But what essentially holds the members of such associations together in mutual loyalty, as I interpret the literature in the light of my own observations of such associations in Ghana, is not self-interest. It is a generalized sentiment of amity which they themselves are apt to identify with the feelings kinsfolk should have for one another. I have met this among Tallensi in Kumasi and Accra. In these cities, lineage, local, totemic, and cult divisions are swept away. There all Tallensi are deemed to be kin to one another as against the rest of the world and the associations they form often even include members of other tribal communities from the north of Ghana. "At home," I have heard it said, "we may be enemies; in Accra we are all kin." Examples of similar attitudes in other West African towns are given in Little's survey; and similar responses of immigrant tribal groups to urban life have been reported from South Africa.[24]

24. Cf., e.g., the interesting description of the *amakhaya* groups of tribal Xhosa immigrants in East London in Mayer, 1961: 99–100. *Amakhaya* are people "of one home," that is, from one rural location, and, says Mayer, they form a "moral community" in the town.

X

Summing up what he describes as "the premises underlying relationship norms," among the Siuai, Oliver writes:

Mankind consists of relatives and strangers. Relatives are usually inter-linked by both blood and marital ties; most of them live nearby, and persons who live nearby are all relatives. Relatives should interact quite frequently and at least in times of crises and on the occasion of one another's rites of passage. Transactions among them should be carried out in a spirit devoid of commerciality—preferably consisting of sharing, nonreciprocable giving, and bequeathing, among closest relatives, or of lending, among more distantly related ones. Among themselves relatives should feel and express emotions of affection or at least amity—colored, when appropriate, by expression of deference, or polite constraint, and of sex avoidance (1955: 454–55).

The argument I have been developing could not be more concisely stated. And it suggests a point which could easily be overlooked: There is a fiduciary element in amity. We do not have to love our kinsfolk, but we expect to be able to trust them in ways that are not automatically possible with non-kinsfolk. That is why agreements in the form of contracts are needed for entering into and maintaining relationships of moral and jural validity with people defined as strangers. Tallensi, certainly, would argue this way, and so, I suspect would most of the tribal peoples I have cited in the course of this discussion.

CHAPTER XIII

Filiation Reconsidered

I

I TURN BACK NOW TO CONSIDER SOME OF THE CONCEPTUAL AND THEORETICAL ISSUES that were sidestepped by the preceding digression. This is not the place to attempt to review all the problems of current theoretical concern in the study of kinship and social organization that have come up in the course of this inquiry,[1] but there are one or two subjects that have not only been central to this inquiry but have also, as we have seen, been central to its theme from Morgan to our own day. It is to some further consideration of these topics that I shall limit myself.

To get the perspective right, I digressed to establish the thesis that the domain of familial and kinship relations, institutions and values, is structurally discrete, that is to say, neither subsumable in any other domain of social life nor reducible to extraneous determinants. What I mean is that the realm of custom, belief, and social organization, which we descriptively identify by the overall rubric of kinship, is both analytically distinguishable and empirically specifiable as a relatively discrete domain of social structure founded upon principles and processes that are irreducible.

This is orthodox enough. It is perhaps not so orthodox today, though our nineteenth century predecessors all assumed it, to assert, as I have done, that a critical fea-

1. The need is ably and judiciously met in Davenport, 1963.

ture of this domain, intrinsic to its constitution and distinctive of its manifestations in social life, is a set of normative premises. I have argued that these premises are focused upon a general and fundamental axiom which I call the axiom of prescriptive altruism or, more briefly, of amity. I ascribe this axiom to the realm of moral values, in contraposition to the realm of jural values ordered to the politico-jural domain. But I cannot emphasize too strongly that this is a methodological and analytical distinction. The actualities of kinship relations and kinship behavior are compounded of elements derived from both domains and deployed in words and acts, beliefs and practices, objects and appurtenances that pertain to both of these and to other domains of social life as well. We are concerned with relations between persons and with the behavior of persons in accordance with discernible rules; and every person is an agent, actual or potential, in all domains. There is no such entity as a kinship person who is not also invested with politico-jural, economic, ritual, etc., identity and responsibility. And, by extension, if a person who is not a kinsman is metaphorically or figuratively placed in a kinship category, an element, or at least a semblance, of kinship amity goes with this.[2] It is conceivable—and I for one would accept—that the axiom of amity reflects biological and psychological parameters of human social existence. Maybe there is sucked in with the mother's milk, as Montaigne opined, the orientation on which it ultimately rests. But this is not my subject. What signifies here is the implication for the problem of "social recognition" which I considered at an earlier stage of this inquiry.

The "social recognition" which converts genealogically identified, imputed, or represented connections into kinship relations presupposes this normative foundation. It means, both for the actor and for the observer, the normative imprimatur of moral and jural values reflected in patterns of customary behavior such as those specified in Radcliffe-Brown's tetrad, and more generally in rules and stipulations that regulate rights and duties, privileges, and claims. The best evidence for this is that when artifiical—so-called fictitious—kinship relations are established by blood brotherhood, or adoption, or "compadrazgo" in Latin American societies, the critical change is in the moral and jural norms thenceforth binding on the persons concerned. Adopted children must behave with the same respect toward their adoptive parents as natural offspring. They cannot normally marry adopted siblings, they inherit like natural children, and so on.[3]

There is no need to expatiate on the incontrovertible principle that all classes and categories of genealogically describable connections are ultimately traceable by the actors to actual, postulated, or figurative parentage and the reproductive cohabitation which is its prerequisite, whether or not infused with mystical notions. This is

2. Examples have previously been given (p. 53). This does not of course hold for the application of kinship notations, as for example a genealogical paradigm, to describe sequences and concatenations of non-human phenomena as in the example quoted in n. 20, p. 53; but it does hold, as I have shown, for charters of political organization framed in genealogical terms that postulate connections and stratification by kinship and descent, which demonstrably reflect synchronic political and territorial relations, and which are not objectively verifiable at the more inclusive levels—as, e.g., among the Tiv and the Cyrenaican Beduin and the Gusii (Bohannan and Bohannan, 1953; Peters, 1960; Mayer, 1949).

3. This is the case among the Iban, but we find exact parallels in other societies including our own. Cf., e.g., the Yakö, as described by Forde, 1950: 303–306.

the basic model. These are the empirical "givens" to which the conventional formula that makes the "parental" or "elementary" or "nuclear" family the fount of kinship has reference. Reduced to its rudimentary postulates, kinship begins from the recognition of mere offspring as children, of their begetters and bearers as parents, and of mating as marriage or its equivalent. It means, at this level, investing individuals with the status, attributes, and properties that make them persons in the domain of familial and kinship institutions. And this does not always follow automatically.

There are in all societies institutionalized procedures for the incorporation of new members into the family and the politico-jural community. The mere fact of birth to a particular parent, or to parents, though indispensable for the assignment of primary kinship status, is not enough. The Ashanti custom of suspending until the eighth day after a child's birth the naming ceremonies which recognize it as human and incorporate it into its family and lineage is not unique, as Van Gennep long ago established.[4]

Progeny becomes a son or daughter by virtue of acts of "social recognition." These are commonly of jural or ritual, or combined jural and ritual form, and are performed by persons entitled and obliged to carry them out. Conversely, genitor is or becomes pater, and in some cases genetrix, mater, by the legitimization of offspring, be it by virtue of precedent or subsequent marriage or such other formal acknowledgment as is customary. The Lozi custom which permits a genitor to legitimize the patrifiliation of his natural offspring by making the appropriate prestations to the mother's jurally responsible kin, without marrying the mother, and the Ashanti custom by which a pre-marital genitor acknowledges paternity by gifts publicly made to the mother and by naming the child, have many parallels in African societies and elsewhere. The gifts given by the *sambandham* husband among the Nayar to acknowledge physical paternity where, in theory, jural paternity is already pre-established by the *tali* tying rite is a striking instance. It implies the notion that there must be a licit genitor behind the legitimate pater, even if it is only the latter who is jurally and ritually recognized.[5] Similar precautions against engendering offspring polluted by incestuous or other illicit sexual liaisons are found in many if not all societies and serve to emphasize the significance of legitimate parentage.

The passage rites that induct a newborn into his primary kinship status may be elaborate and long drawn out (as in Tikopia) or may amount to little more than the bestowal of a name (as in Ashanti), but they serve the same end. And it is structurally

4. Cf. Gluckman 1962b: 1–52 for a critical evaluation of Van Gennep's ideas. "When a child is named" Van Gennep states (1960: 62) "he is both individualized and incorporated into society". In ancient Rome, as Fustel de Coulanges stresses (1956: 53) birth "formed only the physical bond". A son in particular, had to be accepted and ritually initiated into the family cult by the father on the ninth day. A Tallensi infant remains socially marginal, on probation as it were, until its next sibling is conceived, which is the signal for its weaning and recognition as an incipient person. If it dies before this it is unceremoniously buried and does not receive a human funeral. The same custom is found among the LoDagaa (Goody, 1962: 149) and other Voltaic peoples. The probationary period varies widely from culture to culture but the principle is the same.

5. As we can see from the test case of polyandry. Co-husbandship is always strictly regulated; the common wife is never at the promiscuous disposal of all comers. Cf. references below to the Toda and the Lele. This is the point of Malinowski's Principle of Legitimacy.

relevant that they are apt to be more elaborate for firstborn than for later children. For as Tallensi and Tikopia, in common with many other peoples, realize, it is their firstborn children whose birth and legitimization make a married couple into both natural and jurally recognized parents once and for all. Even if they have no other children, or are not survived by living children, their parental status is henceforth irreversible and is given explicit customary recognition in life and when they die. I have dealt with this theme at length for the Tallensi.[6] Thus it is the firstborn who establishes the relationship of filiation once for all in respect of his parents' field of kinship and it is he (or she) who frequently carries the responsibility of representing the whole of his co-filiate sibling group in jural and ritual contexts. It is he who is likely to be principal heir and successor to his father in patrilineal, to a mother's brother in matrilineal, systems and it is upon him therefore that both the continuity and solidarity, and the cleavage and rivalry, between successive generations are apt to be focused.

These considerations point to what has long been recognized in ethnographic description, if not in theory, as the structural nucleus of all kinship systems. I refer to the relationship of filiation to which I have already made frequent allusion in the analysis of our paradigmatic specimens. When I originally proposed the revival of this term (1953a), I stated that "filiation—by contrast with descent—is universally bilateral," but I refrained from closer definition. Later, taking into account subsequent research, I defined filiation as "the relationship created by the fact of being the legitimate child of one's parents."[7] Originally I contrasted filiation with descent

6. Cf. Fortes, 1949c: 233–34, and *passim*. The special significance of firstborn children in Tikopia is discussed in Firth, 1956. This meticulous account of the ceremonies for the social incorporation of a child brings home a point that is apt to be overlooked in describing them as *rites de passage*, for they begin before the birth of a child and are spaced out over two or three years of the child's infancy, marking successive stages of its physical and social maturation. This singling out of the firstborn is extremely common, perhaps universal. The ritually and mystically sanctioned avoidances between Tallensi firstborns and their like sex parents dramatize strikingly the uniqueness of the filio-parental relationship by contrast, especially, with the joking and familiarity relationships of alternate generations, as I note later. Ashanti, similarly, single out a woman's first born (Fortes, 1950: 273). Cf. the eldest child among the Nuer. Evans-Pritchard writes: "The many peculiar prescriptions which adhere to the status of the eldest child may . . . be connected with his pivotal and ambiguous position between the families of his father and mother" (Evans-Pritchard; 1950: 391).

7. Fortes, 1959a: 206, cited above, p. 108. The term "filiation" has long been current in anthropological writings on kinship. French anthropologists use *"filiation"* in a general sense equivalent to the way "descent" has been used by the majority of British and American ethnologists and anthropologists in the past 100 years. (Cf., e.g., Lévi-Strauss's usage, 1949.) But it has a respectable history also in English anthropological writings. Thus McLennan (1876: 285 [1886 ed.]) wrote of the "filiation" of members of the Nayar family to one another. In reviving the term, I have, however, largely followed Malinowski. He used it freely but rather more widely than I propose. Thus, he observes (1935, vol. I, p. 36): "Filiation— if I may use a word covering all traditional and genealogical continuities, that is, covering descent, inheritance, and succession—is matrilineal"; and again (vol. I, p. 37), "two independent principles of filiation can exist side by side." According to the *Oxford English Dictionary*, the term was current in the seventeenth-century, meaning (1) "*Theol*. The process of becoming, or the condition of being, a son", (2) "sonship," (3) "a person's parentage." According to this dictionary, it subsequently came to be used for "descent" or "transmission" and still later for "genealogical" relationship. *Webster's Third International Dictionary* defines filiation as "1 a: relationship esp. of a son to his father b: the relationship between a parent and a child whether legitimate or illegitimate."

in the context of a review of the theory of unilineal descent-group structure. I was specially interested therefore in the function of "complementary filiation"— that is to say, filiation with the parent who does not transmit membership of the unilineal descent group—as the primary mechanism of segmentation within the group. I defined descent as "fundamentally a jural concept . . . [representing] the connecting link between the external, that is political and legal, aspect of . . . unilineal descent groups, and the internal or domestic aspect (1953b: 30). The structural contrast therefore implied was between the external relations of unilineal descent groups taken as units in a system of such units, and their internal constitution. Thus viewed, descent could be regarded as a principle and mechanism of social structure operative in the extra-familial domain of political and jural institutions, whereas filiation and complementary filiation could be regarded as the two components of a mechanism operative primarily within the familial and kinship domain. The foregoing inquiry, however, suggests that this contrast needs qualifications which I will presently note.

In other words, filiation and complementary filiation were associated with processes in the internal structure (as opposed to the external status) of politico-jural groups supposed to be delimited by descent, though they were held to be generated within the "bilateral" familial organization, as a "constant element in the pattern of family relationships" (1953b: 34).

The conceptual and analytical utility of these distinctions has, in the meantime, received voluminous attention, both from the point of view of kinship theory and in the context of ethnographical field research.[8] A major source of confusion, as Leach (1957) trenchantly insisted, has been the ambiguous and loose use of the concept of "descent." Ever since Morgan purported to explain classificatory terminologies by examining their supposed incompatibility with "the nature of descents," anthropologists of different persuasions have used "descent" as a blanket term for analytically distinct variables. Rivers early drew attention to this. Protesting against the habit of confounding "entirely distinct" social processes under the common label, he proposed distinguishing between inheritance, succession, and descent, and confining "descent" to the regulation of membership in unilateral groups.[9] The difficulty arises largely because the actor's kinship concepts translated by the word "descent" are not distinguished from the observer's descriptive constructs and notations to which the same label is attached. An instance is the misinterpretation of conventional notations of kinship terminologies as indicating the existence of unilineal descent groups.

8. I list here, for ease of reference, some of the ethnographic and theoretical contributions toward the clarification of these concepts that I am specially indebted to Barnes, 1962; Brown, 1962; Davenport, 1959; Dunning, 1959; Firth, 1963; Freeman, 1958, 1960, 1961; Goodenough, 1961; Goody, 1961, 1962; Groves, 1963; Leach, 1957, 1960b, 1961a, 1961b, 1962; Murdock, 1960; Robinson, 1962; Scheffler, 1964; Schneider, 1965; M. G. Smith, 1956; Tambiah, 1958. I must make special reference also to Scheffler, 1966, which appeared after this chapter was written.

9. Rivers, 1924: 86. Cf. Leach, 1962, and the critical comment on some of Leach's observations by Forde, 1963. Forde notes (p. 12) that "Rivers did not consider 'unilateral groups' in relation to other discrete genealogically recruited groups, but in relation to overlapping ego-centred kindreds."

The contrast I drew between filiation and descent was meant to disentangle two sets of variables that are, to my mind, erroneously lumped together in theoretical as well as descriptive works. There is now plenty of evidence, as our paradigmatic specimens illustrate, from recent field research as well as from theoretical discussion, in support of discriminating between the configuration of kinship relations that link parent and child *per se*, and so-called "lineal" relations in the more exact sense of "descent." In particular, studies of cognatic and other so-called "non-unilineal" kinship systems have emphasized the value of this distinction.[10] But the traditional use of a portmanteau concept of descent continues to have defenders, and further clarification is therefore needed.

III

I begin with a closer look at the concept of filiation. Though the term is now in general circulation, its most appropriate empirical reference and conceptual status is not unanimously agreed. This must be my excuse for proceeding more laboriously than might seem necessary.

I take filiation to refer most immediately to an empirical isolate that is readily identifiable in all human communities. The facts of parenthood—that is, the complex of activities which includes the begetting, bearing, and rearing of children by specified parental kin—are empirically identifiable in all societies, even if parents and children are not permanently co-resident. At any rate, ethnographers have never failed to find the mother and child couple, and to get evidence of the recognition of genitors and fathers, even in societies where the ostensibly husbandless "matrifocal family" is the common form (cf. Smith, R. T., 1956), or where physiological paternity is ignored or not understood, as classically among the Trobrianders and the Australian aborigines.

After all, the relations of parents and children throughout their life cycle, informal and formal, personal and customary, emotional, intellectual, and practical, mutually consonant and mutually dissonant, form a major part of the descriptive literature of our subject. They also form an inescapable, lifelong part of the day-to-day experience of every one of us as actor and observer. They run through the religious scriptures, the imaginative literature and art, the institutions of law and government, of every civilization of the world from the earliest times till today. Some degree of intuitive understanding of these relations is inevitable and is found throughout mankind.

In developing the brief definition of filiation I proposed in my 1959 paper, I tried to show that the concept had reference to a configuration of affective, moral, jural, and practical relationships and not merely to a unit of genealogical reckoning. To think of filiation as a single-track structural relationship misses the point. For, though it is generated and operates throughout life in the familial domain, it is also decisively shaped by and is necessarily effective in other domains of social life. As I have already emphasized, no one is a person only in the kinship domain. However,

10. This is apparent from the studies of Pehrson, Dunning, and Freeman previously cited. Cf. also Barnes, 1962.

at the most palpable empirical level, we perceive filiation as the nodal mechanism and crucial relationship of intergenerational continuity and social reproduction. In this sense, it is the meeting point of synchronic order and diachronic extension at the core of social structure. For it is by virtue of filiation that each generation of offspring replaces and at the same time perpetuates each generation of parents in dialectical sequence. To ensure this, many societies provide that, where natural reproduction fails in a particular case, artificial or substitute replacement may be resorted to. Adoption is one device; but there are other devices for this as well. Among such are the levirate and the sororate, but most instructive is the placing of a child-bearer in the house of a barren woman. It is found among the Zulu and other African peoples, though it is probably most familiar to us from the biblical story of Rachel and her maidservant Bilhah (Genesis 30).[11] In either case, the effect is to transform a naturally or jurally unfiliated person into a jurally—which commonly means also ritually—filiated member of the parental family. And it is worth stressing that adoption, and analogous institutions, always consist in the creation of a relationship of recognized filiation. A person cannot be adopted into siblingship, for example, to take an obvious contrast.[12] To adopt, one has to have parental status and authority which can be extended to the adoptee; for blood brotherhood, by contrast, the parties must have equal status. In the biblical story, it will be remembered that Rachel, in chagrin over her barrenness, sends her maidservant Bilhah in to her husband Jacob and the child Dan born to Bilhah is counted as Rachel's child.

As it operates in the familial domain, filiation is marked principally by the affective and moral attributes exhibited in the often-described patterns of customary behavior that give vent to the interplay of solidarity and opposition in the relations of successive generations. Intergenerational incest taboos and the concomitant avoidance and respect rules dramatize this situation. As I have already suggested, they underline the singularity of the filio-parental relationships, as against classificatorily like relations between collaterals. An instance more telling, in some ways, than the ritually prescribed avoidances between Tallensi parents and their firstborn children,

11. The custom by which a man may put an extra wife "into the house" of a barren wife to bear children which will be regarded as legally the children of the latter, is found among the Zulu, the Tswana, the Swazi, and other Southern Bantu peoples. Cf. Gluckman, 1950: 185. Schapera (1950: 149) notes that, if, "for purposes of child-bearing, one of the original parties to that marriage is replaced by another person of the same sex, [he or she] . . . is regarded as a bodily substitute, and not as an independent spouse."

12. The principle is obvious in the Roman laws of adoption. But the following examples bring the point home: (a) Powell (1956) reports that younger classificatory siblings are some-times adopted by Trobrianders but they are then addressed and referred to by the kinship terms for children and are so treated. (b) As is well known, adoption is widely practised in Japan to ensure competent succession to male headship of the family and thus its "perpetuation . . . as a corporate group through its name and occupation." Though relatives of appropriate age and generation by kinship or marriage are the preferred adoptees, non-relatives are also adopted. But the point of interest here is that a childless man might adopt a brother "fifteen or twenty years younger" in order to ensure "smooth succession to the status of the headship." He ceases then to be a brother and becomes a *mukoyoshi*, an adoptive son (cf. Befu, 1962: 34, 37, and *passim*). (c) In the traditional family system of southeastern China, it was until quite recently customary for sons to be adopted in order to ensure continuation of the line of succession in the ancestor cult. In this case, however, there was a strict rule that the adoptee should be one of the adoptor's "nearest agnates in the generation next below his" (Freedman, 1966: 7, n. 2).

is reported by Powell (1956) of the Trobrianders. He states that it would be a heinous breach of the incest taboo for a man to have sexual relations with his own daughter, but marriage with a classificatory daughter is tolerated. Mortuary and funeral obligations toward parents, in many societies, bring home the same point.

As we might expect, kinship terminologies reflect these constants, for as we have known since Kroeber first drew attention to it in 1909, the terminological discrimination between parents and their children, whether or not it is generalized by classificatory rules to include collaterals, is a universal and crucial feature of these terminologies. It is very rare indeed (if it occurs at all) for parent and child to designate each other by the same kinship term in reference or to use self-reciprocal kinship terms in address. They may of course be identified with each other by third parties, in accordance with the lineage principle, for example. They may also be accustomed to address each other by personal names or titles, as happens in some circles in our own society and as I have reported is also the practice among the Tallensi, at any rate with regard to the father. But these practices are very different from the use of kinship *terms*, such as father or son, mother and daughter, in reference, for both generations.[13]

The cleavage thus symbolized in kinship terminologies and expressed in incest prohibitions, avoidance and respect rules, residence patterns, economic and ritual activities, etc., etc., pervades the whole life cycle of relations between successive generations. It falls within the familial domain; and it is in this context that filiation normally takes a bilateral, or as I have called it elsewhere (1953b, 1959a), equilateral form. But this is an external view and it can be misleading. Considered from within, as I added, it would be more correct to say that filiation is always complementary.

This, too, is reflected in kinship terminologies. I do not know of any kinship terminology, past or extant, in which male parent and female parent have not been distinguished. The ineluctable complementarity of the sexes by nature, in procreation, and in the tasks of parental care is undoubtedly the basis of this. But custom everywhere prescribes, and the social structure decrees, the form this complementarity will take in a given society. Moral norms and jural institutions are the ultimate arbiters.

The jural dimension is most obviously apparent in the rules and procedures for legitimizing offspring, that is to say, for converting the natural connections of parents and children into the morally and jurally valid relationship of filiation. Though most explicit in societies with differentiated politico-jural institutions, such rules and procedures are quite definite also in kinship polities. "Ideally," says

13. Tallensi sometimes address small babies by the kinship terms for father or mother or grandparent. The infant in these cases, is generally a grandchild of the speaker and is addressed in tones of mixed affection and banter foreshadowing the joking relationship which will presently develop between them. The explanation is that the infant has been taken under the spiritual guardianship of the speaker's deceased parent or grandparent, and is named after that ancestor. The same custom is found among the Ashanti and other Akan peoples. Older informants say that this is not only because the child has been named after a parent's parent or grandparent, but because it is a reincarnation of—in the sense of having the same patri-spirit, and being of the same lineage, as—the parent or grandparent. In neither case, however, will a child be referred to, for the information of a third party, by any other than the appropriate filial terms.

Meggitt, "reproduction exclusively concerns jurally-recognized spouses, and in fact little latitude about this norm is permitted" (1962: 108). Compare Roman law, which, with characteristic exactitude, declared agnation to be a "title in civil law," in other words, a jural status (*Institutes of Justinian*, bk. I, title 15). Bastardy, where this jural category exists, provides an index. Illegitimacy usually means the status of a person who has no jurally or legally recognized pater. Roman law, to turn again to this classical model, defined a person as illegitimate if he had no legal father, as shown by the legal marriage of his parents. Such a person was devoid of agnation, since it was only through the legal father that agnation could be traced. Furthermore, to be legally married both spouses had, in Justinian's time, to be citizens.[14] Slaves could not marry. Similarly, a male slave in Ashanti could not beget offspring who were, strictly speaking, legitimate on the patrifilial side. As we have seen, this would not bar them from attaining citizenship through their mother, if she was a free person; but it would be a spiritual and, from the Ashanti point of view, charac-terological blemish that might impede them from election to high office. To be illegitimate by maternal birth is a contingency that can happen only in very special circumstances in non-Western society. This is not, as Morgan thought and others have echoed since, because birth to the mother is certain in contrast to paternity. The reasons are otherwise.

The child of a Bilhah, born in concubinage by proxy for a legal wife, is not maternally illegitimate. Even the bastard child cared for by the community, who was the prototypical *filius nullius*, or *filius populi* of Blackstonian theory in fifteenth-century England, was not apparently regarded as illegitimate on the mother's side. The child of a slave spouse or concubine would approximate to this. But this followed paradoxically from the fact that a slave, in all slave-holding systems, was himself or herself kinless and stateless, on the one hand, and therefore un-qualified to transmit legitimacy to his or her offspring, while yet subject to the general principles of filiation. He or she therefore transmitted slave status auto-matically to offspring (cf. p. 263, below).

The point is that offspring of unmarried women in tribal and primitive society are not by definition illegitimate on that score, provided that the mother is not banished or otherwise deprived of her filial and sororal status in her natal family, as might happen in retribution for sinful or criminal conception. If she retains her legitimate natal status, she can be deemed to transmit it to her offspring. Thus it is possible for a person to be half-legitimate, so to speak, provided he has been begotten in licit (that is, not incestuous or sacrilegious or, with monogamous marriage in particular, adulterine intercourse). He can, more correctly stated, be quasi-legitimate on the mother's side and this might suffice to give him filial status in his mother's field of

14. Cf. *Institutes of Justinian*, bk. 3, title 2, and title 5, and cf. Buckland 36–55. It is not worth adding examples of this very widely recognized principle that legitimacy is conferred by birth in legal wedlock. It is useful, however, to remind ourselves of the adaptation of this rule to the vagaries of human nature and the accidents of sterility. In ancient Arabia, as Robertson Smith long ago explained (1903: chap. IV) "the fundamental doctrine of Mohammedan law," to wit, that, "the son is reckoned to the bed on which he is born" was firmly upheld (p. 132); hence, "the husband was so indifferent to his wife's fidelity, that he might send her to cohabit with another man to get himself a goodly seed" (p. 139). Tallensi have similar attitudes about adulterine children, especially if they are born to a sterile man (cf. Fortes, 1949c: 23).

consanguineal kinship, as in Ashanti, or quasi-filial status in her consanguineal kinship field in patrilineal systems like that of the Tallensi and the LoWiili. Matrifilial half-legitimacy in these systems rests upon the indefeasible retention by a woman of her filial status in her natal lineage and family throughout her life, and it follows naturally from the postulate that participation in parental status is transmitted to recognized offspring. Its claims strengthened by motives of kinship amity or the desire to recruit offspring to a dying-out descent group, a daughter's half-legitimate child is thus assimilated into its mother's natal family with quasi-filial status which is virtually equivalent to adoption.[15]

But there are systems in which matrifiliation by itself (i.e. without consideration of descent) may suffice to establish the full jural capacity of a person. The Australian custom whereby the father is "thrown away" in assigning persons to subsections, and only matrifiliation is considered, is a case in point. It could be argued that this makes logical sense consistent with the "ignorance" of physiological paternity among Australian aborigines. Nevertheless, this does not mean that patrifiliation, as a jurally and ritually valid relationship with the father, is not recognized. Even with "wrong" marriages it is recognized and determines the assignment of indispensable Kinship and ritual statuses, such as are signified by membership of the patrilodge among the Walbiri.

IV

This points to a principle that must not be lost sight of. It may make a big difference to a person's status in some societies if he is legally fatherless, but it is always assumed and necessarily so that he has been licitly conceived—if not through the agency of a human genitor, then through the intervention of some approved supernatural agency.[16] Illicit conception, as opposed to illegitimate conception, is, as we have seen, usually regarded as either a crime or a sin subject in the extreme case to capital punishment. Where the genitor is known, this may be a factor in his offspring's personal moral obligations, for example, in respect of the incest taboo. Regardless of this, however, there is generally institutional provision for a person illegitimate on his father's side to have a quasi-pater by jural fiction. The requirement that his filiation must be bilateral, notionally, if not *de facto*, for a person to be a fully normal person is thus met.[17] Among the Tallensi and the LoWiili, as we have

15. Cf. Goody, 1962: 352. Goody calls this "institutionalized illegitimacy" by virtue of which a "fatherless child" is deemed to belong to his maternal uncle's patriclan and matriclan and may inherit from him. In early Roman law, it is worth recollecting, "by *ius gentium*, descent was traced from the mother" with regard to the status of a slave. Hence "the child of a female slave . . . was a slave whatever the status of the father" (Buckland: 40).

16. As in the well-known instances of totemistic impregnation believed to happen among some groups of Australian aborigines and the similar theories of the Trobrianders.

17. One of the most interesting observations, in this connection, comes from Dr. Raymond T. Smith's study of the Negro family in the former British territory of British Guiana, to which reference has previously been made. In the early 1950's, when Smith carried out his study, unmarried motherhood was notoriously common in these families. He showed, and others have since confirmed, that the unmarried mother normally lived as a daughter in the "matrifocal family" centered on her own mother. The child of an unmarried mother growing

seen, this role is accepted by the mother's brother or mother's father under whose domestic jurisdiction the child is placed. It is demonstrated in bride-price transactions and other jural and ritual acts which cannot be accomplished without the assumption of paternal responsibility for a dependant.

In cognatic systems of the Iban or Lozi type, the status relations of men and women approach virtually complete equality and symmetry (as opposed to their complementary opposition in Australian systems) in the familial domain and fall little short of this also in the politico-jural domain,[18] in contrast to systems with unilineal politico-jural descent groups—especially patrilineal systems—in which the sexes are jurally and ritually asymmetrically differentiated. Thus in cognatic systems, matrifiliation and patrifiliation tend to have equal weight in the ascription of kinship status. In these circumstances, a jurally fatherless person can by right of matrifilial status frequently acquire politico-jural capacities that are technically supposed to require bilateral legitimacy. Lozi practice seems to approximate to this. The situation could probably not arise among the Iban. Since marriage always takes place between men and women who are cousins of permitted degrees, filiation through either parent or by adoption formally establishes status in the *bilek* and consequently in ego's kindred circle.[19]

With patripotestal marriage, the specific jural procedure which confers patrifiliation is usually quite explicit. Marriage, validated by the appropriate prestations to establish uxorial and genetrical rights is typical. But even where patripotestal marriage is the rule, birth in wedlock is not always a necessary condition for legitimate patrifiliation. As among the Lozi, children premaritally or extramaritally begotten, and therefore *prima facie* illegitimate, can, as I have pointed out, in many African societies be legitimized (even as adults) by redemption prestations. Among the Tallensi, and in other societies with similar patrilineal descent systems, it is possible for a person brought up by a stepfather to legitimize himself retrospectively

18. The classical picture of the Ango-Saxon and Germanic cognatic kinship system, as depicted by Phillpotts (1913), reflects the same picture of symmetrical and equal jural status of the sexes. Freeman's previously cited comparative study of the kindred (1961) brings this out with great clarity.

19. And cf. also the Gonja, as described by E. N. Goody, 1962. Among the Kalinga, whose cognatic kinship system is, as we have seen, very similar to that of the Iban, marriage is also monogamous. But wealthy or otherwise prominent men may have mistresses (*dagdagas*) either before they marry or in addition to their wives. The relationship is usually sanctioned by the man's parents or his wife. Here ostensible illegitimacy by patrifiliation is cancelled out in a cognatic system in which the sexes are jurally equal and the politico-jural authorities are noted as enforcing equitable recognition of offspring. Barton (1949: 59–60) writes that the children of a *dagdagas* "are recognized as relatives" by their father's "legitimate kindred." If one of the parties does not later marry, the *dagdagas* relationship counts as a first marriage and all of a man's property goes to the children of this union.

---

up in such a family would then initially be treated as if it were a child of its maternal grandmother. Later it would learn what its true relationship to its own mother and its grandmother was. However, the interesting point is that it was held to be inconceivable for a child to be fatherless. The genitor was usually known and recognized by the community even if he refused to admit paternity and gave no support to the girl and her child. It was accepted that every child had to have a father in name, if not in practice. This became specially important when children reached school age. Legally fatherless children would then be registered with the surname of their genitor (Smith, 1956; 132–34).

by such payments. This, incidentally, points to the important qualification that filiation, as a source of the credentials I refer to later, is not a function of the relationships between persons and their upbringers but is precisely rooted in jurally
recognized parentage.

The legitimizing procedures followed by an Ashanti genitor not married to the
mother of his offspring, or by the Nayar *sambandham* husband, are on the surface
more ambiguous. Here it would seem that a declaration of paternity, supported by
the conventional gifts to the woman and child, is a voluntary act of conscience, not a
jural procedure. Yet it confers legitimate patrifiliation. We must bear in mind,
however, not only the specific ritual and metaphysical sanctions and the elements of
personal pride that are involved, but also the significance of paternity as the ideological focus of values and social relations critical for the complementary structure of the
universe of kinship and descent relations on which the whole social order is based.
Complementary patrifiliation is not critical for the internal segmentation of an
Ashanti lineage in the same way as matrifiliation is for a Tallensi lineage; but it is not
irrelevant. For as we have seen, it is forbidden for the children of two sisters to have
common patrifiliation.

However, what looms largest in the sanctions for licit and legitimate paternity is
the value attached to the patrilateral connections which counterbalance the individual's politico-jural subordination to his lineage. Such a complementary partition of the field of kinship and descent, as seen from the individual's point of view, or
of the familial domain as seen from the outside, in relation to the total social structure,
is characteristic of many societies of the type represented in our paradigmatic
specimens. What is crucial is the division it represents in the system of norms and
values ordered to this domain, as I have suggested elsewhere (Fortes, 1953b), and
complementary filiation is a key mechanism in this. Nor is it confined to systems like
those of the Ashanti and the Tallensi, in which unilineal descent groups controlling
politico-jural status are counterbalanced by a web of cognatic kinship relations.
Analogous dichotomies are found, as we have seen in the course of our inquiry, in
the social structure, in ritual and totemic institutions, and in the sphere of normative
values in societies as different from these as those of the Australian aborigines.

This brings us back to the proposition that no one can become a complete social
person if he is not presentable as legitimately fathered as well as mothered. He must
have a demonstrable *pater*, ideally one who is individually specified as his responsible upbringer,[20] for he must be equipped to relate himself to other persons

20. This has long been familiar from the Toda arrow-shooting rite by which one of a group
of polyandrous husbands was selected as the official *pater* of their wife's offspring, as Rivers
(1906) reported. A more interesting case is that of the Lele of the Kasai. Among them a village
wife might, at first, have to be sexually available to as many as a dozen men but would end up
as the polyandrous wife of two or three. Though all the husbands were regarded as her children's
fathers and acted as such, it was ultimately the village as a whole, as "an incorporated kinsman" that took responsibility for them. "As husband," Douglas observes, "the village appeared
virile and aggressive. Unity was often sacrificed when rivals quarreled over village-wives. But
when it acted as father, unity was restored" (1963: 137–38). The special significance of this
example is that it shows that fatherhood can be vested in a corporation aggregate, as if it were
a quasi-individual, in a case where the licit genitor is merged in a group of men. It thus paradoxically emphasizes the ideal of the individually designated father.

and to society at large bilaterally, by both matri-kinship and patri-kinship. Lacking either side, he will be handicapped, either in respect of the ritual statuses and moral capacities that every complete person must have (as in Australia) or in the politico-jural and economic capacities and attributes that are indispensable for conducting himself as a normal right-and-duty bearing person.[21]

V

Seen in this context, filiation can be described as a relationship which creates for its bearers a package of jurally, ritually, and morally validated credentials for the rights and duties, privileges and claims that constitute status. They are credentials that entitle the bearer to activate statuses derived from those held by his parents in their respective fields of kinship, descent, and affinal relations, in the first place; but how these credentials, intrafamilially created as they are, are translated into social action and status depends upon the ways in which, and the institutions through which, the familial and kinship domain, on the one side, and the extra-familial, politico-jural domain, on the other, are interrelated. The passage rites of infancy can be understood as the initial steps in the establishment of these credentials and that is why the participation of representatives of both parents and their respective natal families is normally required in these rites.

It is to be noted that the acquisition of these credentials is never open to choice. No one, anywhere, can chose his natural parents; and even adoptive parents are not usually selected by the adoptee—necessarily so with infant adoption. But even where older children, adolescents, and possibly also adults were regularly adopted or adrogated, as in classical Rome, in rural Japan, and among the Andamanese, the decision rested with the adopting parents. There is nothing optative about the initial situation, as Malinowski called it. Herein lie the germs of the involuntary binding force of kinship.

In societies with developed politico-jural constitutions like our own, civic status accrues to a person regardless of his actual parentage, as a rule by right of birth within the territory of the political community, or to a citizen abroad, or by naturalization.[22] Nevertheless, even in these forms of unmediated citizenship a person must produce credentials of filiation in order to qualify for citizenship. A birth certificate may be sufficient—but it is of interest to note that in England it is only since 1953, as a result of a public outcry against the humiliation said to be suffered by persons recorded as illegitimate by birth, that a shortened certificate

---

21. This is best illustrated by matrilineal family systems, as we have seen, since patri-filiation is ostensibly not significant for legitimate status. I have previously indicated that this view is erroneous. The discussion of Trobriand patrifiliation by Marguerite Robinson (1962) confirms this cogently.

22. I cannot refrain from quoting the procedure in France, as reported in Laurence Wylie's delightful study: "A baby formally becomes a member of society within three days after he is born, when his birth is registered by the father or by the doctor at the town hall. His existence is inscribed on the *livret de famille* and he is given *civil status* which will be extremely important for him the rest of his life in any relationship he will have with the government or any of its agencies" (1957: 40).

which does not disclose illegitimate parenthood has been legally valid. All the same, such a certificate implies birth to natural parents and it is only if the living mother of an illegitimate child formally and legally relinquishes her parenthood that such a child can be legally adopted. What I particularly want to draw attention to, however, is that such a certificate is indispensable for claiming legal majority and other citizenship capacities, e.g., the right to vote in a parliamentary election.

The negative case which brings out the significance of filiation as the primary jural and moral credential for personhood in any society is represented again by the status of a slave. A slave, as we have noted, was a non-person in jural and moral terms; that is why he could not, in Justinian's Rome, be a legal husband. And this is typical. Only by defining him thus could he be dealt with as a kind of chattel, transferable by sale or by force. Thus slaves had to be "outsiders" in relation to their owner's society.[23] In Ashanti anyone who was enslaved was by definition kinless, that is, in the first instance, without recognized filiative ties in an Ashanti clan and therefore devoid of citizenship in the political community. He could be employed in responsible service by his owner and many slaves held positions of high trust and influence in the king's court. But he was not *sui iuris*. It was only if he was granted quasi-nepotal status in his owner's family and lineage that he acquired the limited jural autonomy of a lifelong jural minor. And as we have seen, the status—or at best the implicit stigma—of slavery was in theory never extinguishable. It clung to descendants through males of a male slave in theory forever, and put the matrilineal descendants of a female slave under perpetual quasi-servile tutelage. Conversely, no freeborn Ashanti could be enslaved by another Ashanti, but he could be placed in pawn to another Ashanti as security for a loan. He did not thus forfeit his status, either in his lineage or as a free citizen, and this guaranteed his right to be redeemed at any time by the repayment of the loan.[24]

23. As Finley observes: "The slave is an outsider: that alone permits not only his uprooting but also his reduction from a person to a thing which can be owned. . . . Thus, free Greeks who wished to dispose of unwanted children were compelled to resort to the fiction that they had 'exposed' them . . . ; the earliest Roman law code . . . provided that if a Roman were subject to enslavement as a punishment, he had to be sold abroad . . . ; Islamic law always laid down, and usually enforced, the rule that no born Muslim could be enslaved" (1968: article *s.v.* "Slavery" in the *International Encyclopedia of the Social Sciences*, vol. 14, p. 308).

24. Cf. also the following pertinent observation on domestic slavery among the Yao of Malawi, who were both slave traders and slave owners on a considerable scale before the establishment of the British Protectorate in 1891. After pointing out that slaves were given "quasi-child status in the village." Mitchell (1956: 195–96) continues, "The slave descendants as a rule have no relatives in the neighbourhood. The Yao always redeemed uterine kin whom they found in slavery by replacing them with other slaves, usually taken or bought [from other tribes]. . . . Where there are slave-groups in a village to-day, they have frequently been bought or captured in distant places, so that their kinsmen have been unable to trace them." Tallensi slaves were always kinless strangers; no person with accessible kin could be enslaved, for the chances were that if he had accessible kin some connection might be traceable to them from any Tallensi area, and to enslave a kinsman was a sin. Even if no kinship connections could be traced, accessible kin might try to rescue a captured kinsman by force and this would lead to war. They could of course ransom him if they wished. Thus, when, in times of acute famine, Tallensi sometimes sold children into slavery it was always to foreigners. A slave held by a Tallensi was attached to his owner's family and lineage by quasi-filial incorporation, as if he were a kind of illegitimate child (cf. Fortes, 1949c: 25). J. Goody, (1962:

VI

Describing filiation as a package of credentials bestowed by parents acting as the agents of society accentuates its extrafamilial authorization and field of deployment. But the roots must not be overlooked in thus fixing attention on the branches. It must not be forgotten that filiation is the mechanism that insures the replacement—physically, socially and psychologically—of each generation by the next. Offspring are perceived as the replications and extensions of their parents, and this is registered in every domain of social life. Its symbolical representation in beliefs about the identity of the flesh and blood, the bone and spirit of parents and of their children, which we have met with in our ethnographical specimens among peoples as diverse as the Ashanti and the Australian aborigines, reveals the power it has. I do not doubt that here, too, there are biological and psychological parameters behind the cultural representations. The concept of the normal personality as made up on one side of attributes fixed by the flesh and blood passed on by one parent, and on the other, of a spiritual essence or hereditary proclivity derived from the other parent, and sometimes associated with the enduring skeleton, is not uncommon. It is often projected into the religious domain in cults of ancestors and the dead. However, it is the complementarity of these beliefs, and of the ritual practices and values they predicate, as reflections of the structural complementarity of the two sides of parenthood, that I wish to stress. Filiation from this point of view signifies the presumed perpetuation in each person of both his parents in respect of those capacities they are each entitled to bring into the filio-parental relationship by ideological, jural and moral authorization.[25]

The rules and dogmas relating to succession and inheritance in all our paradigmatic specimens corroborate this, especially, of course, those that are crystallized in such variants of the custom of "positional succession" as we found among the Lozi and Ashanti.

The analytical problem is how these originally intrafamilial relations are invested. with extrafamilial structural efficacy as well. The key lies in the regulation of legitimacy and the credentials thus bestowed. But it should be noted that this two-sided. If children acquire credentials for claims on parents and through them on

25. Witness Maine's penetrating observation: "It is an axiom with us that the King never dies, being a Corporation sole. . . . With the Romans it seemed an equally simple and natural process, to eliminate the fact of death from the devolution of rights and obligations. The testator lived on in his heir or in the group of his co-heirs" (1861: chap. VI, p. 182 [1888 ed.]). And again: "The person or class of persons who succeeded did not simply *represent* the deceased, but, in conformity with the theory just delinated, they *continued* his civil life, his legal existence" (*ibid.*: 183; Maine's italics). This was the basis of the principle that the "heir proper" (*suus heres*), is the son who succeeds to his dead father's *potestas* "with no question of acceptance or refusal" (Buckland, 1925, 1947 edn. 187) in his own right, and had, therefore, either to be instituted or else formally disinherited for a will to be valid (Ibid. 195–6).

152) reports that a person thus sold into slavery by a LoWiili parent was deemed to have lost his birthright and could only be received back into his natal community after the performance of special rites and sacrifices for the Earth Shrine.

society, parents, and through them lineages and communities, likewise and co-incidentally, acquire claims on and rights over children, both in the familial domain and in their relations to society at large. The Tallensi rule that a son cannot be *sui iuris* and ritually autonomous while his father is alive, and the parallel notion concerning mothers and daughters, reminiscent as it is of the rule that only the *pater-familias* had full civic status in early Roman law (cf. Buckland: 61) is not unique. Gulliver, for instance, reports of the Arusha that "few men are willing to hazard attempts to deal secretly with a son whose father is alive," and the Harrises make a similar observation for the Taita.[26] Our paradigmatic specimens illustrate this point profusely.[27]

The proverbial Roman *ius vitae necisque* is an extreme case. Ashanti are devoted to children and value large families; but in northern Ashanti, it was formerly the custom to put ninth-born children to death at birth in compliance with magical beliefs which defined them as unlucky, and this custom was enforced by the political authorities, in the last resort. The infanticide of twins and other abnormally born infants for fear of mystical pollution is reported from many societies. Infanticide as formerly practiced in Tikopia is a striking instance of parental right being harnessed to moral values and social responsibility outside the family. Illegitimacy in Tikopia meant birth to an unmarried mother. It was so abhorred that it was obviated by abortion if the pregnant girl could not unequivocally identify the genitor or find a husband; but postnatal infanticide was also practiced, and this for the wholly rational and domestic reason of a family's land being too small to support extra children.[28]

Such rights as these devolve on parents just because parenthood imposes on them the corresponding duties of child rearing. Infanticide of later-born children or of girls, as it was practiced in China, or even of deformed or abnormal children, as in

26. Cf. Gulliver, 1964: 214; Harris and Harris, 1964: 135. The principle is of such generality that it needs no elaboration. It is implicit in our own conception of legal minority until the age of 21. The Chinese parallel to the African examples cited is, however, worth attention. Freedman comments that a married son was potentially a *pater-familias*, but "could realize this status to the full only at the expense of his father, either by breaking away from him (which was legally forbidden if the father was unwilling), or by superseding him" (1966: 45).

27. As with the Ashanti mother's brother's right to pawn a sister's child in order to settle a pressing family debt and the correlative right of a father to protect his child by taking him as a pawn in such a case.

28. Cf. Firth, 1936: 527–30. A comparable African practice is reported for the Kipsigis. I am indebted to Sally Falk Moore for the following reference which is well worth quoting in full: "When an uncircumcised girl is found to be pregnant . . . At the day of parturition . . . Immediately the child's head appears, the old woman who is assisting the girl crams its mouth and nose with mud, so that it may not utter a single cry. If it does, it is considered that all the precautions have been wasted and that the girl is disgraced. This is so, because the child is said to begin life with the first breath of air it draws into its lungs; as it is believed that the spirit of its ancestor also enters its body by the same way. It is this ancestor that the nurse is trying to prevent from entering the child's body; and that is why she tries to stifle the first cry. . . . If this operation has succeeded, the child is said never to have lived, and no disgrace is attached to the girl" (Peristiany, 1939: 53). It has, of course, been well known ever since Carr-Saunders's famous survey, *The Population Problem* (1922), that abortion and infanticide were very widely practiced as means of population control for economic or social reasons among peoples as widely separated in culture and in space as the Eskimo and Chinese and Japanese. I refer to these practices here, however, not for their demographic significance but to illustrate the rights and duties vested in parents by reason of the fact that they become legitimate parents.

parts of West Africa, may be regarded as necessary for the sake of the preserved children.

It is part of the same scheme of reciprocities that where filial inheritance and succession is the rule, potential heirs are obliged to support their parents during their lifetime and, in particular, to perform their obsequies at death.[29] Where ancestor worship prevails, the claims of parents to economic support, respect, and affection during their lifetime are transposed after their death into the onerous and recurrent duties of ritual tendance and sacrificial offerings. The right to inherit may, indeed, be conditional upon accepting such duties of custody of family and lineage sacra.[30] Our paradigmatic specimens provide examples and many more can be cited.[31]

There is no need to add to this random selection of ethnographical examples in order to make my point. Let me repeat: filio-parental relations are intrafamilially generated but are also invariably encapsulated in a hierarchy of extra-familial structural contexts. Isolating them analytically draws attention to the fact that the arrangements filio-parental relations fall into in a given society, and the ways in which they operate, reflect the regulative effect of extra-familial structural and normative principles on their internal structure and normative patterns. It is this that enables the internal structure of filio-parental relations to be articulated with the external social structure. I should make it clear here, by the way, that in speaking of filio-parental relations, I include under this rubric the relations between maternal uncle and sororal nephew among the Ashanti and in other such systems. It must be remembered that it is not only jural authority over his sister's children that is vested in a maternal uncle, but also responsibilities for them which, in patrilineal systems, devolve on the father, for matrilineal descent, where recognized for jural purposes, perpetuates the brother-sister bond, as Radcliffe-Brown emphasized.[32]

29. This was specifically stipulated in Roman law, as we learn from the *Institutes of Gaius* (bk. II, par. 35) and from Maine's discussion of universal succession. How burdensome this can be is well exemplified in Bradbury's analysis (1965) of Edo mortuary ritual.

30. As Fustel de Coulanges, consistently with the paramountcy he attributed to the worship of ancestors and deities in the structure of the family and gens in Greece and Rome, early emphasized (*The Ancient City*, 1956, English trans. New York: Doubleday Anchor ed: pp. 72–84) Maine's analysis of testamentary succession (1861: ch. vi) shows at length how heirship and responsibility for the family *sacra* were "exactly coextensive" in early Roman society.

31. Cf. the discussion of this theme in J. Goody, 1962: chap. XVII. Cf. also Fortes, 1961 and 1965, where I discuss Tallensi filial piety as indicative of these filio-parental relationships. Cf. also the more complex manifestations of this pattern in Chinese ancestor worship as described by Freedman, 1966: 147–53. A pertinent example comes from the Island of Yap in Micronesia. There, it appears, there is no assumption of a biological relationship between father and offspring, as coitus is believed to be irrelevant to conception. The basis of the patrifilial relationship, Schneider reports, is that "the father feeds the child first and creates a debt; the child pays the debt by feeding the father when the child is grown." So central is this reciprocity to the patrifilial relationship that if an old man with no one to care for him is brought food by a young man the latter "thereby becomes his son and inherits the old man's land" (Schneider, 1962: 14, and 6).

32. And it is not only in matrilineal systems that the sibling bond is perpetuated through filio-parental relations. It is a significant element in Australian kinship and marriage institutions, as we have seen, and in the patrilineal avunculate. The wider implications of this factor are persuasively discussed in Sally Falk Moore's comparative study (1964).

VII

The juxtaposition in early Roman law of agnation and cognation provides a useful model of the analytical situation. Justinian's formula is: "Agnates are those cognates who trace their relationship through males, or, in other words, who are cognate through their respective fathers" (*Institutes of Justinian*, bk. 3, title 2). Taking this simply at its face value, we may infer that agnation is regarded as an attribute super-added to the natural bond of cognation, which is the same for both parents.[33] What then is super-added? Clearly it is the jural status in civil law I referred to earlier. Legitimate patrifilial cognation is the credential for this status whereas matrifilial cognation is not; and agnation derives from the agnatic jural status of the father. As we know, it can be conferred by adoption, as well as being attainable by cognatic birth. It is denied to an illegitimate child, who is not deemed to be his father's cognate. It is because a man is *his* father's agnate that he can transmit agnation to his son. And the most important feature of agnation is that it constitutes a son's credential for assuming heirship on his father's demise and succeeding to his estate, perhaps to his rank and his eligibility for office, and, in particular, as Maine stressed (see below) to his paternal authority.[34]

If agnation can be attained only by transmission from a father, we must assume that a father derives his agnatic status from the agnation legitimately held by *his* father, and so on. We could say then that agnatic status is transmitted by serial patrifiliation and is attained by right of patrifilial cognation or adoption—that is, by right of a kinship value added to a recognized genealogical connection. There would be no need to establish a pedigree going back to patrilineal male antecedents of the father in order to qualify for agnatic status if this status is critical for, and can be assumed to hold in every case of, legitimate parenthood.

I am not pretending that this analysis represents accurately the theory behind these Roman concepts as jurists understand and expound it. My purpose is simply to demonstrate a principle by means of a clear-cut model; and I am, in fact, doing no more than restating more moderately an argument put forward by Maine. In a well-known passage he writes as follows:

Cognates then are all those persons who can trace their blood to a single ancestor and ancestress; or, if we take the strict technical meaning of the word in Roman law, they are all who trace their blood to the legitimate marriage of a common pair . . . ; but who are the Agnates? In the first place, they are all the Cognates who trace their connexion exclusively through males . . . all who remain after the descendants of women have been excluded are Agnates, and their connexion together is Agnatic Relationship (1861: 142–43).

After some further discussion of this mode of reckoning kinship Maine goes on:

What then is the reason of this arbitrary inclusion and exclusion? Why should

33. Agnation is derived from *agnasci*, "to be born in addition to," according to *Webster's Third International Dictionary*.

34. I am rashly oversimplifying here to suit my exposition, leaving aside all the complex problems of Roman testamentary succession, in regard to which I have no right to speak with confidence.

a conception of Kinship, so elastic as to include strangers brought into the family by adoption, be nevertheless so narrow as to shut out the descendants of a female member? To solve these questions, we must recur to the Patria Potestas. The foundation of agnation is not the marriage of Father and Mother, but the authority of the Father. All persons are Agnatically connected together who are under the same Paternal Power, or who have been under it, or who might have been under it if their lineal ancestor had lived long enough to exercise his empire. . . . Where the Potestas ends, Kinship ends; so that a son emancipated by his father loses all rights of Agnation. . . . If a woman died unmarried, she could have no legitimate descendants. If she married, her children fell under the Patria Potestas, not of her Father, but of her Husband, and thus were lost to her own family (1861: 143–44).

This argument is connected with the contention that the Patria Potestas is a "capacity inherent" in a man's son or son's son (as *suus heres*) "to become himself the head of a new family and the root of a new set of Parental Powers," whereas a woman lacked this capacity and was under the perpetual tutelage of a male guardian. (The argument is developed *in extenso* by Maine, 1861: 147 ff. and modern scholars concur, see Buckland, 187–189.)

Maine's interpretation of "Parental Powers" and heirship would be understood and accepted in African patrilineal systems. What matters is his emphasis on the specific jural, as opposed to the purely genealogical, significance of agnation in contrast to cognation. Not that cognation is in this context jurally void. Women legitimately born were the agnates of their fathers and of their fathers' agnates, by the same rules that made their brothers agnates. In special circumstances they could even transmit their latent agnation. Thus Justinian transferred "one degree of cognation to the ranks of those who succeed by statutory title."[35] The child of a sister could share with the child of a brother the inheritance of their common uncle if the sister and brother were dead and no other sibling of the deceased would accept the inheritance. The principle recognized here was that siblings by the same father are agnates by filiation regardless of sex, and are deemed to be jurally equivalent in certain situations. There are indications, also, that a relationship parallel to agnation was recognized as derived by matrifiliation and transmitted by women. It has been referred to by the term *enation*.[36] The rule of "*paterna paternus; materna maternus*," which stipulated that whatsoever is derived from the father can pass only to a patrikinsman and what comes from the mother only to a matrikinsman, fits in with the recognition of the dichotomy categorized by the opposition of agnation and enation.

Maine, incidentally, appears to dismiss the facts of biological consanguinity as irrelevant. He speaks almost as if he regarded cognation and agnation as purely juridical categories created by the exercise of paternal authority, hence his emphasis on adoption and its opposite, emancipation. This fits in with his exaggerated respect for "legal fictions."[37] It will be remembered that he lauded these fictions as the

35. *Institutes of Justinian*, bk. 3, title 2; cf. again Allen, on cognation, (1958 edn.: 377).
36. From *enasci, enatus*; according to *Webster's Third International Dictionary*, perhaps translatable as "out-born."
37. Which he defined as ". . . any assumption which conceals, or affects to conceal, the fact that a rule of law has undergone alteration, its letter remaining unchanged, its operation being modified" (1861: 25).

earliest of "agencies by which law is brought into harmony with society" (1861: 24), and in particular by "which family relations . . . [could] be created artificially" (1861: 125). He later described this as "one of the most violent of fictions" (1883: 97 [1886 ed.]). But this fiction is derived from and dependent upon the model presented by the facts of natural parenthood and its normative implications, as Robertson Smith clearly perceived.[38] Indeed Maine himself emphasized the same and attempted to resolve the implicit contradiction in his thesis by the argument that:

Kinship, as the tie binding communities together, tends to be regarded as the same thing with subjection to a common authority. The notions of Power and Consanguinity blend, but they in nowise supersede one another (1875: 68).

It was in this connection that he cited (1883: 289) Morgan's discovery of classificatory kinship as a device to bring into the general fold of the kinship community a range of people who would not by their consanguinity belong there.

Morgan, it will be remembered, extolled the Roman system of kinship nomenclature and the juristic diagrams of the relationships as "beautiful and perfect" (1870: 23); the paragon of all descriptive systems. And what he particularly approved of was the "civil law method" of counting degrees of kinship by steps of parentage,[39] as opposed to the later canon law method of counting downwards from a common ancestor (1870: 25–26). Thus in Roman law a first cousin is in the fourth degree of consanguinity to ego and a sibling in the second degree, whereas in canon law first cousins are of the second degree and a sibling is of first degree.[40] The contrast is instructive, for we can see that the Roman method as Morgan understood it is a filiative calculus, whereas canon law uses a generational and descent calculus. The Roman method connects agnatic cousins by demonstrating the convergence of their respective patrifiliative pedigrees in a common grandfather, the canon law method does so by establishing that they have a common ancestor two generations back. By the Roman method a son is a closer agnatic kinsman—and therefore more eligible successor—than a brother; by canon law, as Morgan describes it, a brother is closer because he is nearer than the son to the common source of their agnation. It is a lineage rather than a filiative calculus.

38. Robertson Smith, 1903: 62. Discussing blood brotherhood and adoption, he comments that they are "evidences of the highest value that the Arabs were incapable of conceiving any absolute social obligation or social unit which was not based on kinship; for a legal fiction is always adopted to reconcile an act with a principle too firmly established to be simply ignored."

39. He describes this method as the only logical and consistent one since it counts by acts of generation.

40. By Roman law the reckoning is *ego, pater* (father)—*avus* (grandfather)—*patruus* (father's brother)—*patrui filius* (father's brother's son). In canon law there are two successive steps of descent from a common grandfather to paternal cousins and one step from parent to siblings (Morgan, 1870: 25–26). The classical Chinese system (as I understand it from discussions with Father Paul Chao, and from his unpublished thesis for the M. Litt. degree, Cambridge, 1967) follows a similar method of reckoning by degrees for example in the laws regulating the length of time and modes of behavior required of kin and affines in mourning for deceased kin. Kroeber observes that, "their system shows how a nondescriptive system was made over into a descriptive one by devices different from and independent of our own. . . ." (Kroeber, 1933: 190, see also Lévi-Strauss 1949, chap. 20.)

VIII

This brings us back to siblingship.[41] By either method of reckoning, siblingship connotes common parentage, which, in terms of the calculus of filiation means co-filiation. Siblings have common filiative credentials, and this is what we subsume under the rubric of the equivalence of siblings. That this equivalence *inter se* in the familial domain is graduated by order of birth and modified in accordance with the values attached to difference of sex in a given society is well known and has been amply considered and illustrated in our inquiry. Here it is more relevant to recollect, also, that siblings may be differentiated *inter se* by the calculus of filiation, as bilaterally co-filiate (full siblings), or unilaterally so (half-siblings), as jurally assimilated (step-siblings), or incorporated (adoptive siblings). The kinship concepts, categories and terminologies of the actors reflect these specifications more or less exhaustively in all societies where they apply; domestic residence patterns, economic arrangements, rules of inheritance and succession, the distribution of ritual roles, the tetrad customs and the norms of morality and of sentiment exhibit their working.[42] And, as we know, it is by the generalization of the model that these categories and relevant indices of the credentials they carry, are extended to build up classificatory kinship structures.

Siblingship, however, is not exhaustively specified by reducing it to common filiative credentials vis-à-vis the parents and through them vis-à-vis society at large. The recognition given to degrees of siblingship testifies to this. Co-filiation does not only relate siblings equally and severally to their parents to give rise to equal and common credentials; it constitutes a special and distinctive bond between siblings which is particularly symbolized, like the bond of filiation itself, by incest taboos and avoidances, and which carries a distinctive credential of its own. The relationship of sibling coevality is a factor of social structure in its own right, standing opposed, indeed, to the intergenerational relationship of filiation. This is the point of Radcliffe-Brown's emphasis on the importance of the sibling group in determining the form of a kinship and descent system; for no single factor is so decisive as the cleavage between successive generations.

We have seen that the paramountcy of the sibling bond is crucial to Ashanti social structure; that the ideal of maintaining the sibling bond in successive generations lies behind the Lozi organization of cognatic relations and is implicit in such institutional devices as the Murngin and Walbiri rules for cousin marriages. The Iban explicitly state this ideal as the main motive for cousin marriage among them, and this is characteristic of cognatic systems of this type in which the sibling bond is stressed as the nodal structural relationship in the kindred. We must not, in this connection, be misled by the apparent attenuation of the sibling bond by classifica-

41. Cf. the discussion of this subject in chap. IV.
42. Particularly well illustrated in what Gluckman has called "the house-property complex" among the Southern Bantu (1950: 195), who rigorously differentiate among sibling groups of common paternal origin by matrifiliation in the assignment of property rights and succession rights. Segmentation by matrifiliation, for example in a Tallensi lineage, is of narrower efficacy.

tory "distance" in systems that have classificatory institutions. I have dealt with this at length in considering Firth's arguments on this subject (pp. 61–63). In descriptive systems like the modern Western European type, the classical Roman type, and such well-known ethnographical examples as that of the Eskimo, the question does not, of course, arise. With classificatory terminologies and institutions, too, as we have seen, the model and touchstone is always actual siblingship by co-filiation.

In elaborating on Radcliffe-Brown's statement, I drew particular attention to the jural evaluation that is added to the familial relationship of siblingship. The test lies in the relative status of cross-siblings. The principle at issue is that siblings are mutually substitutable, regardless of sex, for certain jural and associated ritual purposes, primarily in the familial domain, but by virtue of sanctions in the politico-jural domain. Our paradigmatic specimens provide examples. An excellent illustration is the provision I quoted from the *Institutes of Justinian*, according to which, in certain circumstances, children of a deceased brother and sister were regarded as agnates for inheritance purposes to the exclusion of more distant agnates. Here the difference of sex is deliberately set aside by legal enactment. In tribal society, where jural autonomy is restricted and where citizenship is often mediated through descent groups or local groups, variants of this principle are apt to be accounted for by moral and religious norms. I cite again the Southern Bantu institution of the linked brother and sister. Sister's bride-price cattle are earmarked for brother's wife in implementation of the sibling bond, and the relationship is perpetuated in succeeding generations as the basis of mutual rights and claims in cross-cousin marriage and even in regard to property devolved from the cross-sibling. It is expressed also in ritual relations, and of course in the relations of mother's brother and sister's son, as we have previously seen (cf. Radcliffe-Brown, 1950: 53; Schapera, 1950: 142–44). The Lobedu are typical, and there, we learn, that: "The person responsible for the division of the inheritance in property and wives is the eldest uterine sister of the deceased who acts in consultation with her sisters, especially the cattle-linked sister of the deceased" (Krige, 1964: 182).

But a more pertinent example comes from the previously cited Island of Yap (Schneider, 1962: *passim*). Here we find a political system made up of a number of sovereign villages split in two groups of mutually opposed allies, each occupied by a cluster of genealogically discrete and localized patrilineages of narrow span and shallow depth which own tracts of land subdivided for productive use among its male members. In a way reminiscent of the Yakö, everybody also belongs to one of thirty or forty "named, exogamous, totemic matrilineal clans" that are widely distributed across all the villages, never meet as clans, and are associated with sacred places. Whereas lineage unity and continuity are based on "contractually phrased reciprocities" (see footnote 31, p. 266, above) without any assumption of "biological" relationship, matrilineal clans claim common descent "of the same belly" and are united by "undifferentiated solidarity" exactly in the spirit of the principle of amity. Lineages pursue their sectional interests, villages fight if necessary for their autonomy, the matrilineal clans form the basis—again in a manner well exemplified among the Yakö and other African societies—for countervailing "re-integrative efforts" in crisis.

In the framework of this political structure, the unique relationship of brother and sister stands out as a distinctive familial institution backed by general consensus of jural and moral values. Brother and sister have a specially close relationship coupled with mild avoidance. Brothers must protect sisters, but do not share their food with them. But when the brother dies the sister is entitled to all the products of the land her brother cultivated for a period of one year. The deceased's son must see to this, and thereafter he may appropriate the land. The sister's claim is enforceable; she and her children have the right, which a father also has, to dispossess a man from his land if he is disrespectful or commits a serious offense against customary norms. And these rights and obligations, Schneider demonstrates, arise directly from the relationship of brother and sister "embodied in the relationship of filiation," not from their common lineage membership or common matrilineal clanship. Thus, in the absence of a father's sister, it is not a coeval lineage "sister" but the father's sister's children, and in their absence father's father's sister's children, who exercise these rights over the dead man's sons and his land. Furthermore, if there are no males left to inherit, a sister can take over a deceased's land temporarily and pass it on to her sons.

I am reminded of the theory which Tallensi produce to explain the claims and privileges out-married women retain in their natal families and lineages. They say, as I have recorded elsewhere (1945: 148–49), that but for the accident of birth any woman might have been born a man, that is to say, entitled by birth to the status of her brother. In Ashanti, as we have seen, women do sometimes assume the inheritance of a brother and keep it in trust for their sons to prevent its passing out of the *yafunu* group. Among the patrilineal Akwapim cocoa farmers of Southern Ghana, Dr. Polly Hill reports (1963: 117) that women registered as farm owners generally prove to be daughters of the original purchasers "who are representing their non-resident brothers . . . or wives who have been granted usufructuary rights by their husbands—the farms reverting to their husbands' sons on their deaths." These comparisons suggest the interpretation that a Yap sister assumes the status of a deceased brother—in a sense becomes her brother—for the "inter-regnal" year after his death, and thus asserts symbolically the rights that would have come to her if she had been born a man. The "entitlement through a female" to descent status in patrilineal descent groups in Polynesia, noted by Firth (1957b), and "the sacredness of the father's sister" (Firth, 1936: 209) belong to the same category of structural configurations. The other side of this configuration is well represented in the patrilineal avunculate and has previously been considered.

Granted, then, the distinctive character of siblingship, there is another consideration to be taken into account. Whereas like-sex siblings are potentially, if not always actually, identifiable with one another over the whole range of their status capacities and relationships in all domains of social structure, allowance being made for degrees of co-filiation, opposite-sex siblings are likely to be so identifiable primarily and often solely with respect to their familial relationships. The significant factor is the relative jural status of males and females, assessed, of course, in contexts of relationship where they are otherwise equal in standing. Siblingship and the opposed relationship of marriage are the relevant cases.

It will be recollected that Freeman accounts for the absence of distinctions "based on the sex of the speaker" in Iban kinship terminology by the argument that "males and females have equivalent jural rights" (1960: 77). This hypothesis has wider implications. It accounts for the equality of the credentials derived from matrifiliation on the one hand and patrifiliation on the other—and therefore of the kindred connections and the status capacities that go with them—that are distinctive of such cognatic systems. In these systems, males and females have jural parity in all the dyadic cross-sex configurations—as siblings, as spouses, and as parents. The Lozi approximate to this, at any rate at the village level, and in the familial domain. With the Ashanti, brother and sister have jural equality but not husband and wife or pater and mater in relation to their offspring or to each other. The parity is maintained by a balance of jural and moral values buttressed by ritual and mystical beliefs. In patrilineal systems like that of the Tallensi, the disparity is greater still. Neither as sister nor as wife nor as mother does a woman achieve jural equality with her male partner, though she is never, of course, reduced to the status of a chattel.

IX

How then do the credentials bestowed by filiation operate in other contexts than siblingship? Our paradigmatic specimens provide examples. Matrifiliation in Ashanti corresponds formally to matrifiliation among the Murngin and Walbiri. In both cases it automatically transmits certain status attributes of the mother to the offspring, aligning them as if the offspring were an extension of the mother, socially and personally, but at the same time divided from her by the intergenerational cleavage. More specifically, in Ashanti, matrifiliation is the exclusive and indispensable credential for admission to the lineage and thus to the hierarchy of capacities that makes up citizenship. Similarly, among the Murngin and Walbiri, matrifiliation admits to the externally oriented subsection. Differences arise at the next level. In the Ashanti system there is an intermediate step between matrifiliation and the status of citizenship following from lineage membership. Matrifiliation entitles the bearer to descent status, "enation" comparable to agnation in the Roman system, and it is this that confers lineage membership and citizenship. With the Murngin and Walbiri, assignment to a subsection presupposes alternate subsection assignment of the mother and her mother. This is cumulative filiation, in Barnes's terminology, not matriliny or enation. On another level, matrifiliation produces corresponding credentials in both societies, entitling the bearer to specific claims and capacities, such as the claim of a sister's son to marry a mother's brother's daughter.

A similar analysis can be made of the operation of the credentials conferred by patrifiliation in these societies. But let us rather consider the Lozi case. Here, filiation in its primary form, or in the expanded forms of cumulative filiation, is the credential that gains membership of, and therefore citizenship in a mound village. But by contrast with the unilateral value of the filiative credential for citizenship in Ashanti, Lozi filiation is equilaterally valid as a credential for this status. This is where the possibility of choice particularly emphasized by Leach seems to play a part. But it is choice limited to the village sector of politico-jural status. It is like having a choice between different roads that lead to the same place, as opposed to having a choice between different places to go to. We should remember that village membership, with its implied kinship credentials, does not account for all aspects of a Lozi's politico-jural status. Important attributes of citizenship accrue to him indirectly or directly as a subject of the king, and kinship credentials are not the decisive criteria in this regard.

I drew a comparison, earlier, between the Ashanti lineage and the Lozi village. This applies when we consider them from the outside as constituent units in the system of like units that is the basis of the total polity. But let us consider them again from within. An Ashanti once admitted to his matrilineage exercises the capacities of citizenship and personhood ordered to the lineage system *qua* member of his lineage and through its organization. In marriage, for instance, he must obey the law of lineage exogamy and receive sanction from the lineage elders; in fulfilling his political duties to the chiefdom and exercising the corresponding rights, he must act through his lineage. Precise ritual obligations are likewise identified with his lineage membership, and there is a clear-cut dichotomy between these capacities and responsibilities, on the one side, and their complementary counterparts, ordered to his patrifilial connections, on the other.

A Lozi, by contrast, cannot channel all his corresponding capacities, rights and duties, through the single medium of the village system. In choosing a wife, he must reckon degrees of kinship connection to his great-grandparents to ensure that he is not violating prohibited degrees. Membership of the externally bounded, politically discrete village community is of no avail to him as a guide or normative criterion. And this applies to a large range of his activities. Even within the village, certain claims he may wish to exercise, as for instance to succession to the headship, require the support of a pedigree. Such pedigrees may be reckoned omnilaterally, to borrow the useful term introduced by Barnes, that is, by steps of filiation combined without regard to the sex of the parental generation cited at each step. This accords, as we have seen, with the jural equality of the sexes in cognatic systems of this type. Ashanti, it will be remembered, may also have to adduce pedigrees to authenticate certain claims; but it will be a unilateral (that is, matrilineal) pedigree calculated to demonstrate authentic descent from a founding ancestress of the lineage, not specific genealogical connection with particular persons, as among the Lozi. It will be remembered that Lozi who share a single descent name "are not considered to be a group, nor do they have any specific obligations to each other, nor are there any ritual beliefs or practices attached to any descent-names. Nevertheless, people who share a descent-name feel that they are kinsfolk" (Gluckman, 1959: 172).

It is evident that filiation, however it is geared into the social structure, whether complementarily or equilaterally or otherwise, serves comparable if not identical purposes in all societies in establishing the credentials for the assignment of the primary status attributes that are indispensable for participation as a complete person in the processes of social life.

It is worth repeating, incidentally, that the procedure of establishing claims on the basis of cumulative or serial filiation demonstrated by omnilateral pedigrees is not confined to societies with cognatic systems. In societies with unilineal descent groups, it is often the main instrument by means of which individuals and sibling groups selectively organize and exploit the complementary connections in their field of kinship. The Tallensi illustrate this very clearly. A Tallensi patri-sibling group can be internally divided into matri-sibling segments by the usual criterion of complementary matrifiliation. But both patri-siblings and matri-siblings can be individually distinguished in terms of their structural alignment by the secondary elaboration of their matrilateral identifications. This occurs, appropriately enough, in relation to the ancestor cult. Two full brothers who are in all other respects equivalent and united can, and normally do, have different assemblages of matrilateral ancestors associated with their respective destiny or divining shrines; and these ancestors, who normally include both male and female forbears, must generally be traced, filiative step by step, through the web of kinship (cf. Fortes, 1945, 1949c, 1959a). Full brothers are thus likely to be differentiated from one another by the fact that they owe ritual service to overlapping but disparate clusters of matrilateral ancestors.

The Lozi model for gaining membership in, or to put it from the other side, of recruiting members to, local or political, or economic, or ritual, units and associations has numerous parallels. With modifications, it appears to be common among New Guinea Highland tribes (cf. Barnes, 1962). Among the Chimbu, for example, individuals and families gain entry, or at least attachment to localized, putatively patrilineal clans, and, conversely, depleted clan groups recruit adherents, by exploiting a variety of kinship connections, built up on initial filiative credentials, preferably agnatic (cf. Brown, 1962). Economic and political rights and claims are established by cumulative filiation over successive generations.

The Chimbu have no constituted political or jural authorities at any level of the social structure. Thus it is not a tribe-wide system of government and law, as among the Lozi, but an extensively anastomosing web of kinship and affinal connections, supported by rules of amity as well as by considerations of self-interest and security, that facilitates the migration and mobility of individuals and families among them.

In Polynesian societies, too, filiation seems to have served as a critical credential for entry into and membership of political and territorial units. It seems, according to Firth's latest description, to have been the primary credential for membership of a Maori *hapu*, either immediately, or, as with the Lozi, as the articulating connection for a cumulative pedigree reckoned through either or both male and female antecedents.[43] The further implications of this will be considered in a moment.

43. This was implied in the conjectural analysis I offered of the *hapu* (1959a). H. W. Scheffler carries the discussion further in his incisive paper (1964) where he demonstrates in particular, in what respects it is misleading to regard the *hapu* as a "descent group" organized in terms of "descent concepts" and indicates how filiation enters into its internal structure. Firth, demurring at first from my interpretation, has recently offered the following explanation (1963: 34): "The key to the effective operation of the *hapu* as a corporate group lay in the mechanism for sloughing off potential members. Although a person was entitled to claim membership of a *hapu* through either father or mother, this entitlement was only in the nature of a claim which had to be validated by social action. On the one hand, it required effective acceptance by the body of the members of the *hapu* with whom he or she would have to live, or at least exercise land rights and other rights in common. The most definite mode of social action for validating one's *hapu* claim was, of course, residence. Residence alone without consanguineal kin tie was invalid." A clearer statement of the way filiative credentials and pedigrees serve to gain admission to a "group" but not to fix its boundaries could hardly have been devised.

CHAPTER XIV

Descent and the Corporate Group

I

So far I have considered filiation as the primary credential or set of credentials for activating the initial status relationship of what must necessarily expand into a hierarchy of status relationships for a person to be a complete right- and duty-bearing unit in his society. In contrast to the systems hitherto considered, a system in which simple filiation is the sole and exclusive source of full civic, moral, and ritual status would be one in which no cognizance is taken of ancestry antecedent to the parents for any social purposes. Rights over persons and in property, inheritance and succession, ritual alignments and duties, all such material and institutional representations of status capacities would be determined solely by the recognized relationship of children to their parents. Some features of Australian social systems bear this stamp. Caste membership among the Kandyan Sinhalese and, it would seem, the credentials that determine devolution of property from the parental to the filial generation, seem to fit this pattern. The modern Euro-American family also, in most cases, fits this model, as witness the limitation of the incest taboos and normal intestate inheritance to the nuclear family. The entailed estate, which figures so conspicuously in mid-Victorian novels, is unheard of among ordinary English families today.[1]

---

1. But in England, an intestate inheritance can be claimed by descendants through both males and females of the deceased if no nuclear-family kin survive.

However, one of the clearest examples is provided by the Andamanese as Radcliffe-Brown described them (1922: 75–82). The only significant statuses a person could hold among them were those of parents and children, adults and non-adults, and camp members. The freedom with which children were adopted and moved their residence might also be interpreted as requiring ignorance of or indifference to ancestry antecedent to natural parents. The kinship terminology documents this quite precisely. It will be remembered that the Andaman system is not classificatory, that there are no terms for grandparents other than the honorific terms applicable to all older people, and that ego's terms for parents and children denote specifically the physiological relationships between offspring and genitor, on the one hand, and with the "woman who bore him," on the other—"as opposed to merely juridical relationships," says Radcliffe-Brown. In fact the only relationships that exist inside the family, he notes, are those of husband and wife, parents and children and children of the same parents. Lastly, the only marriages definitely forbidden are with a sibling, a parent's sibling, and a sibling's child. It may well be that their primitive hunting and gathering technology, coupled with the severities of their natural environment, compelled the Andamanese to live in small scattered groups for which the best adapted form of internal social organization was the fluid family system they had. These considerations are not, however, germane to my analysis. More directly relevant is the fact that the sole source of social control among them was the ethic of generosity, buttressed by mythology, and implemented through the medium of ritual beliefs and practices. Males and females seem to have had equal standing and responsibility within this domain; and if this is not the basis of the "bilaterality" of their family organization, it is certainly a contributing factor comparable to the more explicit jural equivalence of the sexes among the Iban.

Though the Andamanese did not recognize pre-parental antecedents for the determination of status credentials, this does not mean that they were ignorant of ancestry in the genealogical sense. They could not but have known that their parents had parents, and so on back to the founding ancestors, supernaturally conceived though they were, referred to in their mythology (Radcliffe-Brown, 1922: chap. IV). In this sense, they might be said to have had a notion of descent. But this is quite a different matter from rules and procedures for the recognition of pre-parental antecedents in the ordering of social relations. Elementary as this point is, it has been one source of confusion in the current controversies revolving around the concept of descent. The main source of confusion has been the failure to discriminate between the observer's construct and concepts, on the one hand, and the actor's rules and procedures, on the other, as these are related, respectively, to the internal order of particular configurations of social relations, and to their external contexts and functions.

The central issue is whether or not it is appropriate conceptually as well as empirically, to apply the concepts of "descent" and "descent group" to "groups" that have been various described as "non-unilinear" or "bilateral" or "ambilineal," etc., with the implication that these "groups" are exactly comparable with the unilineal descent groups we are familiar with from African models. It is argued that these "groups" recruit their members by "descent" and that they are "corporate" in the same way as the paradigmatic African lineages are.

Goodenough (1955) at the outset, described certain land-owning "groups" in Malayo-Polynesian societies as "non-unilinear descent groups." The significant features adduced are that a person is a member of any such "group" by "descent" through either parent. This entitles him or her to a share of the land and to associated privileges; but, by the same rule of "descent" he is equally entitled to membership in several such groups. Furthermore, membership, for example, in the Gilbertese, *oo*, is not terminated by settlement in a different community or atoll. It lasts for as long as the genealogical ties are remembered. And this morphological pattern is accounted for as a "device" "to meet the problem of land distribution in the face of constant fluctuations in kin-group size."

Following this lead, Davenport (1959) attempted to generalize the thesis. "The term 'descent group' serves equally well for both unilinear and non-unilinear types", he contends. He defines descent as "a way in which statuses are ascribed and/or withheld on the basis of kin relationships"—and the two "types" are alike since "one right of membership" is established "albeit through the exercise of choice rather than automatic ascription . . ." in the non-unilinear type. In addition to "descent," there is a factor of "jural exclusiveness," which determines "whether a status is ascribed by only one of the alternative rules of descent at a time, or is simultaneously ascribable to the same individual by more than one."

Murdock, claiming to follow Goodenough, Davenport, and Firth "in preference to Fortes," adds further ambiguity. His principal interest is to classify the various types of "non-unilinear descent groups," and to examine their connection with the cognatic kinship systems in the framework of which they appear. In spite of his protests, he concedes that:

From the point of view of the core individual or siblingship, the membership of the kindred can be defined in terms of serial links of filiation produced by the ramifying intersection of families of procreation and orientation (1960: 4).

Moreover, contrary to Davenport and in agreement with Freeman and Fortes, he concludes that: "A kindred . . . is not, and cannot be, a descent group," or a corporate group, "because of its lack of discreteness." Specifically, he writes:

Wherever kin-group affiliation is nonexclusive, an individual's plural memberships almost inevitably become segregated into one primary membership, which is strongly activated by residence, and one or more secondary memberships in which participation is only partial or occasional (1960: 11).

He refers to "complementary filiation" in unilineal systems in this connection. Unfortunately, he quite misunderstands the nature of complementary filiation in such systems; it is not merely a question of primary membership (whatever that means) and secondary memberships, presumably of the same kind but different only in degree; it is a question of a complementary structural division by which different kinds of rights and duties, privileges and capacities, are assigned to connections through the two parents. Murdock's conclusion is that "ambilineal descent groups" or "ramages" as he prefers to describe them, are "the precise functional equivalents of lineages" (1960: 11).

The same point of view is expressed by, among others, Eggan, who claims that the Sagada of northern Luzon have "a series of bilateral descent groups, which have certain corporate features and act to a degree like unilateral descent groups ..." except that "any individual is potentially a member of a large number of such groups" (1960: 29-30).

Firth's learned contribution (1960), to my mind merely adds to the confusion. He rejects "the limitation of the notion of descent to unilineal groups alone" (p. 23) and instead proposes a number of what he calls "operational criteria" (p. 26) that mark out "bilateral descent groups" (p. 32) within the total universe of kin relations. Among these is "lineality" of which he states: "By definition in terms of continuity, a descent group cannot be non-lineal. It may be unilineal, double unilineal, bilineal, ambilineal, multilineal" (p. 33)—as to which, one might observe, that it is difficult to conceive of a descent group, being "double unilineal"; what we are familiar with is double unilineal *systems* in which there are "patrilineal" descent groups counter-balanced by complementary "matrilineal" descent groups.

Firth purports to demonstrate his thesis by reference to the Maori *hapu*. His description of this unit has already been noted. His conclusion, as I understand it, seems to be that the essential criteria for describing a "group" as a "descent group" are that it is "continuative," "corporate," and "comprises persons organized and united primarily on a consanguineal kin basis." This makes the *hapu* "as a corporate unit of consanguineal kin selectively organized ... functionally equivalent to a lineage." In detail, the "operational criteria" of "common residence and common exercise of land rights" which "assume common recognition of the significance of certain selected genealogies and the genealogical position of every member of the *hapu* therein," "common socio-economic interests," political activities, and "combination for action in respect of external units of the same kind, as in war," make the *hapu* "a corporate kin group closely analogous in most of its activities to the behaviour of a unilineal kin group."

Corporateness, to Firth, here means conformity to these "operational" criteria.[2] To Murdock, incidentally, it has a different meaning. "On the whole," he says,

I agree with Leach that it would be desirable to return essentially to Maine's original definition of a corporation as an estate comprising rights over persons and various forms of real, movable, and incorporeal property in whose assets a number of individuals share in accordance with their respective statuses (1960: 4).

It is beside the point, perhaps, that this was certainly not Maine's concept of a corporation, either aggregate or sole—the essential feature for Maine was the perpetuity of the corporation assured by the laws of intestate succession, as I shall presently show. To the extent, however, to which a criterion of corporateness is

2. The notion of "operational" criteria is difficult to comprehend. In Firth's usage it appears to be equivalent to institutionalized collective activities and patterns of organization and not, as I think is more usual, to the conceptual and analytical operations by means of which a body of raw data is manipulated and arranged to yield general features. By this definition, River's proposal to limit the concept of descent unilaterally is "operational," whereas Firth's usage is loosely functional.

significant for their position, it is evident that Firth and Murdock are not in agreement, except insofar as they both differ radically from Maine, as we shall see.

The argument for "non-unilinear descent groups," by whatever name particular investigators may wish to call them, so influentially advocated, has not lacked other supporters.[3] It is of course open to any of us to use the terminology of description and analysis that most suits his taste and convenience. But this can impede rational discussion.[4] In company with Freeman, Goody, Leach, Schneider, and others, I regard the diffuse and discursive usage of such key concepts as "descent" and "descent groups" as conducive to analytical confusion as well as to misinterpretation of the empirical data of kinship and social organization. It resembles the confusion that arises from equating "democracy" with the rule of "one man, one vote," so that the "democracy" of a one-party state, in which the citizen has the choice of voting for the ruling part or not at all, can be described as "functionally equivalent" to the "democracy" in which the voter has a free choice between different and opposed parties and policies.

It is not merely a question of going back to the proposal Rivers made and Radcliffe-Brown (1929) later supported, of restricting descent to signify only membership of unilateral descent groups. It is rather a question of establishing analytical isolates which accurately identify the mechanisms and processes of social structure exhibited in these "groups" and thus enable us to locate the principles behind them. Therein lies the merit and attraction of Rivers's proposal to those of us whom Schneider has labeled "descent" theorists,[5] but whose real concern is with analytical rigor in structural analysis. Rivers's definition enables us, to put it at its lowest, to distinguish precisely (as the actors themselves do in words and customary action) between lineage relations, norms, and values, on the one hand, and the complementary relations of interpersonal kinship on the other, now known to us from many societies with unilineal descent groups. Questioning it has played a part in raising the problem of the similarities and differences between unilineal descent group structure and the cognatic groups we have been considering.

I must point out however that I have not myself, either in earlier publications in the present treatise, followed Rivers. On the contrary, in defining descent *by contrast with filiation*, rather than in abstract, externally descriptive terms or by reference to some intangible quality such as "lineality," I define it by reference to a feature of internal structural differentiation and opposition that makes "unilineal descent" only a variety of the general category. To repeat what I have stated elsewhere,

whereas filiation is the relation that exists between a person and his parents only,

3. Davenport (1963) gives references. I am indebted to this paper for its clarification of the central issues in this debate.

4. For, as Alice retorted to Humpty Dumpty, "The question is . . . whether you *can* make words mean so many different things."

5. Schneider, 1965. See his references *passim* to Goody, Leach, Gluckman, and myself. There are enough divergencies among those named, even in their approach to kinship and social organizaton, for it to be doubtful if they can be so closely bracketed as Schneider has done. Nevertheless there is a common core to their theoretical orientations and it is shared by a number of other students in this field, including Freeman, Barnes, and Meggitt.

descent refers to a relation mediated by a parent between himself and an ancestor, defined as any genealogical predecessor of the grandparental or earlier generation (1959a: 207).

I particularly emphasized the importance of a "pedigree" as "the charter of its bearer's descent," and I made it clear that, in my view, such a charter of descent might, for some social purposes, in particular societies, take a "unilineal form," but might elsewhere, or for other social purposes, be constructed by the serial combination of mixed forms of filiation. Descent, in this context, serves as an actor-centered instrument for assignment of rights and status or for establishing interpersonal or intergroup connections, and can vary from actor to actor in a "group" constituted by other criteria (such as co-residence) as in the *hapu*.

It is obvious, of course, that any relationship of descent, and consequently the category of descent, implies as a necessary precondition the relationship of filiation. I have dwelt enough on this in the present discussion; what needs some comment is the converse, that is to say, the implication of descent for filiation. I touched on the positive side in my discussion of agnation, and on the negative side, or absence of considerations of descent, in the relations of filiation, in citing the Andamanese system. The point in question is this: where descent—or, alternatively, cumulative filiation—is jurally recognized, a parent transmits to his children (adoptive, as well as natural, of course) not only credentials created by filiation but credentials that derive from pre-parental antecedents—that can, in other words, only be acquired by virtue of recognized, which means legitimate, connection with these antecedents. Membership in a lineage of the Ashanti type is acquired in this way, so that it could be said without distortion that a person becomes a member of his matrilineage not only by primary right of matrifiliation but also by right of his nepotal relationship to his mother's brother which places him in the lineage. The limitation of certain Ashanti offices of state connected with the kingship to *ohene nana*, grandsons of kings, is an example of status assignment by reference to a pre-parental connection that could be described as a link by descent in the elementary sense. In a patrilineal system like that of the Tallensi, whereas a man transmits both lineage membership and patrifiliation, a woman passes on to her children only the connections with her natal kin and especially her brother which she carries over in her familial status as daughter and sister, not in her lineage status. Hence her children do not observe the totemic taboos of her lineage (see Fortes, 1959a). The central African institution of "positional succession," previously referred to, well illustrates the point. At any one time a person of rank or of seniority in his family or clan might simultaneously hold a number of such positions that have devolved on him by succession to sundry predecessors. Devolution by cumulative filiation rather than by a rule of descent best describes the process. For when such a holder of a plurality of positions dies, these are frequently redistributed (as "corporations sole") among several successors selected in accordance with the relevant genealogical criteria. The same principle is involved in systems of succession and inheritance where patrimonial property passes to a brother and personal property to a son on the death of its holder.

What this amounts to is that where descent, or its analog, cumulative filiation, confers credentials for status and, hence, for capacities, rights, and duties, there a specified parent is both a parent and the repository, as it were, and transmitter, of structurally significant ancestry. This underlies systems of succession exemplified in Tswana chiefship, as I have suggested elsewhere (1959a). It is, however, even better illustrated in the law of succession to the British Crown. Here we can observe, with beautiful clarity, how filiation and descent are contrapuntally coupled in the assignment of credentials for eligibility and succession. For practical purposes, eligibility to succeed to the British throne may be said to be confined to the descendants equally through males and females of King Edward VII, great-grandfather of the present reigning monarch. In theory, however, the entire cognatic stock, to use Freeman's term, of Queen Victoria,[6] that is, all persons, male and female, descended from her through males and females, are eligible. We shall see in a moment why more distant collateral lines are in practice not regarded as eligible.

The politico-jural principle that lies behind this segregation by status and rank of the members of this stock from the rest of British society is the rule, embodied in the laws of the land, that males and females are equal in entitlement to hold the office. More fundamentally, this reflects the structural principle of the jural equivalence of siblings, male and female, subject to a ranking order determined by age and sex. Consequently, male and female eligibles are equally entitled to transmit eligibility to all their offspring.

However, though all the descendants of the reigning monarch's great-grandfather are equally eligible to hold the office, they are not equally in line to succeed. As with Tswana chiefship, and by contrast, for instance, with the Ashanti kingship, the royal eligibles fall into a queue order relative to the throne and in accordance with the general principles of eligibility, according to sex. Thus the firstborn son (who may not be first in order of birth in his sibling group if he is preceded by a daughter) of the reigning monarch stands first in the order of succession. He is followed by his *siblings*, males in order of age first, then females in the same order; then come the siblings of the reigning monarch in sequence according to the same rules; and they are followed in the queue by their offspring arranged in accordance with their ranking parent's seniority. The queue order is determined by the computation of degrees of closeness, not to the truncal ancestor, but to the reigning monarch. The computation is by steps of filiation modified by the rule that males take precedence of equally entitled females in accordance with birth order.

Accordingly, the offspring of the reigning monarch are first in line of succession. If they predecease the monarch, their prior right descends to their offspring, who succeed in their place; if they die without issue, then, when the office is vacant, it is treated as if it has lapsed back a generation and therefore passes by cofiliation to to the next qualified sibling of the last reigning monarch. Failing such a sibling, the office is treated as if it lapses back yet another generation, and therefore falls to the next qualified sibling, if one survives, of the last reigning monarch's grandparent. As opposed to the rule of succession in corporate lineages, co-filiation takes precedence of coeval collaterality by descent; and filiation takes precedence of siblingship.

6. Again, this is a *de facto* limitation, for the roots of the cognatic stock, in theory entitled, go back to the Electress Sophia of Hanover by virtue of the Act of Settlement of 1701.

Place in the queue is transmitted by its holder to his or her offspring and they would take precedence of a deceased parent's junior sibling. Order of precedence by birth and sex ranking in the sibling group thus turns into order of precedence *per stirpes*.

The outcome is that the order of succession at a given time becomes: reigning monarch's sons, daughters, their children if any; if none, then the monarch's male siblings, monarch's female siblings, offspring of these siblings in order (a) of their ranking parent's proximity to the throne by sex and age, and in order (b) of their proximity to their parents by sex and age. The reigning monarch's surviving father's brother is further from the throne than is his own sister's son or daughter; but the children of this uncle are closer to the throne, coming as they do *per stirpes* immediately after their father, than is the next oldest surviving sibling of the reigning monarch's father. This is the "Roman" method of computation, which is consistent with the principle that the Crown is a "corporation sole." The office is not in any sense the possession of the whole cognatic stock regarded as an aggregate; they are not, like all qualified members of an Ashanti lineage, relative to the lineage stool, equally entitled to accede, though they are all equally eligible; nor do they have a voice collectively and exclusively in the selection of incumbents for the office. Indeed, with the passage of each generation, the existing queue gets pushed further back, as it were, until junior stirpes are so far behind that their eligibility becomes *de facto* negligible.[7]

In systems of this sort it is easy to see how filiation and descent are differentiated and complementary criteria for the assignment of rank and status. Eligibility is transmitted, to be sure, in the relationship of filiation; but it is jurally definitive because it is derived from pre-parental antecedents who must have held the office. This qualification is important; a pedigree which does not lead back to the purple at some point is not a charter for descent status in this aggregate. In contrast to the dimension of descent, filiation, operating not as a medium for transmitting descent status but as the direct source of credentials for accession, serves as a secondary principle for differentiating among the eligibles, first, by sibling groups and secondly, by individual rank order.[8]

The parallel with the internal structure of the paradigmatic unilineal descent group is striking. Indeed the parallel goes further, though descriptively such a cognatic stock more closely resembles a "ramage" (in Firth's sense) than a classical lineage. As in a lineage system, the in-marrying spouse is ignored in the assignment of descent status or filiative rank. The difference is that sex of parent, and hence of in-marrying spouse, is jurally irrelevant. This is not a "bilateral" or "ambilineal" or "cognatic" mode of descent transmission. If we must have a word for it, we can perhaps call it co-lineal descent; and fully to understand its form we should have to look into the juristic theory of dynastic continuity epitomized in the principle

7. Cf. the interesting discussion of "dynastic shedding" with particular reference to the British Crown and with comparisons to other dynastic systems, in Goody, 1966: 29 ff.

8. A neat parallel is provided by the rules governing succession to the kingship among the Mamprussi of Northern Ghana. Only sons of previous kings may compete for the office. Sons' sons are strictly excluded. They are specially privileged to hold non-royal offices. Cf. Rattray, 1932: vol. II, chaps. LIX and LX.

that "the king never dies," and demonstrated in the rule that the heir apparent, or designated successor, accedes automatically, immediately on the death of his predecessor. Paradoxically, one might say that in their dynastic capacity royals are neither male nor female but simply bearers of the blood royal; and their spouses, correspondingly, are equally consorts regardless of sex.

From the outside, too, there is a resemblance here to a unilineal descent group. There may at one time have been practical advantages such as obviating competitive struggle for the crown, or ensuring the right kind of training for the office, as well as political expediency, in restricting succession thus by heredity. This however is immaterial. What is significant is that the dynasty is set apart from and in contraposition to the rest of the society. The survival of an hereditary peerage and the existence of a large number of non-regal offices of state emphasize the distinction. Naturally, I am not concerned here with the constitutional and social roles of the monarchy or the dynasty, but only with its morphological position in the social system. And in this context the descent rule operates exactly as it does in unilineal descent systems to segregate exclusively the members of the dynasty from the rest of society. Likewise, as in unilineal systems, every royal sibling group is independently connected by complementary filiation with extradynastic kin through whom credentials translatable into status capacities, familial relations, and even rights of inheritance and succession, are acquired.

In one respect, however, the parallel does not hold. The royal equivalent of citizenship is not mediated in any degree or at any level through dynastic membership.

In this model, then, which I have purposely selected for the unusual light it sheds on descent relationships, it is perfectly appropriate to speak of descent both as a variable of structure from the actor's point of view and as a descriptive concept from the observer's point of view. It does not, let me emphasize again, resemble the Maori *hapu* or the Gilbertese *oo*. Intra-dynastic and extra-dynastic filiation and descent do not have equal value as credentials for office or rank, inheritance and succession, or any other extra-familial capacities associated with filiation; a royal has no *de jure* choice, though *de facto* the children of princesses who do not succeed to the crown, follow their fathers in rank and title.[9]

9. The commonest (but not the only) form of inheritance and succession followed in the hereditary peerage of Great Britain is by primogeniture in the "male line," with the usual provision for next-of-kin male line succession by "Roman" reckoning of degrees, if successors first in line fail. This is different from the rule of "general succession" to eligibility for the monarchy. However, royals by matrifiliation can and do succeed to paternal rank and status in accordance with these rules. They do not thereby forfeit their dynastic status. It should be remembered that traditionally, and in theory, a British peerage is "that hereditary and inalienable quality which ennobles the blood of the holder and his heirs" and may not therefore be alienated from the founder's posterity. The same theory presumably applies to the "blood royal" to an even more exalted degree. Succession to the Crown is governed by laws laid down in the Act of Settlement of 1701. But this makes no provision for a royal by birth voluntarily to relinquish this rank however far down the scale of royalty it may be. It is significant of the nature of this status that when King Edward VIII abdicated in 1936 the Declaration of Abdication Act excluded him and his descendants from the succession. (Cf. *Encyclopaedia Britannica*, 1965: vol. 17, pp. 436–40, *s.v.* "Peerage"; vol. 6, pp. 398–99, *s.v.* "Constitution and Constitutional Law"; and vol. 10, pp. 736–37, *s.v.* "Great Britain and Northern Ireland, Kingdom of.")

II

Thus viewed from the outside, the British Royal Family might plausibly be described as a "group of consanguineal kin" who are "operationally" (in Firth's usage) identifiable as united by their name and their common deference to the reigning monarch, and above all by their common interest in the hereditary office they monopolize. And a corresponding description could be applied to an Ashanti lineage, a Lozi village, a Gilbertese *oo*, a Maori *hapu* and a Kandyan *pavula*, etc. But such a description tells us nothing of value about the principles that determine the internal composition and unity of each of these "groups." Are the members of the Royal Family bound to one another because of their common interest in the Crown, or is it because of the independent stipulation that prescribes the specific form of descent relationship they have with one another as a necessary credential for sharing in this common interest?

The comparative evidence amply cited in this inquiry, let alone the evidence of British history, law, and culture leaves no doubt in one's mind that it is the latter. We are dealing with social systems or with sectors of social systems in which a kinship status, in the general sense, is a necessary and indispensable credential for the assumption and exercise of the relevant role. But the credential must be analytically distinguished from the roles it legitimizes and even from the functions it ostensibly fulfills. The universality of filiation as a primary kinship credential testifies to this. For whatever may be the range of legitimate structural spread that is allotted to the familial domain, filiation is the primary source of the kinship statuses that are socially significant; yet the capacities and roles it subserves vary enormously.

The examples we have considered point indisputably to the conclusion that there are critical distinctions between credentials and qualifications for different types of social capacities and status assignment, as evinced, in part, by membership of specified groups or associations. There are those that are exclusive and exhaustive and those that are contingent and elastic; there are credentials that are, in Linton's terms, ascribed or imposed, and those that are achieved; some that are involuntarily binding and some that are voluntarily utilizable. We cannot do justice to the facts if we fail to make these distinctions. Unilineal descent is only one category of the exclusive, exhaustive, ascribed, and binding credentials that are generated by familial relations. The "bilateral" descent of the members of an endogamous caste is an example of another; and we have seen that co-lineal descent also falls under this rubric.

Nor are these distinctions confined to societies or institutions in which kinship is the basic frame of structure. Max Weber (1947: 139–43) drew a similar distinction between "closed" and "open" groups, associations, and social relations. To become a registered member of the British Medical Association, one must have achieved qualifications which are exclusive, though not exhaustive. To say that someone is a registered member of the British Medical Association implies, automatically, that he has a recognized medical qualification. By contrast, knowing that X is a school-teacher or a salesman or a member of a social club implies no exclusive qualifications.

In these cases the decisive criterion is not a credential or a qualification but the fact of admission to an open profession or organization. In the early years of the Massachusetts Bay Colony from the date of the settlement in 1630, Boorstin tells us, "no one could be a 'freeman' of the colony unless he had been admitted to the church. And only 'freemen' could vote or hold office" (1958: 25). An achieved and in part voluntary qualification was necessary and it made both the church and the polity into a closed system; by contrast, anybody can nowadays, merely by purchasing some shares, become a stockholder in a limited liability company.

It is relevant to add that a registered medical practitioner can give up practice in Britain but does not thereby forfeit his professional capacity. He can, of course, be deprived of his right to practice if he commits a crime or an act of moral turpitude deemed to be incompatible with his profession. This is very like the situation of an Ashanti who never loses his lineage status by absence abroad but can be deprived of it for certain kinds of wrongdoing. A schoolteacher, a salesman, a shareholder is free to relinquish or change his place of work, his occupation, or his holdings at will. Similarly, though the parallel is certainly a bit forced, a Lozi is free to change his mound village allegiance when it serves his interests to do so.

These analogies, far fetched though they may seem, are suggestive. The statement that an Ashanti lineage or the British Royal Family constitutes a "descent group" implies the precise information that these groups are made up of persons whose genealogical relations with one another are exclusively and exhaustively specifiable both by any member and by an informed outsider. Anyone acquainted with the rules of exclusion and inclusion can predict the descent group location of a given person. The critical features of politico-jural alignment and a number of rights and duties, privileges and capacities that follow from this, even patterns of customary behavior and observance that go along with it, can be deductively predicted for the actor.

It is not possible similarly to predict, from a knowledge of his genealogical connections, which particular *oo* a Gilbertese will be a member of, or which mound village a Lozi will choose to reside in at a given time. The significant indices are not genealogical connection or descent pedigree but the extra-kinship location of persons by land tenure, by village residence, by membership in a political community and so forth. Alignment by pedigree does not partition either the universe of kinship or the social structure at large by unequivocal intergroup boundary lines. The equivalents of the lineage boundaries are local, or economic, or political, or religious lines of division. Depending upon how we define "functional equivalence," it is arguable that a land-holding-and-using collectivity like the *oo* and a political community like the *hapu* are functionally equivalent to lineages in systems where control over productive resources and relative political autonomy is vested in them. The parallel I suggested between Ashanti lineages and Lozi mound villages (not, be it noted, bearers of common descent names) implies such a comparison. But the association is not mechanically symmetrical. Equivalence of function in this broad descriptive sense does not predicate identity of internal structure for the "groups" that perform these functions. Comparative studies have surely demonstrated this over and over again.

The conclusion, to my mind, seems inescapable that the differences in the internal structure and in the boundary institutions that distinguish the two paradigmatic types of "descent groups" we have been considering are of critical significance both empirically and analytically. There is some advantage therefore, if only for heuristic purposes, in labeling them differently. Extending Rivers' definition somewhat, we might reserve the term "descent group" for all forms of groups in which membership is determined by an exclusive rule of demonstrable or putative descent, in accordance with a specified form of pedigree, from a truncal ancestor or ancestral pair. This would include not only unilineal descent groups but such truly "bilateral" and "multilineal" descent groups as are typified by endogamous local caste groups or sects, or "co-lineal" dynasties. We might then designate the "non-unilineal" category by the general term "cognatic stocks," bearing in mind that cognatic kindreds are not "groups" in the sense of closed and externally distinguishable social entities. However, such niceties of nomenclature are of little importance compared with the correct understanding of the structural principles that underlie the differences.[10] And the crucial distinction is, surely, that "descent groups" are closed by genealogical or quasi-genealogical criteria, whereas "cognatic groups" are open by genealogical reckoning and are closed by non-kinship boundaries.

What, then, of the flexibility of structure supposed to follow from the freedom of choice that is deemed to characterize membership in cognatic groups as opposed to membership in descent groups? I have previously emphasized that—at the limit of the *terminus a quo* of kinship status—no one can choose his parents; and this establishes certain fixed points in his field of kinship relations for the rest of his life. But what is more relevant is the fact, previously adverted to, that lineage membership, in a system of unilineal descent groups, regulates only a part of a person's nexus of statuses, defines only a selection of his rights, duties, and capacities and engenders only one sector of his total social identity. It is, fundamentally, politico-jural status and the capacities entailed by it in other domains of social life that ensue from lineage membership. To recognize this is of such great importance that it cannot be too often emphasized. Morgan understood the principle very well, as we have seen. Yet we still find anthropologists who think of unilineal descent as a device for neatly sorting all the members of a society (regarded as a population rather than as an organized totality) into discrete "groups," like apples in a stack of boxes.[11] Thus misled, they are apt to fall into the trap of thinking of "cognatic groups" as sorted by contrast into "overlapping" compartments, difficult as it is to imagine such an arrangement. The fault lies again in the analytical ambiguity due to failure to distinguish internal structure from external context and to the fallacy

10. I must confess to a slight feeling of levity in proposing to stick to so humdrum a terminology, seeing what a variety of alternatives the authorities I have quoted have offered. In addition to "non-unilinear" which is rejected by Murdock (1960: 2) as being a "negative" term, we have been offered "ramage" (Firth and others), "sept" and sib" (Davenport), "restricted" and "unrestricted" descent groups (Goodenough), as well as the familiar "bilateral" and "ambilineal." In such a forest of terminology it is easy to get lost, as the controversy we have been tracing out shows. Cf. in this connection Leach's remarks, 1962, and the suggestions made in Forde's comment, 1963.

11. This fallacy turns up in the most unexpected quarters. Cf. for instance Schneider (1965: 46 and 75) where the implication is that he considers unilineal descent to "allocate a whole man to a group."

of interpreting genealogically phrased relations as classifications of individuals, not as designations of status.

To be sure, in lineage-based polities, lineage membership forms the indispensable foundation for a person's social existence; but there are components of personhood and areas of social action that are independent of lineage regulation. (There are even elements of civic status in Ashanti, for example, that are not determined by lineage membership, as we have seen.) In these contexts of social relations and normative rules, there is ample scope for freedom of choice, as in patrilaterally ordered relations and activities among the Ashanti, and in matrilateral and local contexts among peoples like the Tallensi. There are even possibilities of choice within the limits of unilineal and other descent group constraints, as studies in the developmental cycle of domestic and family groups have shown (cf. Goody, 1958; Gray and Gulliver, 1964). The principle involved is well, if somewhat sweepingly stated by Leach when he writes that: *"In all viable systems there must be an area where the individual is free to make choices so as to manipulate the system to his own advantage"* (Leach's italics; 1962: 133).

Freedom of choice for the individual or a group is a matter of degree, and the important question always is: How much choice, and in what context of social structure? Demographic limitations may press a man in an Australian tribe to make what may be considered by the strict letter of the prescriptive rules a "wrong" marriage. Some might interpret this as an act of choice. But, as we have seen, choices of this kind never violate such ultimate rules as the incest prohibitions or the moiety division, and it sometimes seems that what looks like a choice can be as plausibly regarded as a response to inescapable limitations.

The same argument applies to the ostensible freedom of choice permitted to members of an *oo*, a *hapu*, and a Lozi mound village. But we must recognize that the choices thus permitted are subject to quite strict structural constraints of a kind corresponding to lineage regulation. In order to have the citizenship status no free person can dispense with if he is to have access to the sources of his livelihood, a Maori must choose to be a member of a *hapu*, a Lozi must choose to belong to a village, a Gilbertese to an *oo*. These rights to choose thus are guaranteed on one side by the politico-jural system, on the other by the limiting credentials of filiation and descent. To choose in defiance of these constraints would be a breach of law that will be punished judicially or otherwise, as Gluckman has shown at length.

III

This brings us back to an issue we have met with several times already. I refer to the attempts to attribute the forms of kinship and descent institutions found in a particular society or type of society to the influence of exogenous parameters such as the ecological or the demographic or the technological conditions and demands to which the society must adapt. Leach's and Worsley's exercises in this direction have previously been discussed. I return to the subject again because of Goodenough's hypothesis (1955: 80–81) that "non-unilinear descent groups" like the *oo* are functionally adaptive, or were formerly so. "The overlapping memberships" he writes "inevitable with unrestricted descent groups make them an excellent vehicle for keeping land holdings equitably distributed throughout the community." By contrast, where there was abundant land and slash-and-burn agriculture unilocal residence and unilinear groups could develop.

The line of argument is typical, and there is no need to multiply examples.[12] Some writers couch the argument in functionalist terms, emphasizing particular economic or technological variables, as Leach and Worsley do. Others take an historical line, as often as not of a speculative nature, as with Goodenough. Then there are the ecological determinists, for example, those who connect band organization specifically with certain types of environmental limitations and opportunities, as in the well-known studies by Julian Steward and his colleagues. An interesting variant of this position is Sahlins' thesis that: "A segmentary lineage system develops in a tribe that intrudes into an already occupied habitat rather than a tribe that expands into an uncontested domain" (1961: 342).[13]

Different aspects are thus emphasized, but the reasoning leads in the same direction. The structure of the descent and kinship groups found in a given environment or area can be explained as having arisen from, or being adapted to, certain modes of exploiting a specialized ecology or technology of production in response, perhaps, to demographic pressures. I think it would now be generally agreed that the comparative evidence is against assumptions of one-way ecological or technological or even economic determinism in the structure of kinship and descent systems. That there are consistent interrelations between forms of social organization and the exploitation of the natural resources available to a community, the population balance, and the other exogenous variables commonly adduced in these discussions, is generally agreed. It was vividly exemplified in Evans-Pritchard's first book on the Nuer and has frequently been demonstrated since.[14] We can say, if we like, that such consistencies reflect the adaptation of social systems to limiting exogenous factors and conditions. Contrariwise, it might be argued that the economic institutions, the technology, the material culture in general of a tribe, and its utilization of natural resources, can just as plausibly be thought of as the media and instrumentalities through which the social organization "does its job of work," in Eggan's telling phrase.[15] Either point of view accords with the thesis that kinship and descent institutions in particular, and social structure more generally, comprise endogenous, independent variables that are not reducible to exogenous forces and conditions.

With regard to the present context of discussion, we need only bear in mind the very wide range of exogenous conditions in which various forms of "bilateral" or

12. Cf. the exchange between Goodenough and Charles Frake on this subject (1956).
13. Sahlins takes the Tiv and Nuer as paradigmatic cases.
14. As, e.g. by Dunning, 1959, and by Pehrson, 1957, with regard to different types of "bilateral" bands. An impressive unilineal example is provided by Stenning's description (1958) of the interdependence of the family cycle, both in its social and in its demographic aspects, and the composition of their herds of cattle at different stages in the cycle of movement from pasture to pasture among the pastoral Fulani of Northeastern Nigeria.
15. Quoted above, p. 44.

cognatic institutions and groups are found. At one end of the scale we find peoples like the Eskimo and the Bushmen who live in small groups at a precarious subsistence level in harsh environments. But at the other extreme are societies like the Iban and the Kalingas with relatively advanced agricultural economies and technologies, the Kandyan Sinhalese, and the equally populous Lozi with their complex political and jural institutions. It is true, of course, that there are important differences, quantitative as well as qualitative, in the ways that bilateral relationships and norms are implemented in the social structure, among these peoples. Nevertheless the central, endogenous core of the social structure in the familial domain is of the same type for all these peoples and for the Euro-American family system.) This is what we have been trying to understand.

With regard to unilineal systems, I myself indulged in the conjecture that "unilineal descent groups are not of significance among peoples who live in small groups, depend on a rudimentary technology, and have little durable property," and I speculated that they occur "in the middle range of relatively homogeneous, pre-capitalistic economies in which there is some degree of technological sophistication and value is attached to rights in durable property" (1953b: 24).

Subsequent research, in particular among peoples with "bilateral" kinship systems who belong to what I called the middle range, has shown how doubtful is the validity of generalizations such as this. I. M. Lewis's comparative analysis (1965) of six well-known patrilineal systems brings this out cogently. His analysis demonstrates that the only "functional" attribute common to all the lineage systems he has considered is the "jural cohesion" of the lineage. And he particularly considers and rejects assumptions of "simple and invariable correlations" between "descent systems and socio-ecological conditions in an adaptive sense" such as those advanced by Sahlins and Steward.[16] It is necessary to remember, by the way, that Sahlins is by no means alone in the approach he develops. To mention only one other instance, Forde, writing with the authority of a pioneer in the modern analysis of African descent group structure, concluded in 1948 that "particular ecological conditions appear to be prerequisite for extensive proliferation of unilineal kin and the formation of large and successively segmented clans." He particularly emphasized "facilities for continued territorial expansion," but added, also, that many other factors "including pre-existing cultural values and the political pressure of external groups" could affect these processes.

As to the influence of "pre-existing cultural values," we have had plenty of evidence for this. The Nuer, the Tallensi, and the Tiv may be said to think agnatically about social relations, like the Romans and Chinese (cf. Fortes, 1961). The paradigm of patrilineal descent is not just a means of picturing their social

16. Lewis is concerned with Sahlins's interpretation of Tiv and Nuer lineage structure referred to above. Sahlins's earlier and more ambitious study of social stratification in, Polynesia, on the same lines, has also been received with strong reservations by experts on that area. Firth, for example (1961), reviewing the book in which Sahlins's thesis is expounded, is critical of the distinction he draws between "ramages" and "descent lines" and does not accept the correlation he claims to exist between these different types of descent groups and different levels of productivity relative to such factors as the quality and availability of land, population density, etc., on different islands.

structure; it is their fundamental guide to conduct and belief in all areas of their social life. Lienhardt's analysis (1961) of the complex religious ideology and symbolism in which the principle of agnation is projected among the Dinka and, to all intents, deified and worshipped, is but one of a number of recent ethnographical expositions of this aspect of descent rules. Similarly, Ashanti, Ndembu, and Nayar, on their part, think, act, and believe in terms of "dogmas" of matriliny.[17] And when we consider peoples like the Kandyan Sinhalese, the Iban, and the Kalingas, we cannot fail to see how differently kindred-oriented premises of thought and conduct about such matters as the regulation of marriage and of land owning and the management of conflicts and disputes, not to speak of ritual relations with gods and ancestors, are from those of descent-oriented premises. The existence of such cultural biases that cannot be accounted for by exogenous parameters has long been recognized and probably nowhere so richly documented as in the literature of the Australian aborigines.

This makes it all the more important to identify and describe the modes of operation of the elementary mechanisms of filiation, siblingship, and descent that are common to different social systems.

IV

Filiation and descent would probably be accepted as endogenous variables that are predominantly if not entirely independent of exogenous forces. It is not quite so straightforward with another variable that has loomed prominently in both descriptive and theoretical studies of kinship and descent institutions in recent years. The notion of the "corporation," "corporate group," or more generally "corporateness," nowadays enters regularly into every description or analysis of kinship and descent institutions. It is indeed so widely and indiscriminately used that it is in danger of becoming quite otiose. Nevertheless, it represents a feature of such importance for our subject that it cannot be overlooked.

Fried (1957) has drawn attention to the fact that a number of different variables is included in the notion of the corporate group as used by different ethnographers, according to the level of the social and political organization represented in the descent group. And one might indeed question whether there is any uniform basis to the corporateness attributed to a Tiv territorial segment, at one level, and to the Tiv tribe as a whole on the more diffuse level of their political organization. Is the corporateness one might attribute to a Nuer major or maximal lineage, which is not territorially fixed and has no focus of constituted authority, comparable to the corporateness of a sedentary, localized lineage of the Tallensi type with its hierarchical internal structure under a recognized lineage head? And what of the corporateness of a Lozi mound village, or a Maori *hapu* in comparison with that of an Ashanti lineage?

If we ignore the casual use of the term "corporate," as the equivalent of what used

17. Cf. in this connection Victor Turner's studies of Ndembu matrilineal symbolism, e.g., 1962.

to be called the "solidarity" of any ongoing association of persons, there appear to be four main models—or to put it in a different idiom, dimensions—of corporateness that figure in discussion and analysis of the ethnographical data. The first, historically speaking, and the one most commonly cited, is the juristic model derived ultimately from Maine, to which I drew special attention in my 1953 paper (p. 26). The crucial feature for Maine is the principle that "corporations never die." This is the connecting link between the common juristic substratum of the "corporation aggregate" and the "corporation sole," the conjunction of which was to Maine the chief test of his theory of the corporation.[18] The perpetuation of a corporation, aggregate or sole, depends, according to this view, on the transmission from generation to generation of the *universitas iuris*, i.e., the "collection of rights and duties united by the single circumstance of their having belonged at one time to some one person"—the "as it were . . . legal clothing of some given individual"—in other words, his total politico-jural status (Maine, 1881: 173). On this view, it is characteristic of corporations that transmission takes place by "universal succession" at one stroke, so that a person's "whole aggregate of rights and duties" passes "at the *same* moment and in virtue of the *same* legal capacity to the recipient" (Maine, 1881: 174), the legitimate heir or group of co-heirs. To see the implications of this we must understand that the *universitas iuris* in the family corporation was held by the paterfamilias not in his own right, but by virtue of his representative capacity as trustee. His death, therefore, was an "immaterial event. . . . The rights and obligations which attach to the deceased [by delegation, as it were, from their real possessor, the corporation] . . . would attach, without breach of continuity, to his successor," for they pertain in fact to the family, "and the family had the distinctive characteristic of a corporation—that it never died" (Maine, 1881: 179).

18. It is as well to place on record the *ipsissima verba* in view of the misinterpretations that have been made at secondhand of Maine's position. This is what Maine says (1861: chap. V, pp. 122–3 [1888 ed.]) "It [i.e., Ancient Law] is so framed as to be adjusted to a system of small independent corporations. . . . Above all it has a peculiarity of which the full importance cannot be shown at present. It takes a view of *life* wholly unlike any which appears in developed jurisprudence. Corporations *never die*, and accordingly primitive law considers the entities with which it deals, *i.e.*, the patriarchal or family groups, as perpetual and inextinguishable. This view is closely allied to the peculiar aspect under which, in very ancient times, moral attributes present themselves. . . . crime is a corporate act. . . . for, as the family group is immortal, and its liability to punishment indefinite, the primitive mind is not perplexed by the questions which become troublesome as soon as the individual is conceived as altogether separate from the group." In this context it will be seen that there is no reference at all either to an estate or to any so-called corporate activities of an economic or political kind. In the next chapter, discussing the devolution of the *universitas juris*, Maine says (p. 180): "It seems, in truth, that the prolongation of a man's legal existence in his heir, or in a group of co-heirs, is neither more nor less than a characteristic of *the family* transferred by a fiction to *the individual*. Succession in corporations is necessarily universal, and the family was a corporation. Corporations never die. The decease of individual members makes no difference to the collective existence of the aggregate body, and does not in any way affect its legal incidents, its faculties or liabilities. And again (p. 181): "A corporation aggregate is a true corporation, but a Corporation sole is an individual, being a member of a series of individuals, who is invested by a fiction with the qualities of a Corporation. I need hardly cite the King or the Parson of a Parish as instances of Corporations sole. The capacity or office is here considered apart from the particular person who from time to time may occupy it, and, this capacity being perpetual, the series of individuals who fill it are clothed with the leading attribute of Corporations—Perpetuity."

Maine's formulation has a long history behind it, going back to Roman times and medieval juristic theory and I shall return to this subject presently. The important point in his view is that rights and duties, office and property, are not the forces that generate corporations but the vehicles and media through the agency of which corporations express their intrinsic perpetuity. However, it is easy to misplace the emphasis and infer that the critical feature is the "estate," that is the body of rights and duties related to property that is held by the corporation and transmitted by succession.

A second model is the political one derived from Max Weber (1947), as I also noted in 1953. Weber's concept of the *"Verband,"* which his English translators render by the term "corporation," puts the emphasis on the collective and associational character of groups which is secondary to Maine's theory. The critical features for Weber lie in the internal structure of the organization. What distinguishes a group as corporate is that there should be "a person or persons in authority—the head of a family, the executive committee of an association, a managing director, a prince, a president, the head of a church—whose action is concerned with carrying into effect the order governing the corporate group" (p. 146). Such a group must be "closed" or must limit membership and the order governing it may be either autonomous (i.e., "established by its own members on their own authority" [p. 148]) or heteronomous with authority over it being imposed from outside. Thus the "system of order which governs corporate action as such" is "an 'administrative' order" (p. 150).

We can see that one significant distinction between Maine's model and Weber's lies in their structural location. Maine's corporation is corporate in relation to the external political and especially jural order; Weber's refers to the internal political and especially administrative constitution and management of such groups. Both, however, are structural models. For anthropologists, Maine's model has one advantage over Weber's. Whereas the latter's analysis is concerned with modern, capitalistic, and industrial forms of corporate organization as his primary data, the former deals with institutions and norms that closely resemble those of contemporary tribal societies. Combinations of these models are common, however, as Leach's grounds (1961) for describing the Kandyan *variga* as a corporate organization illustrate.[19]

The third model, which fits with Radcliffe-Brown's 1950 position, can best be described as a functionalist model. It is eclectic in composition and appears, on the surface, to stand closest to the ethnographical facts. The case for this point of view is persuasively presented by Befu and Plotnicov in their review of the most characteristic ethnographical examples and theoretical statements: They write as follows:

A corporate group should be characterized by reference to its functions—by referring to it as economically, politically, or religiously corporate. A group without important

19. For ease of reference I quote Leach's exact words: "The *variga* is corporate in that its representative leaders (the members of the *variga* court) ultimately decide who is and who is not a member of the group but also because the *variga*, as an aggregate, has title in all the lands of all the villages comprising the *variga*. . . " (p. 78).

economic, political, or religious functions should be regarded, for heuristic purposes, as "non-corporate" (1962: 314).

They arrive at a classification into eight types of corporate descent groups distinguished by the combination each exhibits of the three main functions. And they correlate these types with three levels of unilineal descent group structure: the "minimal," which tends to emphasize the economic functions; the "local," which emphasizes the political function; and the "dispersed," in which the religious functions predominate. The references here are to unilineal descent group systems, but the point of view easily lends itself to extension to "bilateral" kin groups or local or other aggregates. This is the basis of the claims that "non-unilinear" descent groups, by virtue of residing together or collectively owning and distributing land or associating together in a common religious cult, are functionally equivalent to corporate unilineal descent groups. It is consistent also with this point of view to put the emphasis on the "estate" in defining a corporate group, as Murdock does (cited above, p. 279). It is Firth's emphasis, too, as in his statement that "the prime criterion for definition of a group as corporate is that its members collectively exercise a set of rights and may be subject collectively to a set of duties." Though he accepts continuity as a feature of corporate descent groups he insists that this is "secondary to the exercise of their functions" (1959: 216).

It requires little consideration to see how fraught with difficulty what is here called a functionalist, but might more appropriately be described as an instrumentalist, view is in this context. Tallensi *tendaanas* from the Hills are obliged to meet together annually to inaugurate the Sowing Festival by means of collective ritual; they have collective rights to the animals sacrificed; but by no stretch of the term can they be regarded as forming a corporate group (cf. Fortes, 1936). In England and the United States there are interdenominational and interfaith associations of ministers of religion that meet from time to time to discuss and take decisions on common problems; they undoubtedly perform a valuable religious function, but they, too, could hardly be described as a corporate group. One cannot, as we have previously seen, from their functions alone, make inferences as to the composition of, or rules for recruitment to, any "group"—in particular the institutions that maintain its continuity cannot be inferred from a group's functions. But this, as we shall see, is a critical feature for the definition of corporateness.

Similar objections apply to the criterion of collective rights and duties. Partnerships entail such rights and duties. Male and female age regiments among the Tswana and other Southern Bantu peoples have collective rights and duties, but are not normally described as being corporate.

This brings us to the fourth model. Though it would not be inaccurate to describe it as a variant of the functionalist model, it deserves separate recognition. In effect, it can be linked to Radcliffe-Brown's remarks (1935) about corporations forming themselves on the basis of common interests.

The common interests most frequently invoked as central to the process and to the resulting corporate group structure are generally subsumed in the concept of property. The postulate that forms of property and property relations regulate or determine familial and descent group structure has, as we have seen, been a part of

Morgan's legacy that has had a lasting attraction for anthropologists. More specifically, the hypothesis that corporate group structure is primarily definable in terms of, if not generated by, community of property relations, especially with regard to productive resources, has to many seemed almost self-evident. It is reflected in many studies of land-tenure systems in which "tribal," "communal," and "individual" forms of ownership and tenure are compared and contrasted.[20] It is the basis of a theoretical approach to the study of corporate groups that has been expounded with great learning and ethnographical insight by Dr. J. Goody, and I shall take his version as my first example of the property theory.

Rightly critical of the composite definition of the corporate group put forward by Radcliffe-Brown in 1950, Goody originally proposed to "reserve the term 'corporate,' to distinguish those UDGs [Unilineal Descent Groups] in which rights in material objects are vested, or, more precisely, within which property is inherited" (1961: 5).[21]

This formulation is offered in the context of a classification of double-descent systems. Distinguishing between unilineal systems with complementary descent groups and "full double descent systems" Goody takes the "division of property" as "the fundamental feature around which other differences . . . revolve" (1961: 11). For the full development of this useful and strictly operational analysis, we must however turn to his previously cited book (1962). There it is elaborated with reference, on the one hand, to both the legal and the sociological theory of property

20. Cf., e.g., Meek, 1946: *passim*. Since the above was written, Gluckman's authoritative review of the data and theories relating to rights in land, coupled with a reformulation of his analytical scheme of "estates of holding" has become available in his book (1965: chap. 3). Gluckman's scheme of "estates of holding" is the basis of the distinctions between the productive, the local, and the political dimensions of land and territory which figure in most current analyses of the relations between land holding and corporate group structure. (Cf. Goody, 1962: 297.)

21. Several of the commentators on this paper, notably M. G. Smith, expressed reservations about thus limiting the concept of the corporate group. Goody (in common with Fried, 1957, and many others) maintains that Maine, in contrast to Weber, "thought of a corporation in terms of the ownership and transmission of property" (1961: 5). This strikes me as a surprising misinterpretation, due perhaps to confusing property with the *universitas iuris*. Maine's analysis of "The Early History of Property" in chap. VIII of *Ancient Law*, turns on two propositions. The first is that early law recognizes persons only as members of "families," as continuations of their forefathers and as antecedents of their successors. This is a recurrent theme in his analysis of the corporate group. The second proposition is that early law does not distinguish between the Law of Persons and the Law of Things (Maine, 1861: 250–51 [1888 ed.]). "Families" and "communities" come first and the ownership of property is a concomitant of their collective organization in the same way as are rights in persons. Hence, early law is incapable of recognizing distinctions between classes of property (such as movables and immovables) but recognizes instead distinctions between Inheritances and Acquisition, or as we might say patrimonial and individually acquired property. Quoting Hindu law, Maine says: "The inherited property of the father is shared by the children as soon as they are born . . . the acquisitions made by him during his lifetime are wholly his own, and can be transferred by him at pleasure" (*ibid.*, p. 272). In other words, it is status that determines control over property and not the class of property that confers status. This thesis is further developed in Maine, 1875: 107–12 and *passim*. Maine's analysis, it seems to me, closely fits the Ashanti situation and the other ethnographical examples cited by Goody, but is completely at variance with the conclusions Goody draws from it. My interpretation of Maine's theory and its ethnographical implications is much indebted to M. G. Smith's review of the problem, 1956, especially pp. 60–69.

and, on the other, to a wide range of historical, comparative and first-hand ethnographical data. I shall make no pretense of doing justice to this searching study, for there is in it no aspect of the institution of property that is not minutely examined. I shall try only to pick out its implications for Goody's definition of the corporate group.

Goody regards land as the basic immovable property, but other distinctions between productive and non-productive objects of property are also relevant, and he attaches great importance, moreover, to rights over reproductive resources (1962: 295–303). However, the key to the connection between property and corporate groups, as I understand the argument, lies in the process of devolution, more exactly the "process of intergenerational transmission of property (or what we may call corporate transmission, since holder and heir constitute what is, in many senses, the basic corporate unit of the society . . .", (1962: 311–12). There are many variants of this process, some masked by "lateral" transmission, for example, between siblings or forms of partition among co-heirs; but the critical feature is transmission from ascendant to descendant, normally after the holder's death but also *inter vivos* (1962: 314). Examination of the LoWiili and LoDagaa data as special cases confirms the existence of the principle that stresses the obligation and commitment to keep the basic estate intact (1962: 322–23) within the property-holding corporation (1962: 349–53). These are in part obligations to the dead ancestors who "continue to belong to the same corporation as their living descendants; indeed they are its most important members' (1962: 328). Thus the necessity to ensure that there is always an heir becomes of paramount importance for the existence of the corporate group (1962: 353–54). Hence: "In the last analysis, these various mechanisms [i.e., for ensuring heirs and successors] are dependent upon the concept of corporation, the idea that all members of the [LoDagaa] matriclan are entitled to share in the dead man's property." To which is added the rider that "The existence of rights held by members of the whole clan in the property administered by each individual is at once the strength of the corporate ties and the subject of internal disputes" (1962: 354). The analysis concludes with a discussion of the religious obligations, in particular, of heirs to their ancestors, exhibited in their responsibility for sacrifices and associated with the notion of succession as an attribute of the continuity of office linked to descent.

Much of this analysis—for example, with regard to the significance of the ancestors, and the shared rights of clan members in the property of individuals, as well as the relations of holder and heir—confirm what other studies of societies with unilineal descent groups in Africa and elsewhere have previously brought to light. What Goody focuses sharply on, however, is the significance of data of this type for the definition of the corporate group. His contention is that what makes a unilineal descent group into a corporate group is the possession, vested in and shared by all its members, of an estate which consists not merely of a bundle of rights in general, but of rights, specifically, in a definable good or array of goods, namely property—above all, that which has productive and reproductive value. But if I follow him correctly, the fundamental reason why property generates corporation is that it is evaluated as a good or goods that must not be dissipated but must be preserved for the benefit of succeeding generations, and which can be and is preserved by being handed on from generation to generation, presumably in perpetuity. Hence, on the one hand, the cognizance taken of ancestors in reckoning descent as well as by way of ritual duty and, on the other, the critical significance of the nuclear unit of corporation, the relationship of holder and heir. I am not sure if this is an adequate and accurate representation of Goody's theoretical position, but it should suffice to show his commitment to the theory of property as the constitutive principle of the corporate group. Except for this emphasis, crucial as it is, the theory is essentially a reformulation of the Maine model, notably in regard to the key significance attributed to succession.

However, though Goody refrains from comparisons with modern business and industrial corporations, one cannot help being reminded of them, and of the Weberian model, as one follows his argument. Modern corporations can, from a layman's point of view, be characterized as systems of ownership, management, and operation of assemblages of property. Continuity resides in the property, not in the relations among themselves over time of the "corporators." Their only connection with one another is through the plant or the mine or the stock they hold.

In this connection it is interesting to reflect on the parallels with the joint stock company discernible also in Leach's analysis of land holding in Pul Eliya. But in this case it would seem that property rights in valuable farm plots, though devolved by hereditary transmission, militate against the development of unilineal descent corporations. To be sure, the agrarian system of Pul Eliya is very different from that of the LoWiili and LoDagaa. But the concern to retain possession of valuable farm land and transmit it to offspring appears to be a common one. Its achievement through such contrasting forms of familial organization and rules of inheritance must therefore cast doubt on hypotheses that account for unilineal descent corporations by common interests in the preservation of farm land and comparable resources through the succession of generations.

There are, in short, intervening variables that have to be taken into account in attempts to explain the connection between property and descent groups. Some striking evidence for this comes from the study of the establishment of cocoa farming in southern Ghana by Dr. Polly Hill (1963) to which I have previously referred. The farmers who pioneered this development at the turn of the century migrated from villages and towns in a relatively small area of Akwapim in southern Ghana to adjacent territory where they bought forest land and established their cocoa plantations. Operating in the same ecological and economic environment, they necessarily followed the same technical and economic practices in growing, processing, and marketing their cocoa. But there was an important difference in the way different farmers organized the enterprise. The area of Akwapim from which they spread out is occupied by two main culturally and ethnically distinct groups. One group of communities speak Guan dialects and have a patrilineal system of descent, inheritance, and succession; the other group are Akan speakers and have the typical Akan matrilineal familial inheritance, descent, and succession system. Though each group tends to live in its own towns and villages, they are closely contiguous and all form part of a single Akan-type state; and except for the difference in their familial systems and descent bias, their traditional culture and modes of life are much the same.[22]

The forest land taken up by the migrant farmers was acquired by purchase from the chiefdoms that owned the land, and for reasons both of economy and of political expediency in negotiating with the chiefdoms, as well as through traditional custom, the land was acquired in blocks. To this end, two contrasting patterns of organization were followed. One, described by the participants as the "company" system, was followed invariably by groups that came from the patrilineal communities. The other, described as the "family land" system, was the normal form for migrants from the matrilineal communities. And though company lands and family lands were often adjacent blocks, contrasting patterns of land holding emerged and have persisted to the present day.

"A company," says Dr. Hill,

consists of a group of farmers who club together for the sole and commercial purpose of buying cocoa-land. Each individual is concerned to buy land for himself and there is never any intention of joint, or communal, ownership or farming. After the land has been acquired from the vendor stool, each individual member is (sooner or later) allotted a strip, measured along one of the boundaries (the baseline), the width of which is proportionate to the sum of money he subscribes. Each member is then free to do whatever he wishes with his strip; he does not even have to retain it for his own use, but may resell the whole, or part, of it to an outsider of his own choice (1963: 39).

Such a company, adds Dr. Hill, has a leader who collects the subscriptions and buys the land. Once it has been divided up, his role lapses, no successor is appointed, and the company dissolves. These leaders were not selected by kinship or political status. They were men who had "qualities of leadership, enterprise and trustworthiness." Likewise their partners, though often from the same town, might also include outsiders, and if brothers or paternal cousins joined the same company, they subscribed independently and held separate strips of land.

The details of how the strips were measured and laid out from the base line need not be considered here. The result, as the maps reproduced by Dr. Hill show, is a block of land divided into a number of parallel strips of varying widths, demarcated by permanent boundaries, and at any one time individually owned. The strip pattern continues and has been preserved by the operation of the rule of patrifilial devolution to sons only, to which I referred in an earlier context. A man's sons inherit by matrifilial sibling groups, if necessary dividing their strip longitudinally in case they do not want to retain it as a joint possession of a sibling group (Hill, 1963: 114–15).

Let us look now at the "family land" pattern (Hill, 1963: 80–85). The procedures for the purchase were the same as for the company. The initiative in this case was often taken by a man of wealth or enterprise. He might buy the land in his own name or with the help of associates who might contribute to the cost. But these

22. These details are taken from David Brokensha's notes (Hill. 1963: Appdx. I. 4, pp. 27–30).

contributions were not regarded as subscriptions in the contractual and commercial sense that prevailed with the company. They had no relation to the area of land that might be allocated to a contributor. In any case, the associates of the leader were normally members of his own *abusua*, that is, matrilineal lineage, mainly close matrikin, supported sometimes by affines who were frequently cross-cousins, and occasionally by sons. Once occupied, the land is never farmed jointly. In accordance with the usual Akan pattern of lineage land tenure, usufructuary rights are allocated to lineage dependants of the founder and are transmitted to their particular matrilineal heirs. No land can be sold or given to a man's son in gift without the consent of the lineage. The head by seniority is always the manager and all the members have some rights of support from the common pool. And if there is no successor to a particular cultivator, or if a parcel of land is abandoned, it reverts to the lineage pool. Most interesting is the pattern of holdings in this sytem. Instead of neat parallel strips, the land is divided into parcels of different sizes and shapes reminiscent of a patchwork quilt.

A final index of these differences is found in the housing arrangements. The patrilineal-strip-farmers string their dwellings along the base line of their land, each house on its owner's strip. The matrilineal group build in compact clusters at one spot on their land. It would be hard to find more convincing evidence of the independence of corporate descent group structure relatively to property and economic requirements; and there are few better examples of the tenacity and adaptability of traditional forms of familial institutions in the face of the advance of a market economy.

We have had evidence of this before, when I cited some recent research among the Nayar. To return to Goody's thesis, an analogous, though not so explicit a position is taken by Gough in her study of the Nayar of Central Kerala (1961: 339–40 ff.). She uses the term "property group" to designate the most cohesive, co-resident, and legally unitary segment of the maximal lineage, which is distinguished by the fact that it is under the authority of a kāranavan, in contrast to the lineages of higher levels of segmentation which are not joint property owning units. It is significant that she also describes the property group as "the main legal unit" in the caste group. She emphasizes the representative function of the kāranavan in relations with the political authorities and other like units. Furthermore, he is legally responsible for his juniors, and the whole group is answerable for a member who commits a caste offense. Corporateness for Gough is obviously not exhausted by property relations, but includes politico-jural and ritual features that seem to weigh equally with it. (Cf. Freedman, 1966: 36–39, for Chinese parallels.)

Among other studies that bear directly on the property theory, the most important is Goodenough's analysis of the Trukese lineage and property system (1951). Goodenough starts with a definition as follows: "Groups that function as individuals in relation to property will hereafter be referred to as corporations." He continues: "Not any group of persons may hold property as a corporation. The Trukese conceive of a property-holding group as composed fundamentally of siblings" (1951: 30–31). In short, the corporation in Truk is an organized kin group whose core and prototype is a group of own siblings (as among the Ashanti and Tallerzi.)

This organized kin group is a matrilineal lineage of recent common ancestry four to five generations back (1951: 66–67) contained within a hierarchy of such groups connected by locality or by putative common ancestry. The lineage is the basic corporate group; ideally it should be localized in its home locality with land to build on and farm, a meeting house for males, and enough women members to perform essential economic tasks (1951: 127). The lineage has full title to plots of land and trees which are severally exploited by its members but revert to the lineage on the user's death, and, as in other matrilineal systems, there is the countervailing bias of making gifts of personal property to own children who may also inherit such property.

Emphasizing the importance of the sibling group, Goodenough observes that, in a corporate sense, "all the members of a lineage are regarded as siblings" in relation to non-members but internally, generation, age, and sex differences are recognized (1951: 73). The corporate property of the lineage is administered by its most senior male member as its head. In these and other respects, for example, with regard to lineage fission, the picture is closely parallel to the patterns of lineage structure and segmentation known from African matrilineal systems. There are analogies, also, in the political level of the "district." A district is made up of a group of mutually independent matrilineal lineages which are supposed to be the patrilineal descendants, as corporate units, of the chiefly lineage, the head of which is responsible for the welfare of his district like a father for his children (1951: 138). This is an instructive application (emphasizing the corporate "individuality," in Goodenough's terminology, of the lineage) of the principle of complementary filiation in a politico-jural context to counterbalance the intrinsic separatism of the component descent groups. There are other interconnections between lineages in different localities, but what Goodenough particularly insists on is that the lineage is "the cornerstone of the social structure" and that it is a corporation distinguished by the fact that it owns property and is perpetuated by matrilineal descent based on the sibling group as the nuclear corporation. That it is the basis of citizenship is suggested by the observation that: "No individual can exist independent of some lineage affiliation."[23]

Here, I think, we have a rather different presentation of the connection between corporateness and property from that of Goody, one that is closer to Maine and to such African examples as the Ashanti and the Tallensi than to Weber. Here the lineage corporation is shown to be the independent, autonomous, and antecedent variable, and property the dependent one. Property of all kinds can, on Truk, be owned, used, transmitted between generations, and sold in a great variety of combinations of "estates of holding." This has no constitutive effect on the structure and the politico-jural status of the various orders of matrilineal descent groups. The Trukese corporation is, it appears, primarily a unit of politico-jural structure, not a product of property relations. It is not for the sake of creating, preserving, and transmitting an estate that the corporations emerge; on the contrary, they emerge as fixed, enduring, component units of the politico-jural order.

Goodenough's description of the corporation as having "the legal status of an individual"—that is, in relation to like "individuals" in property and other trans-

23. Quoted from Goodenough, 1956, by Schneider, 1961: 214.

actions—is decisive. Underlying it is the principle that the lineage is constituted by the perpetuation by matrilineal descent of the cross-sibling bond; and this is a politico-jural principle, not a function of property relations. It determines membership of a corporation absolutely and exclusively, firstly, in contraposition to like membership, in coordinate units, in a politico-jural system that is based on an association of such units, and, secondly, in complementary balance with other, non-corporational, modes of assigning status to and ordering social relations between persons.

The pattern is the same in principle as among the Nayar, the Ashanti, and the matrilineally organized peoples of Central Africa. The Yao *mbumba*, for example, is a nuclear descent corporation very like the Trukese sibling group.[24] The most revealing case, however, is that of the Plateau Tonga. "A matrilineal group," says Colson,

is a corporate body since it has a common legal personality *vis-à-vis* all other similarly organized bodies. Inheritance, succession, provision and sharing of bride-wealth, vengeance—though to a very attenuated degree today—and a common ritual responsibility, are functions of the group (1958:16).

Tonga "matrilineal groups" range in size from a few adults to around a hundred members and are often widely dispersed. Their genealogical depth varies considerably and tends to be shallow. It is the more significant, therefore, that these groups are regarded as internally undifferentiated for the transmission of rights and status by inheritance and succession. Recruitment by matrilineal descent gives them internal unity, homogeneity and continuity, and their recognition as corporate bodies in external politico-jural and ritual relations and activities is conditional upon this. Considering the moderate subsistence level, the high degree of local and structural mobility, the absence of constituted political authorities and judicial institutions among the Tonga, this is valuable testimony to the power of the dogma of descent as the consolidating principle of corporate group structure.

This description is equally valid for the corporate patrilineal lineage, as among the Tallensi or the Gusii or the Alur. The principle is particularly well exemplified by the Somali institution of the *dia*-payment contract entered into by lineages acting as corporate units vested with politico-jural capacity as autonomous "legal personalities" (cf. Lewis, 1961: chap. 6). In this context, territorial localization can be regarded as a segregative device calculated to affirm the politico-jural autonomy of the corporate lineage vis-a-vis other like units.[25]

To return to the property argument, it is surely indisputable that one and the same

24. The *mbumba*, which Mitchell translates as the "sorority-group," consists normally of a group of sisters and their brother under whose jural control they fall. It is the nucleus of a lineage which goes through a cycle of growth to a three-generation structure, followed by fission and disperion (Mitchell, 1956: 145–52).

25. An excellent example is provided by the Amba of Uganda; cf. Winter, 1958. Cf. also Southall's observation with regard to the Alur that: "The localisation of these lineages clearly re-emphasises their agnatic unity and exclusiveness and turns them into continuously conscious groups. ∴ . . This consistency of the external view of these groups aids their internal consistency and corporate sense . . ." (1956: 48). This principle is fundamental in Tallensi social structure, as I showed at length (1945: esp. chap. XI).

kind of property lends itself to ownership, use, and transmission in a great variety of structural arrangements, for example, by individuals, by partnerships based on contracts that can be dissolved at will, and by corporate groups that are based on non-contractual credentials of membership and are presumed to be indissoluble and perpetual. Conversely, different kinds of property can be dealt with in all of these ways. What is perhaps most open to criticism, I might add, is the elasticity given to the concept of property in the argument. Everything that can be deemed to be owned, from such a non-material possession as a personal name to a large territory, is brought under this rubric.

The value of Goodenough's analysis is that it affords independent confirmation of the conclusion to which the analysis of our paradigmatic specimens has led us. Particular forms of property relations are contingent upon, not constitutive of corporate group structure; and this applies to every aspect of property relations, no matter what may be the customary ways in which title arises and is devolved or disposed of.

We are led back, thus, not only to Maine but to the Roman and medieval jurists and political philosophers whose theories on the nature of the corporation lay behind his researches. My acquaintance with the extensive and specialized scholarship in this field is regrettably superficial; but it is enough to suggest how we might place the conclusions of the present inquiry in a wider analytical perspective. For this purpose there is, to my mind—next to Maine—no better guide than F. W. Maitland.[26]

V

The problem in the forefront of medieval corporation theory was, as Maitland put it, "by what thoughts . . . to distinguish and to reconcile the manyness of the members and the oneness of the body" (1900: xxvii). The problem concerned the whole genus of "corporations aggregate," from the political level of the state to the associational level of the college, the parish, and the guild. The anthropological parallels are obvious, even if we take into account only our paradigmatic specimens. We can say of the Barotse kingdom at one end of the scale and of the Iban *bilek*

26. The medieval theory of the corporation is one of the main themes of Pollock and Maitland, 1895. I am however more particularly indebted to Maitland's own essays on the various aspects of corporation theory in Volume III of his *Collected Essays*, 1911: 210–320. These, together with his introduction to his translation of Gierke, 1900, have been the main stimulus to me.

A representative and extremely useful synopsis of medieval corporation theory is the long excerpt from Gierke's works, entitled "The Idea of Corporation" (in 1961: pp. 611–26). Ernst H. Kantorowicz's profound and fascinating study (1957), though primarily concerned with the intricacies of medieval juristic and theological thought and speculation on the nature of kingship as a corporation sole, is a mine of inspiration from an anthropological point of view. I must add the translation by Ernst Barker of Gierke's *Natural Law and the Theory of Society*, 1500–1800 (1934). There is much to be learned from the translator's review and exegesis in his introduction, but at the abstruse level of this work, Gierke's analysis of medieval corporation theories is too far removed from our ethnographic data to be applicable to the anthropological problems of corporate group structure.

or Walbiri patriline at the other, that, to quote Maitland again, "They seem to be permanently organized groups of men; they seem to be group-units; we seem to attribute acts and intents, rights and wrongs to these groups, to these units" (1900: ix).

The solutions discussed by the medieval jurists revolved around the notion of the "juristic person." Argument raged—and continues in modern jurisprudence—around the question as to whether the "juristic person" is properly to be conceived of as a fictitious legal entity created by the state or "a living organism and a real person, with body and members and a will of its own," as Gierke thought (Maitland, 1900: xxvi). Maitland's compromise is to argue that "what we personify is not the associated group of men but the purpose for which they are associated," and it is on the basis of personified purpose that corporations aggregate, and such corporations sole as the office of the Crown, can be brought together.[27] The significance of adducing "purpose" in this context lies in the implication that corporations have a reality, have capacities to act as units, to exercise rights and fulfill obligations, to sue and to be sued, are even, ultimately, capable of moral and religious wrongdoing, and are not merely a contrivance of the law.[28]

So far, then, transferring the concept of the juristic person to the anthropolgical arena, we could say that it refers to socially recognized entities, that is, either groups organized from within to fulfill defined social purposes, or individuals qualified as if from within, e.g., by birth, to occupy offices that are also endowed from without, with the politico-jural capacities and statuses appropriate to their purposes.

There is, however, another side to this notion which is of direct significance for the anthropological data. It is the idea, as Kantorowicz puts it, of "the identity in succession and the legal immortality of the corporation" with which Maine familiarized us. The point here is that it is not their co-existence as "a plurality of persons collected in one body" that makes a group corporate, but their "plurality in succession," their perpetuity in time. Summing up these ideas, Kantorowicz says that "the most significant feature of the personified collectives and corporate bodies was that they projected into past and future, that they preserved their identity despite changes, and that therefore they were legally immortal" (1957: 310–11).

It is easy to see how closely these conceptions fit our ethnographical data. This may be, in part, because of similar economic patterns, modes of thought and institutions of law and government. A world view bound to the dogma of the descent of all mankind from a divinely created couple of common ancestors, medieval ideas about kingship as personified in the "dignity" represented in the regalia, and the weight given to kinship relations in their social order, have much in

27. Pollock and Maitland, 1895: vol. 1, p. 472. The same point of view is expressed by Barker, 1934: "Translator's Introduction," p. lxxvi.

28. Barker, p. lxxx: "At the end of our argument we are left with a legal world in which there move two sorts of legal persons—the individual legal person, with a legal personality based on the power of purpose which constitutes the essence of an individual; and the group legal person, with a legal personality based on the permanent purpose which constitutes the essence of a group." Both kinds of "legal personality," Barker points out, are in part ascribed by the state.

common with their counterparts in societies such as the Ashanti, the Lozi and the Iban. Be this as it may, it is my contention that the concept of the "juristic person" (taken in a sense free of its more complex jurisprudential refinements) identifies more precisely what is fundamental to the corporation, aggregate as well as sole, as we meet it in our ethnographical data, than does a property, or estate, or functional, or organizational (in Weber's usage) construction.

Our paradigm is the lineage. It is because the lineage, its continuity guaranteed from within by exclusive descent recruitment, is a "juristic person" in its external transactions and status in the politico-jural domain that it has a name, can own property, and must and can act as a unit—to endow with citizenship, or to avenge a wrong done against, any of its members; or to perform the rituals and sacrifices of ancestral and similar cults; or to carry out mortuary and funeral ceremonies for its members or its allies; or to hold and ensure succession to office vested in it. "Thus a lineage," says Evans-Pritchard of the Nuer, in discussing what still remains the classical model, "however far removed from its homeland and however widely separated from its kinsfolk, never becomes entirely absorbed or loses its ritual heritage" (1940: 211). This can be said of descent groups of this kind in many parts of the world. The corporateness of a lineage is shown by its retention of a critical degree of autonomy in external relations, that is, in contraposition to other lineages and to non-lineage contexts of social relations. This is a right sanctioned by the politico-jural organization in the last resort, but the basic condition for this autonomy to be recognized is its internal continuity represented by some notion of common identity analogous to the Ashanti concept of the lineage as "one person" and symbolized very commonly in ritual and mystical beliefs (cf. Fortes, 1953b: 25; and Smith, M. G. 1956: 61).

The notion of a descent group as constituting "one person" takes many forms. The essential idea is that the living plurality of persons constitutes a single body by reason of being the current representation and continuation of a single founder. Whether this is conceptualized and expressed in beliefs about being "the children of so and so," or "of one womb," or "of one blood," or "of one penis," or—more metaphysically—of one spiritual essence or totemic origin, or of common ritual allegiance to ancestors or other supernatural agencies, the implications are the same. The group is one by physical perpetuation and moral identity. This is what links together corporate aggregates as far apart in composition, status, and functions, as the Ashanti lineage and the Walbiri patriline, tenuous as is the corporate quality of the latter in comparison with the former. And this indicates why, as we have several times discovered, the sibling group is commonly regarded as the nuclear, "one person" corporation. For siblings are both a plurality in themselves and by co-filiation a unity. Moreover, they are equal, and a characteristic feature of the corporate group is that its members are equal to one another in jural status regardless of generation, and may be deemed to be representative of the whole group in all external relationships. For this, the sibling group is the perfect model (cf. Fortes, 1945: 32). In descent systems, moreover, it is, as we have seen, the carrier of the descent line and its essential complementary connections. The blood feud in a lineage-based polity, whether or not associated with institutionalized arrangements for alternative compensation through the payment of blood wealth or transfer of persons, is the archetype of how these rules of equality and representation work.

A suggestive pointer to the status of corporate descent groups as juristic persons in a system of corporate groups is found in the weight attached to the relative size of the groups. Where either politico-jural office or important ritual duties are vested in corporate groups, it is not uncommon for a single surviving member of a group to be accepted as its embodiment and representative in relation to other such groups. For just as the individual's personhood cannot normally be terminated except by death or by his removal for other reasons from society, so a corporate group cannot normally be extinguished except by the death of all its members or by its social equivalent, their absorption in other groups. Increasing numbers may of course result in the proliferation of a corporate group. But in a system of corporate groups, proliferation means the multiplication of corporate groups, not the sloughing off of independent individuals.

In corporate groups recruited by credentials of filiation or descent, it is easy to see, as Maine explained, how its members can be thought of as replicating and perpetuating their parents and ancestors, as well as in their turn being the source of identical continuity in their offspring. Where the living are thus decreed by custom to be, and see themselves to be, their progenitors—or at least the jurally and metaphysically significant parts of their progenitors—incarnate, so to speak, extension of the category of the person from the filio-parental relationship to the most distant relationship of actual or presumed kinship is not logically difficult. That is how it comes about that the notion of the juristic person may be extended, in however attenuated a degree, to include the members of a widely dispersed clan, as among the Ashanti and the Alur.

Succession, as all authorities insist, is of key importance in corporate group structure as well as, of course, in the continuity of corporations sole. But it is the instrument for ensuring corporate continuity, given the principle of the corporate identity of organized pluralities, not the foundation of this principle, unless, of course, we subsume the rules of exclusive recruitment under the rubric of succession. With kinship corporations and hereditary offices or statuses, the connection is patent. Its importance is greatest in corporate units of the kind typified by the Iban *bilek*. For the basis of *bilek* corporateness is the headship; filiative recruitment to it is primarily a measure taken both to ensure and to restrict succession to this office in the interest more of preserving the *sacra* of the family than of maintaining its material possessions.[29]

The *bilǝk* is a domestic corporation, but it enables us to understand better the nature of political corporateness as represented in such units as the Lozi mound

---

29. An even better example of a domestic corporation of this type is the Japanese family and *dozoku* group. Befu (1962) demonstrates that the corporate identity of the family centers upon the headship. This explains the exceptional pains taken to ensure competent succession to this office if necessary by adoption (cf. above, p. 256). Befu particularly emphasizes the lack of interest in the blood ties between family heads and their potential successors. Though patrilineal descent and primogenitural succession are the ideals, the critical factor is to find a successor capable of adequately maintaining the family, its name, and in particular its occupation. Property considerations evidently do not count at the family level, and are even less important at the *dozoku* level.

village, the Maori *hapu*, and even an Ashanti chiefdom. In what sense can such units be regarded as comparable juristic persons? The answer lies, I think, in the focal place of supreme office in their structure. From the outside it might seem that it is their territorial boundaries and internal territorial unity that is the basis of their corporateness, corresponding to the descent-bounded unity of the lineage. In fact, it is the ambit of the authority, both politico-jural and ritual, vested in the office of the village chief or, in Ashanti, the stool, that constitutes the boundary of their corporateness. The best evidence for this is the fact that in external relations with other units of the same kind, or with superior political authorities, citizens of these communities can only act in their capacity as citizens (not in private capacities) through their chiefs. The rights and duties, privileges and capacities that accrue equally to all the citizens, or are exercised by them jointly, are validated by their allegiance to the office.[30] Office perpetuated by succession, hereditary or appointive, can serve as the focus for the corporate structure of a heterogeneous or internally differentiated aggregate.

Reduced to its bare essentials, therefore, corporateness, where it exists as a jural category, considered from within, means the perpetuation of an aggregate by exclusive recruitment to restricted membership that carries actual or potential equality of status and mutuality of interests and obligations in its internal affairs. For the corporation sole, it reduces to perpetuation by preordained rules of succession. Considered from without, however, the critical feature is the capacity allocated to a corporate group or office, primarily in the politico-jural domain, to exercise specified rights and fulfill specified duties and responsibilities, either through representatives, or collectively, as a juristic person.[31] Emphasis must be laid on the specification of the rights and duties and responsibilities, for behind each corporator in a corporate group there is still the individual man or woman; behind the king or the chief or the priest there is still the mortal man or woman, moved perhaps by appetite and ambition but, more relevantly, bound also by ties of relationship and loyalty of a personal kind that can at times conflict with the politico-jural and related statuses that pertain to him as a corporator in a particular aggregate, or as holder of an office.[32]

30. The corporateness of the Lele village is of singular interest in this connection. Dr. Douglas (1963: chap. 4) emphasizes especially the role of the semi-hereditary village chiefship as the focus of village continuity and corporate identity in the face of frequently changing composition owing to the mobility of the people. It is rare to find the corporate unity of a heterogeneous aggregate so tangibly displayed and underwritten as in the institution of the village wife and village fatherhood.

31. Maitland, it is of interest to note, quotes with approval the following definition (1900, n. 4, pp. xxxi–xxxii): "Kent, Comment. Lect. 33: 'A corporation is a franchise possessed by one or more individuals, who subsist as a body politic under a special denomination, and are vested, by the policy of the law, with the capacity of perpetual succession, and of acting in several respects, however numerous the association may be, as a single individual.' " This is perhaps as good a general definition as could be devised. More recent authorities use the same criteria in defining modern industrial corporations, cf. e.g., Eells, 1962: 57.

32. The contradictions posed by this disjunction are reflected in the elaborate juristic, political and theological controversies of the middle ages concerning the king's "two bodies" expounded and dissected by Kantorowicz. Though it is not the subject of such sophisticated disputations in African societies, the underlying notion of this dichotomy is patent enough in African institutions of kingship and other forms of high office. Cf. Forde and Kaberry,

We can see now why kindreds in cognatic systems do not emerge as corporate groups. One reason is that they cannot be perpetuated by exclusive recruitment; the other reason is that they have no focus in a perpetual office or its equivalent. They cannot be conceptualized as perpetual persons. The individualistic, erratic, and arbitrary ways in which blood vengeance is pursued among peoples like the Kalingas (the tendency to orient blood vengeance to locally aggregated kindred relatives, the inhibiting effect of intercalary kindred connections, and the emergence of local leaders as mediators) reflect this structural constraint.

Granted the foregoing analysis, there remains one cardinal consideration. Corporations do not exist in a void. They have functions; they normally have names; they have posessions, be it only something as incorporeal as their names or some shared moral privilege like the inter-clan joking partnerships and funeral obligations that are found in both East and West Africa; they have rights and duties. Above all, there is often, and not only in tribal society, a scheme of differentially exclusive associations between corporate groups or offices and divisions of religious cult, or places of worship, or distinctive ritual prescriptions and practices, or metaphysical beliefs, as in some varieties of what is conventionally called totemism. Corporations subserve particular ends in the social life of a people. They have reality, they work and are displayed only by virtue of the customary clothing, as Maine might have said, more generally by virtue of the cultural media and equipment of the society in which they are recognized. We can neither observe nor understand them if we take account only of the form and ignore the contents of their mode of existence. But as I have argued throughout this inquiry, it is essential for an analytical theory of social structure to distinguish consistently and as strictly as our tools of analysis permit between social relations and structural configurations, on the one side, and the innumerable and protean contexts of action, belief, and practice, as well as the natural environment, in which they necessarily and inevitably become manifest.

With reference in particular to the corporate group and its estate, Maine has the apposite formula (1861: 185, 188). The material possessions of the Roman family, he avers, form only "an adjunct or an appendage of the Family"; it is succession that regulates the devolution of the family. "The goods descend no doubt to the Heir, but that is only because the government of the family carries with it in its devolution the power of disposing of the common stock." This could well describe the Iban *bilek*, the Japanese family, and the other types of corporate group we have been considering. What in the last resort constitutes the basic estate of every corporate group is its members, and its most valuable asset is the power and right vested in it by politico-jural (and usually also mystical) sanctions of disposing over them, in the first place for the reproductive ends of maintaining the corporation and, secondly, for productive and defensive ends. The frequent association of corporateness with rules of exogamy or endogamy, and more particularly with the rule of what is commonly called collective responsibility, mark the exercise of these prerogatives in external relations

---

1967. It is fundamental to the institution of the "Divine Kingship," as Evans-Pritchard showed (1948). Cf. also Fortes, 1962b.

with other like bodies and society at large; mourning customs and the jural distinctions between in-group and out-group homicide are frequent indices of their
internal recognition.

My conclusion, then, is that the essential defining characteristic of the corporation,
aggregate or sole, as we meet it in our ethnographic observations, is its endowment
with the status corresponding to that of the "juristic person," as described by jurists
like Maitland. The critical feature is that it is an ideally perpetual "right-and-duty-
bearing unit" in the politico-jural domain. It is by this criterion that the Iban *bilek*,
the Lozi mound village, the Ashanti lineage and the Maori *hapu* can be regarded as
"functionally equivalent" despite the differences between their respective structural
boundaries, and not by reference to their kinship constitution or their control over
property or their internal administrative structure. As to the ultimate source of the
notion of the corporation as a person, Maitland's question as to whether ". . . the
right-and-duty-bearing group must be for the philosopher an ultimate and unanalysable moral unit: as ultimate and unanalysable. . . . as the man" (1911: 319)
shows where the problem lies. What our investigation has shown is that an answer
can at least be attempted if we begin from the foundations of personhood and status
in the domain of kinship and descent institutions and values.

VI

I cannot end this inquiry without a reminder of the limits I have deliberately set
for it. The subject of marriage, or as it is now commonly described, of alliance, is
only adverted to, not systematically considered. This will seem a serious omission
to scholars who regard alliance as the crux of kinship structure. But I do not do so.
My interest lies in the institutions that are indispensable for the continuity through
time without which there can be no ongoing society. Hence I regard the succession
of generations in the process of physical and social reproduction focused in the
relationships of filiation and descent as the keystone of kinship structure. For this
process to go on, institutionalized forms of alliance are not essential. What is indispensable is parenthood, and for this any form of permitted procreative cohabitation is sufficient.

I have refrained, also, from attempting to answer the question that has absorbed
some of our greatest authorities from the time of Morgan until today. I refer to the
question of why—or, more correctly, how it has come about that—some peoples
have patrilineal descent institutions whereas others have matrilineal or double
descent systems and yet others lack kinship institutions of these types altogether. I
have contented myself with arguing that recourse to exogenous determinants or
historical antecedents to account for structural forms is at best of doubtful validity
and at worst utterly fallacious.

The fact is that an analytical method such as the one I have followed is not
calculated to yield answers to questions of this sort. Given its strictly synchronic
frame of reference, it can reveal principles of contemporaneous interdependence and
divergence in the relations of the elements and constituents of a social system at a

given time. It cannot answer questions of historical origins. It can reveal consistencies and covariations over a connected period of time; it cannot provide evidence of unobservable antecedents.

What I have endeavored to demonstrate is that (given its economy and world-view) the social structure of every society has two basic and irreducible dimensions, or, more concretely, that it comprises two basic orders of social relations, institutions, and norms. Familial domain and politico-jural domain, kinship and polity, moral order and legal order are alternative ways of designating this dichotomy of structural features, depending on which aspect one wishes to emphasize. The important point, however, is that these two orders of relations, institutions, and norms are, as I have shown, analytically distinguishable in every society. They may be so fused together in the actualities of conduct and behavior as to be superficially indistinguishable; but closer investigation never fails to differentiate between them.

I have particularly stressed the complementary association of kinship and polity in social structure. This is not adventitious; it is a defining characteristic of their functional relationship. They stand for polar constellations of institutions and social relations that maintain a distinctive structural balance in a given community at a given time. By this I mean not a state corresponding to a mechanical equilibrium, but rather a state analogous to the balance between the genotype and the phenotype of an organism in a given environment. Where kinship is the all-pervasive source of social order, polity may be masked and apparently curbed; but it is, nevertheless, as effective a component of the social order as the genotype is of an organism that may be phenotypically unrecognizable in an adverse environment; and the converse applies where polity is *prima facie* all-pervasive and dominant.

I regard it as now established that the elementary components of patrifiliation and matrifiliation, and hence of agnatic, enatic, and cognatic modes of reckoning kinship are, like genes in the individual organism invariably present in all familial systems. The institutional patterns that emerge in a given social system can be understood as resulting from or reflecting the balance of interdependence and integration, on the one hand, and of divergence and segregation, on the other, arrived at in the tasks assigned to each of these elements. It is a common observation that the balance can vary in opposite directions even in neighboring communities of identical, or at least closely similar culture, living in the same environment and by the same technology. Such geographically graded shifts of structural balance can readily be shown to be consistent with shifts in patterns of government or economic organization, or world-view and to fit the developmental cycle of the family. But as to which is cause and which is effect, or, more generally, as to what lies behind such variations, we are still, I believe, in the realm of guesswork.

The analytical method enables us to delineate the particular balance of kinship and politico-jural variables that underlies the matrilineally centred social system of the Ashanti or the corporate organization of the Lozi village, and to contrast it with the balance reflected in patrilineally centred social systems like that of the Tallensi or cognatic systems like that of the Iban. But as to determining causal agencies, we can but speculate; and, so far, no hypothesis advanced to account for the origin or emergence of these types of structural arrangements, even when recorded historical data are available, has been more than plausible guesswork. As often as not, moreover, the hypothesis is arrived at by recourse to the traditional trick of transposing observable synchronic association into a conjectural diachronic sequence. With regard to these matters, for the time being at any rate, *ignoramus*.

Bibliography

Aberle, David F.
   1961. Matrilineal descent in cross-cultural perspective. In David M. Schneider and Kathleen Gough (Eds.), *Matrilineal kinship*. Berkeley: University of California Press.
Abrahams, R. G.
   1967. *The political organization of Unyamwezi*. Cambridge Studies in Social Anthropology, No. 1. Cambridge: Cambridge University Press.
Ackerman, Charles.
   1964. Structure and statistics: the Purum case. *American Anthropologist*, 66: 53–65. Discussion of "The Purum case." *American Anthropologist*, 66: 1351–1386.
Allen, Carleton Kemp.
   1927. *Law in the making*. 6th ed., 1958. Oxford: Clarendon Press.
Apter, David E.
   1955. *The Gold Coast in transition*. Princeton, N.J.: Princeton University Press. (Revised 1963 as *Ghana in transition*. New York: Atheneum.)
Aquinas, St. Thomas.
   1964. *Ethicorum Aristotelis ad Nicomachum expositio (Commentary on the Nichomachean Ethics)*. Transl. by C. I. Litzinger. 2 vols. Chicago: Henry Regnery.
Aristotle.
   The Politics and Economics. Translated by Edward Walford. Bohn's Classical Library. 1889 ed. London: George Bell & Sons.

Bachofen, Johann Jakob.

1861. *Das Mutterrrecht*. Stuttgart: Krais & Hoffmann.

Bacon, Sir Francis.

1625. Essays (1906 edition). New York: Dutton & Co.

Banton, Michael (Ed.).

1965. *The relevance of models for social anthropology*. A.S.A. monographs No. 1. London: Tavistock Publications. New York: Frederick Praeger.

Barker, Ernest.

1934. Translator's introduction to *Natural Law and the theory of society, 1500–1800*, by Otto Gierke. Cambridge: Cambridge University Press.

Barnes, H. E. (Ed.).

1948. *An introduction to the history of sociology*. Chicago: University of Chicago Press.

Barnes, J. A.

1960. Marriage and residential continuity. *American Anthropologist*, 62: 850–866.

1962. African models in the New Guinea highlands. *Man*, 62 (2): 5–9.

Barnett, S. A. (Ed.).

1958. *A century of Darwin*. London: Heinemann.

Barton, Roy Franklin.

1949. *The Kalingas: their institutions and custom law*. Chicago: University of Chicago Press.

Basehart, Harry W.

1961. Ashanti. In David M. Schneider and Kathleen Gough (Eds.), *Matrilineal kinship*. Berkeley: University of California Press.

Beattie, J. H. M.

1957. Nyoro kinship. *Africa*, 27: 317–40.

1958. Nyoro marriage and affinity. *Africa*, 28: 1–22.

1964. Kinship and social anthropology. *Man*, 64 (130): 101–103.

Befu, Harumi.

1962. Corporate emphasis and patterns of descent in the Japanese family. In Robert J. Smith and Richard K. Beardsley (Eds.), *Japanese culture: its development and characteristics*. Chicago: Aldine Publishing Company.

Befu, Harumi, and Leonard Plotnicov.

1962. Types of corporate unilineal descent groups. *American Anthropologist*, 64: 313–27.

Berndt, Ronald M.

1955. Murngin (Wulamba) social organization. *American Anthropologist*, 57: 84–106.

Bohannan, Laura, and Paul Bohannan.

1953. *The Tiv of Central Nigeria*. Ethnographic Survey of Africa, Vol. 3, part 8. London: International African Institute.

Bohannan, Paul.

1955. Some principles of exchange and investment among the Tiv. *American Anthropologist*, 57: 60–70.

Boorstin, Daniel J.

1958. *The Americans: the colonial experience*. New York: Random House.

Bosman, Willem.

1705. *A new and accurate description of the coast of Guinea*. London: J. Knapton and D. Midwinter.

(Reprinted 1814. In John Pinkerton (Ed.), *A general collection of the best and most interesting voyages and travels in all parts of the world*, Vol. 16. London: Longman, Hurst, Rees & Co.)

Bourret, F. M.

1949. *The Gold Coast: a survey of the Gold Coast and British Togoland 1919–1946.* Stanford, Calif.: Stanford University Press. (Revised 1960 as *Ghana: the road to independence, 1919–1957.* Stanford, Calif.: Stanford University Press.)

Bowdich, T. E.

1819. *Mission from Cape Coast Castle to Ashantee.* London: J. Murray. (3rd ed., 1966, W. E. F. Ward (Ed.). London: Frank Cass. Reprint of 1819 ed.)

Bradbury, R. E.

1965. Father and senior son in Edo mortuary ritual. In M. Fortes and G. Dieterlen (Eds.), *African systems of thought.* London: Oxford University Press.

Braithwaite, Richard B.

1953. *Scientific Explanation: a study of the function of theory, probability and law in science.* Cambridge: Cambridge University Press.

Briffault, Robert.

1927. *The mothers: a study of the origins of sentiments and institutions.* 3 vols. London: Allen & Unwin.

Brookfield, H. C., and Paula Brown.

1963. *Struggle for land: agriculture and group territories among the Chimbu of the New Guinea highlands.* London: Oxford University Press.

Brown, Paula.

1962. Non-agnates among the patrilineal Chimbu. *Journal of the Polynesian Society*, 71: 57–69.

Brown, Robert R.

1963. *Explanation in social science.* Chicago: Aldine Publishing Company. London: Routledge & Kegan Paul.

Bryson, Gladys.

1945. *Man and society: the Scottish inquiry of the 18th century.* Princeton, N.J.: Princeton University Press.

Buckland, W. W.

1925. *A manual of Roman private law.* Cambridge: Cambridge University Press. (Reprinted 1947.)

Burridge, Kenelm.

1960. *Mambu: a Melanesian millennium.* London: Methuen.

Burrow, J. W.

1966. *Evolution and society: a study in Victorian social theory.* Cambridge: Cambridge University Press.

Busia, Kofi Abrefa

1951. *The position of the chief in the modern political system of Ashanti: a study of the influence of contemporary social changes on Ashanti political institutions.* London: Oxford University Press.

1954. The Ashanti of the Gold Coast. In Daryll Forde (Ed.), *African worlds: studies in the cosmological ideas and social values of African peoples.* London: Oxford University Press.

Carr, E. H.

1961. *What is history?* London: Macmillan.

Carr-Saunders, A. M.

　　1922. *The population problem: a study in human evolution.* Oxford: Clarendon Press.

Chao, Paul.

　　1967. *Filial piety and ancestor worship in the context of the Chinese family system.* Unpublished M.Litt. dissertation, University of Cambridge.

Childe, V. Gordon.

　　1951. *Social evolution.* London: Watts & Co.

Christaller, Rev. J. G.

　　1881. *Dictionary of the Asante and Fante language called Tshi (Twi).* (2nd ed., rev. and enl. 1933. Basel: Printed for the Basel Evangelical Missionary Society by Friedrich Reinhardt Ltd.)

Christensen, James Boyd.

　　1954. *Double descent among the Fanti.* Behavior Science Monographs. New Haven: Human Relations Area Files.

Claridge, William Walton.

　　1915. *A history of the Gold Coast and Ashanti: from the earliest times to the commencement of the twentieth century.* 2 vols. London: J. Murray. (2nd ed., 1964, London: Frank Cass.)

Cockcroft, Sir John.

　　1950. Nuclear reactors. In J. L. Crammer and R. E. Peierls (Eds.), *Atomic Energy.* Harmondsworth, England: Penguin Books.

Cohn, Bernard S.

　　1962. Review of *Pul Eliya,* by E. R. Leach. *Journal of the American Oriental Society,* 82: 104–106.

Colson, Elizabeth.

　　1955. Ancestral spirits and social structure among the plateau Tonga. *International archives of ethnography,* 47: 21–68.

　　1958. *Marriage and the family among the Plateau Tonga of Northern Rhodesia.* Manchester: Manchester University Press.

Colson, Elizabeth, and Max Gluckman (Eds.).

　　1951. *Seven tribes of British Central Africa.* London: Oxford University Press.

Constitution and constitutional law.

　　1965. Article in *Encyclopaedia Britannica,* Vol. 6, pp. 398–399.

Crammer, J. L., and R. E. Peierls (Eds.)

　　1950. *Atomic energy.* Harmondsworth, England: Penguin Books.

Cumming, Elaine, and David M. Schneider, 1961. Sibling solidarity: a property of American kinship. *American Anthropologist,* 63: 498–507.

Danquah, J. B.

　　Discipline and inheritance: the dual family system of the Akan people. Unpublished manuscript. Cited by Meyerowitz (1951).

　　1944. *The Akan doctrine of God.* London: Butterworth Press.

Darwin, Charles.

　　1859. *Origin of species.* London: J. Murray.

　　1871. *The descent of man, and selection in relation to sex.* London: J. Murray.

Davenport, William.

　　1959. Nonunilinear descent and descent groups. *American Anthropologist,* 61: 557–572.

　　1963. Social organization. In Bernard J. Siegel (Ed.), *Biennial review of anthropology.* Stanford, Calif.: Stanford University Press.

Debrunner, Rev. Hans W.

1959. *Witchcraft in Ghana: a study on the belief in destructive witches and its effect on the Akan tribes.* Accra, Ghana: Presbyterian Book Depot.

Dixon, Roland B.

1919. Some aspects of the scientific work of Lewis Henry Morgan. In "The Morgan Centennial Celebration" at Wells College, Aurora, N.Y. *Transactions of the N.Y. State Archaeological Association,* Rochester, N.Y.

Douglas, Mary.

1963. *The Lele of the Kasai.* London: Oxford University Press.

Dumont, Louis.

1953. The Dravidian kinship terminology as an expression of marriage. *Man,* 53 (54): 34-39.

1957. *Hierarchy and marriage alliance in South Indian kinship.* Occasional Papers of the Royal Anthropological Institute, no. 12. London: Royal Anthropological Institute.

Dunning, R. W.

1959. *Social and economic change among the northern Ojibwa.* Toronto: University of Toronto Press.

Eells, Richard.

1962. *The government of corporations.* New York: Free Press of Glencoe.

Eggan, Fred.

1937. The Cheyenne and Arapaho kinship system. In Fred Eggan (Ed.), *Social anthropology of North American tribes,* pp. 35-95. Chicago: University of Chicago Press.

1950. *Social organization of the Western Pueblos.* Chicago: University of Chicago Press.

1955. Social anthropology: methods and results. In Fred Eggan (Ed.), *Social anthropology of North American tribes.* 1955 ed. pp. 485-551. Chicago: University of Chicago Press.

1960. The Sagada Igorots of northern Luzon. In G. P. Murdock (Ed.), *Social structure in Southeast Asia,* Ch. 3. New York: Wenner-Gren Foundation for Anthropological Research.

Eggan, Fred (Ed.).

1937. *Social anthropology of North American Tribes* (2nd enlarged ed. 1955). Chicago: University of Chicago Press.

Elkin, Adolphus Peter.

1938. *The Australian Aborigines: how to understand them.* Sydney: Angus & Robertson, Ltd.

Emmet, Dorothy.

1958. *Function, purpose and power: some concepts in the study of individuals and societies.* London: Macmillan.

Evans-Pritchard, E. E.

1933. Zande blood-brotherhood. *Africa,* 6: 369-401. (Reprinted in *Idem,* 1962, Ch. 7.)

1937. *Witchcraft, oracles and magic among the Azande.* Oxford: Clarendon Press.

1940. *The Nuer: a description of the modes of livelihood and political institutions of a Nilotic people.* Oxford: Clarendon Press.

1948. *The divine kingship of the Shilluk of the Nilotic Sudan.* Cambridge: Cambridge University Press.

1950. Kinship and the local community among the Nuer. In A. R. Radcliffe-Brown and Daryll Forde (Eds.), *African systems of kinship and marriage*. London: Oxford University Press.

1951a. *Social anthropology*. London: Cohen and West.

1951b. *Kinship and marriage among the Nuer*. Oxford: Clarendon Press.

1956. *Nuer religion*. Oxford: Clarendon Press.

1962. *Essays in social anthropology*. London: Faber & Faber.

Field, M. J.

1960. *Search for security: an ethno-psychiatric study of rural Ghana*. London: Faber & Faber.

Finley, M. I.

1968. Slavery. *International Encyclopaedia of the Social Sciences*. Vol. 14. New York: Macmillan.

Firth, Raymond.

1929. *Primitive economics of the New Zealand Maori*. London: Routledge & Sons.

1930. Marriage and the classificatory system of relationship. *Journal of the Royal Anthropological Institute*, 60: 235–268.

1936. *We, the Tikopia: a sociological study of kinship in primitive Polynesia*. Preface by Bronislaw Malinowski. London: Allen & Unwin.

1939. *Primitive Polynesian economy*. 2nd ed., 1965. London: Routledge & Sons.

1951. Review of *The web of kinship among the Tallensi*, by M. Fortes. *Africa*, 21: 155–159.

1954. Social organization and social change. *Journal of the Royal Anthropological Institute*, 84: 1–20.

1955. Some principles of social organization. *Journal of the Royal Anthropological Institute*, 85: 1–18.

1956. Ceremonies for children and social frequency in Tikopia. *Oceania*, 27: 12–55. Reprinted in *Idem* 1967. *Tikopia ritual and belief. q.v.*

1957b. A note on descent groups in Polynesia. *Man*, 57 (2): 4–8.

1959a. *Economics of the New Zealand Maori*. Wellington, N.Z.: R. E. Owen, Gov't Printer. (2nd ed., 1929, *Primitive economics of the New Zealand Maori*.)

1959b. *Social change in Tikopia: re-study of a Polynesian community after a generation*. London: Allen & Unwin.

1961. Review of *Social stratification in Polynesia*, by Marshall D. Sahlins, in *American Anthropologist*, 63: 610–612.

1963. Bilateral descent groups: an operational viewpoint. In I. Schapera (Ed.), *Studies in kinship and marriage*. Occasional Papers of the Royal Anthropological Institute, no. 16. London: Royal Anthropological Institute.

1967. *Tikopia ritual and belief*. London: Allen & Unwin.

Firth, Raymond (Ed.).

1957a. *Man and culture*. London: Routledge & Kegan Paul.

Fisher, H. A. L. (Ed.)

1911. The collected papers of Frederic William Maitland. 3 Vols. Cambridge: Cambridge University Press.

Forde, Daryll.

1948. The integration of anthropological studies. *Journal of the Royal Anthropological Institute*, 78: 1–10.

1950. Double descent among the Yakö. In A. R. Radcliffe-Brown and Daryll

Forde (Eds.), *African systems of kinship and marriage*. London: Oxford University Press.

1963. On some further unconsidered spects of descent. *Man*, 63 (9): 12–13.

Forde, Daryll (Ed.).

1954. *African worlds: studies in the cosmological ideas and social values of Africa peoples*. London: Oxford University Press.

Forde, Daryll, and P. M. Kaberry (Eds.).

1967. *West African kingdoms in the nineteenth century*. London: Oxford University Press.

Fortes, Meyer.

1936. Ritual festivals and social cohesion in the hinterland of the Gold Coast. *American Anthropologist*, N.S. 38: 590–604.

1945. *The dynamics of clanship among the Tallensi*. London: Oxford University Press.

1948. The Ashanti social survey: a preliminary report. *Rhodes-Livingstone Journal*, 6: 1–36.

1949a. Time and social structure: an Ashanti case study. In Meyer Fortes (Ed.), *Social structure: studies presented to A. R. Radcliffe-Brown*. Oxford: Clarendon Press.

1949c. *The web of kinship among the Tallensi*. London: Oxford University Press.

1950. Kinship and marriage among the Ashanti. In A. R. Radcliffe-Brown and Daryll Forde (Eds.), *African systems of kinship and marriage*. London: Oxford University Press.

1953a. Inaugural Lecture, *Social anthropology at Cambridge since 1900*. Cambridge: Cambridge University Press.

1953b. The structure of unilineal descent groups. *American Anthropologist*, 55: 17–41.

1953c. Analysis and description in social anthropology. *The Advancement of Science*, 10: 190–201.

1955. Radcliffe-Brown's contributions to the study of social organization. *British Journal of Sociology*, 6: 16–30.

1957. Malinowski and the study of kinship. In R. Firth (Ed.), *Man and culture*. London: Routledge & Kegan Paul.

1958. Introduction to Jack Goody (Ed.), *The developmental cycle in domestic groups*. Cambridge Papers in Social Anthropology, No. 1. Cambridge: Cambridge University Press.

1959a. Descent, filiation and affinity: a rejoinder to Dr. Leach. 2 parts. *Man*, 59 (309): 193–197, and 59 (331): 206–212.

1959b. *Oedipus and Job in West African religion*. Cambridge: Cambridge University Press.

1961. Pietas in ancestor worship. *Journal of the Royal Anthropological Institute*, 91: 166–191.

1962b. Ritual and office in tribal society. In Max Gluckman (Ed.), *Essays on the ritual of social relations*. Manchester: Manchester University Press.

1963. The "submerged descent line" in Ashanti. In I. Schapera (Ed.), *Studies in kinship and marriage*. Occasional Papers of the Royal Anthropological Institute, no. 16. London: Royal Anthropological Institute.

1965. Some reflections on ancestor worship in Africa. In M. Fortes and G. Dieterlen (Eds.), *African systems of thought*. London: Oxford University Press.

Fortes, Meyer, *et al.*

1954. A demographic field study in Ashanti. In Frank Lorimer (Ed.), *Culture and human fertility*. Paris: Unesco.

Fortes, Meyer (Ed.).

1949b. *Social structure: studies presented to A. R. Radcliffe-Brown*. Oxford: Clarendon Press.

1962a. *Marriage in tribal societies*. Cambridge Papers in Social Anthropology, No. 3. Cambridge: Cambridge University Press.

Fortes, M., and G. Dieterlen (Eds.).

1965. *African systems of thought*. Studies presented and discussed at the Third International African Seminar in Salisbury, December 1960. London: Oxford University Press.

Fortes, M., and E. E. Evans-Pritchard (Eds.).

1940. *African political systems*. London: Oxford University Press.

Fortes, Meyer, and Doris Y. Mayer.

1966. Psychosis and social change among the Tallensi of Northern Ghana. *Cahiers d'Études Africaines*, 6: 5–40.

Frake, Charles O.

1960. The Eastern Subanun of Mindanao. In G. P. Murdock (Ed.), *Social structure in Southeast Asia*. New York: Wenner-Gren Foundation for Anthropological Research.

Frake, Charles, and Ward Goodenough.

1956. Malayo-Polynesian land tenure. *American Anthropologist*, 58: 170–176. (An exchange of communications over Goodenough, 1955.)

Frazer, Sir James G.

1890. *The golden bough*. New York and London: Macmillan.

1910. *Totemism and exogamy*. London: Macmillan.

Freedman, Maurice.

1966. *Chinese lineage and society: Fukien and Kwangtung*. London School of Economics Monographs on Social Anthropology, no. 33. London: Athlone Press.

Freeman, J. D.

1953. *Family and kin among the Iban of Sarawak*, unpublished Ph.D. dissertation, University of Cambridge.

1955. *Iban agriculture: a report on the shifting cultivation of hill rice by the Iban of Sarawak*. London: Her Majesty's Stationery Office.

1958. The family system of the Iban of Borneo. In Jack Goody (Ed.), *The developmental cycle in domestic groups*. Cambridge Papers in Social Anthropology, No. 1. Cambridge: Cambridge University Press.

1960. The Iban of Western Borneo. In G. P. Murdock (Ed.), *Social Structure in Southeast Asia*. New York: Wenner-Gren Foundation for Anthropological Research.

1961. On the concept of the kindred. *Journal of the Royal Anthropological Institute*, 91: 192–220.

Freud, Sigmund.

1913. *Totem and taboo*. (Originally published, Vienna: Hugo Heller.) (1950, English transl. by James Strachey. London: Routledge & Kegan Paul.)

Fried, Morton H.

1957. The classification of corporate unilineal descent groups. *Journal of the Royal Anthropological Institute*, 87: 1–29.

Furnivall, John Sydenham.

1948. *Colonial policy and practice: a comparative study of Burma and Netherlands India.* Cambridge: Cambridge University Press.

Fustel de Coulanges, Numa Denis.

1864. *La cité antique.* Transl. by Willard Small as *The ancient city.* Garden City, N.Y.: Doubleday Anchor Books, 1956.

Gellner, Ernest.

1960. The concept of kinship. *Philosophy of Science,* 27: 187–204.

Gibbs, James L., Jr.

1963. The Kpelle moot: a therapeutic model for the informal settlement of disputes. *Africa,* 33: 1–11.

Gierke, Otto.

1900. *Political theories of the Middle Age.* 1927 ed., transl. and with an introduction by F. W. Maitland. Cambridge: Cambridge University Press.

1934. *Natural Law and the theory of society, 1500–1800.* 2 vols. Trans. and with an introduction by Ernest Barker. Cambridge: Cambridge University Press.

1961. The idea of corporation. In Talcott Parsons *et al.* (Eds.), *Theories of society: foundations of modern sociological theory.* Vol. 1, Part 2, D, II, 1. New York: Free Press.

Gluckman, Max.

1941. *Economy of the central Barotse Plain.* Rhodes-Livingstone Paper, no. 7. Livingstone, Northern Rhodesia: Rhodes-Livingstone Institute.

1943. *Essays on Lozi land and royal property.* Rhodes-Livingstone Paper, no. 10. Livingstone, Northern Rhodesia: Rhodes-Livingstone Institute.

1950. Kinship and marriage among the Lozi of Northern Rhodesia and the Zulu of Natal. In A. R. Radcliffe-Brown and Daryll Forde (Eds.), *African systems of kinship and marriage.* London: Oxford University Press.

1955. *The judicial process among the Barotse of Northern Rhodesia.* Manchester: Manchester University Press.

1962b. Les rites de passage. In Max Gluckman (Ed.), *Essays on the ritual of social relations.* Manchester: Manchester University Press.

1963. *Order and rebellion in tribal Africa.* New York: Free Press of Glencoe.

1965. *The ideas in Barotse jurisprudence.* New Haven, Conn.: Yale University Press.

Gluckman, Max (Ed.).

1962a. *Essays on the ritual of social relations.* Manchester: Manchester University Press.

Goodenough, Ward H.

1951. *Property, kin, and community on Truk.* Yale University Publications in Anthropology, No. 46. New Haven, Conn.: Yale University Press.

1955. A problem in Malayo-Polynesian social organization. *American Anthropologist,* 57: 71–83.

1956. Residence rules. *Southwestern Journal of Anthropology,* 12: 22–37.

1961. Review of *Social structure in Southeast Asia* by G. P. Murdock (Ed.). *American Anthropologist,* 63: 1341–1347.

Goody, Esther N.

1962. Conjugal separation and divorce among the Gonja of northern Ghana. In Meyer Fortes (Ed.), *Marriage in tribal societies.* Cambridge Papers in Social Anthropology, No. 3. Cambridge: Cambridge University Press.

Goody, Jack.

1957a. Anomie in Ashanti? *Africa*, 27: 356–363.

1957b. Fields of social control among the LoDagaba. *Journal of the Royal Anthropological Institute*, 87: 75–104.

1958. The fission of domestic groups among the LoDagaba. In Jack Goody (Ed.), *The developmental cycle in domestic groups*. Cambridge Papers in Social Anthropology, No. 1. Cambridge: Cambridge University Press.

1959. The mother's brother and the sister's son in West Africa. *Journal of the Royal Anthropological Institute*, 89: 61–88.

1961. The classification of double descent systems. *Current Anthropology*, 2: 3–25.

1962. *Death, property and the ancestors*. Stanford, Calif.: Stanford University Press.

Goody, Jack, (Ed.).

1958. *The developmental cycle in domestic groups:* Cambridge Papers in Social Anthropology, No. 1. Cambridge: Cambridge University Press.

1966. *Succession to high office*. Cambridge Papers in Social Anthropology, no. 4. Cambridge: Cambridge University Press.

Gough, E. Kathleen.

1959. The Nayars and the definition of marriage. *Journal of the Royal Anthropological Institute*, 89: 23–34.

1960. Caste in a Tanjore village. In E. R. Leach (Ed.), *Aspects of caste in south India, Ceylon and north-west Pakistan*. Cambridge Papers in Social Anthropology, No. 2. Cambridge: Cambridge University Press.

1961. Nayar: central Kerala. In David M. Schneider and E. Kathleen Gough (Eds.), *Matrilineal kinship*. Berkeley: University of California Press.

Gray, Robert F., and P. H. Gulliver. (Eds.).

1964. *The family estate in Africa: studies in the role of property in family structure and lineage continuity*. London: Routledge & Kegan Paul; Boston: Boston University Press.

Great Britain and Northern Ireland, Kingdom of.

1965. Article in *Encyclopaedia Britannica*, Vol. 10, pp. 736–737.

Groves, Murray.

1963. The nature of Fijian society. (Review of *Moala* by M. Sahlins, 1962.) *Journal of Polynesian Society*, 72: 272–291.

Gulliver, P. H.

1964. The Arusha family. In Robert F. Gray and P. H. Gulliver (Eds.), *The family estate in Africa*. London: Routledge & Kegan Paul.

Hailey, Lord.

1938. *An African survey: a study of problems arising in Africa south of the Sahara*. London: Oxford University Press. (1956 ed.; rev., 1957.)

1951. *Native administration in the British African territories*. Part 3. London: H.M. Stationery Office.

Hallowell, A. Irving.

1943. The nature and function of property as a social institution. *Journal of Legal and Political Sociology*, 1: 115–138. (Reprinted in *Idem*, 1954, Ch. 12.)

1954. *Culture and Experience*. Philadelphia: University of Pennsylvania Press.

Harris, Grace.

1962. Taita bridewealth and affinal relationships. In Meyer Fortes (Ed.), *Marriage in tribal societies*. Cambridge Papers in Social Anthropology, No. 3. Cambridge: Cambridge University Press.

Harris, Alfred, and Grace Harris.

1964. Property and the cycle of domestic groups in Taita. In Robert F. Gray and P. H. Gulliver (Eds.), *The family estate in Africa.* London: Routledge & Kegan Paul.

Herskovits, Melville Jean.

1940. *The economic life of primitive peoples.* New York: Alfred A. Knopf.

Hiatt, Lester Richard.

1962. Local organization among the Australian Aborigines. *Oceania*, 32: 267–286.

1965. *Kinship and conflict: a study of an aboriginal community in northern Arnhem Land.* Canberra: Australian National University.

Hill, Polly.

1963. *The migrant cocoa-farmers of southern Ghana: a study in rural capitalism.* Cambridge: Cambridge University Press.

Hoebel, E. Adamson.

1954. *The law of primitive man: a study in comparative legal dynamics.* Cambridge, Mass.: Harvard University Press.

Hogbin, H. Ian.

1934. *Law and order in Polynesia: a study of primitive legal institutions.* Introduction by Bronislaw Malinowski. London: Christophers.

Homans, G., and D. Schneider.

1955. *Marriage, authority and final causes: a study of unilateral cross-cousin marriage.* Glencoe, Ill.: Free Press.

Hutton, J. H.

1946. *Caste in India: its nature, function, and origins.* Cambridge: Cambridge University Press.

Huxley, Julian.

1942. *Evolution: the modern synthesis.* New York and London: Harper & Brothers.

Jacobs, A. C.

1932. Illegitimacy. *Encyclopedia of Social Science.* 1937 and 1957 eds. Vol. 7: 579–586. New York: Macmillan.

Josselin de Jong, J. P. B. de.

1952. *Lévi-Strauss's theory on kinship and marriage.* Leiden: E. J. Brill. (Mededelingen van Het Rijksmuseum voor Volkenkunde, Leiden, No. 10.)

Kantorowicz, Ernst H.

1957. *The king's two bodies: a study in mediaeval political theology.* Princeton, N.J.: Princeton University Press.

Kimble, David.

1963. *A political history of Ghana: the rise of Gold Coast nationalism, 1850–1928.* Oxford: Clarendon Press.

Köbben, André J.

1952. New ways of presenting an old idea: the statistical method in social anthropology. *Journal of the Royal Anthropological Institute*, 82: 129–146.

Kohler, R.

1897. Zur Urgeschichte der Ehe. *Zeitschrift für Vergleichende Rechtswissenschaft,* (Stuttgart), Bd. 11.

Krige, Eileen Jensen.

1964. Property, cross-cousin marriage, and the family cycle among the Lobedu. In Robert F. Gray and P. H. Gulliver (Eds.), *The family estate in Africa.* London: Routledge & Kegan Paul.

Kroeber, Alfred L.

1909. Classificatory systems of relationship. *Journal of the Royal Anthropological Institute*, 39: 77–84.

1933. Process in the Chinese kinship system. *American Anthropologist*, 35: 151–57. Condensed and reprinted in *Idem* 1952, ch. 22.

1939. Basic and secondary patterns of social structure (1938). *Journal of the Royal Anthropological Institute*, 68: 299–309. Reprinted in *Idem* 1952, ch. 26.

1950. The history and present orientation of cultural anthropology. In *Idem* 1952, ch. 17.

1950/1951. Reality culture and value culture. In *Idem* 1952, ch. 18.

1952. *The nature of culture*. Chicago: University of Chicago Press.

Kroeber, Alfred L. (Ed.).

1953. *Anthropology today: an encyclopedic inventory*. Chicago: University of Chicago Press.

Kurankyi-Taylor, E.

1951. *Ashanti indigenous legal institutions and their present role*. Unpublished Ph.D. dissertation, University of Cambridge.

Kyerematen, A. A. Y.

1950. *Inter-state boundary litigation in Ashanti*. Unpublished B.Litt. dissertation, Oxford University.

1964. *Panoply of Ghana: ornamental art in Ghanian tradition and culture*. New York: Praeger.

La Fontaine, Jean.

1962. Gisu marriage and affinal relations. In Meyer Fortes (Ed.), *Marriage in tribal societies*. Cambridge Papers in Social Anthropology, No. 3. Cambridge: Cambridge University Press.

Lawrence, Peter.

1951. *Social structure and social control among the Garia*. Unpublished Ph.D. dissertation, Cambridge University.

1955. *Land tenure among the Garia: the traditional system of a New Guinea people*. A.N.U. Social Science Monographs, no. 4. Canberra: Australian National University.

1965–66. The Garia of the Madang District. *Anthropological Forum*, 1: 373–392.

Leach, E. R.

1951. The structural implications of matrilateral cross-cousin marriage. *Journal of the Royal Anthropological Institute*, 81: 23–55. Reprinted in *Idem* 1961b, ch. 3.

1954. *Political systems of highland Burma: a study of Kachin social structure*. Cambridge, Mass.: Harvard University Press.

1957. Aspects of bridewealth and marriage stability among the Kachin and Lakher. *Man*, 57 (59): 50–55. Reprinted in *Idem* 1961b, ch. 5.

1958. Concerning Trobriand clans and the kinship category *tabu*. In Jack Goody (ed.), *The developmental cycle in domestic groups*. Cambridge Papers in Social Anthropology, No. 1. *q.v.*

1960b. The Sinhalese of the dry zone of Northern Ceylon. In G. P. Murdock (Ed.), *Social structure in southeast Asia*, ch. 7. *q.v.*

1961a. *Pul Eliya, a village in Ceylon: a study of land tenure and kinship*. Cambridge: Cambridge University Press.

1961b. *Rethinking anthropology*. London: University of London, Athlone Press.

1962. On certain unconsidered aspects of double descent systems. *Man*, 62(214): 130–134.

Leach, E. R. (Ed.).

1960a. *Aspects of caste in south India, Ceylon and north-west Pakistan.* Cambridge Papers in Social Anthropology, No. 2. Cambridge: Cambridge University Press.

Lévi-Strauss, Claude.

1949. *Les structures élémentaires de la parenté.* Paris: Presse Universitaires de France.

1953. Social structure. In A. L. Kroeber (Ed.), *Anthropology today: an encyclopedic inventory.* Chicago: University of Chicago Press.

1958a. L'analyse structurale en linguistique et en anthropologie. In 1958b, pp. 37–62. (Originally published in *Word*, 1945, 1: 1–21.)

1958b. *Anthropologie structurale.* Paris: Librarie Plon.

Lewis, I. M.

1961. *A pastoral democracy: a study of pastoralism and politics among the northern Somali of the Horn of Africa.* London: Oxford University Press.

1965. Problems in the comparative study of unilineal descent. In Michael Banton (ed.), *The relevance of models for social anthropology.* London: Tavistock Publications. New York: Frederick Praeger. A.S.A. Monographs, no. 1.

Lewis, I. M. (Ed.).

1966. *Islam in tropical Africa.* London: Oxford University Press.

Lienhardt, Godfrey.

1961. *Divinity and experience: the religion of the Dinka.* Oxford: Clarendon Press.

Little, Kenneth.

1965. *West African urbanization: a study of voluntary associations in social change.* Cambridge: Cambridge University Press.

Lloyd, Peter Cutt.

1962. *Yoruba land law.* London: Oxford University Press.

Lorimer, Frank (Ed.).

1954. *Culture and human fertility: a study of the relation of cultural conditions to fertility in non-industrial and transitional societies.* Paris: Unesco.

Lounsbury, Floyd.

1956. A semantic analysis of the Pawnee kinship usage. *Language*, 32: 158–194.

1962. Review of *Structure and sentiment* by R. Needham. *American Anthropologist*, 64: 1302–1310.

Lowie, Robert H.

1920. *Primitive society.* New York: Boni & Liveright.

1936. Lewis H. Morgan in historical perspective. In R. H. Lowie (Ed.), *Essays in anthropology presented to A. L. Kroeber.* Berkeley: University of California Press.

1937. *History of ethnological theory* (8th printing, 1960. New York: Holt-Rinehart.

1948. *Social organization.* New York: Rinehart & Co.

1959. *Robert H. Lowie; ethnologist.* Berkeley: University of California Press.

Lowie, R. H. (Ed.).

1936. *Essays in anthropology presented to A. L. Kroeber.* Berkeley: University of California Press.

Lubbock, Sir John (Lord Avebury).

1870. *The origin of civilisation and the primitive condition of man.* London: Longmans, Green & Co.

Lystad, Robert A.

    1958. *The Ashanti: a proud people*. New Brunswick, N.J.: Rutgers University Press.

McLennan, John F.

    1876. *Studies in ancient history*. London: Bernard Quaritch. (Comprising a reprint of *Primitive marriage*. 1865. New ed., 1886. London: Macmillan.)

McLeod, Malcolm D.

    1965. *A survey of the literature on witchcraft in Ghana (excluding the Northern Region) with particular reference to the Akans*. Unpublished B. Litt. thesis, Oxford University.

Maine, Sir Henry.

    1861. *Ancient law*. London: Murray. (1888 ed. New York: Henry Holt.)

    1875. *Lectures on the early history of institutions*. London: Murray. (7th ed. 1897.)

    1883. *Dissertations on early law and custom*. London: Murray. (1886 ed. New York: Henry Holt.)

Maitland, Frederic William.

    1900. Translator's Introduction to *Political theories of the Middle Age*, by Otto Gierke. Cambridge: Cambridge University Press. (1927 ed.)

    1911. *The Collected Papers of Frederic William Maitland*. Edited by H. A. L. Fisher. 3 Vols. Cambridge: Cambridge University Press.

    1913. *The constitutional history of England*. Cambridge: Cambridge University Press.

Malinowski, Bronislaw.

    1913. *The family among the Australian Aborigines*. London: University of London Press.

    1922. *Argonauts of the Western Pacific*. London: Routledge & Kegan Paul.

    1926. *Crime and custom in savage society*. London: Kegan Paul, Trench, Trubner & Co. Ltd.

    1927a. *Sex and repression in savage society*. London: Kegan Paul, Trench, Trubner & Co. Ltd.

    1927b. *The father in primitive psychology*. London: Kegan Paul, Trench, Trubner & Co. Ltd.

    1929a. *The sexual life of savages in north-western Melanesia*. London: G. Routledge & Sons. (3rd ed., 1932. London: Routledge & Kegan Paul. Special foreword by Malinowski.)

    1929b. Article s.v. Kinship. *Encyclopaedia Britannica*, Vol. 13, pp. 403–409. 14th ed.

    1930. Kinship. *Man*, 30 (17): 19–20.

    1935. *Coral gardens and their magic*. 2 vols. New York: American Book.

    1944. *A scientific theory of culture and other essays*. Chapel Hill: University of North Carolina Press.

Marriott, McKim, *et al.*

    1959. *Caste*, in *Man in India*, 39 (2): 92–162.

Marett, R. R.

    1936. *Tylor*. London: Chapman and Hall.

Marwick, M. G.

    1965. *Sorcery in its social setting: a study of the Northern Rhodesian Cewa*. Manchester: Manchester University Press.

Marx, Karl.

1888. Theses on Feuerbach, 1845. (Reprinted in *Handbook of Marxism*, selected by Emile Burns, London: Victor Gollancz, 1935, p. 228–231.)

Mauss, Marcel.

1925. Essai sur le Don: Forme et Raison de l'Échange dans les Sociétés Archaïques. *L'Année Sociologique*, Nouvelle Série, 1: 30–186. English translation by I. Cunnison: *The Gift*, 1954, London: Cohen & West.

Mayer, Philip.

1949. *The lineage principle in Gusii society*. International African Institute Memorandum, No. 24. London: Oxford University Press.

1950. Privileged obstruction of marriage rites among the Gusii. *Africa*, 20: 113–125.

1961. *Townsmen or tribesmen: conservatism and the process of urbanization in a South African city*. Cape Town: Oxford University Press.

Meek, C. K.

1946. *Land law and custom in the colonies*. London: Oxford University Press. (2nd ed., 1949.)

Meggitt, Mervyn J.

1958. The Enga of the New Guinea Highlands: some preliminary observations. *Oceania*, 28: 253–330.

1962. *Desert people: a study of the Walbiri Aborigines of central Australia*. Sydney: Angus & Robertson, Ltd.

1964. Indigenous forms of government among the Australian Aborigines. *Bijdragen Tot de Taal-, Land- en Volkenkunde*, 120: 163–180. (The Hague: Martinus Nijhoff.)

Meyerowitz, Eva L. R.

1951. *The sacred state of the Akan*. London: Faber & Faber.

1952. *Akan traditions of origin*. London: Faber & Faber.

Middleton, John.

1958. The political system of the Lugbara of the Nile-Congo divide. In John Middleton and David Tait (Eds.), *Tribes without rulers*. London: Routledge & Kegan Paul.

Middleton, John, and David Tait (Eds.).

1958. *Tribes without rulers: studies in African segmentary systems*. Introduction by Middleton and Tait. London: Routledge & Kegan Paul.

Middleton, John, and E. H. Winter (Eds.).

1963. *Witchcraft and sorcery in East Africa*. London: Routledge & Kegan Paul.

Mitchell, J. Clyde.

1956. *The Yao village: a study in the social structure of a Nyasaland tribe*. Manchester: Manchester University Press.

Moore, Sally Falk.

1964. Descent and symbolic filiation. *American Anthropologist*. 66: 1308–1320.

Morgan, Lewis H.

1851. *League of the Ho-de-no-sau-nee or Iroquois*. Rochester: Sage and Brothers. (1904 ed., rev. New York: Dodd, Mead.)

1870. *Systems of consanguinity and affinity of the human family*. *Smithsonian Contributions to Knowledge*, 17: 4–602.

1877. *Ancient society*. New York: Henry Holt (1878 ed. New York: Henry Holt.) (Definitive ed. 1964, edited by Leslie A. White for the John Harvard Library. Cambridge, Mass.: The Belknap Press of Harvard University Press.)

Morrison, Philip.
  1950. The physics of the bomb. In J. L. Crammer and R. E. Peierls. (Eds.), *Atomic energy*. Harmondsworth, England: Penguin Books.
Murdock, George P.
  1949. *Social structure*. New York: Macmillan.
  1959. *Africa: its people and their culture history*. New York: McGraw-Hill.
  1960. Cognatic forms of social organization. Introduction to G. P. Murdock (Ed.), *Social structure in Southeast Asia*.
Murdock, George Peter (Ed.)
  1960. *Social structure in Southeast Asia*. Viking Fund publications in Anthropology, No. 29. New York: Wenner-Gren Foundation for Anthropological Research.
Nakane, Chie.
  1962. The Nayar family in a disintegrating matrilineal system. *Interntional Journal of Comparative Sociology*, 3: 17–28.
Needham, Rodney.
  1954. The system of teknonyms and death-names of ·the Penan. *Southwestern Journal of Anthropology*, 10 (4): 416–431.
  1962. *Structure and sentiment: a test case in social anthropology*. Chicago: University of Chicago Press.
Needham, Rodney, et al.
  1964. The Purum case (discussion by Ackerman, *et al.*, *American Anthropologist*, 66: 1351–1381).
Nimkoff, Meyer F. (Ed.).
  1965. *Comparative family systems*. Boston: Houghton, Mifflin.
Oberg, K.
  1940. The kingdom of Ankole in Uganda. In Meyer Fortes and E. E. Evans-Pritchard (Eds.), *African political systems*. London: Oxford University Press.
Oliver, Douglas L.
  1955. *A Solomon Island society: kinship and leadership among the Siuai of Bougainville*. Cambridge, Mass.: Harvard University Press.
  1962. Review of *Pul Eliya* by E. R. Leach. *American Anthropologist*, 64: 621–22.
Parsons, Talcott, and Edward A. Shils (Eds.).
  1951. *Toward a general theory of action*. Cambridge, Mass.: Harvard University Press.
Parsons, Talcott, et al. (Eds.).
  1961. *Theories of society: foundations of modern sociological theory*. 2 vols. New York: Free Press.
Pedersen, Johannes.
  1920. *Israel: its life and culture*. Translated 1926. London: Oxford University Press. (New ed., 1959.)
Peerage.
  1965. Article in *Encyclopaedia Britannica*, Vol. 17, pp. 436–440.
Pehrson, Robert N.
  1954. Bilateral kin grouping as a structural type: a preliminary statement. *University of Manilla Journal of East Asiatic Studies*, 3: 199–202.
  1957. *The bilateral network of social relations in Könkäma Lapp district*. Indiana University Publications, Slavic and East European Series, vol. 5. Bloomington: University of Indiana Press.
Peristiany, J. G.
  1939. *The social institutions of the Kipsigis*. London: Routledge & Kegan Paul.

Perregaux, Edmond.

1906. *Chez les Achanti*. Neuchatel, Switzerland: Paul Attinger.

Peters, Emrys.

1960. The proliferation of segments in the lineage of the Bedouin in Cyrenaica. *Journal of the Royal Anthropological Institute*, 90: 29–53.

Phillpotts, Bertha S.

1913. *Kindred and clan in the Middle Ages and after: a study of the sociology of the Teutonic races*. Cambridge: Cambridge University Press.

Picken, Lawrence.

1960. *The organization of cells and other organisms*. Oxford: Clarendon Press.

Pollock, F., and F. W. Maitland.

1895. *The history of English law before the time of Edward I*. 2 vols. Cambridge: Cambridge University Press. (2nd ed., 1905.)

Popper, K. R.

1945. *The open society and its enemies*. London: G. Routledge & Sons, Ltd.

Powell, H. A.

1956. *Present day social structure in the Trobriand Islands*. Unpublished Ph.D. thesis, University of London.

1960. Competitive leadership in Trobriand political organization. *Journal of the Royal Anthropological Institute*, 90: 118–145.

Radcliffe-Brown, A. R.

1913. Three tribes of western Australia. *Journal of the Royal Anthropological Institute*, 43: 143–194.

1922. *The Andaman Islanders*. London: Cambridge University Press.

1924. The mother's brother in South Africa. *South African Journal of Science*, 21: 542–55. Reprinted in *Idem* 1952, ch. 1.

1929. A further note on Ambrym. *Man*, 29 (35): 50–53.

1930–31. The social organization of Australian tribes. 4 parts. *Oceania*, I: 34–63; 206–246; 322–341; 426–456.

1935. Patrilineal and matrilineal succession. *The Iowa Law Review*, 20: 286–303. Reprinted in *Idem* 1952, ch. 2.

1936. The development of social anthropology. Unpublished lecture, Chicago, December 1936.

1939. *Taboo*. Cambridge: Cambridge University Press. Reprinted in *Idem* 1952, ch. 7.

1940a. On joking relationships. *Africa*, 13: 195–210. Reprinted in *Idem* 1952, ch. 4.

1940b. On social structure. *Journal of the Royal Anthropological Institute*, 70: 1–12. Reprinted in *Idem* 1952, ch. 10.

1941. The study of kinship systems. *Journal of the Royal Anthropological Institute*, 71: 1–18. Reprinted in *Idem* 1952, ch. 3.

1949. A further note on joking relationships. *Africa*, 19: 133–140. Reprinted in *Idem* 1952, ch. 5.

1951. Murngin social organization. *American Anthropologist*, 53: 37–55.

1952. *Structure and function in primitive society: essays and addresses*. Foreword by E. E. Evans-Pritchard and Fred Eggan. Glencoe, Ill.: Free Press.

1953. Dravidian kinship terminology. *Man*, 53 (169): 112. (Reply to Dumont, *Man*, 53(54).)

1957. *A natural science of society*. New York: Free Press. (Lectures recorded in 1937.)

Radcliffe-Brown, A. R., and Daryll Forde (Eds.).

    1950. *African systems of kinship and marriage*. London: Oxford University Press.

Rattray, Robert Sutherland.

    1916. *Ashanti proverbs*. Oxford: Clarendon Press.

    1923. *Ashanti*. Oxford: Clarendon Press.

    1927. *Religion and art in Ashanti*. Oxford: Clarendon Press.

    1929. *Ashanti law and constitution*. Oxford: Clarendon Press.

    1932. *The tribes of the Ashanti hinterland*. 2 vols. Oxford: Clarendon Press.

Redfield, Robert.

    1953a. *The primitive world and its transformations*. Ithaca, New York: Cornell University Press.

    1953b. Relations of anthropology to the social sciences and to the humanities. In A. L. Kroeber (Ed.), *Anthropology today*. Chicago: University of Chicago Press.

Resek, Carl.

    1960. *Lewis Henry Morgan, American scholar*. Chicago: University of Chicago Press.

Richards, Audrey I.

    1939. *Land, labour and diet in Northern Rhodesia: an economic study of the Bemba tribe*. London: Oxford University Press.

    1950. Some types of family structure amongst the central Bantu. In A. R. Radcliffe-Brown, and Daryll Forde (Eds.), *African systems of kinship and marriage*. London: Oxford University Press.

Rivers, W. H. R.

    1906. *The Todas*. London: Macmillan.

    1914a. *Kinship and social organisation*. London: Constable & Co. Ltd.

    1914b. *The history of Melanesian society*. 2 Vols., Cambridge: Cambridge University Press.

    1924. *Social organization*. Edited by W. J. Perry. New York: Alfred A. Knopf; London: Kegan Paul, Trench, Trubner & Co. Ltd. (Posthumously published lectures.)

Robertson Smith, William.

    1885. *Kinship and marriage in early Arabia*. Cambridge: Cambridge University Press. (1903 ed. London: A. & C. Black.)

Robinson, Marguerite S.

    1962. Complementary filiation and marriage in the Trobriand Islands: a re-examination of Malinowski's material. In Meyer Fortes (Ed.), *Marriage in tribal societies*. Cambridge Papers in Social Anthropology, No. 3. Cambridge: Cambridge University Press.

Romney, A. Kimball, and Phillip J. Epling.

    1958. A simplified model of Kariera kinship. *American Anthropologist*, 60: 59–74.

Rose, Frederick G. G.

    1960. *Classification of kin, age structure and marriage among the Groote Eylandt Aborigines: a study in method and theory of Australian kinship*. Berlin: Akademie Verlag.

Russell, Bertrand.

    1919. *Introduction to mathematical philosophy*. London: Allen & Unwin.

Sahlins, Marshall D.

    1958. *Social stratification in Polynesia*. Seattle: University of Washington Press.

    1961. The segmentary lineage: an organization of predatory expansion. *American Anthropologist*, 63: 322–345.

1962. *Moala: culture and nature on a Fijian island.* Ann Arbor: University of Michigan Press.

Salisbury, Richard Frank.

1962. *From stone to steel: economic consequences of a technological change in New Guinea.* Melbourne: Melbourne University Press.

Sarbah, John Mensah.

1897. *Fanti customary laws: a brief introduction to the principles of the native laws and customs of the Fanti and Akan sections of the Gold Coast, with a selection of cases thereon decided in the law courts.* London: Clowes & Sons.

Sarpong, Fr. Peter.

1965. *Girls' nubility rites in Ashanti.* Unpublished B.Litt. thesis, Oxford University.

Saussure, Ferdinand de.

1916. *Course in general linguistics* (English translation from the French by Wade Baskin) New York: Philosophical Library, 1959.

Schapera, I.

1938. *A handbook of Tswana law and custom.* London: Oxford University Press. (2nd ed., 1955.)

1950. Kinship and marriage among the Tswana. In A. R. Radcliffe-Brown and Daryll Forde (Eds.), *African systems of kinship and marriage.* London: Oxford University Press.

1956. *Government and politics in tribal societies.* London: C. A. Watts & Co.

1957. Marriage of near kin among the Tswana. *Africa,* 27: 139–159.

1962. Should anthropologists be historians? *Journal of the Royal Anthropological Institute,* 92: 143–156.

Schapera, I. (Ed.).

1963. *Studies in kinship and marriage.* Occasional Papers of the Royal Anthropological Institute, no. 16. London: Royal Anthropological Institute.

Scheffler, H. W.

1964. Descent concepts and descent groups: the Maori case. *Journal of Polynesian Society,* 73: 126–133.

1966. Ancestor worship in anthropology: or, observations on descent and descent groups. *Current Anthropology,* 7: 541–51.

Schneider, David M.

1962. Double descent on Yap. *Journal of the Polynesian Society,* 71: 1–24.

1965. Some muddles in the models: or, how the system really works. In Michael Banton (Ed.), *The relevance of models for social anthropology.* Association of Social Anthropologists Monographs, No. 1. London: Tavistock Publications; New York: Praeger.

Schneider, David M., and E. Kathleen Gough (Eds.).

1961. *Matrilineal kinship.* Berkeley: University of California Press.

Service, Elman R.

1960. Kinship terminology and evolution. *American Anthropologist,* 62: 747–763.

Siegel, Bernard J. (Ed.).

1963. *Biennial review of anthropology.* Stanford, Calif.: Stanford University Press.

Simmel, Georg.

1922. Die Kreuzung sozialer Kreise. *Soziologie,* 305–344, Muenchen: Duncker & Humblot. Translated by Reinhard Bendix as "The web of group-affiliations" published together with his essay, "Conflict." New York: The Free Press. 1955.

Skinner, Elliott P.

1964. *The Mossi of the upper Volta: the political development of a Sudanese people.* Stanford, Calif.: Stanford University Press.

Smith, Edwin William.

1926. *The Golden stool: some aspects of the conflict of cultures in Africa.* London: Holborn.

Smith, Michael G.

1956. On segmentary lineage systems. *Journal of the Royal Anthropological Institute*, 86: 39–79.

Smith, Raymond Thomas.

1956. *The Negro family in British Guiana: Family structure and social status in the villages.* London: Routledge & Kegan Paul.

Smith, Robert J., and Richard K. Beardsley (Eds.).

1962. *Japanese culture: its development and characteristics.* Chicago: Aldine Publishing Company.

Southall, Aidan W.

1956. *Alur society: a study in processes and types of domination.* Cambridge: W. Heffer & Sons.

Spiro, Melford E.

1958. *Children of the kibbutz.* Cambridge, Mass.: Harvard University Press.

Spoehr, Alexander.

1950. Observations on the study of kinship. *American Anthropologist*, 52: 1–15.

Stanner, W. E. H.

1936. Murinbata kinship and totemism. *Oceania*, 7: 186–216.

Starcke, C. N.

(1888.) 1891. *La famille primitive: ses origines et son développement.* Paris: Félix Alcan.

Stenning, Derrick J.

1958. Household viability among the pastoral Fulani. In Jack Goody (Ed.), *The developmental cycle in domestic groups.* Cambridge Papers in Social Anthropology, No. 1. Cambridge: Cambridge University Press.

Stern, Bernhard J.

1931. *Lewis Henry Morgan: social evolutionist.* Chicago: University of Chicago Press.

Stevenson, H. N. C.

1954. Status evaluation in the Hindu caste system. *Journal of the Royal Anthropological Institute*, 84: 45–65.

Tait, David.

1961. *The Konkomba of northern Ghana.* (Posthumous monograph, edited by Jack Goody.) London: Oxford University Press.

Talmon, Yonina.

1965. The family in a revolutionary movement—the case of the kibbutz in Israel. In Meyer F. Nimkoff (Ed.), *Comparative family systems.* Boston: Houghton, Mifflin.

Tambiah, S. J.

1958. The structure of kinship and its relationship to land possession and residence in Pata Dumbara, central Ceylon. *Journal of the Royal Anthropological Institute*, 88: 21–44.

1965. Kinship fact and fiction in relation to the Kandyan Sinhalese. *Journal of the Royal Anthropological Institute*, 95: 131–173.

Tauxier, Louis.

1932. *Religion, mœurs et coutumes des Agnis de la Côte-d'Ivoire (Indénié et Sanwi)*. Paris: P. Geuthner.

Tax, Sol.

1937. Some problems of social organization. In Fred Eggan (Ed.), *Social anthropology of North American tribes*. Chicago: University of Chicago Press.

1955. From Lafitau to Radcliffe-Brown: a short history of the study of social organization. In Fred Eggan (Ed.), *Social anthropology of North American tribes* (1955 ed.). Chicago: University of Chicago Press.

Teggart, Frederick John.

1925. *Theory of history*. New Haven, Conn.: Yale University Press.

Tegnaeus, Harry.

1952. *Blood-brothers: an ethno-sociological study of the institution of blood-brotherhood, with reference to Africa*. New York: Philosophical Library.

Thomson, Donald Ferguson.

1946. Names and naming in the Wik Monkan tribes. *Journal of the Royal Anthropological Institute*, 76: 157–167.

1949. *Economic structure and the ceremonial exchange cycle in Arnhem Land*. Melbourne: Macmillan.

Thomson, George.

1949. *Studies in ancient Greek society. Vol 1. The prehistoric Aegean*. London: Lawrence and Wishart.

Turner, Victor W.

1957. *Schism and continuity in an African society: a study of Ndembu village life*. Manchester: Manchester University Press.

1962. Three symbols of *passage* in Ndembu circumcision ritual: an interpretation. In Max Gluckman (Ed.), *Studies on the ritual of social relations*. Manchester: Manchester University Press.

Tylor, E. B.

1865. *Researches into the early history of mankind and the development of civilization*. London: Murray.

1871. *Primitive culture*. 2 vols. London: Murray.

1889. On a method of investigating the development of institutions; applied to laws of marriage and descent. *Journal of the Anthropological Institute*, 18: 245–269.

Van Gennep, Arnold.

1960. *The rites of passage* (translated by Monika B. Vizedom and Gabrielle L. Caffee from the French) London: Routledge & Kegan Paul.

Vinogradoff, Sir Paul.

1914. *Common sense in law*. London: Oxford University Press. (3rd ed., 1959.)

Voegelin, Charles F., and Florence M. Voegelin.

1957. *Hopi domains: a lexical approach to the problem of selection*. Indiana University Publications in Anthropology and Linguistics, Memoir 14. (Supplement to *International Journal of American Linguistics*, 23(2).) Baltimore: Waverly Press.

Ward, Barbara.

1956. Some observations on religious cults in Ashanti. *Africa*, 26: 47–61.

Ward, W. E. F.

1948. *A history of the Gold Coast*, London: Allen & Unwin. (Revised 1958 as *A history of Ghana*.)

Warner, William Lloyd.

1937. *A black civilization*. New York: Harper.

Warrington, Captain J. C.

1934, revised 1942. Notes of an enquiry into Ashanti native custom. Unpublished manuscript originally filed in the Office of the Chief Commissioner for Ashanti, Kumasi, Ghana.

Weber, Max.

1947. *The theory of social and economic organization*. Trans. by A. M. Henderson and Talcott Parsons and ed. by Talcott Parsons. New York: Free Press.

Westermarck, Edvard.

1891. *The history of human marriage*. London: Macmillan.

White, Leslie A.

1948. Lewis H. Morgan: pioneer in the theory of social evolution. In H. E. Barnes (Ed.), *Introduction of the history of sociology*. Chicago: University of Chicago Press.

1957. How Morgan came to write "Systems of consanguinity and affinity." *Papers of the Michigan Academy of Science, Arts and Letters*, 42: 257–268.

1958. What is a classificatory kinship term? *Southwestern Journal of Anthropology* 14: 378–385.

1964. Introduction to *Ancient Society*, by Lewis H. Morgan. John Harvard Library. Cambridge Mass.: The Belknap Press of Harvard University Press.

Whitehead, Alfred North, and Bertrand Russell.

1910–1913. *Principia mathematica*. Cambridge: Cambridge University Press.

Wilks, Ivor.

1964. Ashanti government in the nineteenth century. Draft Paper No. 3, Institute of African Studies, University of Ghana, Legon, Ghana. (Published 1967 under title: Ashanti Government. In Forde, Daryll and P. M. Kaberry (Eds.), *West African kingdoms in the nineteenth century*. London: Oxford University Press: 206–238.)

1966. Aspects of Bureaucratization in Ashanti in the nineteenth century. *Journal of African History*, 7.

1966. The position of Muslims in metropolitan Ashanti in the early nineteenth century. In I. M. Lewis (Ed.), *Islam in tropical Africa*. London: Oxford University Press.

Wilson, Monica.

1950. Nyakyusa kinship. In A. R. Radcliffe-Brown and Daryll Forde (Eds.), *African systems of kinship and marriage*. London: Oxford University Press.

1951. *Good company: a study of Nyakyusa age-villages*. London: Oxford University Press.

Winter, Edward.

1958. The aboriginal political structure of Bwamba. In John Middleton and David Tait (Eds.), *Tribes without rulers*. London: Routledge & Kegan Paul.

Worsley, P. M.

1956. The kinship system of the Tallensi: a revaluation. *Journal of the Royal Anthropological Institute*, 86: 37–75.

Wylie, Laurence.

1957. *Village in the Vaucluse*. Cambridge, Mass.: Harvard University Press.

Yalman, Nur.
　　1962. The structure of the Sinhalese kindred: a re-examination of the Dravidian terminology. *American Anthropologist*, 64: 548–575.
Young, Michael, and Peter Willmott.
　　1957. *Family and kinship in East London*. London: Routledge & Kegan Paul. (1962. Baltimore: Penguin Books.)

Index